Honor, Symbols, and War

Honor, Symbols, and War

Barry O'Neill

Ann Arbor

THE UNIVERSITY OF MICHIGAN PRESS

First paperback edition 2001
Copyright © by the University of Michigan 1999
All rights reserved
Published in the United States of America by
The University of Michigan Press
Manufactured in the United States of America
∞ Printed on acid-free paper

2004   2003   2002   2001   5   4   3   2

A CIP catalog record for this book is available from the British Library.

Library of Congress Cataloging-in-Publication Data

O'Neill, Barry, 1945–
    Honor, symbols, and war / Barry O'Neill.
        p.   cm.
    Includes bibliographical references and index.
    ISBN 0-472-10959-6 (alk. paper)
    1. International relations—Psychological aspects.
    2. International relations—Decision making.   3. Symbolism in
politics.   4. Honor.   I. Title.
    JZ1253.O54   1999
    327.1′01′4—dc21   99-27077
                                                           CIP

ISBN 0-472-08786-X (pbk. : alk. paper)

In memory of my mother and father

Contents

Preface

When Soviet nuclear missiles were discovered in Cuba, Sir Harold MacMillan suggested a plan to ease the crisis. He would immobilize Britain's 60 Thor missiles on the condition that Premier Khrushchev would withdraw the Soviet deployment. In a letter to President Kennedy, MacMillan stated that his undertaking would be both "symbolic and real," and "might be helpful to save the Russians' face." Kennedy opposed the idea because he saw a different symbolic suggestion in it—that Soviet protection of Cuba could be traded for Western defense of Europe (*Press Association Newsfile,* Jan. 10, 1993).

In March 1982, during the crisis over the Falklands/Malvinas, an Argentinean scrap-metal dealer landed a party on an outlying island to salvage an old whaling station. He had notified the British Embassy of the trip, but when his workers raised the national flag, shot some of the local deer, and ignored other points of British sovereignty, Britain dispatched marines to remove them. The spiral of reactions ended in war (Freedman and Gamba-Stonehouse 1991; Perez de Cuellar 1997.)

Putting the right symbolic nuances in their words and actions is a regular concern of foreign policy practitioners. They also worry about intangible goals like saving face and preserving national honor and prestige, but these subjects have not been emphasized by international relations theory. This book analyzes symbolism in international relations and examines four status regulators that rely on symbolism: honor, social face, prestige, and moral authority. My aim is to treat the topics more precisely than has been done before.

This book's thesis is that to understand symbolism one must distinguish three types: value, message, and focal symbols. Value symbols, which are discussed only briefly, involve the association of the party's identity and values with certain actions or objects. Message symbols are ways of communicating. Communication in a regular language is based on the precedent of the use of its words and grammar, but the mechanism of symbolic communication is different, involving prototypes, metaphors and metonymies. I show some regularly used symbolic techniques. Focal symbols are events, often not deliberate acts by any agent, that induce observers to adopt a common judgment about what move they will make in an important situation. They establish a focal point through a certain part/whole mechanism that can be called symbolic.

I argue that message and focal symbolism can explain a diverse set of international phenomena, including contests in armaments, actions around leadership, moves in prenegotiations, symbolic arms control agreements, and states' responses to tension during a crisis. Moreover, it can explain these behaviors within a strategic paradigm, without introducing assumptions about emotion or rhetoric or psychological associations. Nonstrategic approaches are also necessary, of course, but it is important to establish that parties would continue to engage in symbolic behavior even if they were fully aware of their situation and were focused on the consequences of their actions.

Concerning the status regulators, my thesis is that their importance has been understated. If rhetorical appeals to national honor are less common nowadays, this is mostly a change in vocabulary. Leaders talk about showing "will," "resolve," "strength," or "credibility," but their patterns of behavior are typical of past disputes over honor. As with symbolism, the status regulators can be analyzed strategically—this approach is just as appropriate for them as for resources, interests or military power. Through definitions and game models I draw distinctions among them and show their relationships. Honor is an internal quality of the individual that can only be estimated by the rest of society. It involves, in part, the individual's desire to be seen as honorable, and this self-referential property is the key to proving one's honor and judging another person's honor. Social face is the group's expectation about how it will treat the individual in direct interactions. Unlike honor, it is not about the individual's internal character; social face is set by precedents of the group's past treatment and sets a precedent for the future. Prestige is the belief among the members that the person is admired—each one's belief that the rest of the group believes that the individual possesses a desirable trait. It is like face in that it involves the group's expectations about its own expectations, but it is based more on deeds done or objects acquired than on precedent. Moral authority is the kind of prestige that one gains by keeping the group's norms. It confers influence over further cases when the norms are unclear, and so is important in an understanding of normative change. The theories developed for these status regulators explain various international phenomena such as the tendency to perceive other states' actions as challenges, international commitments, insults, and the unusual nature of international apologies.

The analysis leads to a series of policy conclusions concerning the prospects of using arms control for symbolic purposes, the danger of using insults as diplomatic tools, and the importance of not identifying a challenge as such on the record. Understanding the most common forms of symbolic messages should help leaders avoid sending messages that are misunderstood. The most significant conclusion in my view involves the issue of proliferation. The focus of the final chapter is the symbolism and status aspects around nuclear weapons, and the danger that these may induce the "haves" to hold on to them unnecessarily and other nations to acquire them and engage in arms competitions. I argue that the symbolism of honor and challenges was at the center of one episode in the U.S./Soviet arms race, the 1980s deployment of missiles in Europe.

The three methodologies used here are the theory of games, the philosophy of language, and cognitive linguistics. Past game-theoretical models of communication have tended to ask about the credibility of the messages, but here I look at how we understand their meaning. Past game models looked at the persuasiveness of assertions, for example, that one is resolved to win a conflict. I consider a wider variety of communicative acts than assertions, including challenges, promises, insults and apologies, the kind of speech that goes beyond expressing the speaker's beliefs and brings things about in the world of social relations.

I hope to make the methodological point that game theory can be applied to broader issues in the social sciences than the literature has seen so far, and that it can be combined with findings in the social and behavioral sciences in significant ways. Game-theoretical methods are not bound to a rational choice account of motivation or perception. Appendix A describes some developments in game theory that allow this extension.

In its concerns if not its style, this work has much in common with post-structuralist approaches. It emphasizes social perceptions, language, and the social rules. Moral authority is tied in with norms and normative regimes, which are clarified here by comparing them with the equilibria of repeated games. What might be called a "social construction," a "shared understanding," or "convergent beliefs" can be interpreted nonmetaphorically with a precise model of beliefs about beliefs, using the method of interactive belief systems.

Most of the material presented here is accessible to nonmathematical readers. Some acquaintance with a Nash equilibrium would be helpful, but appendix B explains that concept, as well as the notion of an interactive belief system. The necessary concepts from philosophy, psychology, and linguistics are explained as they appear.

This work is written as a contribution to the theory of international relations and diplomacy, but it also deals with social interaction in general. I hope that its findings will be useful to other disciplines such as cultural anthropology, sociology, social psychology, and political behavior.

Warm appreciation is conveyed to Robert Aumann, Steve Brams, Dov Samet, Avner Shaked, and Martin Shubik for their constant personal support. Many of the topics develop the ideas of Robert Jervis, who seems to have a game-theoretic intuition about international situations without the mathematics. Thomas Schelling's influence is clear in his willingness to bring together disparate aspects under a strategic analysis. The final chapter on nuclear thought-styles was shaped by Lynn Eden's work, with her special merging of history, technology, and organization theory. Neta Crawford read the whole manuscript carefully and gave me excellent suggestions. Many others have contributed through their suggestions and support: Dilip Abreu, Leslie Arwin, Rudolf Avenhaus, Neylan Bali, Dieter Balkenborg, Jeremy Bulow, George Bunn, Martha Burns, Erhan Cinlar, Carol Cohn, George Downs, Jonathan Feinstein, Harriet Friedmann, Raymond Garthoff, Charles Glaser, Gary Goertz, Sue Golding, Danny Goldstick, Tad Homer-Dixon, Michael Intriligator, Catherine Kelleher, Marc Kilgour, Audrey Kurth-Cronin, Jonathan Mercer, Jennifer Milliken, Barry Nalebuff, Georg Noldeke, Catharine O'Neill, David Pearce, Scott Plous, Ted Postol, Bob Powell, Daniel Probst, Anatol Rapoport, Scott Sagan, Prudence Shaw, Jim Sutterlin, Eric van Damme, Steve van Evera, Alex Wendt, Brad Westerfield, Philip Winsor, as well as the dear residents of Sweet's Mill. I want to express my special appreciation to Ellen Cohn for her love and support through good times and difficult ones.

Financial assistance was provided by the Social Science Research Council/ MacArthur Foundation, the Stanford Center for International Security and Co-operation, and Bonn University. It is recognized and appreciated.

One consequence of the Cold War ending has been the end of many working relationships. To those just mentioned who come to read this I send warm greetings and my wish to see them again. Many of us have peace as the underlying concern of our professional lives. Working on these subjects requires faith that understanding war will help us avoid it. This is only partly grounded in the evidence, and we are discouraged again and again to see the folly return. However, we must attack the problem as well as we can, following our interests and skills. This book was written in the hope that a better theoretical knowledge of symbols and honor may help.

Part I

Symbols

CHAPTER 1

Symbolism: Introduction

The idea of symbolism arises across the social sciences, but a solid definition of it is difficult to find. Some writers treat it as the basis of society, but they often give no definition of it or they define it in obscure and figurative language. A symbol "stands for" an idea. However, "stands for" is a metaphor, and its root meaning is unclear. A symbol "calls" an idea "to mind," but apple pie calls ice cream to mind without the help of symbolism. After attending a conference on symbolism, anthropologist Melford Spiro complained that the participants had much of interest to say but had given so little attention to defining the term that it was not clear that they were talking about the same subject (quoted by Firth 1973, 54). The semiotician Umberto Eco (1984) recounts a 1920s debate transcribed in a French philosophical dictionary (Lalande 1926). After each definition, the dictionary offered a Talmud-like discussion by a group of academics. In the case of symbolism, for each criterion that one commentator suggested, someone else had a counterexample, and in the end a symbol was everything and nothing. To Eco the exchange read like an absurdist play.

An Approach to Defining Symbolism

Reckless of the past, I will try to make the idea of symbolism precise. I use three techniques that should increase the prospects of success. First, the notion is split into subtypes. Some of the more enlightening past discussions have done this, such as Sapir's distinction between referential and condensation symbols,[1] which influenced the work of Victor Turner and Murray Edelman. The three va-

---

1. Sapir's *referential* symbols are "agreed upon as economical devices for purposes of reference" (1937). Examples are oral speech or the telegraph code. *Condensation* symbols are "substitutive behavior for direct expression, allowing for the ready release of emotional tension." These correspond most closely to our message and value symbols.

rieties I see as prevalent in international relations will be termed *message symbols, focal symbols,* and *value symbols.*

Second, the definitions of the types will be grounded on systematically collected facts. Computer databases of news articles were searched and hundreds of examples of symbols in international relations discourse were assembled. The corpus of real examples suggests the regularities that should be included in a definition and shows counterexamples to mistaken definitions. The third feature is the use of game theory. Many past definitions were put in terms as obscure as the concept to be defined. With game theory, the definition can be embedded in a well-studied framework: utilities, probabilities, and strategies. Focal symbolism and message symbolism are essentially social phenomena, and game theory is a precise way to formulate interactive decisions.

Family Resemblances

Most writers recognize the existence of subtypes of symbolism, but the procedure here is more radical. Rather than starting with a general definition of symbolism and then dividing it into types, I will work out each type first and the general concept will follow. The reason lies in the structure of the idea of symbolism. A common way to define a formal concept is to give a list of its required properties. This is the norm in mathematics: being a pentagon, or an open set, or an associative group involves features A and B and C, and so on. However, it does not work well for naturally occurring concepts. Symbolism, in particular, is not based on a checklist but on a *family resemblance.*[2] Consider the imaginary concept of "pifflishness." Say it is based on a set of features, five in number, and an object is "pifflish" if it possesses four of the five. The set of pifflish objects is well defined and forms a psychologically natural cluster, since its members are similar to each other: they share at least three of the five features. It would not be surprising that a language would have a single name for them all. Still, a checklist approach would not work.

There is no set that is necessary and sufficient. Wittgenstein's metaphor of a family is apt. The resemblance among a group of brothers and sisters cannot be stated as a core set of if-and-only-if features. Not every member has the nose or the eyes or the forehead, but they all look alike.

A modification of the pifflish example shows a stronger difference between

---

2. The concept of a family resemblance was introduced by Wittgenstein and amplified by Eco (1984), Lakoff (1987), and others.

family resemblances and the checklist approach. One can imagine a concept requiring four out of five features where two of the features are logically incompatible, making it impossible to possess all five. There would then be two types of pifflish entities, one group with one feature and the other group with the other. All pifflish objects possess the remaining three elements, so all are similar to each other. The concept of symbolism has this property of including contradictory features, and this fact may have caused the bedlam around a definition. Two defining features of symbols are that they have an innate connection to their referent and that they are arbitrary. The Swiss pioneer of semiotics, Ferdinand de Saussure (1922), endorsed the first condition, stating that a symbol must be connected to its referent either by similarity or by a part/whole relation. His example was the figure of Justice, blind and holding a balance scale, which map into properties of abstract justice. Working independently in the United States, C. S. Peirce (1931) stated that a symbol must be arbitrary, like the shape of the letter *a*. The field of semiotics continues to quote both definitions as authoritative, and this contradiction may have deterred writers from working out a more precise account.[3] The resolution of the puzzle is to assemble the general notion from its subtypes.

There are some common meanings of symbolism that will not be used here, because they are so broad that the word would do no work. A symbol is sometimes just an abbreviated code, a prestipulated designator for something lengthier, an alternative to listing the details. Central in this meaning is the arbitrariness emphasized by Peirce—the more the code is simply stipulated, the more it deserves the name "symbol." The character א is a symbol when it means infinity in a mathematical formula but not when it appears in a Hebrew word, where its role evolved and is now established by precedent. In another usage of some philosophers, all words or letters are symbols since all language is conventional. Political science has also produced some uselessly general senses of the word. Some authors have associated symbolism with anything not encompassed by calculated self-interest, such as behavior involving norms or "psychological" factors.

The three important meanings are message symbols, focal symbols, and value symbols. The first two are treated in the next four chapters. Value symbols will enter the discussion, but we have less to say about them directly.

---

3. A modern semiotic definition in Peirce's direction is given by Sebeok (1986), who calls a symbol "a sign without either similarity or contiguity, but only with a conventional link between its signifier and its denotata, and with an intensional class for its designatum."

Message Symbols

In May 1994, Nelson Mandela was to be sworn in as president of South Africa. In a gesture of "hope and reconciliation," he invited James Gregory, his white jailer for the previous 20 years, to attend the ceremony. The meaning of his act was clear. What was puzzling was why the world could immediately understand it. There was no prevalent custom of leaders inviting their jailers to their presidential inaugurations. Symbols are often compared to language, but somehow this kind of language is understandable the first time it is used.

Other examples of message symbols are a leader's gift to another to show international friendship, or a visit to another nation's war memorial. These are messages without words, but not every nonlinguistic communication counts as symbolic. A wink, or a discrete clearing of one's throat, or a come-here wave of the hand are not symbols. What makes some communications symbolic? If their message is not in a known language, how can we understand them? And why not just say it in words?

Mandela's inauguration message involved a unique symbol, but some symbols are used so often that they move toward conventions. At that point their connection with their meaning is immediately understood without the decoding methods typically used for symbols. Chapter 3 traces the evolution of the Gulf War yellow ribbons to see what induced shifts on the continuum between symbols and conventions and what was lost or gained.

Focal Symbols

As Jervis (1989) has pointed out, some symbols are different from Mandela's in that they have no sender. The *New York Times* reported that on the morning of August 27, 1991, "in a surrender viewed by the Latvians as highly symbolic, the Soviet Army turned over the very image of its privileged status, its spacious officers' club in the heart of Riga. Its loss to the occupying Soviet Army in 1940 was a major blow to the national pride, because it had been built by contributions by the Latvian public to serve as a national cultural center." The Soviet military was not trying to communicate something to Latvians. Most likely, its action was just part of the withdrawal, and Soviet authorities did not expect the populace to take special notice. Still it was symbolic, so an account of the phenomenon must go beyond one of sending messages. It was a *focal symbol*, defined in chapter 4 as one that induces the observers to commonly expect a certain outcome in a game they will be playing with each other, through considering a certain part/whole relationship and each others' views of the same.

Focal symbolism is important in bargaining. In the prenegotiation phase, questions regarding the shape of a table induce joint expectations, self-fulfilling ones, about who will give in later on the real issue. Focal symbolism also figures in international crises. In a game model of chapter 5, chance events like an unintended border clash symbolically suggest war and raise tension, inducing one of the players to preemptively attack. The theory of symbolism shows how a pre-crisis arms control agreement, even a purely symbolic one, might hold tension down and preserve peace in the crisis.

Value Symbols

The core properties of a value symbol are affect and polysemy. It has affect in the sense that people hold a strong attitude toward the ideas it represents, and the symbol itself comes to be valued by the group. A flag generates the same positive response as the country it stands for. The affect can be negative, of course, like the reaction of most Americans over the years to the symbol of Fidel Castro.

"Polysemy" means multiplicity of meaning. A value symbol unites various ideas under one cognitive entity, and thus creates a synergy among the emotions attached to each of them. A national flag represents its country in the geographical sense, as well as its history, culture, and institutions. When these are united in the flag, the group's positive attitude toward each is augmented by the rest. A value symbol can function at the individual level—some are even purely private. When one is shared, however, the common attachment influences the individual's sense of identity in the group (Schuessler 1994). When a person acts symbolically in the value sense, it is to express who he or she is, rather than to bring about external consequences. The polysemy property of value symbols is parallel to message symbols and focal symbols, which represent general ideas by concrete actions or events.

Value symbols get "reified," that is, thought of and spoken of as if they were single, tangible objects. Some American lawmakers have tried to criminalize burning the U.S. flag. A flag burner might reply that he or she did not intend to burn *the* flag, only *a* flag, that there are plenty of others left. However, the attitude is that each flag is in a unity with the whole. When language uses the definite article, *the* flag, that is a signal that a reified value symbol has emerged.

The three categories of symbolism are not exclusive, and sometimes the same event involves several types. The emotional power of value symbols promotes their use as message symbols, as when someone waves or burns the flag to make a political point. Focal symbols acquire strong values, and certain grand ones of recent decades, the construction and demolition of the Berlin Wall or Nixon's visit to China, have influenced history. However, to clarify the dynamics of symbolism, these episodes may be too grand. They have acquired so many associations that it is hard to untangle the dynamics of each kind of symbolism. It is better to look at small and passing symbolic events, and this approach is developed in the next chapter.

CHAPTER 2

Message Symbols in Practice

In a tale that has been told in many countries, an emperor sends word to the local rabbi that he must come to his court and answer three questions, otherwise he will be put to death. The questions and the rabbi's answers will be in signs. The rabbi is in despair, when a young man of the congregation, a lowly poultry dealer, offers to go instead. When the poultry dealer arrives at the emperor's court, the emperor lifts up one finger. The young man holds up two. The emperor holds up an egg, and the dealer pulls a piece of cheese out of his pocket. Finally, the emperor takes a handful of wheat and throws it on the floor; the young man picks up the grains one by one and puts them in his kerchief. The emperor declares himself satisfied. Afterward, the rabbi wants to know what happened. "He pointed to me with one finger," says the young man, "meaning he would take my eye out, so I held up two to say that I would take out both of his. He offered me some food, but I showed him I had some. Then he spilled some wheat on the floor, but I thought it would be a sin to waste it, so I picked it up." When the emperor's courtiers ask him what the exchange meant, he explains, "I held up one finger to say that I am the one ruler here; he replied that there are two: God reigns in heaven as I do on earth. Then I wanted him to tell me whether this egg is from a white or brown hen, and he answered me back: Is this cheese from a white or black goat? I showed him that God had scattered the Jews, and he replied that the Messiah will come and gather them together again."

If national leaders are very lucky even their misunderstandings will bring harmony. More realistically they should understand symbolic communication and its pitfalls. This chapter asks: What are the grammar and vocabulary of international symbols? It gives examples of how messages are translated into symbolic form, how receivers extract their meaning, and how ambiguities arise. It surveys several hundred international symbolic messages gleaned from newspaper articles. The data lead to the theoretical discussion of the next chapter.

Communicating clearly, which is the focus here, is different from communicating credibly. The credibility question asks why the receiver should believe what the sender is saying, and many game models have addressed it. However, this chapter is concerned with how the receiver understands what the sender is saying. Also, it does not ask what message content ought to be sent—the strategic use of symbolism for a certain goal will come later in connection with honor and face.

The Database

A collection of message symbols was assembled from the Nexis electronic database of newspapers and magazines. Nexis accepts a phrase from the user and retrieves articles that have it anywhere in their text. It contains all issues of several hundred publications back to the early 1980s and is so large that the problem is discrimination. Asking for any article with the words *symbol* or *symbolism*, might return a million or so items, and many of them would not involve message symbols. I searched for phrases that were likely to be associated with message symbols: the expressions *symbolic gesture* and *symbolic message* along with terms like *premier* or *secretary of state* gave items that were almost always appropriate. Of course, the miss rate was high—many message symbols were reported without using these words—but the goal was to get a large body of data, not a complete one. The years 1980 to 1995 yielded about 680 different international message symbols.[1]

Some Rough Definitions

Before the items are described, some approximate definitions will be given of the mechanisms behind symbolic messages. Details are postponed to chapter 3, but having the basic ideas now will allow a grouping of the data according to the mechanisms used. A *prototype* is a semispecific instance used in place of a more abstract idea to help us manipulate it mentally. A robin, more than an ostrich, is prototypical of birds, and if we wanted to engage in reasoning about

---

1. It would be tempting to draw statistical inferences about what symbolic messages get sent and how often different nations use different techniques of symbolism or send various kinds of content, but that would be asking too much of the data. The sample was not a random one. The news sources in Nexis were not spread evenly over countries, and the search phrases may have systematically selected certain kinds of message symbols. Some data are better than none, however, and the 680 items can tell us roughly the form and content of what gets sent.

birds, we might think specifically about robins. Some prototypes represent classes of objects, and others are used for intangible ideas. The latter are *proto-typical scenarios* and for concepts like love, envy, or anger, they give us a specific, mentally manipulable script. A *metonymy* is the choice of a part to suggest the whole. A *conceptual metaphor* is a mapping that translates an extended set of ideas from one domain into those in another. Life becomes a journey; or money a liquid, so one can talk about "liquidity" or "cash flow." According to the the-ory developed in the next chapter, the simplest kind of symbolic message is sent by taking a prototypical story or category, choosing an action that is a part of the prototype, and performing that action. The action performed is the message symbol. The sender and receiver know the prototype and also have higher-level knowledge about each other's knowledge of the prototype and this situation al-lows the receiver to reason from the message to the prototype it probably came from, and from there to the sender's meaning. A head of state uses the proto-typical scenario of friendship—dines at the house of a former adversary, rec-ognizing that among the things that friends typically do, is invite each other to dinner. For some symbolic messages, another element, a metaphor, appears in the chain of logic between the prototype and the intended meaning. In this ex-ample, the metaphor is the mapping of international activities to interpersonal ones. A state is like a person, a country is like a person's house, dining together is typical of friends, so the message symbol is understood as meaning that our nations are allied.

The examples that follow, then, were described by the press between 1980 and 1995 as symbolic messages or symbolic gestures, except where noted. The survey shows that the bulk of the messages sent can be accounted for by a rela-tively short list of prototypes, metonymies, and metaphors.

Scenarios and Metaphors

The COUNTRY-AS-A-PERSON metaphor was the most frequent in the sample. The reason for its popularity is evident: it transfers the international domain to the interpersonal one, where the symbol sender can use the many prototypes around social relations. It includes two submetaphors. One can be termed A-COUNTRY-AS-A-SPECIFIC-PERSON. Saddam must get out of Kuwait, said Bush, but no one was so obtuse as to counter that Saddam was not in Kuwait, that he had made a short visit in August 1990 but had flown home. The other subtype is A-COUNTRY-AS-AN-UNSPECIFIED-PERSON, and it has various aspects: one thinks of countries as "friendly" or "hostile," of those with large militaries as "strong." Industrialization is maturity and other nations are "underdeveloped." The national person does not always have a gender, but when it does it is more likely to be male, especially in the context of war. Occasionally it is female (Milliken and Sylvan 1991; Rohrer 1995; Weber 1994, 1995), as in the 1990 talk of the "rape" of Kuwait.

These examples show that conceptual metaphors occur in networks, with some that overlap or represent subcases of others. Treating a nation as its leader allows war to become a physical fight between people and the United States to "push" Saddam out of Kuwait or deal him a "knockout punch." The metaphor A-COUNTRY-AS-A-PERSON is linked to A-WAR-AS-A-GAME and to another metaphor that came up often in the data, A-TERRITORY-AS-A-HOUSE. Examples from this network will be described first.

A-COUNTRY-AS-A-SPECIFIC-PERSON:
The Friendship Scenario

In this case the political leader generates a symbol by selecting an action from the prototypical scenario of friendship and support. What do we think of friends as typically doing?

> They get together and are seen together;
> they engage in social activities together—taking trips, dining, staying at each other's houses;
> they join and help one another on tasks;
> they do favors for one another;
> they use various conventions that signal friendship, like greetings, handshakes, embraces, or gifts.

In regard to meeting and being seen together, the database contains 72 meetings of international figures described as symbolic messages or gestures. Of these, 16 involved public association. In July 1994, after North Korean president Kim's death, some of his advisors stood with his son around the bier, to show that the latter had the support of the apparatus. A common form was appearing at a joint news conference. Engaging in leisure activities together came up six times and included a leader traveling with, eating with, enjoying recreation with, or staying over with another. In April 1987, U.S. Secretary of State James Baker attended Seder dinner with Jewish refuseniks.

Conventional signals of personal friendship appeared in many examples:

there were 13 symbolic handshakes and embraces, 6 instances of symbolic gift giving, and 4 examples of using titles or salutes or friendly appellations to show the respect concomitant with friendship. Examples were the Arafat/Rabin handshake of 1994 and Nelson Mandela's display at the May 1994 opening of the South African Parliament when he walked across the floor to embrace his rival Mangosuthu Buthelezi. In May 1988, the mayors of Istanbul and Athens played backgammon and, the newspapers noted, called each other by their first names. A related symbol of approval, although not friendship, was German premier Kohl's 1994 promise to shake the hand of the last Soviet soldier to leave German soil.

A recurrent pattern, of which there were 13 instances, involved an important person doing something for another country, by means of an action that would normally be performed by someone of lesser status. When a leader does the deed in person, the act is lifted out of bureaucratic routine to tap the COUNTRY-AS-ITS-LEADER subtype. The deviation from regular practice and the person's high position are clues that a symbolic message is being sent. It is hard otherwise to explain why in November 1992 Russian president Yeltsin went to South Korea and personally delivered to the president the black box from the downed KAL 007 airliner. In July 1994, the FBI director in Moscow personally received files on former Russian citizens accused of gang activity in the United States. After sacred Bolivian weavings were recovered from American art dealers, in October 1992, U.S. treasury secretary Nicholas Brady turned them over in person to Bolivian president Jaime Paz Zamora. The previous month, French president Mitterand had personally returned two historical cultural documents to South Korean officials. Prototypically, important people spend their time on important business.

A-COUNTRY-AS-ITS-LEADER: The Leader's Personal
Implementation Symbolizing Important National Policy

In some examples that are related but outside the friendship scenario, a leader personally implements some decision to endorse it as important national policy. In August 1990, at an air base in the central Amazon, Brazilian president Fernando Collor shoveled cement into a shaft that the previous military government had built to conduct a nuclear test. The symbol was repeated at another site the following year. (His actions may have been *only* symbolic—according to Krasno 1994, the test sites were quietly kept functional.) In August 1989, the leader of the Hungarian Democratic Reform Party personally opened a padlocked gate to allow East German refugees to enter Hungary. In January 1993, as U.S. marines left Somalia, two local leaders tore down the barricades separating parts of their city as a symbolic gesture of reconciliation.

A-COUNTRY-AS-A-SPECIFIC-PERSON: Visits to Recognize
Another Nation's Status

Symbolic messages often draw on prototypes around status. An important expectation in some cultures involves who acts as the host. A friend of mine who came from Europe to New Haven, Connecticut, in the 1940s, remembers her difficult adjustment as a young faculty wife. She and her husband were invited to social dinners, but when she tried to reciprocate, her invitations were politely but repeatedly declined. She discovered the reason years later: those higher up entertain those lower down but not the reverse. This rule has lost some force, but the idea is still around in other contexts—if the company president wants to meet with a lower employee, it is the employee who goes to the president's office.

Visiting another's country is therefore a statement of the other's importance. The database includes 74 trips to visit described as symbolic. In February 1993, the Lebanese prime minister expressed a wish that the U.S. secretary of state would come to Beirut to symbolically recognize Lebanon's sovereignty. In January 1992, the premier of Japan visited Kyongju, the historical site of the kingdom that first unified Korea. By recognizing the importance of the city, he was symbolically accepting Korean unity, sending the message that, contrary to Koreans' suspicions, Japan sincerely wished to see their country united. Another pattern, related to chapter 12's discussion of prestige, is to reward a country by arranging an important meeting there. In November 1989, it was proposed to hold a PLO/Israel meeting in Cairo to recognize Egypt's contributions to peace.

The rule of visiting to show respect also applies to individuals. In 1985, Senator Edward Kennedy spent the first night of his visit to South Africa at Bishop Tutu's home, signaling his friendship and recognizing Tutu's importance. (Here there was no COUNTRY-AS-A-PERSON metaphor—the senator was speaking for himself.) In February 1989, President Bush visited Beijing and invited a dissident Chinese astrophysicist to a dinner as support for human rights.

Some messages have caused trouble because they were ambiguous as to which prototype was intended. In June 1992, U.S. Secretary of State James Baker visited Beirut to meet the Lebanese president. He meant it as a recognition of Lebanon's independence, but some critics saw it as friendship with a puppet of Syria. Baker arrived there directly from Damascus, and this element was taken as supporting the worse interpretation. More than communications that succeed, misunderstandings like these hold lessons for diplomats.

A-COUNTRY-AS-A-SPECIFIC-PERSON: Metaphors Not Involving the Leader

The elements mapped in a conceptual metaphor are flexible. The scheme of TERRITORY-AS-A-HOUSE could have the territory be a country or a city; in the COUNTRY-AS-A-PERSON metaphor, the person is usually the leader, but it could be some other citizen, perhaps a diplomatic representative. Twenty-three acts involved diplomatic recognition and representation. Ronald Reagan's 1986 choice of Edward Perkins, an African American, as ambassador to South Africa was seen as symbolic. A prototypical angry gesture is refusing to talk to someone, so refusing to grant diplomatic recognition can be a sign of disapproval. In June 1987, the French government signaled its displeasure with apartheid by refusing to accept South African envoys. Just as one would walk out of a friend's house after a serious argument, international censure is expressed by an ambassador returning home. In the converse of the friendship scenario, disapproval is conveyed by refusing to deal with someone.

Sometimes a country does a favor to another country's citizen or group as a positive symbol toward the country. Favors to private individuals yielded 42 symbols in the corpus. The beneficiaries included family members who were reunited or persons needing medical care who were given visitors' visas. In November 1985, Andrei Sakharov's wife, Yelena Bonner, was allowed to travel to the United States for treatment. Deported individuals were allowed to return or political prisoners were released as symbolic gestures, the latter action used frequently in Israeli/Palestinian relations.

A-COUNTRY-AS-A-NONSPECIFIC-PERSON: Friendship, Support, Status, and Hostility

If the symbolic action is done by normal functionaries, the metaphor A-COUNTRY-AS-ITS-LEADER does not apply. Instead the whole country can be interpreted as the person. There were 36 instances of countries participating in tasks interpreted as symbolic shows of support. Examples were a French/West German army brigade conducting joint maneuvers in 1987 and the May 1994 proposal to send North Korean lumberjacks to work in South Korea. Similarly, Belize offered to send troops to help the U.S. contingent in Haiti.

Favors to a country in the form of aid and trade were continually described as symbolic—the database contained 33 instances. The international help sent as symbolic gestures was the prototypical kind by which people help people. As symbols, nations would offer food or medicine, not a favorable exchange rate in a trade deal. Examples were U.S. air drops of food and medicine over eastern Bosnia or the provision of supplies to Afghanistan in 1992. Unfriendly symbolic gestures numbered 35, and involved sanctions and embargoes.

The GOING-TO-WAR Scenario

The data suggest that leaders hold a prototypical scenario for going to war. The resulting symbolic messages use only a metonymy and a prototype—the scenario is at the international level, so there is no need for a metaphor to map events down to the interpersonal level. The scenario involves several steps, including using harsh language; cutting economic, social and diplomatic ties; making plans with allies; augmenting and mobilizing one's forces, moving them up to the other's border, and then attacking. That is the prototype for actually going to war—to send a warning a state selects one or more of the preparations. Weapons procurement, military operations, and military aid, including reductions or cancellations of aid, were described as symbolic 36 times. Shows of force are an element of this prototypical set, and the database contained 73 examples, such as countries moving troops near Iraq or to Bosnia, or the United States sending Patriot missiles to Saudi Arabia and South Korea.[2] Token acts of violence, of which 19 were described as symbolic, included the U.S. attack on Libya and the bombing of Iraq following the allegation that Saddam Hussein had plotted to kill George Bush.

The TERRITORY-AS-A-HOUSE Metaphor

Chilton (1996) argues that metaphors around TERRITORY-AS-A-HOUSE were at the basis of Cold War thinking. The common phrase "national security" taps it—one "secures" one's house against outside entry by building it solidly and locking it. Like many metaphors, it can be misleading. The idea that one must seal one's nation against outside dangers induces a focus on external threats like invasions instead of serious internal dangers like poverty, drug use, or lack of resources for education or science. Usages like "international security" or "global security" try to fix this fault by implying that it is the whole that must be secured, not individual nations. However, the metaphor counterposes an in-

---

2. Vagts (1956) gives many examples of military shows of force over the last two centuries.

side to an outside, so these are oxymorons without a coherent source domain to exploit.

The metaphor makes geography symbolically important in the symbolic message. There were 16 messages that gave prominence to national borders—many symbolic actions were performed at borders instead of in national capitals. In August 1994, Jordanians and Israelis stood in rows and exchanged gifts across their common border to symbolize the new peace. The same month, U.S. secretary of state Warren Christopher crossed from Israel to Jordan on a newly constructed road linking the two countries. Allowing free travel within one's country is like hospitality in one's home. Israel made such a gesture in August 1994, when King Hussein piloted his own airplane over Jerusalem. Travel between countries symbolizes friendship, and ending travel means a chill. In September 1990, the United Nations voted to cut air links to Iraq and Kuwait. The TERRITORY-AS-A-HOUSE metaphor also leads to the practice of presenting keys to cities. During a February 1993 visit, the premier of Hungary was given the key to Bangkok. In October 1985, Queen Elizabeth received the key to Belize City.

The NORMAL-ACTIVITY and INDEPENDENCE Scenarios

A symbolic message, more than an explicit statement, must be interpreted by considering its context. Some actions are thought of as the routine activities of life, and continuing to perform them in an extreme situation makes a point. Ten remarkably normal activities were described as symbolic. In October 1990, the staff of the American embassy in Kuwait had been stuck there for months. They shampooed their hair and washed their cars as a gesture of resistance, as if they were not severely low on water. In October 1991, Saddam Hussein walked across a repaired Baghdad bridge, symbolically asserting that Iraq had recovered from the air attacks of the Gulf War. In September 1993, during his battle with the Russian Parliament, Boris Yeltsin took a stroll around Pushkin Square. These daily activities were seen as symbolic because of their context.

A variant involves acting differently to show independence. Five instances were recorded, such as Palestine in 1990 instituting its own summer time system to separate itself from Israel. Estonia had done the same in 1988 vis-à-vis the Soviet Union. A good example, not in the database, comes from UN secretary-general Perez de Cuellar (1997), who in 1986 was invited to join the foreign ministers associated with the Contadora Group in a series of visits to five Central American countries to advance the peace process for that region. The group was to travel together, but concerned about perceptions of his independence, he arranged to travel in a separate aircraft, which would land at a different time than the foreign ministers' plane. In each national capital he insisted on a separate appointment with the president.

Getting One's Action Recognized as Symbolic

Belize offered troops to help the United States in Haiti, but what could they have added to America's military power? The event illustrates a prevalent phenomenon. Since a symbolic message is usually not an expression in the language, the intended receiver may not spot that it is a message at all. It is the sender's job to get the message recognized as such, and one way is to choose an action that in itself is ineffective. Belize's soldiers would make no real difference, so the audience looks for another explanation for the offer and recognizes it as symbolic. Declaring a cease-fire when hostilities have already stopped, declaring oneself nuclear-free when one never had an interest in those weapons, or signing a treaty to ban an inconsequential weapon all call for a symbolic interpretation since these actions have no other point. This practice is the source of usages like "merely symbolic" or "purely symbolic," and one might be tempted to include ineffectiveness as a requirement for symbolism. If symbols were unimportant by definition, however, the present study would be hard to justify. In the scheme used here, actions are symbolic not *because* they are ineffectual; ineffectualness is a device used sometimes to ensure that the actions get spotted as messages.

A related technique would be not only abiding by a treaty but surpassing it, for example, opening one's territory to verification beyond an arms treaty's provisions to show enthusiasm for the current agreement or an expanded one. The United States and Britain, for example, allowed inspections of their civilian nuclear plants beyond the requirements of the Non-Proliferation Treaty.

An action will be more likely to be recognized as a message if it is extreme or bizarre. National leaders are constrained by the decorum of their office, but others can use striking images. There were 36 nongovernmental demonstrations in the corpus, such as that of the intellectuals who floated wreaths down the Danube to show support for the Bosnian people. The pope, who inhabits a world of ritual, released white doves from his window each year to symbolize his hope for peace. In April 1993 in Kuwait, 30 Kuwaiti babies born during or after the Iraqi occupation were brought to a memorial for U.S. war dead, with the symbolic meaning that American soldiers had not died in vain. A dramatic technique is to pack many commonly used symbolic themes into one action. An example including aid to individuals, performing a task jointly to show friendship, doing something for the first time, and carrying out details personally was the August 1988 plan of Soviet cosmonauts to deploy a U.S. satellite into orbit from their space station. They went outside to personally release the satellite, which extended communication to doctors in remote areas.

The use of special dates emphasizes the symbolic nature of an event. Leaders called for peace on the fiftieth anniversary of World War II. In February 1986, Gorbachev made a progressive speech on the anniversary of Khrushchev's Secret Speech. Still, the most straightforward way to get a symbol recognized as such is to announce that it is a symbol—the famous handshake between Arafat and Rabin was presented that way well before their meeting.

The Symbolic Use of Language

Sometimes language is used symbolically, and this fact shows that symbolism cannot be defined simply as communication outside of language. A linguistic act can be symbolic in two ways: through the form of its language or through the meaning. There were eight examples of form, such as ex-Eastern bloc countries dropping the prefix "People's Republic of ____," Leningrad reverting to St. Petersburg, and the Strategic Defense Initiative being renamed the Ballistic Missile Defense Organization. In September 1990, Premier Yon of North Korea addressed his South Korean counterpart as "President," symbolically recognizing his legitimacy.

Classes of Speech Acts

Speech that was symbolic for its semantic meaning occurred 60 times in the database. Language performs several different tasks beyond asserting the speaker's beliefs, and the symbolic messages can be grouped by the kind of task they performed. One set of categories is[3]

> assertives, which assert the sender's belief in an idea;
> directives, which request or order the receiver to do something;
> commissives, which commit the sender to some action;
> expressives, conveying the sender's attitudes or feelings, such as congratulations or expressions of gratitude;
> effectives, which bring about a state of affairs, such as knighting or inaugurating someone;

---

3. The original set of speech act categories was due to Austin (1962), but the one used here is closer to Searle's as modified by Clark (1985).

verdictives, in which the sender announces a judgment and thereby determines an institution's policy, for example, declaring a winner where "the
decision of the judges is final."

The symbolic messages that follow are grouped by the typical purpose of
their language act, not by what the message was trying to accomplish on the particular occasion. A leader who offers hospitality to another is making a statement of friendship and therefore performing an expressive. Linguistically, however, an offer is a commissive, so that is the category used for the symbol here.

Expressives are statements of attitudes or feelings. There were 17, including declarations of support or approval labeled symbolic, many of them resolutions passed by legislatures. Countries sent apologies for past harms and offered condolences for losses. In October 1993, Premier Yeltsin apologized to
Japan for the death of sixty thousand Japanese war prisoners held in the Soviet
Union. In July 1994, President Clinton sent condolences on the death of North
Korea's Great Leader Kim, and in February 1994 during a visit to Jordan, the
prime minister of Israel offered condolences to King Hussein on the death of
his son. The press described these instances as symbolic because they were more
than messages between individuals. The sender was performing an element of
the friendship prototype and tapping the COUNTRY-AS-A-SPECIFIC-PERSON
metaphor as well. Clinton was expressing a U.S. desire to maintain ties with
North Korea, and Israel's act was seen as indicating a wish for renewed friendly
relations.

An example of an expressive in a symbolic mode was King Juan Carlos's
1991 apology for the expulsion of Spanish Jews during the Inquisition. Normally the apology comes from the perpetrators and normally it is delivered to
the victims, but here both were long gone. Other common aspects of an apology, like punishing the guilty or making restitution (chap. 11), could no longer
be undertaken. Therefore, as a speech act the king's apology was clearly defective. It made sense only as a symbolic message, part of a scenario involving
friendship and reconciliation. Just as Belize's offer of troops was notable for its
insignificance, the flaws in Juan Carlos's apology alerted the audience to a symbolic meaning.

Commissives, which pledge the speaker to a course of action, numbered 15.
Belize's offer of military support was one. To get one's promise spotted as symbolic, one can include clear flaws—make it extremely vague, or make it empty
by putting no time limit on its fulfillment, or make a commitment to an action
beyond one's control, perhaps to something far in the future. Examples were

Premier Kohl's 1990 promise that Polish borders are safe forever, the 1992 nonaggression statements issued by the two Koreas, and Jordan's 1992 promise to negotiate a peace treaty with Israel. For Kohl's or the two Koreas' pledges, the ultimate fulfillment was not up to the person announcing the promise, and likewise Jordan could not sign a peace treaty alone. In July 1994, a group of Americans in Haiti opposed to U.S. intervention offered themselves as human shields. The offer could not have been accepted, and thus was seen as symbolic.

Directives include requests, commands, and invitations (the latter might also be viewed as commissives, as promises of hospitable treatment.) There were 12 instances, such as Central American nations setting a deadline for the Nicaraguan Contras to disarm, the U.S. Senate Foreign Relations Committee calling on President Reagan to reduce American involvement in the Iran-Iraq War, or the Senate calling for a comprehensive nuclear test ban. These directives were recognized as symbolic because they clearly had no force, unlike normal directives. They appeal to the scenario of how one tries to get someone to change course, one element of which is calling on the individual to do so.

Twelve instances of effectives appeared, including the United Nations setting up a war crimes tribunal for the Balkans and making 1993 the Year of Indigenous Peoples, and the U.S. Senate in 1986 ratifying the Genocide Treaty. In 1990 the Lithuanian legislature voted to secede from the Soviet Union. These acts were seen as symbolic just because they were really "ineffectives"—the party making the proclamation was not in a position to bring it about.

Verdictives, slightly different from effectives, are declarations of judgments that determine institutional policy. In 1987 the U.S. State Department announced that Kurt Waldheim's past made him ineligible to enter the country. As Austrian head of state, Waldheim was immune from being barred, so the audience had to look for a symbolic meaning. In August 1993, the State Department declared that Sudan was a supporter of terrorism, with the congressionally mandated consequence that foreign aid would end. The action was interpreted as symbolic because aid was already very small.

The final category is assertives, statements implying the speaker's belief in certain facts. Greek prime minister Papandreou was alleged to have claimed that the Korean airliner downed by the Soviet Union was a spy plane. When one person is a friend or supporter of another, a stereotypical behavior is to agree with what that individual says. A newspaper writer implied that this disloyal leader of a NATO state was symbolically expressing support for the Soviet Union. This was the lone example of an assertive in the corpus, but it is notable that every category of language act was used symbolically at least once.

Ceremonies and Awards

Thirty-five instances of symbolic gestures involved ceremonies or awards. A head of state frequently visited a gravesite or memorial to lay a wreath, the visitor often being from a former enemy state in the war being commemorated. Ceremonies tended to symbolism of all three kinds, and they will be discussed further in the next chapter, after the concept of focal symbolism has been developed.

Grammars for Symbols

Some messages in the corpus showed the beginnings of a symbolic grammar. Two phenomena in particular appeared: the use of intensifiers, analogous to words like *very,* or *definitely,* and the combination of established symbols to generate new meanings. The Gulf War yellow ribbons showed the use of an intensifier—if one ribbon is a welcome, one hundred ribbons make an enthusiastic one.

Many symbols were emphasized through an action being a "first"—18 had this feature. In November 1989, the United States and USSR cosponsored a United Nations resolution for the first time, marking the end of the Cold War. In July 1989, George Bush became the first U.S. president to address the Polish parliament, and in February 1994, the queen was the first British monarch to visit Russia since the revolution. All these were described by the press as symbolic messages or gestures. In a historic example from outside the database it was reported that Richard Nixon, when his plane landed in China, made sure that he was the first one down the stairs and the first to shake hands with his hosts (Ambrose 1989, 512–13). This was meant to intensify the symbolism.

A frequent element in grammars is the national flag. The flag is not a communicative act in itself—one must do something with it, like wave it, salute it, pledge allegiance to it, fly it over a certain building, or burn it. For message symbols, a flag functions like a word in a sentence, the whole action being the message. Flags alone are value symbols, like the pope's doves or the queen's very person, so using them in a message symbol has the effect of putting an emotionally powerful word into a speech. Across the world, nations hold protocols for their flags' treatment, and the details suggest a grammar. It is proscribed to fly one national flag below another in time of peace, or to use it in advertising, or to let it touch the ground (McCaffree and Innis 1985). In 1987 during the Iran-Iraq war, a major international event was the reflagging of Kuwaiti tankers in the Gulf with American flags to communicate that the United States intended to protect them (Gamlen and Rogers 1993). A 1988 proposal for the Olympic Games was to have athletes from the two Koreas march together behind the Olympic flag. Often the shapes and colors in the design have meaning (Firth 1973), and some symbolic gestures involved including elements that recognized national groups. In the early 1960s a new Canadian flag was proposed that showed three blue maple leaves attached together in the pattern of a fleur-de-lis, the point being the unity of Canada's English and French cultures. In February 1992 on Independence Day, Sri Lankans flew black flags in place of their national flag to express their opposition to the government.

The Berlin Wall appeared in a network of symbols and showed the development of a grammar. It also showed how a grammar can span the three varieties of symbolism. The wall was built in 1961, but long before that, the city itself had been a symbolic outpost against communist expansion. This meaning was supported by the symbolic drama of the Berlin airlift, and the value associations generated probably had the historical consequence of reducing the cloud over Germany after World War II (Sutterlin and Klein 1989). When the wall was built, many Western politicians visited it immediately to demand strong action, but Konrad Adenauer, in the middle of an election campaign, failed to do so. His omission became symbolic, in the focal sense, of his complacency. The wall's strong value symbolism distorted history in the popular mind—many recountings of President Kennedy's "I am a Berliner" speech place it at the wall, rather than at its actual location at City Hall. The wall physically divided Berlin, but as a focal symbol it divided Germany and Europe. It was put into message symbols: political rallies and musical concerts were held there, and toward the end, it was decorated with miles of graffiti. The focal and message importance of its demolition under Gorbachev was at least as important as that of its construction. The rubble was used to build roads connecting the sectors that it had previously divided.

Conclusion

The forms of symbolism in the database are diverse but they can be categorized under a few headings. A practical question is whether a symbolic message will be understood correctly, but the method used here does not answer that directly, since it does not give us access to the intention of the sender or the interpretation of the receiver. However, their problem is one of coordination, of generating common understanding, and their expectations will be set by what has typically been done in the past. The information here can help guide the construction of a message symbol by showing the most commonly used techniques.

CHAPTER 3

Message Symbols in Theory

The introduction described President Mandela's eloquent gesture of inviting his white jailer to his inauguration. It was indisputably symbolic, but the puzzle is how we could understand it. It was not an expression in an established language or a convention based on precedent. Nor was the action of French president Mitterand, who, during the 1992 siege of Sarajevo, flew into the city's airport, announcing that his act symbolized the need to help people in danger. Mitterand compared the city to the Warsaw Ghetto, which had been a short flight from Paris but was ignored by the European leaders at the time. After his speech at the airport, he flew home. His action was symbolic rather than directly functional—he might have done more direct good for Sarajevo by staying in Paris and arranging for substantial measures. Its symbolic meaning was immediately understandable, even though there was no convention that leaders visit the airports of countries in distress.

This chapter asks: How can a nonlinguistic action carry a message? How can an unprecedented action be understood without a grammar? And what does it means for a message to be delivered "symbolically"? As to the third question, one cannot say that symbolism is simply communication outside a natural language. The last chapter cited condolences, apologies, and congratulations delivered verbally that the press described as symbolic. Conversely, if I frown at someone's remark, I am communicating outside an established language but not symbolically, except in the weakest sense of the word. Communicating outside of a natural language is not necessary or sufficient for symbolism.

This chapter defines the concept of a communicative act, possibly delivered outside of language, and then defines a symbolic message as a kind of communicative act. The elements of the definition are explained through three international examples. Finally, the chapter discusses the symbolic communication/conventional language distinction as a continuum. The Gulf War practice of displaying yellow ribbons has moved back and forth along the continuum over its evolution and shows the advantages and limits of sending messages symbolically.

Definition of a Communicative Act

The first step is to define communication without language. This issue was analyzed by the philosopher Paul Grice (1957) and those who developed his ideas.[1] Grice distinguished different kinds of meaning. The weakest sense, called *natural meaning*, involves simple inference, the way in which red spots "mean" measles. As an example of the second sense, suppose we are having a spat on the telephone and I hang up on you, and later I do not invite you to my party. My actions mean something to you as messages. Of course, they also "mean" something in the weak sense, as information relevant to some significant fact, that you will not be going to my party. But hanging up the phone is more than a piece of evidence that I am angry, it is my way of saying it. The meaning intended by the sender in a communication is *utterance meaning*. However, the term *utterance* is not apt here, since message symbols are often not uttered, so I will use *communicative meaning*. In line with this terminology and with Recanati (1993), I use *communicative act*, in place of "utterance," for an action that has this kind of meaning.

The third sense is *semantic meaning*, where a sentence in a language means what it literally says.[2] It is different from communicative meaning. "It's getting late," taken semantically, refers to the time of day, but when whispered to someone at a party, it has the communicative meaning that the person wants to go home.

The focus here is on the second kind of meaning, communicative meaning, since it allows an action to carry a message. An action carries a message by virtue

---

1. Grice's idea is adapted here for the present purpose. Schiffer (1972) revised Grice's definition to deal with speech acts other than assertions, and his modification is relevant here since future chapters will treat the meaning of challenges, apologies, and other performatives. Grice's definition was revised in another way by Strawson (1964), Schiffer (1972), and others in response to a series of increasingly complex counterexamples as to whether the sender was communicating simply an intention or an intention to communicate an intention, etc. The version here is close to Harman's (1974), which circumvented these complexities using recursiveness—the speaker is viewed as having an intention to communicate that very intention. Some philosophers find recursiveness objectionable, but I do not, since it places clear limits on the concept's meaning and can be understood and manipulated easily. Avramides (1989) and Recanati (1993) review developments of Grice's idea.

2. The distinction is similar to Austin's idea that saying something involves both an *illocutionary* and *a locutionary* act (1962).

of the actor's intention. An intention possesses three components: an initiating action, a chain of causes and effects, and a goal. The actor performs the action because of an expectation that it will trigger the causal chain and so bring about the goal or at least increase its likelihood. An initiating action is a communicative act if it is meant to initiate a causal chain of a certain kind. The sender must hold the intention that the action will cause the receiver to become aware of that very intention and that, *on account of recognizing that intention*, the receiver will believe something or do something. That is, the sender wants the receiver to follow a certain sequence of logic, one step of which is recognizing that the sender intends the receiver to follow it, and the conclusion is a belief or an action.

The self-reference in the definition makes it confusing, but an example will clarify it. When Sylvania withdraws an ambassador from Freedonia, that is likely to be a communicative act meaning displeasure. Freedonia forms certain expectations about Sylvania's viewpoint, and Sylvania intended Freedonia to do so and intended that Freedonia thereby recognize that intention. Recognition of the Sylvanian intention was a necessary step in Freedonia's thinking, otherwise it would miss Sylvania's meaning. Contrast this with Sylvania making military preparations that Freedonia observes and takes to mean that Sylvania is planning a war. Here Sylvania's intention in making the preparations does not necessarily include that Freedonia recognize that intention. Sylvania may be unconcerned about what Freedonia does or does not conclude. The military preparations have "natural" meaning in that they are relevant evidence but are not a communicative act.

The war preparations would constitute a communicative act if they were diplomatic signals, and this fact might suggest a simpler criterion: a communicative act is one intended to convey information. However, a modification of the example shows that this condition is not enough. Suppose Sylvania's military preparations were discovered by a Freedonian spy who sends word back home. In fact, it is a trick: Sylvania knew the spy was watching and would convey the information. The whole point of Sylvania's preparations was to convince Freedonia that it was planning a war. The military preparations are not a message, even though they were performed to send information. The sender's intention must be to communicate by having that very intention recognized.

DEFINITION: Sender X's action A is a *communicative act* to receiver Y, means that X holds an intention whose initiating action is A, whose goal is to induce Y to believe something or to do something, and whose planned causal chain involves action A causing Y's knowledge of this intention.

The sender's "reflexive intention" will be called the *communicative inten-tion*. The definition allows that a communicative intention might not be just that the receiver believe something—it might be that the receiver do something in response to a question or an order or a request, as with Mitterand's visit to Sarajevo. A communicative act meant to produce a belief is called an *assertive* communicative act, after Schiffer (1972),[3] and one calling for an action is an *im-perative* one. The *meaning* of a communicative act is the propositional content of the intended belief or the action to be done, and a receiver who recognizes the intention *understands the meaning*.[4]

The Interaction of Metaphors, Prototypes, and Metonymies in Message Symbols

Three examples show how the elements work together to produce a symbolic message.

Clinton's Hospitality

In February 1994, Britain's prime minister John Major visited the United States. In what the press described as a "symbolic gesture," President Clinton suggested that he stay at the White House and that they take a ride together on the presi-dential plane and travel to Pennsylvania to see places where Major's ancestors had worked. Clinton's message seemed to be that the nations were close allies. It was an important one to send in the context of recent frictions—against British objections, the United States had granted a visa to a Sinn Fein leader, and Britain had resisted U.S. calls for air strikes in Bosnia.

Clinton's action involved a metaphor, a prototype, and a metonymy. Clin-ton was appealing to a metaphor that maps nations into persons. The persons were the nations' leader, Clinton or Major. Relations among elements are also

---

3. This assertive/imperative distinction is different from the assertive/directive distinction of the last chapter. The former was applied to performative verbs like *promise* or *offer condolences*. This one applies to communicative acts in general. It classifies even a promise as an assertive, since a promise is meant to induce the receiver to believe it will be kept. These terms are used here in spite of the possible confusion to stay in accord with the original sources.

4. This definition involves a recursive element, so one might suspect that it leads to proposi-tions like those of "common knowledge" situations: "X knows that Y knows that X knows. . . ." It does, but ones that are slightly different. One can make a plausible assumption about the logic of intentions—that intending a goal through a causal chain implies intending each element of the chain—and another about a receiver's reason for drawing conclusions—that having a reason im-plies knowing that one has it. Then X's communicative act to Y means that "X intends that Y know . . . that X intends that Y know X's intention."

mapped: one nation being an ally of another is mapped into friendship between the leaders. Clinton's prototype involved the everyday concept of friendship. If one were asked for ways to express friendship, they might be the following: associate with the person; call, write or visit; engage in pleasant activities together; extend hospitality; eat meals with the person; express interest in the other's personal life; and so on. The symbol's metonymic aspect was the choice of items from this list. Some choices were more suitable than others in the situation— writing a chatty letter would not have had a public effect, so Clinton invited Major to stay at his house.

These are the ways to be a friend in stereotype, but there are ways to be one in fact. A person sometimes prefers to be alone. Could Clinton have announced that he was letting Major stay home and rest in the English countryside, to show Anglo-American friendship? This would have made a poor symbolic gesture because it is not part of the friendship prototype. One says, "I'm his friend, but I didn't invite him over." "But" signals that this is contrary to expectations (Lakoff 1987).

The structure of Clinton's symbol is shown in figure 1. To generate it, he worked bottom to top, but to decode it the audience goes downward. For a symbol to be understood, the decoding path must be reasonably unique given evidence from the context and other clues. Clinton made remarks that steered the audience to the right meaning. Also helpful was the prevalence of the technique of having leaders stand for their nations in international symbolic messages.

Definition of a Symbolic Message

Recalling that a communicative intention is the one the receiver is intended to recognize as a step in understanding the meaning, the definition follows.

DEFINITION: X's action A is a *symbolic message* (or *message symbol* or *symbolic communicative* act) to receiver Y, means that A is a communicative act from X to Y, and X's communicative intention involves Y understanding the meaning by recognizing that X chose A as a metonymy from a prototype of the meaning or from a prototype transformed by a metaphor.

Prototypes and Prototypical Scenarios

Mitterand's and Mandela's symbols are more complicated than Clinton's, and to analyze them, some elements in the definition must be developed. The first notion is that of a prototype. Prototypes and allied concepts have been increas-

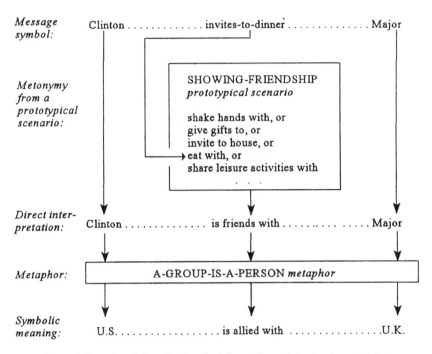

Message symbol: Clinton . . . . invites-to-dinner . . . . Major

Metonymy from a prototypical scenario:

SHOWING-FRIENDSHIP
prototypical scenario

shake hands with, or
give gifts to, or
invite to house, or
eat with, or
share leisure activities with

. . .

Direct inter-pretation: Clinton . . . . is friends with . . . . Major

Metaphor: A-GROUP-IS-A-PERSON *metaphor*

Symbolic meaning: U.S. . . . . is allied with . . . . .U.K.

Fig. 1.   The train of thought that deciphers Clinton's invitation to Major

ingly used in cognitive psychology to explain how our thought processes organize and manipulate categories (Lakoff 1987; Medin and Ross 1992). They are alternatives to the classical view of categorization that saw concepts as having boundaries, usually specified by a list of features. A classical category would be triangles, which are plane figures, closed, with three straight lines. If each requirement is met, the object is a triangle. One alternative to this is the concept of family resemblances, discussed for the definition of symbolism (chap. 1), where a concept is defined by some number of a set of attributes. The notion of prototypes is more radical. One version is that we hold in mind a typical member (a prototype) of the category, then determine an object's membership by comparing it for similarity with the example. The understanding of the concept of a bird, for instance, draws on the properties of a typical bird. Just how the prototypes are chosen and just what rules of comparison are used to determine membership are deeper issues—adequate theories of categorization can become complicated—but most modern approaches are based on the idea of a prototype or a related concept like an exemplar, a stereotype, a scheme or a script.

The modern theory was prompted by a number of difficulties with the classical approach. A theory that a category is a list of features was put in doubt by the difficulty of coming up with such a list even for simple concepts. What are necessary and sufficient conditions to be a chair or an elephant? If an elephant with wings flew over, would it be an elephant with wings or some other kind of animal, like an elephant but with wings? The claim that prototypes are psychologically real draws support from different experiments, beginning with those of Rosch and her collaborators (1976, 1978). Subjects showed reliability in rating specific objects as "typical" of their category. They were ready and consistent in answering questions like, Which is a better example of a fruit: a pineapple or an orange? These questions do not even make sense under the old view, where something is either a fruit or not. Other evidence for the reality of prototypes comes from studies of concept acquisition by young children, who learn the prototypical members first. The concept of a prototype also seems to have a role in psychological tasks other than categorization, like logic, induction, generalization, and remembering.

A category of objects often relies on a prototypical member, but a category of emotions or activities relies on a prototypical scenario. Anger or romantic love, for example, evade definition and are understood by semispecific stories centering on a typical event of anger or love (Kovecses 1986, 1990; Lakoff 1987). In the case of anger, the cast includes two people, the transgressor A and the transgressee B. The story starts with A committing an unjust harm against B. Then B takes offense and becomes emotionally and physically agitated. B's state causes and somewhat excuses the next event in the scenario, B's taking an action against A. In taking retribution B "gets even with" A, that is, does something back more or less proportional to the transgression. Through this response, B's anger is released and stability is restored. This is the prototypical scenario for anger—it describes the pattern that is expected. One can be angry without following the script exactly: I can be angry with myself, or I can be angry but not try to get even. The word *but* suggests that we have expectations that are being crossed, that the case does not fit the prototypical scenario.

Prototypes, either as objects or scenarios, are not entirely specific. A chair is prototypical furniture, but we do not have to picture the exact style or the kind of wood or the color. The question is then how specific the prototype is to be. Rosch and her colleagues argued that a prototype's level of specificity is chosen to maximize its operating efficiency in use. It is the best trade-off between two goals: having a manageable number of prototypes which are not too laden with details, and being able to draw many logical consequences from a mental representation. The specificity of our image of a robin allows us to deduce things about birds. Not all our deductions will be correct—penguins do not appear in the spring, or eat worms—but they are generally accurate. The preferred level for prototypes is called the basic level. Concepts below that level, like the idea of a certain subspecies of robin, are *subordinate;* concepts lying above it are *superordinate.* Clinton's symbolic gesture had the concept of interpersonal friendship as superordinate and the various ways of being friends—inviting someone to one's house, engaging in leisure activities—as basic and prototypical.

Prototypes and prototypical scenarios are cultural entities. Individuals can be confident that others know them. As an ideal, one can assume that prototypes and prototypical scenarios are *common knowledge* for a group, meaning that everyone knows them, everyone knows that everyone knows them, ad infinitum.[5] To the degree that the world knows that Clinton knows that friends invite friends to dinner, and Clinton knows this, and so on—all can be confident that the message received was the one sent. Also, for the purpose of explaining symbols, the different rules about prototypes and prototypical scenarios preclude us from postulating them in an ad hoc way. The prototype must be prominent through the culture, or there will not be common knowledge of it, and it will not be understood.

Metonymies

The second element of message symbols is *metonymy,* the use of a part to represent the whole. To say "my blood was boiling" can mean that I am angry. The phrase chooses an element of the prototypical scenario for anger, an internal sensation of a physiological response. In visiting Sarajevo, Mitterand took an element of the scenario of helping a friend in need—paying a visit—to represent friendship. Other examples are removing a sentry post at the Berlin Wall to celebrate the end of communist rule or the United States ordering a review of aid to Yemen as a message of disapproval for its stand in the Gulf War. Metonymies were traditionally literary devices, but evidence has grown that they influence our patterns of thought. Like prototypes and metaphors, they make their referents easier to manipulate (Lakoff and Johnson 1980, chap. 8; Lakoff 1987).

---

5. The idea of common knowledge is a technical one here. It means something different from the usual sense, that the idea is widely known. It is usually attributed to Lewis (1969), although Friedell seems to have formalized it earlier (1967, 1969). They wrote independently, but both were influenced by Schelling. Friedell was also inspired by Abelson and Rosenberg's symbolic psychologic (1958). Binmore (1992) gives an introduction to the idea, and Geanakoplos (1994) reviews recent findings. To be practical, the concept should be understood as allowing less than full certainty and the possibility that the belief is mistaken, so here the phrase *common belief* will often be used.

Conceptual Metaphors

In its literary usage, a metaphor is a specific expression, a figure of speech, like "the shadow of your smile," or "my wild Irish rose." A *conceptual metaphor,* as defined by Reddy (1979), is a way of thinking, an extended mapping that takes one conceptual domain into another. People think and speak in the *source* domain, the easier one to manipulate, and the mapping allows them to draw inferences about the *target* domain, the one of real interest. Like prototypes, metaphors are cultural entities, often used in language, and people know that they are commonly understood.

The standard naming rule for a conceptual metaphor follows the pattern THE-TARGET-AS-A-SOURCE. The naming rule reminds us that the metaphor involves a general mapping, a constellation of ways of talking and thinking, not a specific expression in the language. Reddy did a thorough study of INFORMA-TION-AS-A-CONDUIT, in which communicating information is mapped into sending an object or material to someone. In 1990, George Bush wanted to "get the message through" to Saddam that he must leave Kuwait. People talk of the need to "package" the message right and to make sure it does not get "distorted."

Conceptual metaphors help us understand a complicated target domain, but the mapping is usually imperfect and leads to systematic errors. In the case of Bush's attempt to "get the message through," it is possible that Saddam understood what Bush was saying, that he was ready to go to war but did not find the statement fully credible. A message's meaning and its credibility are different. The first may get through, but the second might not arrive with it. The metaphor's source domain of sending objects or material through a conduit cannot express this distinction, and the metaphor induces the user to overlook that there are really two tasks to accomplish.

Prototypes operate at the basic level of thought, but metaphors operate at a superordinate level (Lakoff 1987). The metaphor LOVE-AS-A-VEHICLE leads to expressions like "traveling down the road of life together"—here the vehicle is a car—or love "ending up on the rocks"—now it is a boat. For A-GROUP-AS-A-SPECIFIC-PERSON, the group may be a state, as when Clinton represents the United States, or it may be a group within a state, as in Mandela's symbolic act.

As well as the metaphors that arose in chapter 2, some others are common in international relations writings. Goertz (1994) describes THE-CONTEXT-FOR-A-POLICY-DECISION-AS-A-BARRIER, as when one talks of obstacles to its success, and WAR-AS-A-DISEASE. Milliken (1996) discusses the use of the latter metaphor during the Vietnam War. The idea of the spread of proliferation of nuclear weapons also draws on a biological metaphor. Another example is A-POLICY-AS-A-PATH (Chilton 1989), as when two nations are "on the road to war," and WAR-AS-A-GAME (Lakoff 1991; Cohn 1994; Milliken 1996), as when one missile "takes out" another. The latter is a good (or bad) example of how a metaphor can lead to false thinking. It would be hard to choose a winner in the Iran-Iraq war. Calling it a tie is the only way to satisfy the metaphor, but the two countries were devastated by this tie. The metaphor makes wars seem less horrific.

Having elaborated on these components, we can now analyze Mitterand's trip to Sarajevo and Mandela's invitation to his jailer.

Mitterand's Visit to Sarajevo Airport

Mitterand's visit drew on a particular subscenario of the friendship prototype, how one responds to friends in need. If one were asked for ways to do this, the ways might be to write a letter or telephone them, visit them, listen to them, give them advice, comfort them, or try to supply their needs. As the metonymic aspect of his symbol, Mitterand chose the visit.

Clinton's gesture to Major meant that their countries *were* friends, but Mitterand was saying that in general European countries *should* help Bosnia in its crisis. It was an imperative communicative act, rather than an assertive one. The difference cannot be deciphered from the action alone—the audience must know some context—and Mitterand's verbal explanation helped as well. He emphasized how his short flight from Paris showed that Bosnia was part of Europe. It is as close as Warsaw, he stated, recalling an event where evil was tolerated to the world's regret. He not only stated the symbol's meaning but explained its various symbolic elements to enhance its impact.

Mandela's Inauguration

Mandela's symbolic gesture exploited two prototypes. One is the scenario of reconciliation. It is a simple pattern involving a wrong, a restoration of justice, a gesture offering reconciliation, and an acceptance. The other involves how reconciliation is offered, the gesture-of-reconciliation prototype. In Mandela's case, he invited Gregory to a ceremony marking an important event in his life, as one would invite a friend to one's marriage.

Mandela's metaphor is A-COUNTRY-AS-A-SPECIFIC-PERSON. The black majority in South Africa is Mandela, the white citizenry is James Gregory, and one's domination over another is mapped into someone holding someone in jail. The

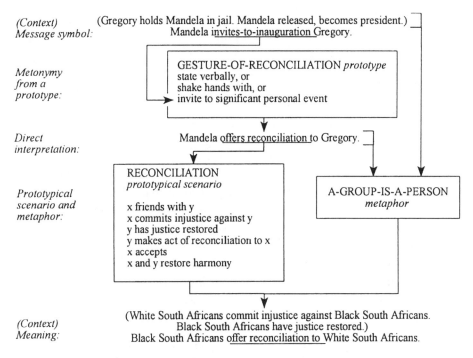

(Context)   (Gregory holds Mandela in jail. Mandela released, becomes president.)
Message symbol: Mandela invites-to-inauguration Gregory.

Metonymy   GESTURE-OF-RECONCILIATION *prototype*
from a   state verbally, or
prototype: shake hands with, or
          invite to significant personal event

Direct   Mandela offers reconciliation to Gregory.
interpretation:

          RECONCILIATION
Prototypical   *prototypical scenario*   A-GROUP-IS-A-PERSON
scenario and   *metaphor*
metaphor: x friends with y
          x commits injustice against y
          y has justice restored
          y makes act of reconciliation to x
          x accepts
          x and y restore harmony

          (White South Africans commit injustice against Black South Africans.
(Context)   Black South Africans have justice restored.)
Meaning: Black South Africans offer reconciliation to White South Africans.

Fig. 2.   Deciphering Mandela's symbolic invitation. The operations involving the prototype, prototypical scenario, and metaphor are applied both to the symbol and the context.

metaphor's role is more complicated here, because the mapping is to be applied not just to the message itself, Mandela's invitation, but to elements in the context in which it was sent, the history of the races in South Africa (fig. 2).

Mandela's invitation, though a recognized kind of reconciliatory gesture, is ambiguous. Taken alone, it might be a flaunting of his victory or an act of personal friendship. The receiver will have more confidence in an interpretation that fits more aspects of the action. Reconciliation is the typical first act of a new leader like Mandela. Gregory's role as the jailer is a salient feature that must be interpreted in any explanation of Mandela's symbolism. The fact that the invitation involved a public ceremony also alerted the audience to expect a symbolic message. A dinner invitation or a gift would have fit the prototype, but a gesture around Mandela's inauguration underlines the connection with his ascension to leadership. It makes it clear that he is signaling as a national leader, sending a symbolic message about the two races, not just about two individuals. It is not a perfect isomorphism since not every element of the reconciliation scenario can be mapped—there was no previous time at which the two men, or races, were friends—but enough fits to make the meaning clear.

The Symbol/Convention Continuum

In symbolic communication, then, a common knowledge of metonymies, prototypes, and metaphors leads the receiver to understand the message. When a symbol is used often enough, the steps drop out, and the receiver comes to recognize the meaning directly. The symbol becomes conventionalized. Why do people choose to say something symbolically, rather than just say it? Looking at conventionalization helps us answer this, since a symbol that has turned into a convention "just says it." Do conventions sometimes move back to become symbols? The yellow ribbons displayed in the United States during the Gulf War had different positions on the symbolic/conventional continuum over their history, and this section looks at the causes and consequences of their shifts.

Definition of Meaning by Convention

"Convention" cannot be taken in a literal sense. Most conventions did not start with a gathering of people who agreed to follow the practice. The use of a red flare on a road or the order of the alphabet sprang up somehow, and users continued to follow them because of precedent. Whatever conventions are, they are different from symbols. The red flare on the road means caution but does not symbolize it. According to the following definition, the essential feature is how people understand the meaning.

DEFINITION: A communicative act has meaning *by convention*, if the group understands the meaning by recognizing it as based on an agreement or a stipulation or a precedent.[6] Such an act is called a *conventional communication.*

---

6. As far as the users are concerned, a conventional communication appears more arbitrary than a symbol, so this concept of convention is like Peirce's concept of symbol. Arbitrariness was a major element in David Lewis's definition of convention (1969), but the present definition is more influenced by Schiffer's (1972). Lewis's approach does well for many coordination problems but has been criticized when applied to language, where it is not clear that a speaker's goal is always to coordinate at least in any reasonable sense. Lewis required that a convention be a regularity, constantly used in the group, and the focus of the present definition is that this regularity must have come about in a certain way. It has a narrower range than Lewis's, because it refers only to communications, not practices in general.

Evolution of the Gulf War Yellow Ribbons

The history of the ribbons suggests that two forces were moving the practice back and forth between a symbol and a convention. People understood the meaning of wearing the ribbons through some prototypical scenario or story that they called to mind. Over time the story faded, and people came to understand the meaning by precedent. That is, the practice moved toward a convention.

Intermittently, the convention was inserted into a plot—it was used in a folkstory, a song or a movie. Traditional and popular plots tend to be dramatic and emotional and to exploit cultural stereotypes and prototypical scenarios. The convention's use in a story line refreshed the symbolic aspects of the colored ribbon motif, and the popular mind again saw it as a metonymy drawn from the prototypes in the story. It moved back to a symbol.

Also important for the symbolic practice's survival was the fact that its use in a plot increased its connection with strong emotions and so its power as a value symbol. Moreover, if the movie or story or song became widely known, people had the confidence to use the element as a metonymy. These dynamics can be examined in detail for the yellow ribbons since they entered the historical record, the older uses set down as songs and stories and the newer ones described by the media.[7]

The Gulf War ribbons descended from a similar practice during the Iran hostage crisis, and this, in turn, came from two strands of tradition (fig. 3). One involved traditional and popular songs telling of wearing various colors to express love for an absent partner. The other included songs and stories in which a husband passed by his home on a train or bus and his wife sent momentous news to him, coding her message into a colored signal.

The first theme, wearing colored ribbons for an absent loved one, goes at least as far back as Shakespeare's time. In *Othello*, Desdemona refers to an old lyric song about a forsaken lover who wears a green laurel branch. Different embodiments of the idea have been used in traditional songs over the centuries. Through the present century, college students sang a mildly risqué version,

7. When Americans began displaying yellow ribbons around the Iranian hostage crisis in 1979, news reporters and the curious public contacted the Library of Congress for information, and were directed to the Library's Archive of Folksong, which became a hub for collecting and relaying the information. When the Gulf crisis broke out, the Archive had that role again. The account here is taken in part from the articles of the late Gerald Parsons, music archivist at the Library (1981, 1991), as well as Santino (1992), Tuleja (1994), Larsen (1994), Heilbronn (1994), Dunn (1991), Soens (1992), and Adams (1994).

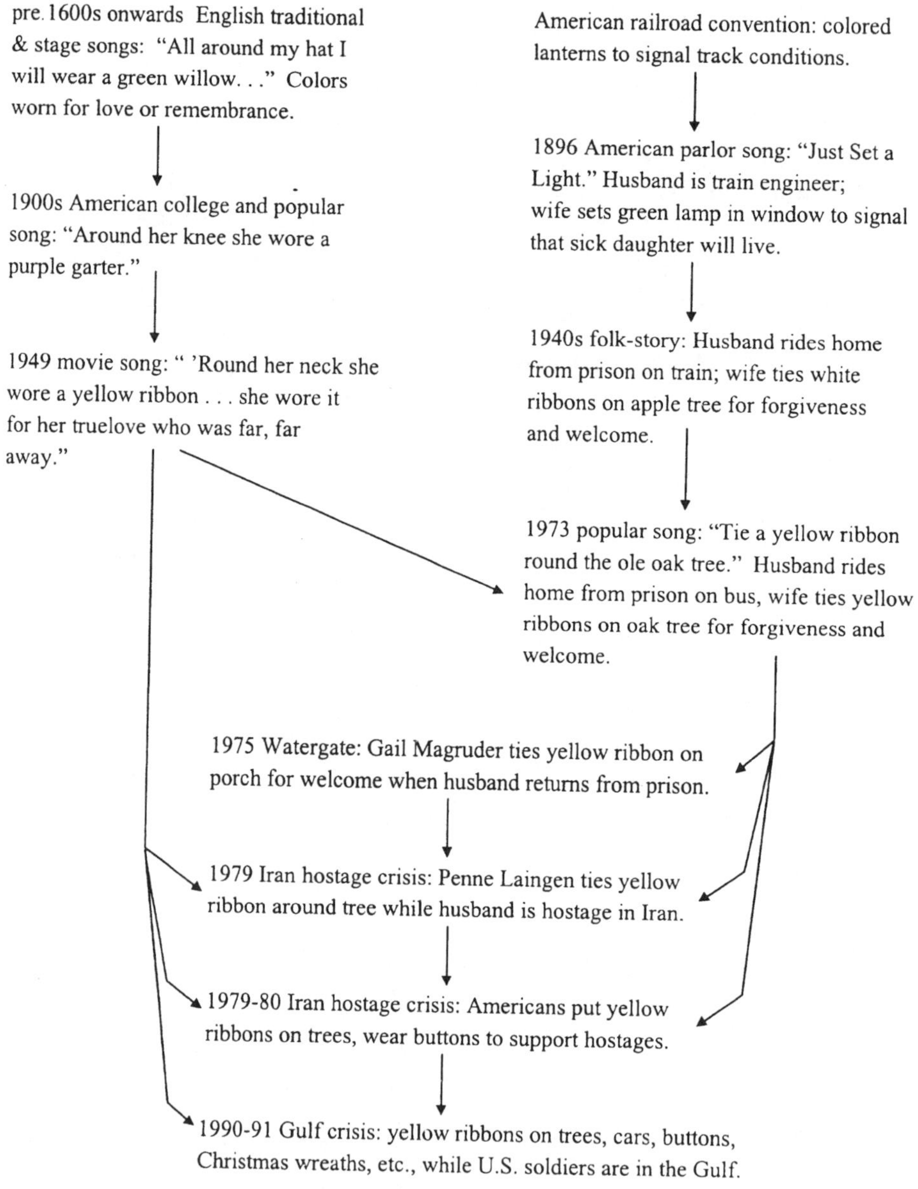

pre.1600s onwards English traditional
& stage songs: "All around my hat I
will wear a green willow. . ." Colors
worn for love or remembrance.

1900s American college and popular
song: "Around her knee she wore a
purple garter."

1949 movie song: " 'Round her neck she
wore a yellow ribbon . . . she wore it
for her truelove who was far, far
away."

American railroad convention: colored
lanterns to signal track conditions.

1896 American parlor song: "Just Set a
Light." Husband is train engineer;
wife sets green lamp in window to signal
that sick daughter will live.

1940s folk-story: Husband rides home
from prison on train; wife ties white
ribbons on apple tree for forgiveness
and welcome.

1973 popular song: "Tie a yellow ribbon
round the ole oak tree." Husband rides
home from prison on bus, wife ties yellow
ribbons on oak tree for forgiveness and
welcome.

1975 Watergate: Gail Magruder ties yellow ribbon on
porch for welcome when husband returns from prison.

1979 Iran hostage crisis: Penne Laingen ties yellow
ribbon around tree while husband is hostage in Iran.

1979-80 Iran hostage crisis: Americans put yellow
ribbons on trees, wear buttons to support hostages.

1990-91 Gulf crisis: yellow ribbons on trees, cars, buttons,
Christmas wreaths, etc., while U.S. soldiers are in the Gulf.

Fig. 3.   Evolution of the Gulf War yellow ribbons

"Around her leg she wore a purple garter, . . . She wore it for her Williams man so far, far away," or a crimson garter for Harvard, or other colors for other colleges. Tin Pan Alley versions were sent to the copyright office, the earliest submitted in 1917. The song was also used by soldiers as a marching cadence (Soens 1992). It was the theme of a 1949 John Wayne movie, *She Wore a Yellow Ribbon,* about wives and sweethearts whose true loves were soldiers who went off to battle Indians. The song became a popular hit that year, recorded by the Andrews Sisters and others and again in 1961 by Mitch Miller. In 1975, a version closer to the one used by Shakespeare rose on the British hit parade. It is clear that wearing ribbons for a soldier away at war has been a recurrent and widely known theme, so someone using it symbolically in the right context could expect the message to get through.

The other ancestral branch of the yellow ribbons had a wife signaling to a husband riding by on a train or bus. This also seems to have involved a song that descended from a practice. "Just Set a Light" was a sentimental parlor piece from 1896, which my mother sang to me as she learned it from her mother. A train engineer must make a night run, although his young daughter lies sick near death. His wife is to put a lantern in the window: if my darling is dead show the red, he tells her, if she is alive show the green. The climax is the sight of the green lantern. Gussie Davis, one of the song's composers, had worked as a railroad porter and it seems likely that he was inspired by the practice of using colored lights to show safety or danger on the tracks ahead (Cohen 1981). Cohen cites another symbolic rendering of the custom, in a nineteenth-century poem, "Will the Lights Be White?" by Cy Warman (1911). Warman went through a series of railroad color codes representing the troubles of life, and finally asked if he would see white lamps, meaning "go ahead," to welcome him into heaven. Again one finds an association of the practice with certain stories and emotions.

The song of the green lantern probably influenced a progenitor of the Gulf War yellow ribbons. This was a folk story, circulated at least as far back as the 1940s, about two men who strike up a conversation on a train. One has just been released from prison and says he is worried that his wife will not take him back. He has written her a letter telling her to tie a white ribbon around the apple tree in their front yard if she has forgiven him. If the tree is bare, he will ride on to start a new life somewhere else. He is too anxious to look, so his fellow passenger tells him the scene: the apple tree is covered with ribbons. The story was retold in newspaper columns and in sermons and made into a television play in 1972 starring James Earl Jones as the ex-con.[8]

8. There is no direct evidence that the song "Just Set a Light" was the ancestor of the folk story, but the two share the unusual theme of a wife sending a crucial message encoded into colors to her

These two strands, the 1940s story of the men on the train and the cycle of songs related to "She Wore a Yellow Ribbon," were brought together in 1973. Professional songwriters Irwin Levine and Larry Brown wrote "Tie a Yellow Ribbon Round the Ole Oak Tree." Brown had heard the story in Vietnam but he put the convict on a bus instead of a train and had his conversation with the driver instead of a fellow passenger. The signal around the tree, which was a "white kerchief" in the story as it had reached Brown, became a yellow ribbon. The songwriters changed the color to yellow because of popular consciousness of the 1949 song, because it seemed more romantic than white, and because it fit the meter. Their song became a radio hit and continues to be popular with orchestras playing for dances, so again it had a wider social base, broader than the typical popular or rock song.

The idea in the song had descended from practices: wearing colored ribbons or setting out warning lanterns. In January 1975, the plot element of ribbon tying was turned into a practice. When Watergate figure Jeb Magruder was released from prison, his wife, Gail, tied yellow ribbons on their front porch to welcome him home. This was a close parallel to the song. In April 1979 during the Iranian hostage crisis, Penne Laingen put a yellow ribbon on a tree in her yard, meant to stay there until her husband, Bruce, came home from captivity and untied it. Her inspiration was a television report about Gail Magruder's welcome for her husband. Her uncertain memory of the 1973 song lyrics was that they told of a prisoner, and she felt this fit the plight of her husband. Her idea of him coming back to untie the ribbon was not in the song but faintly suggested "She Wore a Yellow Ribbon." On December 10, 1979, in a *Washington Post* article "Coping with IRage," Barbara Parker suggested that Americans who were frustrated over the standoff could follow Penne Laingen's example. An association of support for the hostages' families ordered lapel pins depicting yellow ribbons and distributed them across the country to grassroots organizations like Boy Scout troops and to visible local celebrities like television weathercasters.

The hostage crisis ended in January 1981, but eleven years later the ribbons were revived. In 1990 as U.S. troops left for Saudi Arabia, ribbons appeared on trees, utility poles and the radio aerials of cars. The practice took on new forms, with newspapers drawing yellow ribbon banners across their mastheads and supermarkets putting pictures of ribbons on shopping bags and loading yellow tapes in their cash registers. When the bombing of Iraq started, the yellow storm

---

husband as he passes by on a train. Both end with the dramatic sight of the good news. A contrivance in the story also suggests that it was borrowed from the song—the daughter's recovery could not be foreknown, but one would expect that the prisoner's wife could have expressed her state of mind in a letter.

intensified. A Buffalo television channel wrapped its news desk in a large yellow bow (Hallin and Gitlin 1993). The largest ribbon manufacturer reported a one-year sales increase from five million to fifty million yards (roughly the circumference of the earth) (Larsen 1994), and when the supply of ribbon ran out, other materials, like paper, nylon, or plastic "Do Not Cross" tape, were conscripted. The ribbon decorations continued after the war to welcome the troops home. On July 4, Ross Perot bankrolled a project to wrap the Texas state capitol building in yellow.

Colored ribbons have been adapted to other meanings since, during the Somalian intervention and in November 1994 when a U.S. helicopter pilot was held in North Korea. Yellow ribbons have been displayed during searches for missing children or for friends lost at sea, and at murder trials they have been worn by family members of the victim.

Symbols versus Conventions: Why Say It Symbolically?

The Gulf War ribbons' ancestors moved back and forth between conventions and symbols. When the conventional practice was put into popular songs and stories, it became associated with metaphors and prototypes. Embedding it in a plot enriched its associations, which encouraged its symbolic use, where the latter evoked those associations. In the railroad song and poem, the colored warning lights become linked to the metaphor LIFE-AS-A-JOURNEY. "Life is like a mountain railroad," says another old song, in which the signals mean life or death on the tracks ahead. The folk story and song of the husband's return connected the ribbons to prototypes about ways to welcome someone home. Generally one can meet the person at the station, invite the person's friends over for a party, or decorate the house for a celebration. The last was the metonymy for the ribbons' appearance in the plot, and so the story and song connected them with the welcome home prototype. When yellow ribbons were used during the Iranian hostage crisis, they were very much a message symbol. Americans recognized the intended prototype and knew that others would see this too, because of the song's wide circulation.

To a large extent the process is cyclical—if the practice has associations that are too clear at the time, it will not be flexible enough for the details of the current context. As time passes, and knowledge of the song or story fades, the practice becomes a convention and more flexible in its meaning. Then it can be used in a new way. Sometimes this is explained by stipulation. The railroad engineer on the night run and the husband on the bus told their wives what the color code meant, and they were also telling the listeners this repeatedly in the chorus.

The association of the ribbons with forgiving a prisoner had to wane before they could be used for soldiers in the Gulf. By 1990, people were somewhat less conscious of the song and could base their interpretation of the ribboning more on the 1979 Iranian crisis. The 1979 use of ribbons was then a precedent, another basis of a convention. Those conventional communications that are based on precedents are understood because of the similarities of contexts between the precedent and the current situation. This is a different mechanism than the symbolic one of prototypes, metaphors, and metonymies. Wearers in 1990 could expect that their ribbons would be understood since the Gulf situation was similar to the 1979 Iranian crisis. They saw their country confronting another Middle Eastern tyrant and their loved ones being taken away from home for an indefinite time, and these similarities invoked the precedent. Other military actions had been conducted in Grenada, Lebanon, and Panama, but the ribbons had not appeared because the contexts were less similar.

A first generalization about conventions versus symbols is this: *A practice that appears in a conventional communication rather than in a message symbol is more flexible in acquiring new meanings.* The structure of prototypes and metaphors for symbols constrains the meaning more tightly than the mechanism of precedents for conventions. During the ribbons' evolution, their meaning shifted from unrequited love to forgiveness to support for soldiers to welcome home, and in recent uses back to lamenting the loss of a relative. The meaning fit what the context required, as long as it was not too great a step from the previous meaning. Gail Magruder, under the influence of the 1973 song, was showing acceptance of a husband in prison for a crime, but the song's connection to Penne Laingen's situation was looser—her husband was a captive, but he did not need forgiveness. The shift in meaning was possible to the degree that the audience used the precedent of Magruder rather than the plot of the song. Compared to the ribbons used in the Iranian hostage crisis, the Gulf War ribbons were one step further from the song—the soldiers were away from home but not captives. For a convention, each new usage forms a precedent for the next.

Other offshoots showed the meanings became more adaptable when the memory of the song had waned. From the fall of 1991, red ribbons were used for the fight against AIDS (Fleury 1992), white ribbons for opposition to violence against women, red ribbons around car aerials for opposition to drunk driving, green for environmentalism, and blue for survivors of child abuse. These meanings trace back to the song but have nothing to do with decorating a house or welcoming someone home.

A second generalization is that *a practice that appears in a conventional com-*

munication rather than in a message symbol is more flexible in changing its form. Under the influence of the 1973 song, Gail Magruder and Penne Laingen each tied a ribbon on a tree in her front yard, but later the ribbons were tied to radio aerials or Christmas decorations or became simply yellow supermarket tape. Their form moved away from the one in the song but remained understandable through a chain of precedents.

This flexibility increased the potential users. Boose (1993) believed that tying the ribbons in a bow had a suggestion of the feminine, of women who must stay at home waiting for the men at war. The college songs bring out the feminine connection, with ribbons in crucial places to be untied when the lover returns and the early users, Magruder and Laingen, were wives waiting at home. If the ribbons had kept that association, their use would have been limited. Picturing the ribbons on lapel buttons and bumper stickers helped to defeminize them.

A third generalization is that *message symbols can convey their meaning with more emotion and convey the emotion more accurately.* The lump-in-the-throat plot of the popular song put feeling into ribbon tying. Associating the message with the song's plot also conveyed the welcome-home emotion better than just asserting it.[9]

Americans seemed to want their symbol to have a value component and to see it as an old custom. Many people who called the Library of Congress for information already knew what they wanted to hear and were looking for an authority to back them up (Parsons 1991). They insisted that the yellow ribbons had been around since American soldiers marched off in the Civil War, perhaps as far back as the War of 1812. The claim of an historical tradition was made in newspaper columns and even in academic articles, but it is almost surely false. Library of Congress researchers found no evidence in nineteenth-century letters, diaries, photographs, or fiction. The military connection comes from this century, with the soldier's marching song and the John Wayne movie, and one suspects that belief in an old tradition is a fuzzy confusion of the movie with history, just as the popular mind moved President Kennedy's speech to the Berlin Wall. Some of those who put up ribbon assemblages misremembered the 1973 song as referring to a returning Vietnam veteran, not a convict, and claimed the song recorded a real incident in Brunswick, Georgia (Heilbronn 1994).[10]

A final generalization is that *a symbolic message can be more ambiguous than*

---

9. A movement in England to mount paper Union Jacks in windows during the Gulf War did not spread (Verkuyten 1995).

10. In spite of this, yellow ribbons have not yet passed the "definite article" test for a value symbol: one can speak of "the flag" and "the dove of peace" but not "the yellow ribbon."

a conventional communication. This is often an advantage. The ribbons expressed any or all of these stances: opposition to Saddam, support for Bush's policies, personal support for the troops, a hope that they would return safely, and solidarity with the rest of America. Some people interviewed by Heilbronn saw the ribbons as making up for the shabby treatment of the soldiers who returned from Vietnam. The ribbons were promises that things would be different, and many who had doubts about the Gulf War itself put them up anyway. The symbol's ambiguity had the advantage that America could feel united emotionally without really being united politically.

Overall, yellow ribbons were more attractive as symbols than conventions because of the imprecision of their message and the strong values conveyed by their association with prototypical stories. The same traits apply to many examples of the last chapter and are typical reasons for choosing symbolism over direct language for a message.

CHAPTER 4

Focal Symbols

The introduction described how the Soviet army gave up its officers' club and Latvians got back their cultural center after 50 years. The action was symbolic but it could not have been a symbolic message since the Soviet military did not aim to communicate anything. This was an example of a focal symbol, which is, roughly speaking, an event that establishes a focal point in a game through an analogy or a prototype.[1]

A focal point is an outcome that develops because players commonly expect it, based on their beliefs about others' beliefs about extra-game factors. (Some examples will be given shortly.) Outcomes become focal in other ways: by their prominence, by agreement among the players, or by precedent. When a focal point is generated by a focal symbol, however, the mechanism in play is a particular one that deserves to be called symbolic. The players' common expectation is produced by their consideration of a certain member/set relationship. The member is the focal symbol and the larger set is a class of events that either show an analogical similarity to it or, in some cases, is the class of events for which the symbol is a prototype. In turn, this set is associated with a particular game outcome and so leads the players to develop self-fulfilling expectations of that outcome.

In the officers' club example, by the end of August 1991 Latvia was assured of its own government and the debate turned to the degree to which other forms of Soviet influence would be acceptable. When the Soviet army left the club, Latvians saw an analogy with the Soviet withdrawal from their country because of the structural similarity. Latvians surmised about each other that they were

---

1. The concept of focal point is connected to that of a Nash equilibrium. The latter is described in detail in appendix B, but here it can be summarized as a set of moves, one for each player, that no player would want to change if he or she knew the others' moves. If the outcome is a Nash equilibrium, the expectations produced by the focal point are consistent—if a player believes the others will do their part, that player has the incentive to choose consistent with the outcome as well.

thinking on similar lines, and each was more confident to act for independence. A move that might have left someone isolated and vulnerable now had an expectation of support, thanks to the focal point generated by the symbol.

First this chapter will elaborate on the difference between focal symbols and message symbols, then it will distinguish focal symbols and focal points in general. It will give some examples of focal symbolism and finally a definition. Jervis (1989) discussed a series of examples, and the present definition allows an account of two of these—symbolic leadership and prenegotiation symbols—as forms of focal symbolism. Official ceremonies are then interpreted as a mélange of focal, message, and value symbolism. The next chapter will present crisis tension as focal symbolism, and symbolic contests will be discussed briefly in chapter 13.

Focal Symbols Compared with Message Symbols

Message and focal symbols share a common consequence—people get mutual understanding of each other's thinking. A message symbol causes a convergence of beliefs between the sender and receiver, but focal symbols do not require a sender. There is convergence of beliefs in the group, but it comes from an external event. The failure of President Carter's mission to free the Iranian hostages was taken to symbolize his foreign policy frustrations, but the failure was not a communication from Carter. It resulted from a dust storm, a mechanical fault in a helicopter, and various human decisions. None of these involved the self-referential intention characteristic of sending a message.

Sometimes the distinction between focal symbols and message symbols is subtle, as when the symbol is an intentional act but the intention does not include the communication of that intention. A major symbol of the Gulf War was the perceived success of the Patriot missiles in downing Iraqi Scuds. Many Americans connected the Patriots with the superiority of U.S. technology over Saddam's raw force. They knew that others saw it this way, and these beliefs mobilized support for the war. George Bush had put the Patriots in place deliberately, and it is likely that he hoped that their success would be taken symbolically, but Americans did not interpret that success as a communication from their president about what he wanted them to believe. The Patriots were a focal symbol, not a message symbol.

It is remarkable that this form of agentless symbolism has been so overlooked. The only exception I know of is Jervis's discussion. The explanation may lie in the emphases of the particular disciplines that study symbols. Semiotics, allied fields of philosophy, linguistics, and anthropological studies of ritual generally look at repeated behaviors, but focal symbols tend to be specific events. International relations scholars and historians deal with specific events but tend not to be concerned with the theoretical aspects of symbolism. Other studies of symbolism have come from the structural study of myth, the theory of literary criticism, religious studies, and the sociology of symbolic interaction, but these emphasize communication and tend not to look at focal symbolism.

Focal Symbols Compared with Focal Points

"Focal symbolism" alludes to Schelling's idea of focal points in games (1960). This section discusses how a focal symbol determines a focal point through symbolic processes. In 1957 Schelling put a now-famous question to some colleagues at Yale: you arranged to meet someone in New York City at a certain time but forgot to agree where, and now you must choose a place, hoping that your friend makes the same choice. They were not necessarily to answer the first place that came into their minds. Instead they were to consider how their friend would see the problem, knowing that they both were going through the same mental process. Most of them chose the clock in the middle of Grand Central Station. Perhaps they figured that people generally meet there, or perhaps that the clock is large and impressive. Or perhaps the key was that Grand Central is where one gets off the train from New Haven.[2] None of these reasons involve the abstract properties of the game; the players are going outside the game to solve it.

Even when there are strong game-theoretical reasons for choosing one outcome, the contextual factors might prevail and lead to another. Suppose that there were exactly one other place to meet, the Cloisters, and both knew it to be a pleasant site that would give each higher utilities (matrix 1). Each friend might still choose the clock. Focality can be more powerful than high payoffs.

Definition of a Focal Point

A focal point will be defined as an outcome that players believe to be more likely based on extra-game-theoretic factors.[3] A further condition is that this greater likelihood be based not just on their beliefs about the extra-game factors but on their beliefs about other players' beliefs about them. Suppose I think my friend

---

2. Pairs of students from other cities, however, are usually able to select a common meeting place based on their local knowledge.

3. Mehta, Starmer, and Sugden (1994) use the term *Schelling salience* for roughly the present concept. Here the term *salience* is saved for the immediate psychological impact of a stimulus, without any cogitations about what others might be thinking.

	Go to Grand Central	Go to the Cloisters
Go to Grand Central	*1, 1*	0, 0
Go to the Cloisters	0, 0	*2, 2*

Matrix 1.   Where to meet in New York, a game with a focal point. Nash equilibrium outcomes (see this chap., n. 1) are italicized.

will reflexively stop at the clock since it is the first thing he comes on when he steps off the train. Unknown to me, he reasons the same way, and we meet. Going to the clock is then not a focal point. Simply forming an opinion about each other's action is not enough. There must be higher level thinking about each other's thinking for the outcome to be a focal point.

DEFINITION: A *focal point* is a game outcome that the players perceive as more likely due to their beliefs about each other's beliefs about each others' consideration of extra-game-theoretic factors (or higher-order beliefs about these factors).

Contrast the general focal *point* of the clock at Grand Central with the focal *symbol* of the officers' club in Riga. To represent the Latvian situation as a game, the innocent simplification is made that the country has exactly two citizens who are deciding whether they can rely on each other to join the push for full independence. The game is depicted here as a Stag Hunt,[4] shown in matrix 2 and discussed in appendix B, and it has two pure strategy equilibria. One equilibrium is the mutually beneficial one of jointly acting for independence, and the other is the inefficient one of both doing nothing. It is assumed that the outcome will be one or the other—that the Latvians understand each other well enough to know their expectations in the game following their observation of the Soviet withdrawal. The Soviet withdrawal from the club symbolically suggests the upper left equilibrium as a focal point because of its analogy to the larger Soviet withdrawal from Latvia. Both events have similar structures involving giving up power and leaving, and the analogical mapping is further supported by the context—the club was already established as a symbol of Latvian

---

4. The Stag Hunt has been used to represent social movements (e.g., Chong 1993). Brown (1965) used it to model a lynch mob.

	Push for independence	Stay silent
Push for independence	*4, 4* (Soviet withdrawal)	1, 3 (vulnerability for one)
Stay silent	3, 1 (vulnerability for one)	*2, 2* (mutual inaction)

Matrix 2. Outcomes and payoffs for a game involving Latvians' decisions on collective action. Nash equilibrium outcomes are italicized.

national culture. This is different from the focal point of the clock in Grand Central. It is not in any larger class of analogous events that selects it as a place to meet. It is focal for other reasons, either precedent or salience or physical centrality.

The officers' club example was a collective action problem that involved a focal symbol. Other collective action examples have involved focal points that were not focal symbols, and the two processes can be compared. Marketplaces, statues, or historic sites provide locations for political demonstrations (Karklins and Petersen 1993), and the likely reason is their prominence, their centrality, or for the statues, their historical associations. Lohmann (1992, forthcoming) discusses the growth of weekly demonstrations in Leipzig for East German independence. Each protest march seemed to grow based on how many people had shown up the previous week. Anything that publicly distinguishes an outcome might make it focal—Tilly (1978) notes that traditional holidays often provide the dates for spontaneous political demonstrations. These examples have the elements of higher-level knowledge playing a role but lack the requirement that the larger set is evoked by an analogy or prototype.

Besides analogy there is another mechanism that produces focal symbols. It involves prototypes, often combined with metonymies. After the breakup of the Soviet Union, Ukraine's nuclear warheads came to symbolize its sovereignty. By holding the kind of weapon that many powerful sovereign states possess, the country had one element from the prototype of a powerful state (Sagan 1996). Power could not be symbolized by a large shoe industry, for example. The difference between analogy and prototype as symbolic mechanisms is that the former involves structure and the latter overall similarity of surface features. The former can generate a class of like objects not contemplated before, but prototypes must be preestablished in the culture. The common element between the mechanisms is the connection of the symbol to the outcome through a larger class of events. A symbol must stand for something broader. If there were no such class in the players' minds, if the connection between the event and the outcome were just a matter of similarity, this might constitute precedent but not symbolism.

Definition of a Focal Symbol

Roughly, a focal symbol is an event, not necessarily brought about by any player, that establishes a focal point in the game by generating the higher order beliefs that the players are following a certain logic that connects the symbol to a larger set and that set, in turn, to the outcome.

DEFINITION: Suppose S is an event, M is a class of events containing S, and G is a game. Then S is a *focal symbol* with meaning M if the following mechanism leads to a focal point in G through each player's belief that the mechanism is in operation and belief in other players' beliefs in that: the occurrence of S evokes the larger class M in players' minds through analogy or prototypicality, and M evokes the focal point of G.

In the definition, an *event* means an occurrence at a relatively specific time and place. In the officers' club example, S is the Soviet Army's withdrawal from the club, and M is the set of events, the general Soviet withdrawal from Latvia.

How Focal Symbols Get Noticed

To become a focal symbol, the event must first get noticed, and players must believe that others have noticed it. A focal symbol gets noticed in two ways. Sometimes players are looking for it because they face a coordination problem, and sometimes it forces itself on their consciousness. In the latter case, the event is said to be *salient*, meaning that one pays attention to it without a deliberate decision to do so. Salience has often been used as an explanatory variable in the psychology of perception. For the Gestalt psychologists of the early part of the century it was what differentiated a perceived figure from the background, and social psychologists have used it to explain perceived group differences and identities (Taylor and Fiske 1978). It is different from focality in that it is a one-person concept, so levels of belief are not involved. When Schelling asked his respondents to guess where their friend would go to meet them in New York, he was tapping focality, not salience.

Some focal symbols are innately salient—the Berlin Wall was miles of concrete and wire meandering through the city. Others are made salient by the context. A striking symbol of the Gulf War was the photograph of U.S. marines disembarking from helicopters in Kuwait City. Readers recalled the opposite scene at the end of the Vietnam War, when helicopters took soldiers and refugees from the roof of the Saigon embassy. The 1991 helicopters became symbolic of America's liberation from the "Vietnam syndrome."

How Focal Symbols Evoke or Construct Their Meaning

After a focal symbol has been discovered, it must evoke the larger class that is its meaning. The two mechanisms, prototypicality and analogy, will be described in detail.

Prototypical Focal Symbols

Here the class of events to be evoked is a concept already familiar to the audience. A prototypical object or scenario was defined as a specific example used in our thinking for a wider category (chap. 3). This is the mode by which Che Guevara was a symbol of Latin American revolution and Nelson Mandela was a symbol of resistance to apartheid. There are different ways in which items become prototypical. Some are *central* in their category, in the sense that they are fairly similar to the other members. As a bird, a robin is a better example than a penguin, because of its physical features and behavior.[5] Prototypicality can arise from an object's function: as a prototype for furniture, a chair is better than a telephone or a rug, and a gun is better than a whip as a prototype of a weapon. In other cases a category is brought to mind by an *ideal* member. The story of Tristram and Isolde symbolizes romantic love, although their love was never consummated and so lacked a central feature of such a relationship. It had one core feature to a high and pure degree, selfless devotion. A third way to stand for a category is as a *stereotype*. The item's prominence is socially based, ingrained in the group's thought patterns, and the group is conscious of that fact. Compared to prototypes by centrality or to ideals, a stereotype's status is less due to its innate features. It represents its class somewhat by convention and precedent. Racial, political, and occupational groups usually have stereotypes. Central prototypes, ideal prototypes, and stereotypical prototypes all involve the linking of a specific member to a larger category (Lakoff 1987).

---

5. The idea of centrality is that if one constructed a psychological space based on placing similar entities close together, the prototypes would lie in the middle. When subjects were given somewhat similar tasks, judging what is a typical tool, fruit, flower, etc. (e.g., McEvoy and Nelson 1984), they gave prototypes that seemed to be based on centrality.

Analogical Focal Symbols

Unlike a prototypical symbol, one based on analogy constructs a new class on the occasion. Borrowing Lakoff and Johnson's phrase from their study of metaphor (1980), an analogical focal symbol can "create similarity." The essence of analogy, as the concept is used here, is a mapping based on similarity of structure meant to resolve some specific question (Gentner 1989; Holyoak and Thagard 1995).

What does it mean to say events have a similar structure? An event can be described in terms of objects, features of these objects, and relationships among these objects. An object might be the Berlin Wall. A feature is a property of a single object, like its size or shape or material. Relations hold between or among objects (the East German government *constructs* the Berlin Wall, a flag *flies over* an embassy).[6] Two structures are isomorphic if there is a mapping of objects into objects, features into features, and relations into relations such that when features or relations hold among certain objects before the mapping, the mapped versions of those features, relations, and objects also hold. Electrical current is isomorphic to water flow in that one can map electrons into water, voltage into height of the water's source, and electrical current into water flow, so that truths in the first system are also valid in the second.[7] The greater the height of the water (voltage) the greater the flow (electrical current). (Isomorphism will be clarified in the Berlin Wall example of fig. 5.)

Rules for Analogies: Structural Similarity, Systematicity,
and the Persistence of Causation

A strong analogy depends on the successful mapping of the pattern of relations. Features are less important. Gentner labeled this the *principle of structural similarity,* and it is illustrated by an experiment by Goldstone, Medin, and Gentner (1991). Subjects were shown stimuli of columns of geometrical shapes (fig. 4)

---

6. There are many ways to do this, and formally, one could turn any relationship into a feature by defining $X(y)$ to mean that country y is under attack by x. Features, however, are supposed to refer to general properties, not specific entities, and the representation is supposed to reflect what is psychologically natural.

7. Very often the isomorphism is not exact. Real-life analogies will be imperfect or incomplete—higher voltage does not mean that current moves faster, so speed of movement cannot be mapped. Sometimes elements are not mapped one to one. Holyoak and Spelman's article (1992) asked, "If Saddam is Hitler, who is George Bush?" Bush's role shared features with Roosevelt's and Churchill's. Instead of making a definite choice, subjects seemed to use both to support the analogy with World War II, which was so influential before the Gulf War.

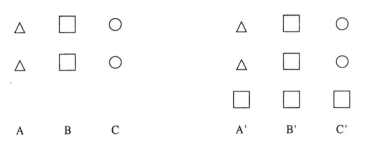

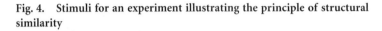

Fig. 4. **Stimuli for an experiment illustrating the principle of structural similarity**

and asked whether column A was more similar to B or to C. Twenty-three of the 28 subjects judged A more similar to B—two triangles were more like two squares. However, with A', B' and C' the same as before with an added common shape, all twenty-eight subjects judged A' to be more similar to C'. Why should adding a common element change the similarities? The suggested explanation was that subjects compared the right-hand group of columns not by its features, "square," "triangle," and so on, but by relations among its elements, "same as" or "different from." Relationally, A' and C' were more similar. One might think that similarity involves adding up the similar features, but evidently it does not. Analogical reasoning depends more on the structural pattern of the relations.

Another regularity in analogies is the *principle of systematicity* (Holyoak and Thagard 1995). Given alternative domains to map a source into (which would be alternative symbolic meanings in the case of analogical focal symbols), people choose the one that maximizes the *amount* of structure that can be mapped. They attribute more confidence to an inference based on a wider analogy.

A third principle is the *persistence of causation,* that it is generally mapped into itself (Gentner 1989). Water flow might be mapped into electrical current, but the mapped version of voltage will still *cause* the mapped version of current.

Pragmatic considerations are also important—when deliberating a move in a coordination game, players would choose an analogy that solves the problem under consideration. The question at issue must be mapped into one to which the player, and everyone else, knows the answer. To summarize, analogical arguments gain strength from the extent of the mappings, the similarity of mapped features and relationships, and most importantly, the isomorphism of structures. In analogical focal symbols, these make us more confident that others see the symbol as we do.

An Analogical Focal Symbol: The Berlin Wall

Through the Cold War, a dominant symbol was the Berlin Wall. Chapter 2 discussed its features as a message symbol. As a focal symbol it represented the division of East and West and the suppression of human rights under communism. One mapping is straightforward (fig. 5).[8] East Berlin becomes the Eastern bloc, and West Berlin becomes the Western bloc. The wall becomes the division of the world into free and suppressed. As is required, however, causation is mapped into causation.

Focal symbols can draw on several analogies simultaneously. The wall could be thought of as dividing Germany, or Berlin, or one could see a more feature-oriented analogy between the wall and a prison. This analogy shows the unimportance of features relative to structure. Berlin, a city, is mapped into Europe, a region of nations. Bricks and mortar are put into correspondence with Soviet policies. The analogy is strong nevertheless, because the structure of the two diagrams is the same.

Symbolic Leadership

One variety of focal symbolism involves leadership. The country's citizens draw an analogy between the leader's actions and their own and tend to follow the leader's example. There is less problem of getting the event noticed: a leader's deeds are immediately salient. Chapter 12 will examine a positive aspect of this leadership as "moral authority," but sometimes an unwanted analogy is drawn—a leader tries to send a symbolic message or to do something or to believe something but uses a form that has an unwanted focal meaning. In September 1993, Yitzhak Rabin and Yassar Arafat met at the White House to sign a peace declaration and ended the ceremony with the famous handshake. Rabin, who had previously declared that he would never shake Arafat's hand, said he had done it unwillingly but could not refuse in front of the U.S. president and the world (*MacNeil-Lehrer Report*, September 13, 1993). He had not meant the handshake the way the world took it. His words were ineffective, however, and even people who were aware of this disavowal saw the handshake as symbolically important.

Jervis (1989) points to a conflict of symbolism around Ronald Reagan's 1985 visit to Bitburg, Germany. After Reagan announced that he planned to lay

---

8. Figure 5's way of presenting the structure is essentially a visual version of the predicate calculus (Rumelhart and Levin 1975; Gentner 1989).

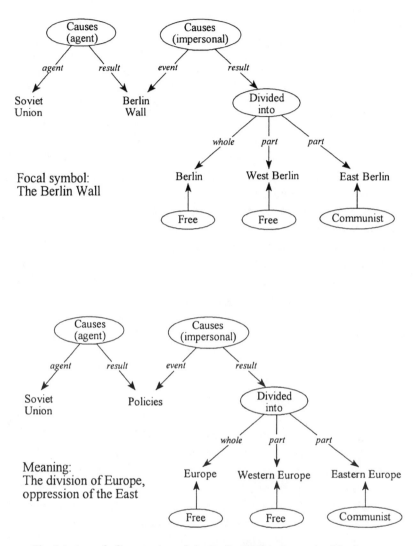

Fig. 5. A symbolic meaning of the Berlin Wall is determined by its analogical similarity to a larger class of Soviet actions.

a wreath at a military cemetery, it was revealed that the cemetery contained the graves of several dozen SS officers. Speaking at a White House ceremony, Elie Wiesel, a Holocaust survivor, warned that "for the sake of history, a U.S. president should not bow down before SS graves." A public debate arose on what a visit would really mean, Reagan maintaining that his message was not toleration for the SS but abhorrence of war. Critics replied that whatever he intended, the action would indeed mean toleration of the SS. To avoid embarrassing the German chancellor, Reagan went to the cemetery but stopped as well at the Bergen-Belsen death camp. The ceremony at Bitburg was altered so that the American and German leaders were not photographed shaking hands; two World War II soldiers stood between them and shook hands in their place (Hilberg 1986; Levkov 1987; Schmitt 1989). Figure 6 shows two examples of symbolic handshakes.

In a parallel controversy that year, on the anniversary of Japan's surrender Yasuhiro Nakasone became the first postwar Japanese prime minister to visit the Yasukuni Shrine in Tokyo (Tsumagari 1994). The souls of 2.6 million war dead spiritually reside there, among them Prime Minister Tojo and 13 others who were convicted as war criminals. Some commentators saw Nakasone's visit as promoting militarization, and some opposition leaders objected that it violated the constitutional prohibition against state support of any religion. Government officials insisted that the visit was not a religious act, only a remembrance of the dead, that it continued a long-standing practice of visits by cabinet members. Like Reagan, Nakasone went ahead with the ceremony but tried to diminish its connection to the unwanted meaning by altering its details. He bowed only once before placing a wreath, where Shinto ritual involves two bows, clapping hands, and bowing again. The principle of structural similarity, however, says that changing surface features like bows and handshakes will be ineffective in determining analogies. It is the structure that is important. Indeed, the changes did not placate Nakasone's critics, and only one such visit has been made since, in 1996 by Prime Minister Hashimoto, who tried to undo the semblance of an official visit by going there on his birthday.

The crucial issue was not how onlookers saw the leaders' intentions in making the visits but how onlookers expected each other to act as a consequence of knowing about the visits. When critics charged that the Bitburg visit would "rehabilitate the SS," they were implying that observers would have lower expectations that others would act forcefully on issues connected to the memory of the Holocaust. Reagan and Nakasone's "symbolic leadership" spoke louder than their words in citizens' collective action games and made the undesirable outcomes more focal.

Fig. 6. Symbolism in handshakes. (*Top*): French President François Mitterand and German Chancellor Helmut Kohl meet at the World War I battlefield of Verdun (September 1984). (*Bottom*): Reagan and Kohl at Bitburg observing former soldiers Ridgeway (*left*) and Steinhoff shaking hands (May 1985). (Photos copyright Presse- und Informationsamt der Bundesregierung, Bonn.)

The Bitburg situation can be represented as involving choices by two citizens—Reagan himself is not a player. They observe the leader's choice, then choose a position themselves on a question evoking the memory of Nazism, such as German military activity outside the NATO area or laws against neofascist revival parties. Each citizen takes a lenient or a strict position. The players' preferences are different: the row player prefers a lenient policy and the column player would rather see a strict one, it is assumed, but above all they want to be in step with each other. Also they do not want an open conflict. Also they must commit themselves to actions before knowing the other's move. A game with these abstract features is known as Battle-of-the-Sexes (matrix 3).[9] If the leader has done something in public that has a structure of toleration or one of militancy, like visiting the cemetery or refusing to visit it, this influences each citizen's expectations of the other's action in that direction. Each chooses that position, expecting the other to do the same. The basis of their reasoning is the analogy between the leader's action and the current issue, through the larger class of events involving toleration. The followers are looking to their leader for coordination, and interpreting the latter's action through an analogy.

Ceremonies

International ceremonies are held for various reasons.[10] They are meant to bring things about, and on this account they can be grouped using the categories of language acts listed in chapter 2. Six categories were given but most ceremonies can be accounted for by three of these.

> *Commissive ceremonies*
>   make agreements, such as treaties or surrenders;
> *Effective ceremonies*
>   install officials, like an ambassador;
>   render honors or give awards;
> *Expressive ceremonies*
>   welcome, show hospitality to, or bid farewell to someone during state
>   visits;

9. The name comes from Braithwaite (1955), whose couple wish to spend the evening together, but he would rather go to the opera while she prefers the prizefight.

10. This list was generated by searching for international ceremonies reported in the Nexis database.

	Lenient	Strict
Lenient	*2, 1*	0, 0
Strict	0, 0	*1, 2*

Matrix 3. Two citizens choose positions on the tolerance of Nazism, a game that might have a focal point established by symbolism. Equilibrium outcomes are italicized.

commemorate events or people; these include ceremonies on the anniversaries of war events or at the funerals of leaders.

These tasks could be done unceremoniously—documents could be signed and mailed, or awards simply handed over, or heads of state picked up at the airport with no pomp or ritual. Do the symbolic elements promote the functions of the ceremony, or are they just entertainment? The answer may lie in the study of religious rituals since international ceremonies seem to be their secular counterparts. Concerning rituals, Whitehead (1927, 61) commented that their symbolic elements "run wild like the vegetation in a tropical forest." Turner (1967) viewed symbols as the building blocks, the basic meaningful components, of rituals. At secular ceremonies too, one finds symbols upon symbols. At the July 1991 signing of the START Treaty, George Bush and Mikhail Gorbachev used pens made from the debris of missiles destroyed under the recent Intermediate-Range Nuclear Forces Treaty. The pens were mounted in a holder showing St. George slaying the dragon. In Christian art, this motif corresponds to St. Michael the Archangel battling Satan, and the design seemed to play on the leaders' first names, as they banished the evil of war with their missile-pen lances.

One way to discern the purpose of symbols at ceremonies is to look at the features they share with rituals, to see whether symbolism's religious functions have secular counterparts. The following list of general properties of ceremonies includes ideas from Turner (1967), Skorupski (1976), and Moore and Myerhoff (1977), as well as other ideas suggested by the database of message symbols.

1. Religious and secular ceremonies often reaffirm the social order, symbolically recognizing the positions of individuals within the societal hierarchy. Traditional values and historical roots are reemphasized, verbally in speeches and symbolically in actions.

2. Ceremonies often include performative language, such as words that install a leader or make an agreement. In religious rituals, the effectives invoke magic, but those in nation-state rituals are based on the power of participants in their official roles.

3. Ceremonies are often repetitive in their setting, content or form. Many are performed on anniversaries. Any spontaneity, such as exuberance or applause, comes at prescribed times.

4. Ceremonies often involve behavior or objects reserved for the occasion. Certain rooms or desks are regularly used for treaty-signing. They correspond to the sacred objects of a religious ritual.

5. The staging and presentation are dramatic and evocative, perhaps with band music, parades, decorations or elaborate dress.

6. A ceremony has a well-defined beginning and ending.

7. Ceremonies include an audience—private ceremonies are the exception. The audience symbolically represents the broader group, watching and noting what is being committed to or effectuated at the ceremony.

Points 3, 4, and 5, involving the repetitive or special nature of ceremonies and rituals, seem related to making commitments. They make a promise more credible by tying it to other promises made in the same fashion. Breaking the current promise would cause the group to distrust past and future promises. Following point 7, the physical presence of various delegates means not only that they observe the ceremony but, significant for a game-theoretical analysis of commitments, they observe each other observing it. The value symbols of point 1 are included as guarantors of the promise made. Some of the structures at commissive ceremonies also suggest focal symbolism, in that they parallel the structure of the society that is being committed by its leader—representatives of various concerned groups are present to symbolically witness and accept an agreement.

Ceremonies affirm the social order using focal and message symbolism. Rules prescribe who sits where at official dinners (McCaffree and Innis 1985), as well as who sits behind the podium during speeches. Who speaks is important—participating in a treaty ceremony is taken as standing in the group and support for the agreement. Controversy can arise over just what social order is being affirmed—who can attend the ceremony and in what capacity these individuals are to attend. Should Lithuania send a representative to the commemoration of the Warsaw Uprising? Should Germany's premier be invited to D-day remembrance services? Should the Russian delegate to the ratification of the Middle East Peace Accords stand on the platform with the signing party or down on the White House lawn? A historical example was Emperor Hirohito's attending Japan's surrender on the USS *Missouri* but not having to step up and sign the document. Ceremonies with structures that parallel some important aspect of the society are frequent among indigenous peoples (Turner 1967), and the phenomenon appears, if somewhat less strongly, in official ceremonies.

Focal Symbolism in Prenegotiation

In most examples so far, the players had no influence over the symbolic event. It came about by chance or by the action of nonplayers, like Soviet policymakers for Latvia, the U.S. president, or the Japanese premier. Sometimes, however, the symbolic event is determined by the individuals who will play the significant game, then the symbol can be chosen to influence the game's outcome. One can illustrate this point by positing two games played in sequence. The first is the *symbolic precursor* game, where the players make their moves in the knowledge that the outcome will influence the play of the second more important game, through the mechanism of focal symbolism.

Participants in negotiations often start by bargaining over symbolism, hoping to gain an advantage in the real confrontation. In 1968, as deaths mounted in Vietnam, representatives in Paris argued about whether the negotiating table would be square, oval, diamond shaped, or round. The U.S. and South Vietnamese governments worried that a square table would symbolically imply an equal negotiating status for the Viet Cong and would raise expectations that the Viet Cong's demands would be satisfied (*New York Times,* January 17, 1969, p. 3).

A negotiation often resembles a Chicken game, where one side or the other must compromise to avoid a mutual loss. Chicken has multiple equilibria and so is open to the influence of symbols. An excellent precedent for one Chicken game is a previous one, so yielding in the precursor game establishes a focal point in the later game. Jervis (1989) cites a symbolic example from August 1986, just before the Reagan-Gorbachev summit. The United States arrested a Soviet embassy aide, Gennady Zakharov, for receiving classified material. The Soviet Union reacted by seizing Nicholas Daniloff, a U.S. reporter who had been an intermediary for the CIA (Garthoff 1994). The two governments began bargaining over who would be released first and how many Soviet dissidents would be freed at the same time. Some American commentators worried that the Soviet Union would see the Daniloff negotiations as a measure of U.S. resoluteness at the summit. On the face of it, this seems far fetched. After many years of dealing with the United States, why would Soviet leaders look to this event to judge America's true fiber? A focal symbolism argument, however, suggests that the Daniloff case's publicity and proximity to the summit made it salient. Its structure made it a member of the larger class of U.S./USSR negotiations, and it became a focal for the summit negotiations. The issue was not one of each side learning about the other's characteristic resolve by looking at accumulated evidence. It was each side forming expectations about the other's current expectation, a phenomenon that is less stable.

Parties sometimes try to counter the focal symbolism of early negotiation moves. In March 1982, the deputy foreign minister of Argentina, Enrique Ros, proposed that negotiations be held over the Falklands, and he included a common phrase, that they be initiated "without prejudice to the rights, claims or position of the parties and without prejudgment of the outcome" (Perez de Cuellar 1997). This did not change the structure of the situation and so might not have worked any better than President Reagan's or Premier Nakasone's alterations in their ceremonies.

The line between simple precedent and symbolic precedent is not always sharp. If one party allows discussion of an item at the early stages of a negotiation, the other side can expect it to be on the table in the main rounds (Stein 1989). This might plausibly be viewed as invoking an analogical larger class involving the party's resoluteness, and so constituting a focal symbol, or it might not. In other cases, the focal symbolism is clear, as when the precursor game is in a domain very dissimilar on the surface to the significant negotiation, and their connection is through their parallel abstract structures. The word *precedent* would not apply between events so different at the level of their features and the explanation must be symbolism. Frequently parties quarrel about where their negotiations will be held. Each is reluctant to travel to the other's homeland, and even a meeting in a nearby capital is resisted, since most of those states have become involved in some way in the dispute. A focal symbolism interpretation would point to the analogy between physically going to the other's geographical location in the prenegotiation and moving toward the other's bargaining position in the real session. The problem is solved if parties choose a site that is neutral and far away, and many negotiators from Middle East and African countries have settled their differences in Geneva or Oslo (Ulriksen 1994).

CHAPTER 5

International Tension and Trust

Roughly speaking, international tension is a shared worry about an imminent conflict. This chapter shows how tension can be influenced by focal symbols. It gives a strategic account of how trust-building events carried out before a crisis, like arms control agreements, can have symbolic value in reducing tension. Finally, the chapter derives principles that would help governments reduce tension during a crisis. One principle, of course, is that leaders should attend to the symbolism of their actions. Another is that if leaders take an action that might increase tension, they should avoid making it a "public" one, in a certain defined sense.

The model of tension is based on three ideas:

tension involves worry shared by adversaries about an imminent war;
the worry itself may contribute to starting a war;
tension is spoken of as a single feature of the current situation.

An aim of the model is to include these three features. The last point means that tension does not vary from one country to the next. One speaks of the tension between two parties, not "Serbian tension" versus "Austrian tension." A metaphor of chapter 3 saw war as a disease, and if a war is about to "break out" in the international body, tension is the system's temperature.

The chapter starts with somewhat inadequate models of tension based on continuous versions of Chicken and reaches a full-fledged model using a continuous Stag Hunt. Chicken-type games are representative of the crisis models that have appeared in the literature and are included as a contrast with the present approach. In Chicken-based models each state is hoping the other will back down as tension rises. By staying in, a state may gain the prize, but that keeps the crisis going and risks the outbreak of a war. Chicken models do not show the full concept of tension, since they do not portray it as a reason that war starts. In fact, worry about a war promotes peace in these models because it induces the states to back down.

In contrast to a Chicken model, the continuous Stag Hunt makes tension the cause of war. The states decide whether to start a war, not whether to back down. The ideal outcome for both is that they both remain patient until the crisis ends; the only motive for starting a war is fear that the other is about to attack. The threshold for attack is determined partly by the focal symbolism of random events happening during the crisis.

Symbolic Events and International Tension

Unexpected events can raise or lower the worry about war, and their connection to tension is often a symbolic one. During the 1962 Cuban missile crisis, a U-2 reconnaissance plane took off from Alaska to collect radioactive samples from a Soviet nuclear test. Near the North Pole, the pilot was unable to use his magnetic compass, and a bright aurora borealis prevented him from navigating by the stars. Thinking he was returning home, he flew into the Soviet Union. Soviet radar station operators took the plane to be on reconnaissance preliminary to a strategic bombing attack, and MiG fighters took off to shoot it down. The U-2 pilot realized his error and turned around, but by then U.S. fighters had scrambled. Because of the crisis, the interceptors took off with nuclear air-to-air missiles installed. The U-2's fuel was spent, but it made visual contact with the U.S. fighters and glided back to its base. Khrushchev complained of the incident in a letter to Kennedy, "What is this, a provocation? One of your planes violates our frontier during this anxious time we are all experiencing, when everything has been put into combat readiness." Sagan (1993) uncovered the story by locating and interviewing the pilot of the stray U-2, and received further information from Soviet sources.

When incidents like this happen, they are said to "increase tension," or "deepen the crisis," or "move the world closer to war." Sometimes an event is both a result of tension and a cause of it. In the Dogger Bank incident of 1904, a Russian warship was so edgy about the Japanese navy that it mistakenly attacked and sank a British fishing trawler. The action was obviously a misunderstanding, but it led to public meetings in Trafalgar Square and induced the Admiralty to "put the Home Channel and Mediterranean fleets on a war footing." According to Connaughton (1988), "War between Britain and Russia appeared imminent."

This cannot be message symbolism if the parties recognize that no message is being sent. The genre at work is the focal variety, based on analogy involving structural similarity. In the Dogger Bank incident, the sinking of the British trawler was analogous to the kinds of events that would happen in a naval war, and the U-2 flying over the Soviet Union was like a war where hostile aircraft fly into each other's country and are engaged by the defenses. Some economics models involve an arbitrary extraneous event influencing actions through mutual expectations, so-called sunspot phenomena, and in principle, international tension could rise and fall as leaders watch sunspots, but in fact they go by those events that are symbolically connected to war. Leaders alter their expectations of each other's actions based on the inference that the other is doing the same.

Often the symbol does more than raise tension symbolically. It changes other aspects of the situation, as when a state mobilizes its army or takes an action that provokes another's anger. Perhaps this is why one can search historical sources on events like the stray U-2 and the Dogger Bank incident and find no suggestion that symbolism was involved. Historical explanations have focused on other aspects. The thesis here is that while objective military or emotional factors may be involved, there is more, and to judge a symbolic explanation, one first needs an account of how it might operate. The full-fledged model (example 4) will involve "pure" tension, without objective or emotional elements. The mutual alarm comes from external symbolic events, randomly generated and commonly known to be undeliberate.

Tension as an Explanation in International Relations Theory

Tension is common in everyday talk about conflict, but it is rare in current international relations theory. It was more frequent thirty years ago, and one can speculate about why it has waned. From the late 1950s to the early 1970s, systems thinking was influential, spread by the writings of Karl Deutsch, David Singer, Morton Kaplan, Anatol Rapoport, David Easton, and others. The approach was congenial to one feature of tension—that it pertains to the whole situation. Several authors included tension as an explanatory variable for war (Singer 1958; Osgood 1962, 114; Holsti 1962; Bergeron 1971; Newcombe and Wert 1972; Goldmann 1974), and others used system-level concepts that seemed very close, like Quincy Wright's "international atmosphere" (1957), or Klingberg's nondirectional measures of friendship or hostility between pre–World War II governments (1941, 1965). Tension's focus on the whole system was attractive to 1960s peace-oriented researchers, because it ascribed the arms race largely to interactions more than individual states, counterbalancing the Cold War attitudes that blamed the adversary.

The early work on peace research saw interaction among those using mathematics, quantitative analysis and systems theory. Systems theory declined, and the other two strains separated, each putting less emphasis on tension. The quantitative researchers emphasized data, and at first some generated "barometric" measures to study the progress of a crisis, like the rate of exchange of dipomatic messages, the number of hostile acts back and forth, or physiological indices of the stress in leader's voices (Wiegele 1973, 1985). Holsti (1972) looked at the sense of time pressure expressed in diplomatic measures, and consistent with the notion of tension, he graphed it not just for individual states but for the whole system (fig. 7). More recently, however, crisis intensity measures like Leng's (1993) presented data only for each state. It would have been easy to aggregrate the single values to get a tension measure for the entire system, but without systems theory hypotheses behind their research, researchers kept their analysis at the level of individual states.

The formal modelers used game and decision analysis to study the outbreak of war. They looked at individual choices, and the notion of tension "in the atmosphere" was unappealing. The concept also seemed bound up with emotions, like anxiety and fear, which were not congenial to their method.

In the last two decades crises have been studied increasingly using the psychology of decision behavior. A conceptual cousin of tension is "stress," which is thought to lead to conflict by distorting leaders' decisions (Brecher 1980, 1993; Holsti and George 1975). Unlike tension, stress is not a decision variable—leaders do not weigh it in as a reason for or against war. It is an outside influence on decision quality (Lebow 1981; Janis 1989).

Those researchers who have discussed tension by name have treated it as noncognitive and have not focused on it. Snyder and Diesing talked about the "*feeling* of tension" between states (1977, 9) but referred to tension itself as the "intensity of conflict *behavior*" (1977, 15, my emphasis). Neither concept involved the probability of war. In defining a crisis, some writers required a high probability of war (e.g., Snyder and Diesing 1977, 7; Brecher, Wilkenfeld, and Moser 1988, 4; Brecher and Wilkenfeld 1997), but did not analyze that probability further.

The present theory is meant to go back to the original conception. Tension is a certain probability, a kind of entity familiar in decision theory, and it is a property of the whole system. The different parties may have special knowledge of how far they can be pushed before acting, and so they may assess different in-

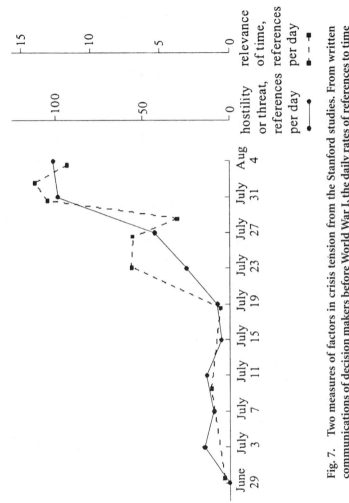

Fig. 7. Two measures of factors in crisis tension from the Stanford studies. From written communications of decision makers before World War I, the daily rates of references to time as a factor in decision making (Holsti 1969), and to hostility or threat (Zinnes 1972).

dividual probabilities of war, but "tension" is used for the probability held by an outside observer.

The model allows two definitions of the term. Tension can be *the probability at a certain time that the crisis will eventually end in war*. This is the conditional probability of ultimate war, given that the crisis is in its current state. An alternative meaning is *the relative likelihood of an immediate war at a certain time*. This could be called the "hazard rate," or what an actuary might call the "force of mortality." To distinguish the two, the probability of eventual war is called *prospective tension*, and the other is *instantaneous tension*. Both are functions of time, changing as the crisis progresses.

Although the model focuses on cognitive aspects, tension is more than that. Calling it "worry" about war associates it with preoccupation, aversive feeling and a distortion of judgment that might prompt someone to act rashly. Holsti (1962) quotes the Japanese war minister, who wanted to go ahead in 1941 despite the United States' great advantage: "Once in a while it is necessary for one to close one's eyes and jump from the stage of the Kiyomizu Temple." These emotional and performance components are important, but here a major part of the message is that tension has a strategic basis.

Tension in Chicken-Based Crisis Models

Past game models of crises could often be seen as basically games of Chicken (matrix 1 and appendix B) sometimes extended to two or more stages. Two simple examples of this general kind are given now.

> EXAMPLE 1: CONTINUOUS-TIME BRINKMANSHIP WITH COMPLETE
>   INFORMATION

Two players face each other, and one will gain a prize if the other backs down. Each has value 1 for the prize and 0 for backing down. At some unknown time uniformly selected between 0 and 1, a war will start if neither player has backed down by then. Neither knows when a war will send them "over the brink."[1] A war gives -1 to both.

An equilibrium is a rule telling each player when to back down if the other has not done so already. The game has exactly one equilibrium that is symmet-

---

1. Still the game is termed *complete information* because the rules do not give a player any private information unknown to the other.

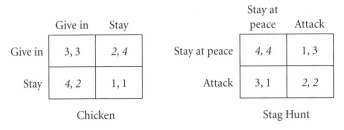

	Give in	Stay
Give in	3, 3	2, 4
Stay	4, 2	1, 1

Chicken

	Stay at peace	Attack
Stay at peace	4, 4	1, 3
Attack	3, 1	2, 2

Stag Hunt

Matrices 1 and 2.   Chicken and Stag Hunt representations of crises. Outcomes from pure strategy Nash equilibria are italicized.

ric.[2] It is in mixed strategies (defined in appendix B), that direct each player to choose a backdown time uniformly between 0 and 1.

The value of tension according to each definition can be calculated for this equilibrium. While the game is on, the prospective tension is a constant ⅓, since there are three events that happen at random times with the same uniform distribution: a war breaking out and one or the other player dropping out. The probability that a war will be the first of these is ⅓. As long as the crisis is on, the instantaneous tension is $1/(1 - t)$. War initially breaks out at rate 1 per unit time, but as the crisis proceeds, it becomes increasingly likely to happen in the next moment. Since war is not a consequence of the players' strategies, this formula holds whether players are using the equilibrium strategies or not.

EXAMPLE 2: CONTINUOUS-TIME BRINKMANSHIP WITH INCOMPLETE INFORMATION

The second model requires a more complicated calculation to determine the tension, but it is closer to the crisis models in the literature. A version of Powell's analysis of "brinkmanship with two-sided information" (1988, 1990) is used. In his model, three events occur in a sequence: each of two players chooses whether to give in; then war has a chance to break out. This sequence makes up one stage of the game, and it is repeated a certain number of times. To represent the idea that the crisis deepens the longer it continues, Powell postulates that at each stage, war's probability increases in constant increments: δ, 2δ, 3δ, ... This assumption puts a bound on the number of stages, since if no one capitulates, war becomes certain. Each of Powell's players can be of two types, with

2. Derivations of this and the other equilibria are in appendix C.

High or Low Resolve, as determined by their relative payoffs for the outcomes. The High Resolve type is more motivated to risk war rather than to give in, so each time a player opts to stay in the crisis, the other will raise its estimate that the player has High Resolve.

In Powell's model, prospective tension can change only at those discrete times when something can happen, and instantaneous tension is zero except at the times when a war could break out. Here his model will be made continuous in time and in players' types. Each player's private value for the prize is chosen independently from a uniform distribution on $(0, 1)$, and a player gets 0 for quitting and -1 for a war. As in example 1, war will occur at some time between 0 and 1, and this is parallel to Powell's model, in that war breaks out at an increasing rate: in a small interval time $(t, t + t)$ the likelihood of war breaking out is $t/(1 - t)$. If two or more events happen simultaneously, players get the average of the payoffs, although the exact rule will not matter much, since at the equilibrium the likelihood of simultaneous events will be zero. The game is then played as follows.

> Stage 1: The players learn their own respective values v_1 and v_2 in $(0,1)$ for the prize; each holds a uniform distribution on $(0,1)$ for the other's value.
>
> Stage 2: At some time in $[0,1]$, a war may start or either player can drop out, and such an event ends the game.
>
> Payoffs: If a war starts, each gets -1, or if player i drops out, player i gets 0 and the other player j gets v_j. Simultaneous events yield the average of the payoffs.

A Nash equilibrium for this game takes the form of a pair of strategies, each telling a player what to do as a function of that player's prize value (appendix B). The only symmetrical equilibrium is that both players do the following: for a prize value v, plan to quit at time $(v - 1) e^v + 1$. Figure 8a graphs this function. The equilibrium is strict, in the sense that deviating from it would lead to a nonzero expected loss. The function rises over time, meaning that those who value the prize more highly will hold out longer. Still, no matter how low a player values the prize, the player should stay in the crisis for some positive time, since the other possibly values it even less. Those with a low value give up very quickly: if a player holds value .1, that is, at the 10th percentile, and a war happens over a period of one year, the player should wait two days and then give in.

The instantaneous tension is $1/(1 - t)$ for as long as the crisis is on. This starts at 0 and goes off to infinite tension as the time approaches 1. The prospec-

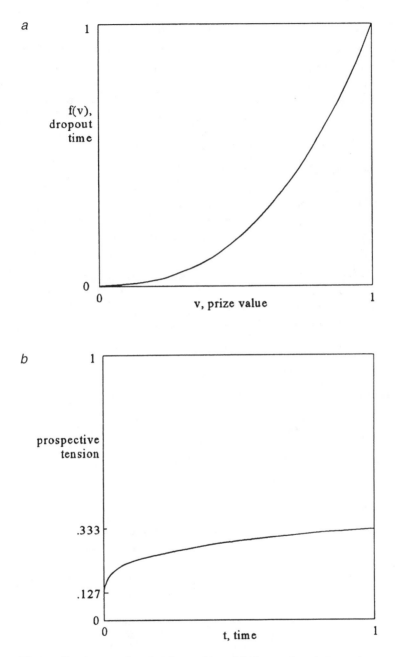

Fig. 8. Continuous-time brinkmanship with incomplete information: *a*, the symmetrical equilibrium strategy; *b*, prospective tension

tive tension over time is graphed in figure 8*b*. This is the probability of eventual war. At the start it is only .127. The world is optimistic, since it expects that one player or the other will drop out in the first half of the interval. The median dropout time for a player is .176 (found by substituting $v = .5$ in the formula for the strategy), so one or the other ought to end the crisis before a war. If neither drops out, prospective tension rises toward an asymptote of ⅓. Near the end, the three events that would end the crisis become equally likely.

Tension in Stag Hunt–Based Crisis Models

The Chicken models yield measures of tension, but they do not embody the concept's full character since worry has no role in causing the war. In the Stag Hunt–based games, it is peace that comes probabilistically, and it is the players who start the war. They do it in response to tension.

Matrix 2 shows the payoffs of a single-play Stag Hunt where players have complete information about each other's payoffs. A Chicken game corresponding roughly to the previous example is added for comparison. In the Stag Hunt models, tension is produced by a first-strike advantage. Each fears that the other is about to attack and, if there is a war, knows it is better to be the one starting it (in the matrix, a payoff of 3 is better than 1). The less hope one holds that the crisis will end peacefully, the greater the incentive to attack. If both knew the other would not attack, each would prefer to refrain—this would yield the ideal outcome of 4 for both. However, they would be consistent in their beliefs if they both expected an attack. The Stag Hunt game embodies the notions of trust and distrust, which are central to war and peace. The fact that Chicken-type games predominate in game literature on crises may be due to theorists' traditional feeling that the Stag Hunt is trivial, that the inefficient equilibrium is somehow irrational. In my view, this has been a mistake, for reasons presented in appendix B.

Matrix 2 is not quite the game that players face in the next two examples. They do not choose actions at a single time—they choose when to preempt from a continuum. Another difference is that in the simple Stag Hunt models, both know what the other gets from striking first, but in these models they are unsure of that value.

EXAMPLE 3: A CONTINUOUS-TIME STAG HUNT WITHOUT SYMBOLISM

STAGE 1: The players learn their respective values a_1 and a_2 for striking first; each holds a uniform distribution on (0,1) for the other's value.

TABLE 1.   Payoffs for the Outcomes of the Continuous-Time Chicken and Stag Hunt

Both drop out	1 drops out		Peace	2 attacks 1
$v_1/2, v_2/2$	$0, v_2$		1, 1	$0, a_2$
2 drops out	War		1 attacks 2	Both attack
$v_1, 0$	$-1, -1$		$a_1, 0$	$a_1/2, a_2/2$

STAGE 2: The crisis starts at time $t = 0$; peace comes randomly at constant rate 1; each player can attack at any time during the game; peace or an attack ends the game.

PAYOFFS: Peace gives each 1, or if player i attacked j, the payoffs are a_i to i and 0 to j. When events happen simultaneously, players get the average payoffs.

Table 1 *(right)* summarizes the payoff information, again comparing it with the Chicken model *(left)*. Note that it is not a game matrix since neither side knows all the values in it and neither chooses a row or column. They choose a time from a continuum.

An equilibrium in this game is a pair of functions giving the time when each player is to attack, if peace has not come and if the other player has not attacked. This time is a function of the player's first-strike payoff a_i. It might be infinity, meaning never attack at all. There is a continuum of equilibria determined by the choice of a parameter c in the interval [.693, 1] (fig. 9).[3] They are ordered by peacefulness, in the sense that an equilibrium with higher c will tell a player with a given first-strike payoff to wait at least as long before striking.[4] Figure 9 also shows that the higher a_i is, the earlier the player's patience runs out. This

---

3. It may seem odd that the continuous Stag Hunt has an infinity of equilibria, but the single equilibrium described for the continuous Chicken was an artifact of requiring symmetry. The basic Stag Hunt and Chicken games have three (pure or mixed strategy) equilibria, but for Chicken only one of these is symmetrical (appendix B). Nalebuff and Riley (1985) discuss the asymmetrical equilibria in a Chicken game somewhat similar to the one defined here.

4. The value of c is interpretable as the time the person with the lowest value for striking first would wait.

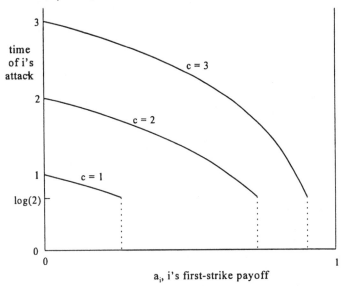

Fig. 9. Three members of the family of symmetrical equilibrium strategies in the continuous-time Stag Hunt without symbolism (example 3)

makes sense—the less the player has to lose by striking first compared to getting to a peaceful outcome, the more readily the player will strike. An unexpected result is that a substantial set of individuals give peace no chance and attack immediately. Finally, the figure shows that if neither player attacks as soon as the crisis starts, there is a period of .693 time units during which no one strikes. This is the eye of a storm, and if the peace does not arrive, the danger of an attack resumes.

Sample curves in figures 10 and 11 show the prospective and instantaneous tensions at various equilibria. Both are rising. That prospective tension should increase makes sense since the only reason that someone would strike now rather than waiting and hoping for peace is that the situation will be getting more dangerous.

EXAMPLE 4: A CONTINUOUS-TIME STAG HUNT WITH SYMBOLISM

This model adds a variable symbolic of war, which fluctuates randomly during the crisis. The actors use its value and perhaps its history to decide at each moment whether to strike. At the initiation of the crisis, the cue event takes some positive value, which can be set arbitrarily at 1, and then makes small equal steps up and down equiprobably in a random walk. Here the limit of the process

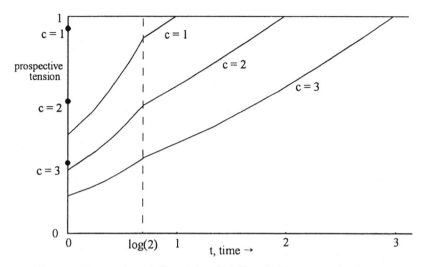

Fig. 10. Prospective tension, the probability of ultimate war, in the continuous-time Stag Hunt without symbolism

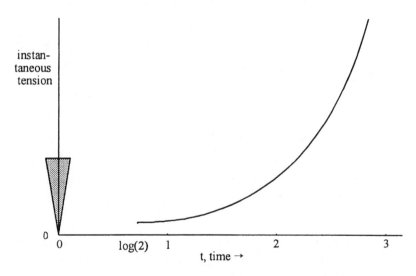

Fig. 11. Instantaneous tension in the continuous-time Stag Hunt without symbolism (example 3), for the equilibrium $c = 3$. There is an atom at $t = 0$, whose probability is indicated by the area of the triangle.

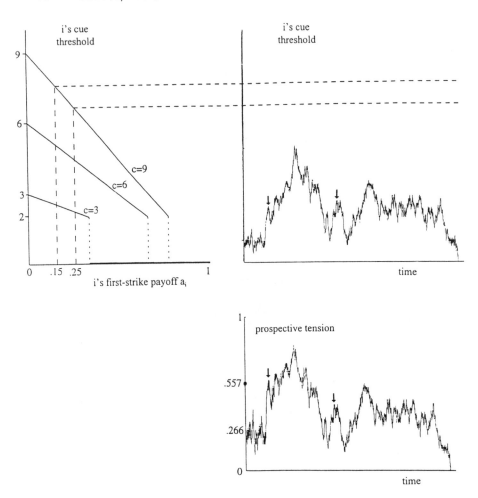

Fig. 12.   Examples of symmetrical equilibrium strategies *(upper left)* in the continuous-time Stag Hunt with symbolism (example 4). The course of a game is shown for the equilibrium $c = 9$ and the first-strike payoffs $a_1 = .15$ and $a_2 = .25$. The cue variable *(upper left)* does not reach the threshold of either player. Prospective tension *(lower left)* is slightly different from the cue.

is taken, as the rate of stepping grows and the step size shrinks keeping the standard deviation of the movement after a unit of time constant at 1. In real crises, it would be discrete events that influence tension, but for simplicity here the cue variable changes continuously over time. This is standard Brownian motion as would be produced by random changes of direction that are infinitely many and infinitely small. The cue variable is sure to reach zero at some point, and then the crisis is assumed to be over.[5] Figure 12 *(upper right)* shows a sample path that terminates when the process arrives at zero.

The difference with the last example is that the players are not looking at their watches to decide to attack but at the symbolic cue variable. A Nash equilibrium takes the form of a pair of functions, each of which tells its player to attack when the cue reaches a certain threshold. Here a family of equilibria arises, as shown in figure 12 *(upper left)*, again depending on the parameter c. A player sets the threshold at a linear decreasing function $c(1 - a_i)$ of the first-strike payoff a_i, and a player whose threshold would be below 2 sets it at 0. Since the cue starts at 1, some players will strike immediately, but if there is no war at the opening of the crisis, there is sure to be none until the cue variable rises above 2. Again there is an eye of the storm. A higher value of c means that players are more trusting of each not to strike and that peace is more likely. Setting c to infinity is the equilibrium of both ignoring the cue and simply waiting for peace.

Figure 12 *(upper left)* takes a sample path of the cue variable, and shows the dynamics of play for the equilibrium $c = 9$ and first-strike payoffs $a_1 = .15$ and $a_2 = .25$. These payoffs determine the threshold values for the cue variable shown, and if the latter rises above the lower of those thresholds, the player will start a war. The crisis is very dramatic, with events happening that greatly increase tension, but the first-strike advantage is low and both players stay at peace.

Instantaneous tension cannot be defined in the model, for reasons discussed in appendix C. Figure 12 *(lower right)* also shows the prospective tension, the likelihood at each time of eventual war. It is a function of the cue variable up to that point. It starts high at $t = 0$, then drops if neither attacks immediately. It then follows a path somewhat similar to the cue variable's, but there is a slight difference. The tension is a function not only of the cue's current value but of its history. Note that in the top right-hand graph of figure 12, the cue variable reaches an early peak, then a very high value, then a second peak. (The first and third peaks are indicated by arrows.) At the latter peak, the cue has a slightly higher value than at the first, but the tension, in the bottom graph, is lower than it was at the first. The world is less worried the latter time, because it has already seen tension climb higher with neither player attacking. It has lowered its estimate of each player's first-strike payoff.

---

5. The time for this random process to touch zero is exponential, so the event of the crisis ending behaves probabilistically in a way identical to the constant rate of ending in example 3.

Precrisis Symbolism: The Value of Arms Agreements

The full-fledged model of tension, example 4, has two outside, nonstrategic factors that influence the outcome. One is the random cue event that the players are watching, and the other is the trust parameter c that sets the equilibrium. How are these determined? As to the random cue event, the argument has been that it is chosen for its symbolism. The U-2 overflight during the Cuban missile crisis, being analogous to war, would mean a jump in the cue.

To determine c, if symbolism is in play it must involve events before the crisis that set the overall atmosphere of trust. An example would be the symbolism created by an arms treaty. The literature on arms control has debated whether arms control should be promoted for its symbolism. Some writers have derided this idea, holding that agreements are worthless unless they limit dangerous weapons. Jervis (1989, 221–23) countered that the symbolism of agreements is as least as important as the content, noting that during the Reagan administration, the military were supportive of strategic arms treaties but the civilian officials in the Pentagon saw them as lowering the country's guard. Some of them might have been happier to have seen the United States behind in weapons in an unconstrained competition than equal in an arms control regime. An interpretation is that the civilian hawks were more concerned about symbolism. Another example of the symbolic importance of an arms treaty was the Rush-Bagot agreement of 1817, which limited naval armaments on the Great Lakes (O'Neill 1991a). It has been seriously violated over most of its duration but constantly praised. Various incoming Canadian prime ministers intended to renegotiate it and bring it into accord with practice, but realized it was more prudent not to raise the history of its violation, since its value was what it meant symbolically. "Confidence-building measures" (Krepon 1995), agreements to share knowledge and build trust, are another example. Proposals like notification of exercises and accommodation of observers seem to suggest cooperation over weaponry. If the two sides are able to do this in peacetime, each is slow to believe that the purely technical preemptive advantage of their weaponry will start a war.

The full-fledged model gives a natural way to interpret the symbolic value of arms control (fig. 13). Its precrisis symbolism selects an equilibrium with a higher value of c, one for which a given tension-producing crisis event is less provocative. This combines with events during the crisis (the cue variable) and players' private first-strike payoffs to determine war or peace. The model does not prove that symbolic treaties will help states get through a crisis, but it shows that a strategic argument can be constructed to support the idea, without appeals to irrationality or "psychology."

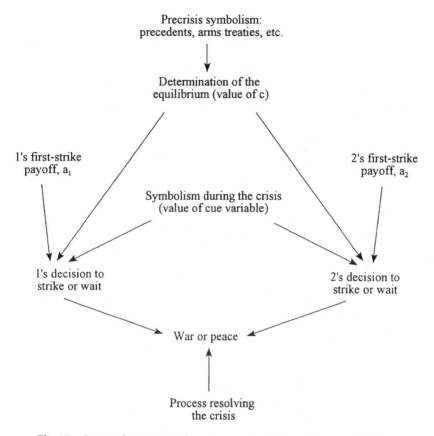

Fig. 13.   Interactions among the components of the continuous-time Stag Hunt with symbolism (example 4)

The Tension Metaphor

Crisis tension is part of a conceptual metaphor, and like other metaphors, it clarifies and distorts the truth. Where it is accurate or misleading can be gleaned by comparing it with the model. The metaphor of tension can be seen as part of a broader metaphor that maps a harmonious state into a physical object.[6] It could be called A-MENTAL-STATE-AS-AN-OBJECT. Ending the harmonious state corresponds to destroying the object. The point of the metaphor is that the destruction of harmony is not easy to reverse. Just as it is hard to put a broken object back together, hostilities that have started are hard to stop.

---

6. People also talk about feeling "tense." This too seems to come from the idea of physical stretching, according to the historical citations in the *Oxford English Dictionary*.

The general metaphor has two subgroups. One maps within-an-individual mental conditions into an object that gets smashed or breaks apart. Accordingly, a person is said to be "together" or to be "fragile," to "fall apart," "fall to pieces," be "crushed," or "shattered" by a bad experience. The other subgroup deals with relations among two or more parties and maps them into physical connections— an individual is said to be "well-connected," to have "close ties" to another. The relation between a pair of people here becomes an elongated object, sometimes stringlike, and rather than getting crushed or broken into pieces, it is stretched and snaps. A situation is "taut," relations are "strained," nations "sever diplomatic ties."[7] The metaphor of international tension is in the second group.

The model's definition of tension as a whole-system property fits the metaphor, since the tension in a string or rod is the same at either end. The formal definition of tension that is closest to the mechanical metaphor is the instantaneous variety. The prospective variety would have a string break not in response to the force at the moment but by looking ahead to a coming increase and preemptively breaking now. Strings do not do this, but national leaders do. The analysis suggests that, in spite of the metaphor, leaders can compensate for a current tense time by announcing steps now that would increase trust, even if these become operative only later on in the crisis. Another element left out of the metaphor is that leaders use private knowledge that may lead them to different probabilities than an outside observer holds. The tension metaphor does not capture all the aspects of the decision to preempt, but it does contain the important idea that worry is mutual to a significant degree and can itself cause war.

The Role of Public Events

The opposite of crisis tension is trust, the belief that the other side will be patient. Trust is represented by the mutually beneficial outcome of a Stag Hunt game. The logic of the game shows the connection between tension, trust, and common knowledge. If the two governments hold high probabilities that the other side will stay at peace, this confidence can be unstable in that each player may start to worry. Each will worry not just about the other's actions but about whether the other is starting to worry, since worry may lead to preemption. What the situation requires is confidence at higher levels of knowledge: player A should believe that B believes that A will stay at peace, and so on up the lad-

---

7. Sometimes the metaphor involves an object but is nonspecific about the "shape" of a social relationship: "Distrust wrecked their marriage."

der of beliefs about beliefs. Trust is stabilized by the common knowledge of trust; one might even define it as requiring common knowledge of trust.

Some events influence only the lowest order of knowledge, and some have consequences up the hierarchy. The importance of symbolic events is that they change beliefs at various levels. Some tension events operate only at the lower levels of belief. Sagan's investigations (1993) revealed that during the Cuban missile crisis, in the predawn hours of October 26, 1962, an Atlas intercontinental missile was launched from Vandenberg Air Force Base in California. It was a test firing, part of a program that had been laid out before the crisis, which, evidently, no official had thought to cancel. Its reentry vehicle contained only instruments, but missiles at adjacent launch facilities carried nuclear warheads. Sagan speculates that a Soviet base watcher might have seen the firing and called home an alarming report. From the viewpoint of this analysis, the missile launch is an event that may have altered beliefs about U.S. actions but probably not higher-order beliefs about beliefs. Although the Soviet decision makers might have learned of it, the United States could not know that they had the information, the Soviet Union could not know that the United States knew that the Soviet Union knew it, and so on.

This distinction can be made by defining a *public event,* one whose very occurrence in the context makes it common belief among the decision makers.[8] The Atlas launch was not a public event, and so its interactive epistemology was different from the U-2 overflight, the signing of an arms treaty, or a friendly visit by a national leader. When the latter occur, they are known to have happened, and known to be known, and so on. Other things equal, this gives them more impact on trust or tension than the Atlas launch. Getting through a crisis may mean paying special attention to those public events that are liable to increase tension.

---

8. This definition of public event is conceptually identical to the one used in the literature on common knowledge (Geanakoplos 1994), although there, for formal reasons, it is not defined as relative to a context.

Part II

Honor, Face, and Prestige

CHAPTER 6

What Is National Honor?

In *Duck Soup*, the Four Marx Brothers poke fun at statesmen's concern with their national honor. Groucho, as the prime minister of Freedonia, summons the Sylvanian ambassador specifically to deliver an insult. He tries "baboon," "swine," "worm," until for some reason, "upstart" does it. Faces are ceremonially slapped and the cry rings round the palace that this means war!

Even in the 1930s, the idea of a war over honor was inane enough for a Marx Brothers movie, and nowadays the conviction is that leaders save their violence for goals that matter. Honor talk is heard occasionally—before the 1993 U.S. expedition to Somalia, for example—but it is usually taken as rhetoric, to rally the public behind a policy justified on practical grounds. Veblen (1917), anticipating the modern attitude, saw honor as just a rhetoric of complaint: "National honor . . . is not known to serve any material or otherwise useful end apart from affording a practicable grievance consequent upon its infraction."

This chapter's thesis is that a version of honor is still in play. It is a primitive one, constructed as the common denominator of the elements of honor within various societies and transformed by its use in the international system. Honor still matters, however—it is simply the name that has changed.

In 1969, while the Vietnam War was rending American society, the *New York Times* surveyed those who continued to support U.S. policy. It reported that "time and again people who hate the war talk about national prestige" (November 16, 1969, p. 62, quoted in McGinn 1972). More evidence comes from Henry Kissinger, who wrote in his memoirs as if honor had kept the country trapped in Vietnam (1979, 228), "No serious policymaker could allow himself to succumb to the fashionable debunking of 'prestige,' or 'honor' or 'credibility.'" In a study of some ancient and modern wars, historian Donald Kagan (1995) wrote, "The reader may be surprised by how small a role . . . considerations of practical utility and material gain, and even ambition for power itself, play in bringing on wars, and how often some aspect of honor is decisive." The basic dynamics of honor may still be operating in a different vocabulary, he suggested, perhaps as "ideology."

Herman Kahn (1984) described a 1963 seminar he had conducted for government leaders. He had given the participants a scenario in which the Soviet Union had destroyed the major capitals of Europe and the American president could either retaliate with nuclear weapons or do nothing at all. Retaliation would destroy the Soviet Union's population but not its missiles and would trigger a counterstrike that would incinerate American cities. What should the president do? Four attendees thought he should attack in spite of the consequences. They were Gerald Ford, Melvin Laird, Henry Jackson, and Bourke Hickenlooper. Three of these would later assume positions important to U.S. defense policy, Jackson as the preeminent Senate defense critic, Laird as secretary of defense, and Ford as president. Herman Kahn, hard line but practical, was dismayed at their preoccupation with the reputation of a country that would no longer exist and hoped that they changed their minds when they assumed greater power. Perhaps they did, but his exercise showed their concern with national honor even in the face of nuclear destruction.

The vocabulary of President Wilson's day included "honor," "insult" and "self-respect"; now countries "show resolve" or "show national will," they worry about "credibility" and "reputation," or they avoid an "image of weakness." Concern with "national humiliation" was seen as a major factor in the 1967 Middle East War (Stein 1985, 57; Cohen 1990), and the Cuban missile crisis (Steinberg 1991). The question is this: Vocabulary aside, is the structure of modern behavior around war isomorphic to honor behavior in societies? A clearer theory is needed, since as long as honor remains nebulous, its role is hard to determine. The chapter identifies the common elements of honor across various societies and sets up a game model to reproduce many of them and show how they fit together.

The Elements of Honor

The thesis is that international society takes the common denominator of the elements of honor cultures. These can be identified from various sources: studies in social history and anthropology, social psychology, legal studies of honor as one's good name, especially from Germany, nineteenth-century studies of ethics, and long tracts on challenges and duels, especially from Renaissance Italy and Spain, where these matters were set into law.[1] Not all the elements are seen

---

1. Frank Stewart (1994) gives an excellent critical survey of the literature on honor.

in any one honor-based society, but overall they seem to lie at the core of the concept.

The behavior required by honor depends on the person's gender. The honorable man is supposed to respond violently to threats to his honor; he is true to his social class, his leader, and his country, while the honorable woman is true to her husband and family. Feminist theorists have discussed how international relations are shaped by male attitudes and behavior (e.g., Cohn 1987, 1993; Peterson 1992). Indeed the male version of societal honor is closer to the one nations seem to follow and is the kind examined here.

The first element deals with honor's content. Honor has a "Don't Tread on Me" component or, better, "Don't Tread on Me or Mine."

(E1) Honor requires

> trueness to one's word when given on one's honor;
> readiness to defend one's home, and the rights of oneself and one's group, and to avenge violations;
> social grace, in the case of aristocratic honor;
> sometimes nonvoluntary traits, like noble birth or physical strength.

At the national level also, honor means that one is willing to defend an ally. On receiving word that Germany wanted Britain to promise neutrality in case of a war with France over its colonies, British secretary of state Lord Grey telegraphed his ambassador in Vienna, "From the material point of view such a proposal is unacceptable, for France would be so crushed as to lose her position as a Great Power, and become subordinate to German policy without further territory in Europe being taken from her. But apart from that, for us to make this bargain with Germany at the expense of France would be a disgrace from which the good name of this country would never recover" (Albertini 1952–1957, vol. 2, 633).

The second element makes honor dichotomous—either one has it or not.

(E2) Having honor is associated with personhood, autonomy, group membership, and sexual identity.

A man who has lost honor is treated as a nonperson in many societies, ignored rather than punished. One does not talk to him and, in Montenegrin society, reaches behind one's back to hand him a drink (Boehm 1983). Consistent with treating honor as personhood is that adults start with a presumption of holding it and, barring an event that puts it in question, in many societies need to do nothing to acquire or maintain it. This is reflected in the metaphorical expressions of "staining," "blemishing," or "tarnishing" one's honor. Hardin (1995) sees honor as a "norm of exclusion" and dueling as a device primarily to set the honor-group apart.

Another consequence of E2 is that someone outside the social class possessing honor has no privilege to issue a challenge (e.g., Peristiany 1966, 31). In Renaissance Italy, a challenge from a woman, a cleric, or a commoner could be ignored.

The connection of national honor and autonomy becomes clear when states are pressed to submit disputes to arbitration. In the affair of the U.S. warship *Alabama*, Lord Russell (quoted in Perla 1918, 106) responded that "England's honor can never be made the subject of arbitration." Heinrich von Treitschke (1916, 29) refused arbitration on the grounds of autonomy, "Were we to commit the folly of treating the Alsace-Lorraine problem as an open question, by submitting it to arbitration, who would seriously believe that the award could be impartial? It is, moreover, a point of honor for a State to solve such difficulties for itself." At the 1899 Hague Conference, the Arbitration Treaty required signators to arrange an international commission to engage in fact-finding in case of an impending war. Some smaller nations claimed that this presented a threat to their sovereignty, and Romania had a phrase added that exempted disputes involving crucial interests or honor (Holls 1900). Those least able to defend their sovereignty were the most concerned about it and defined it as part of their national honor.

The next element introduces a reputational component.

(E3) Honor involves caring that one has a commonly known reputation for honor.

An episode from the Roman historian Livy illustrates that honor must be visible (Nobili 1550). Lucretia was the wife of a nobleman in the era of the Roman kings, about 500 B.C. A prince of the ruling Tarquins visited her while her husband was away and demanded her favors. If she refused, he would kill her, as well as her male slave, and leave their bodies side by side with the implication of adultery. Lucretia had a choice of losing her reputation for fidelity or being unfaithful in fact. She yielded to Tarquin. She then summoned her husband and relatives and described the outrage. After receiving promises of vengeance, she drew a dagger and took her own life. When Lucretia chose her good name over actual virtue, neither her family nor Livy reproached her for it, and she became a heroine to his readers.

It is the duty of the honorable person to generate common knowledge that he is honorable, to assure everyone that he would be willing to defend the group.

If each member knows that others are confident in the given member, they too will be steady. This requirement differentiates honor from virtue, whose test is sometimes described as doing what one would do even if no one were watching. The need to assure others of one's honor generates the norm of responding to a challenge[2] and the norm in many cultures of maintaining publicly a proper style of life and a graceful demeanor, as stated in E1 (Peristiany and Pitt-Rivers 1992). Another consequence of E3 is that honor comes to depend only on behavior *commonly known* to be publicly observed. In the context of Renaissance England, James (1986, 229) writes, "Men of honor could (and did) lie, cheat, deceive, plot, treason, seduce, and commit adultery, without incurring dishonor. Such activities were of course immoral, and might compromise the perpetrator's religious status, bringing his eternal salvation into question. But as long as they were not attributed to him in a public way, honor was not brought into question." The group meant to hold a high opinion of the honor possessor is typically a well-defined one, those others that hold honor. Following Stewart (1994), it is called the *honor group.*

The need for national honor to be visible was emphasized by von Treitschke (1916, 550, quoted by Thayer 1918). "Whoever attacks the honor of a state even in its externals, thereby impugns the essential character of the state. To attribute to the state a too irritable sense of honor is to ignore the moral laws of politics. A state must have a very highly developed sense of honor if it is not to be false to its nature. It is not a violet that blooms in the shade; its power is to be displayed proudly and brilliantly; it cannot permit this power to be questioned even symbolically."

Element E3 introduces a circularity in honor, and this self-reference may have prompted some authors to avoid a definition, or state a confused one, or just discard the concept. Perla (1918, 56) noted, "The attitude of men toward honor therefore becomes a matter of 'loyalty to loyalty,' or loyalty for loyalty's sake rather than loyalty to an ideal involved in a specific case." This argument led him to reject the notion as incoherent. Loyalty to loyalty, in his view, makes honor an excuse for wars that are really prompted by anger or greed. In E3, the idea is put more accurately as loyalty to *others' perceptions of* loyalty, as well as (not "rather than") loyalty to certain ideals.

The self-reference of honor, as asserted by E3, means that honor-conscious people worry about others' beliefs about their own attitudes. Germany's request

---

2. From the *Decameron*, Patrizi cites the story of Agilulf, king of the Lombards, who was "reputed most wise because, not being able to take secret vengeance for an offense to the honor of his wife, he bore the injury patiently to avoid publicity" (1553). This is a case of reputation counting more than revenge.

for a British promise of neutrality induced Lord Grey to start worrying about German beliefs about British beliefs: "The proposal made to us meant everlasting dishonour if we accepted it. . . . Did Bethmann Hollweg not understand, could he not see, that he was making an offer that would dishonour us if we agreed to it? What sort of man was it who could not see that? Or did he think so badly of us that he thought we should not see it? Every thought the telegram suggested pointed to despair" (*British Documents* XI, 293, 506–7, quoted by Albertini 1952–1957, 632.) We cannot compromise our honor. What must they be thinking of us for them even to consider that we might do so?

A consequence of E3 can govern behavior when two principles of honor come into conflict. An official who no longer supports government policy is caught between loyalty to the group and honesty and can maintain honor only by resigning. Cyrus Vance resigned as secretary of state because he had opposed President Carter's commando raid to free the Iranian hostages. As with Lucretia, his only option was to withdraw. Honor functions differently from morality in this regard. When moral principles come into conflict, one chooses the lesser evil. One's conscience is the accepted judge of morality, but society judges honor, and one cannot necessarily trust one's own judgment about what society will say.

(E4) The group acts as if the traits, virtues, and values that make up the content of honor are one or at least strongly covarying.

This is the *unity of honor.* Honor may involve assorted traits, as listed in E1 and E3 and others, and in theory, an individual could possess some and not others. However, E4 asserts that they are treated as present or absent as a whole.

The unity of honor is often contradicted by evidence, so how does the idea survive? Three factors sustain it. First, a culture socializes its members to follow the whole set of honorable behaviors, and this makes contrary evidence less likely. Second, honor deals with inner motives and character that influence behavior only indirectly, so an observer has some room to interpret another's actions in a way consistent with the unity of honor (Miller 1993). Finally, the unity of honor is a *social fact*, in that everyone expects everyone else to act on it. They may not believe it privately, and may even reject it openly and verbally, but they follow it in their public actions.

(E5) Regarding the importance of honor in society:

> *it is normative, that is, supported by guilt, shame, and others' dispositions to reward and punish;*

> *it accrues to groups as well as individuals, and one member can honor or dis-*
>   *honor the group;*
> *it is often seen as sacred.*

Honor is normative in both individual and social ways. Individually, those who have it feel proud, and those without it feel guilty.[3] Shame is a social response (Lewis 1971). It includes the wish to avoid other group members (Boehm 1983, 80). This reaction fits the idea of E2, that honor is like group membership, in that those who lose honor want to withdraw.

Honor is normative in a social way, also in that possessing it legitimizes one's claim to certain benefits from others. Other members feel that they *ought* to favor the honorable; conversely, losing honor means losing the right to respectful treatment.

Since the honor of the individual and the group reflect on each other, the whole group has an inducement to pressure the individual to behave correctly. Honor and dishonor extend into the past and future—one can tarnish ancestors or descendants even though they have no part in one's act. Demosthenes wrote, "There is a thing which Athens has always placed above success and that is honor, the elevated feeling of what she owes to her traditions in the past and to her good name in the future" (1993). Terraillon (1912, 251) called it "the government of the living by the dead," and Groucho refused to make up with the Sylvanian ambassador, "My ancestors would rise out of their graves, and I'd just have to bury them again."

Tying honor to one's ancestors makes it like religion. In many religions, norms are reinforced by linking them to God's will; the traits of honor are linked through the principle of the unity of honor, and this interconnection makes it more important to keep each individual norm. Honor is regarded as sacred, lying at the core of the individual's self-esteem and connecting the meaning of the person's life with the group over time.

(E6) Preserving one's reputation for honor often requires publicly enduring some cost or risk, often by participating in violence.

A fair fight was required by most cultures, but in Albania, one could sneak up and shoot the offender in the back (Hasluck 1981, 228). This custom seems

---

3. Peristiany and Pitt-Rivers (1992), writing of Mediterranean society, distinguish guilt and shame in a different way but argue that the difference does not matter, "Guilt related to the lack of virtue, shame to the loss of precedence or face. . . . the function of the concept of honor is precisely, despite the frailty of the logic involved, to equate them. . . ." Translated into our terms, this is an expression of E4, the unity of honor.

to promise honor without risk, but the murderer had to leave a token at the scene to reveal his identity, so the victim's kin could take their vengeance in turn. "It was everywhere 'held dishonorable' to kill and not to tell," according to Hasluck, so there was no safe route to keep one's honor.[4]

In some medieval societies honor was shown by going to war or hunting wild boar with minimal weapons or engaging in dangerous jousts. Jousts were public (Vale 1981), often symbolically observed by other knights and the monarch. These honor-proving deeds were undertaken on the person's initiative, but there were others, like dueling, that required a cue, like a challenge. In some societies, an insult to oneself or one's family was a cue for violence. Internationally, honor is linked with violence through its emphasis in military culture and during times of war.

The Basic Game of Honor

Some of these elements can be incorporated into a game. The game takes account of E3, E4, and E6, which are, respectively, that honorable people care what others think, that honor is treated as a unified bundle of virtues, and that honorable people pay a cost to prove it. It uses the idea of showing some innate quality by paying a cost, which was introduced to the political science literature by Schelling (1960) and discussed more explicitly by Jervis (1971), and independently since the late 1970s it has become widespread in the economics game literature. Later the game will be extended to include other points, the variability of honor's importance across societies and the institutions of challenges and oath taking.

The simplest model assumes the individual is worried about only two things: reputation for honor and the cost of engaging in some risky activity like a joust. There are no other goals related to honor or self-interest. A nonnegative real number h is the individual's personal honor or *sense of honor*, a term of Frank Stewart's (1994), and it measures the degree to which the individual values honor relative to self-interest goals, like the cost of conflict. The cost c might be the risk of a joust, for example, which we assume that the person is required to do on the proper occasion, as a way of showing honor.

The individual knows the coefficient h exactly, it is assumed, but the pub-

---

4. Some social institutions have been called *honor* but are quite different. Kathleen Stuart (1993) describes craft guilds of sixteenth- to eighteenth-century Germany where dishonor spread like a disease, often by inadvertent social contact with animal skinners or executioners. As in the common pattern, this dishonor meant exclusion from the group, but it could not be avoided by challenges and violence. It could be restored by a proclamation from a high authority

lic is uncertain about it.[5] They all share the same probability distribution for h. Since by E3, an honorable person wants to be recognized as honorable, it is assumed that the individual cares about the audience's expectation of that distribution. This will depend on what the public has seen the person do. If the public's evidence is that the person has performed action A, the expectation is designated $E[H \mid A]$, read "the expectation of H given A." Capitalizing H indicates that it is an unknown variable that the public estimates, different from h, which is a number. This expectation is the individual's *social honor* or *reputation for honor*.

The two available actions are Jousting and Not Jousting, and their payoffs to the individual are

for Jousting: $h\,E[H \mid \text{Joust}] - c$;

for Not Jousting: $h\,E[H \mid \text{Not Joust}]$.

The essential point is that the individual's reputation $E[H \mid -]$ has been multiplied by h. The more honorable the person is, the more he cares about reputation for honor.

To summarize, the stages in the game are

STAGE 1: The individual learns his sense of honor h.
STAGE 2: The individual chooses Joust or Not Joust.
PAYOFFS: The audience observes the choice and reestimates the individual's honor; the latter receives a payoff that depends on the cost paid and the audience's opinion, as specified previously.

This game has two kinds of equilibria, summarized in figure 14. The first involves a threshold rule: all observers expect that a person whose honor lies below some cutoff h^* will Not Joust, but one with honor at or above h^*, will at-

---

5. The alternative, which is *not* knowing our own h, would lead to a model of "self-respect," where we learn about ourselves from our actions in critical moral situations and attach a value to what we learn. Over the years, self-respect has been tied with honor in foreign policy debates. Grover Cleveland, vowing to defend Venezuelan territory against British claims, told Congress (Cleveland 1913), "I am firm in my conviction that there is no calamity which a nation can invite which equals that which follows from supine submission to wrong and injustice, and the consequent loss of national self-respect and honor, beneath which are shielded and defended a people's safety and greatness." In June 1995, Bob Dole asked the U.S. Senate, "What would the consequences be on our national self-respect—on the nation's soul—of a preventable Serbian victory, followed by 'cleansing massacres'?"

General
payoffs:

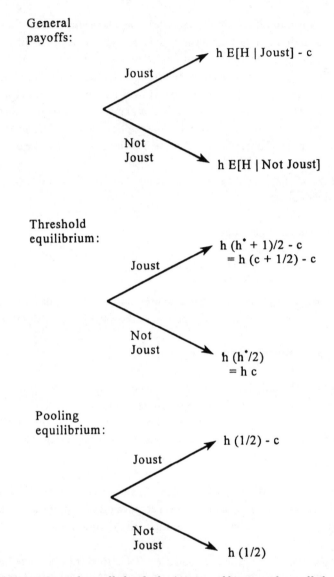

Joust

h E[H | Joust] - c

Not
Joust

h E[H | Not Joust]

Threshold
equilibrium:

Joust

h (h* + 1)/2 - c
= h (c + 1/2) - c

Not
Joust

h (h*/2)
= h c

Pooling
equilibrium:

Joust

h (1/2) - c

Not
Joust

h (1/2)

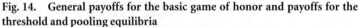

**Fig. 14.   General payoffs for the basic game of honor and payoffs for the
threshold and pooling equilibria**

tach enough importance to reputation to choose Joust. (The prescription for
exactly h^* is not important because that event has zero probability.) By the rules
for revising probabilities, choosing Not Joust induces the public to reestimate
the individual's honor at $h^*/2$, less than before the test, while jousting gives a

new estimate of $(1 + h^*)/2$, which is higher. Substituting these values in the formulas for the payoffs allows us to be more specific about the payoffs when players believe the threshold equilibrium is in effect.

for Jousting: $h(1 + h^*)/2 - c$

for Not Jousting: $h h^*/2$.

These expressions allow a calculation of the cutoff h^*. At the threshold equilibrium, a person whose honor is exactly at h^* will be indifferent between jousting and not jousting. Equating the two expectations and substituting $h = h^*$, gives $h^* = 2c$. Thus he jousts when honor is equal to or greater than $2c$.[6] (This conclusion assumes $c \leq \frac{1}{2}$, since otherwise h^* would go beyond the possible range of honor; for $c > \frac{1}{2}$ the only equilibrium is Not Joust.) The threshold h^* determines his estimated honor in society's eyes. By choosing Joust, the individual will enjoy a reputation for personal honor $c + \frac{1}{2}$, [$= (1 + h^*)/2$ with $h^* = 2c$], which is higher than before, but choosing Not Joust drops estimated honor to c, [$= h^*/2$ with $h^* = 2c$], which is lower than the original $\frac{1}{2}$.

A second type of equilibrium involves never jousting no matter what one's personal honor. Such equilibria are called *pooling equilibria,* since players' actions do not reveal their types, as if they were mixed in a pool. The audience's part of the equilibrium is to keep its estimate at $\frac{1}{2}$ if it sees Not Joust and adopt some partly arbitrary estimate after seeing Joust.[7] Estimating the value at $\frac{1}{2}$ will do here—the audience views jousting as irrelevant to honor and continues to hold its original opinion of h after seeing a joust. The individual has no motive to joust, since it involves a cost with no benefit.

The existence of two equilibria means that in some cultures committing a certain deed gains one honor and in other cultures it does nothing.

The game has two unusual features. One is that the payoffs at an outcome depend on players' beliefs, which change depending on the equilibrium.[8] It is

---

6. There is another equilibrium identical to this, except that Not Joust, rather than Joust, is chosen exactly at cutoff. The distinction will be ignored here since the difference arises with zero probability.

7. The latter cannot be calculated by the axioms of probability, since not jousting is a zero probability event. It can be set arbitrarily as long as it is low enough to give no one an incentive to joust: the most honor-conscious person, someone with h close to 1, gets approximate benefit $E[H \mid \text{Joust}] - c$ from jousting, and $\frac{1}{2}$ from not, and this implies that $E[H \mid \text{Joust}] < c + \frac{1}{2}$.

8. Allowing beliefs directly into the utility function has some unusual consequences when the beliefs are determined by moves in the game. Standard techniques like backward induction sometimes do not work, and an equilibrium may not exist (Geanakoplos, Pearce, and Stacchetti

natural that an equilibrium depends on the payoffs, but here the reverse relation holds too. The other feature is that one player has no moves; the audience's behavior is defined by what it believes rather than what it does. This approach is consistent with newer definitions that see an equilibrium as a consistent set of actions and/or beliefs (app. B).

Extensions: Nonreputational Honor Goals, Differing
Importance of Honor Across Societies

The basic model included only one honor-related goal, enhancing one's reputation for honor, and only one thing to do to pursue it. In accordance with element E1 there may be other honor goals. Suppose the real number x_j measures the degree to which an action A_j achieves other honor-related goals other than reputation. A high value of x_j means that doing A_j is important according to the society's principles around honor, for example, that i's action A_j contributes to defending the group. Individual i's total weight for the honor-related consequences of i's actions is then $h_i \{E[H_i \mid A_j] + x_j\}$. (By the principle of unity all honor goals are multiplied by the same constant h_i. The scale for x is chosen so that the rate of proportionality is 1. A subscript has been added to personal honor to show it is a property of the individual.) The utility of other self-interest (non-honor-related) consequences of action A_j are y_j. The individual will choose an action that maximizes $h_i \{E[H_i \mid A_j] + x_j\} + y_j$, which can be determined as before.

Element E5 noted that some cultural practices seem designed to bolster the importance of honor. The basic model can be extended to reflect the degree of importance the culture places on honor. "Importance" means the weight placed on honor in the payoff, other things equal. A player's payoffs can be changed to $k\, h_i\, E[H_i \mid \text{Joust}] - c$, and $k\, h_i\, E[H_i \mid \text{Not Joust}]$ where k measures the cultural importance and has no subscript because it holds across people. The threshold for jousting is calculated as $h^* = 2c/k$. For a given cost of proving honor, the more important honor is, the less the individual's paying the cost increases the audience's estimate. This is ironical, but the logic of the model shows that it is reasonable.

1989; see also Gilboa and Schmeidler 1988; Nalebuff 1991; and Bernheim 1994). Geanakoplos, Pearce, and Stacchetti extend the Nash equilibrium concept to what they call a *psychological equilibrium,* but this is not an ideal name from my viewpoint—all equilibria are psychological in that they use subjective probabilities and utilities. Their concept is similar to the one used here, although it applies only to games of complete information.

Is Honor Personal or Social?

The model offers an answer to an ancient question: Does honor reside in one's character or in one's reputation as granted by society? The Italian Renaissance writer Valmarana (1598) stated that honor results from personal virtue like the casting of a shadow. He was assuming that society's judgment is as reliable as the laws of optics, but Lucretia's story shows that this is not so. Writing on the nobility of the Italian Renaissance, Burckhardt (1929) recognized the puzzle, calling honor an "enigmatic mixture of conscience and egotism," but he proposed no solution. The anthropologist Jean Peristiany (1966, 21) equivocated on the personal/social question: "Honor is the value of a person in his own eyes but also in the eyes of society. It is his estimation of his own worth, his claim to pride, but it is also the acknowledgment of that claim, his excellence recognized by society, his right to pride." Virtue becomes *self-perceived* virtue here, which is equated with socially perceived virtue. The stance of some writers (e.g., Miller 1993, writing on Icelandic sagas) is that the individual-versus-social question cannot even be asked in honor societies, where social perception and individual perception of virtue are one in the members' eyes. This overstates the principle of the unity of honor. The dual-nature question has been raised constantly by those writing within honor cultures, for example, in the tracts of the Italian Renaissance (Bryson 1935).

As quoted earlier, Perla dismissed honor on the grounds that it was circular. In *Henry IV,* Part I, Falstaff rejects it because it is purely social perception. He must decide whether to go into battle, and to rationalize the safer choice, he runs through a "catechism" of questions. Honor cannot cure wounds or set broken legs, he says. It is held by the dead, but they cannot feel it or hear it, and they lose it at the whim of living detractors. It is just a word, a mere "scutcheon," a coat of arms. His dismissal can be answered by the model, which suggests that there are two concepts of honor: an individual's personal trait h, and the society's estimate of it $E[H \mid$ the individual's actions]. They become linked because the person makes a choice based on their product.

Is National Honor a Sham?

An important question is whether a system of national honor promotes or endangers peace, especially given that details of the system may be changed when it is raised to the national level. Josiah Royce (1914, xxiv) wrote, "What is called national honor is at present altogether too much a matter of capricious private and often merely personal judgement simply because the nations are not as yet self-conscious moral beings." Perla (1918), writing toward the end of World War I, saw international honor as a sham, since clear principles about what it meant were lacking. A monk knows what he is promising by the vows of poverty, chastity, and obedience, and a physician understands what the code of ethics calls for. However, when a government holds that "national honor is the sublime ideal for which it is ever ready to suffer annihilation if necessary, that it is one thing which it can never consent to arbitrate, we know almost nothing about the implications which the phrase comprises." He allowed that a legitimate system of national honor was possible and hoped that when the war was over the code could be based on pacific values.

Perla was overstating the point. Not every invocation of national honor has been bellicose. In keeping with E1, it has sometimes meant fidelity to moral principles, for example, England's honorable duties to help Armenians in the early part of this century, or oppose slavery in the last one, as he indicates. On the other hand, part of his case must be granted. There is an unavoidable problem in transferring honor up to the international system. Many societal honor systems call for obedience and loyalty to those in authority, loyalty to one's patron, lord, or king, or in military codes, to one's country. These requirements reinforce the social hierarchy by making loyalty an expression of who the person is.

(E7) Honor reconciles autonomous action with obedience to a hierarchical order by making obedience the individual's duty.

A system of honor is like a shell that can be filled in different ways. Some societies have changed honor's content but retained its structure. Nye (1993, chap. 3) recounts how the code of French feudal society provided a structure for postrevolutionary bourgeois honor. The original concept involved personal courage and prowess in battle, the latter sexual power, fidelity of one's wife, and discipline and reliability in public and commercial life.

The fact of this kind of evolution makes it plausible that an honor system might be moved up to the level of international society, but it suggests that there would be changes in content. It turns out that some elements in the structure of honor change as well—some are lost, and others are deemphasized. In the international system, there can be no duty owed to some higher power, as there is no higher power. Honor is left to be an assertion of autonomy. The German theorist and teacher Heinrich von Treitschke (1916) commented after the seizure of Alsace, "The world will recognize that in disregarding the will of the Alsatians of today we are only fulfilling an injunction imposed by our national honor." In the dispute between Germany and England over a treaty concerning Morocco, the kaiser announced, "Germany has risen to a world power and our honor demands that we be consulted in any further exploitation of the globe" (von Bulow 1914, 96, quoted in Perla 1918). International honor tells a powerful nation that it has a right to have its way, but it puts no corresponding duty on that country or anyone else to comply with a social order. Contrary to Perla, the problem of honor at the international level is less that its content disappears and more that those components that support reconciliation and peace get left behind. More of this phenomenon—the withering of the pacific features of honor—will be seen in the next chapter on challenges.

CHAPTER 7

Challenges to Honor

Challenges, at least perceived ones, have often triggered international disputes. Before the War of 1812, the United States took England's impressment of its sailors as a symbolic denial of its sovereign status. Another instance was the 1979 seizure by Iranian students of the staff of the American embassy in Tehran. This chapter asks what challenges are and whether states really challenge each other's honor. The practical issues treated are the following: What makes a challenge compelling or weak, and how can the impact of another's challenge be weakened so as to avoid one's being forced into a fight?

The Form of Challenges to Honor

Challenges are a recurring element in honor-based societies.

(E8) Procedures often exist for making and responding to challenges; accepting a challenge incurs some cost or risk, and not accepting means a loss of honor.

Challenges can be separated according to whether they are substantial or not. A substantial challenge is one that does real harm to some interest that the receiver is honor bound to defend, such as his home or family members. The point of doing the harm is to convey a symbolic message. Internationally, this might involve injuring or killing another government's officials—Luard (1986, 115–16) lists some wars that started in this way. Nonsubstantial challenges are those that do not harm the individual's interests directly but can do reputational damage if they are not answered. They can be symbolic or conventional actions or explicit words of challenging. A symbolic/conventional challenge might be touching another's moustache (in Montenegro, Hasluck 1981, 145), pulling another's nose (in the antebellum American South, Greenberg 1990, 1996), or staring at a rival (in U.S. inner cities, Anderson 1994). A challenge in explicit verbal

101

form would be a statement like "I challenge you," or in Renaissance Italy, "You lie in your throat," or between children today, "I dare you." Children, or adults in a bar, sometimes say, "I bet you won't" do some action. This is a *performative*, a special sentence, typically in the first person, that in its utterance accomplishes the social task it is naming.

This chapter will concentrate on performatives like "I challenge you. . . ." The fact that this kind works suggests that harm is not a necessary component, nor is symbolism. Although symbolism is a focus of this book, at this point it is a complication. The linguistic challenges are full-fledged, and what they tell us can be applied to the others.

Purely verbal challenges are puzzling. Somehow, a recitation of words forces someone to do something that is risky or costly. One of the cleverest instances in literature appears in the medieval poem *Sir Gawain and the Green Knight*, a story that will be used later in the chapter to show some of challenging's finer points. The Green Knight, a giant and completely green, shows up at King Arthur's Christmas feast and offers a bizarre, apparently suicidal game. He wants an exchange of blows, with both parties using his large green ax, and he stipulates that his opponent must go first. When no one accepts, he furrows his green brow and taunts the company,

> What, is þis Arþureȝ hous, quoþ þe haþel þenne
> þat al þe rouse rennes þurȝ ryalmes so mony?
> Where is now your sourquydrye and your conquestes
> Your gryndellayk and your greme and your grete wordes?
> Now is þe reuel and þe renoun of þe Rounde Table
> Ouerwalt wyth a worde of on wyȝes speche
> For al dares for drede withoute dynt schewed.
> (309–15, from Tolkien and Gordon 1925)

"This is surely not Arthur's house renowned through many kingdoms," he is saying. "The Round Table's pride and fierceness and bragging talk have vanished, its fame has been upset by one man's speech, *by words alone*, for all are cowering without a blow being dealt." He is raising a central question of this chapter: How can a mere verbal formula, with no factual evidence against the hearer's honor, force the person to risk his life?

Do States Really Challenge Each Other's Honor?

The relevant question is not whether the honor of states is challenged, but whether they see it as challenged. Some actions perceived as challenges might not have been intended as such, but if they led to violence, the honor system may have been in operation, at least from the challengee's viewpoint.

Compared to theories of war causation that involve gross national product, alliance structure, or the degree of democracy, it is harder to measure directly the importance of challenges and honor. One must look at diverse evidence, such as the vocabulary used between the parties, the internal discussions of the event by policymakers, and the kinds of actions taken. The honor model is a guide to the relevant features, which include the existence of commitments, the superficiality of the challenge, the pressure to make a violent response, the challenger's construal of what the response is supposed to be showing, and various metaphors in the leaders' language that suggest the within-society prototypical scenario of a dispute over honor.

Sometimes a leader cites honor explicitly. During World War I, Germany's U-boat campaign led to the sinking of the *Lusitania,* and when President Wilson called on Congress to declare war, he explained why the enemy would be Germany alone, for the present (*Cong. Rec.,* 65th Congress, vol. 55, pt. 1, 1917, 118–20): "I have said nothing of the governments allied with the Imperial Government of Germany because they have not made war upon us or challenged us to defend our right and our honor." More often, concepts around honor are named, but not honor itself. On October 22, 1962, at the start of the Cuban missile crisis, President Kennedy went on the radio to explain his stance (U.S. Department of State 1961): "This secret, swift and extraordinary build-up of communist missiles . . . is a deliberately provocative and unjustified change in the status quo which cannot be accepted by this country if our courage and our commitments are ever to be trusted again by either friend or foe." When a commitment is based on honor, it can become the object of a challenge and have implications for the world's judgment of one's mettle.

Another event suggesting a challenge to honor was the August 1964 encounter between North Vietnamese torpedo boats and U.S. destroyers in the Gulf of Tonkin. The formality of declaring war had fallen out of use, but a rough equivalent in the United States was a congressional resolution granting the president the power to wage war. In the week following the incident, Lyndon Johnson used several forums to make his case for a wider war and frequently construed the North Vietnamese action as a challenge.[1] On August 5, he told an audience at Syracuse University that this was "the same challenge that we have faced with courage and we have met with strength in Greece and Turkey, in Berlin and Korea, in Lebanon and Cuba." Congress acceded, and on signing the

---

1. Historians have questioned Johnson's sincerity in describing the encounter, but that is another issue. Many in Congress believed him and his resolution passed almost unanimously.

resolution on August 10, he stated, "Our nation was faced by the challenge of deliberate and unprovoked acts of aggression in Southeast Asia." This fits the definition of a challenge to honor, that one's response will form part of a public history that others will use in their assessments.

Of course, the word *challenge* has a usage unconnected to honorable reputation; it is sometimes simply an impediment to a goal. However, that interpretation does not fit here. The attacks were not described as functional moves with objective consequences that had to be undone. Johnson constantly talked as if North Vietnam's actions were messages that the United States must answer. They required "a response," "a positive reply." "That reply is being given as I speak to you tonight" (Johnson 1965, Address to the Nation, August 4, 1964). "The attacks have been answered . . . aggression unchallenged is aggression unleashed. . . . that is why we have answered this aggression with action," he told the Syracuse audience. In his phrasing, U.S. retaliation was meant to show something to a wide audience. A resolution in Congress would "affirm the national determination that all attacks will be met." Congress should act promptly "to give convincing evidence to the aggressive Communist nations, and to the world as a whole, that our policy in southeast Asia will be carried forward." The agenda was transmitting information to the world, not bringing about a military outcome. Johnson cited the U.S. commitment to South Vietnam as a reason for his response (Johnson 1964, Message to Congress, August 5, 1964): "America keeps her word. Here as elsewhere, we must and shall honor our commitments." This is consistent with the oath-taking feature of many honor systems, discussed in the next chapter. That a response was necessary even though no damage had been done to the U.S. ships fits the property that challenges can be nonsubstantial.[2]

Another piece of evidence that honor was involved was the U.S. administration's view of Hanoi's motive for its actions. Publicly, Washington avoided explanations, and at the United Nations Adlai Stevenson described the incident as just another example of Hanoi's violent ways (U.S. Department of State 1964, 273). Privately, however, on August 5, Walter Rostow wrote a memo to Secretary of State Dean Rusk (*Foreign Relations of the United States,* vol. 1, 639) suggesting that Hanoi had been hoping that "a US failure to react sharply to these attacks might have persuaded the Khanh government [of South Vietnam] that further reliance on the US was unprofitable and that Saigon should seek the best terms it could with Hanoi." Rusk seemed to accept this. Three days later, he tried to send a message to North Vietnam through a Canadian emissary. The North

---

2. Nisbett and Cohen (1996) argue that the culture of honor is stronger in the U.S. South, and present evidence that the positions of Southern politicians, like Johnson, tend to reflect it.

Vietnamese prime minister was to be told that the United States saw the incident as an attempt either to provoke it or to portray it as a "paper tiger" (651–53). Rusk was sending his interpretation of the action back to North Vietnam in order to clarify the meaning of the U.S. response. His understanding, that Hanoi sought to unmask the United States before its allies, is the typical motive for a challenge to honor.[3]

The vocabulary of challenging has become rarer, but the old mechanism seems to persist with new words. In the 1980s, the Reagan administration pushed for strong action against Nicaragua and sent military support to the rulers of El Salvador. The Salvadoran government had one of the worst human rights records and had been sponsoring death squads to eliminate its political opposition, so U.S. policy was hard to rationalize from democratic values. Except for Panama, Central America did not occupy a geographically strategic position, and it had no vital raw materials that gave the United States an objective reason to worry about its own security. How was the policy justified? Many administration supporters used a vocabulary suggesting honor. In the examples that follow, most taken from Schoultz (1987), each writer claims that strong action in Central America proves that America possesses a certain trait, which I have put in italics.

> When engaged in a conflict for global stakes, what may appear as a marginal interest will be invested with a significance it would not otherwise have, for almost any challenge is likely to be seen by the challenger and by third parties as a test of one's *will.* . . . In Central America there are no vital raw materials or minerals whose loss might provide the basis for legitimate security concerns. Yet Central America bears geographic proximity to the United States, and historically it has long been regarded as falling within our sphere of influence. . . . [If] the Soviet Union observes our passivity to events in our own backyard that signal the loss of American control, what conclusions might it draw about our probable passivity in other, far more difficult areas? (Tucker 1981, 144–45, 176–77, 180)

> The decline of U.S. pre-eminence in the region—an area traditionally in the U.S. sphere of influence—and of its ability to deny interference in the region by other powers, threatens to be interpreted as an indication of U.S. *weakness* in absolute terms. (Hayes 1980, 135)

---

3. Milliken (1996) gives other examples of prestige and credibility talk in the U.S. administration during the Vietnam War.

The United States cannot afford to wear blinders ignoring Cuban and Soviet efforts in the region. We must consider the serious consequences of any perception of *weakness* in an area acknowledged to be basic to US security and how our European allies in NATO might question *our resolve* in Europe if we appear indifferent to the spread of communism in our own backyard. (Dickens 1980, 210)

The crisis is on our doorstep. Beyond the issue of US security interests in the Central American-Caribbean region, our *credibility* world wide is engaged. The triumph of hostile forces in what the Soviets call the "strategic rear" of the United States would be read as a sign of US *impotence*. (*Report of the National Bipartisan Commission on Central America* [Kissinger Commission 1984, 93])

An image of *weakness or incompetence,* or of an inability to effectively influence the course of events in an area so close, so traditionally dominated by Washington, and so weak in its own right should be avoided. (Millett 1982, 81)

If Central America were to fall, what would be the consequences for our position in Asia, Europe, and for alliances such as NATO? . . . Our *credibility* would collapse, our alliances would crumble, and the safety of our homeland would be put in jeopardy. (Ronald Reagan's address to a joint session of Congress, April 1983. *Weekly Compilation of Presidential Documents,* May 2, 1983, 613–14)

This kind of talk is recurrent in U.S. foreign policy, and other examples can be garnered from debates over the MX missile, Saddam Hussein's invasion of Kuwait, the intermediate-range nuclear missiles in Europe, and bombing raids in reprisals for terrorism.

The quotes show several features of honor behavior. Choosing an unimportant context to deliver an important demonstration fits with the nonsubstantial nature of challenges. As in a challenge to honor, the question is what others will think, not whether the event is intended as a challenge—by declaring Central America to be a test of American commitments, the U.S. administration is making it that. A goal of the demonstration is the trust and respect of the world to enhance the defense of oneself and one's allies, as in societal honor. In line with the TERRITORY-AS-A-HOUSE metaphor, there is an emphasis on events in the U.S. "sphere of influence" and "backyard" and events "on our doorstep." Some quotes hint that gender identity is also at stake, following the second element of the last chapter. The reference to credibility recalls the link of honor to commitment making.

There is a notable variety of words for what a bold action will prove: *strength, will, credibility,* or other traits. Writers move from one to another so smoothly that the words seem synonymous. They appear to be manifestations of one unnamed central quality. Also, the character traits that the strong action is supposed to show seem elliptical. Writers worry about "reputation," but reputation for what? America should show her "will" and "resolve," but will and resolve to do what? If it is to act in Latin America, that is odd, given the area is a marginal interest as Tucker and others suggest. Is the goal to show willingness to act where U.S. interests are *not* at stake? If so, what is the limit of this kind of argument? The problem is that the speakers leave a blank after the key words. This is the same self-referential pattern as arose for honor, which is the desire to be seen as honorable, and the blanks would be filled in following this account of honor. Having "resolve" involves being ready to show others that one has resolve.

The oft-cited rationale of "credibility" is another one that leaves a blank. Some fact or assertion is to be believed, but which one is not specified. Perhaps the issue is "general credibility," which in the speaker's mental model is a broad attribute of a state. Following the COUNTRY-AS-AN-UNSPECIFIED-PERSON metaphor, there would be a "national personality," where some nations are characteristically truthful and others are ready to lie. However, this account does not fit other aspects of U.S. foreign policy at the time. While the administration was trying to establish "credibility" in Latin America, it was lobbying Congress to allow it to violate the Anti-Ballistic Missile Treaty. Even if it did not see its plans as a treaty violation, most other nations did, so this threatened U.S. credibility, in the sense of a general trait. The Reagan administration treated credibility around the ABM Treaty and around Central America as unconnected. The U.S. administration's position was not consistent with its belief in a national trait of honesty, but with the idea that certain commitments, those to defend certain kinds of interests, had to be kept. The historian Mervyn James (1986, 229) stated that English nobility would "lie, cheat, deceive, plot, treason, seduce, and commit adultery without incurring dishonor." The U.S. concern for credibility focused just on the commitments that such a society would see as points of honor.

The Nature of Challenges to Honor

Philosophers and linguists concerned with speech acts have not paid much attention to challenges, but they have provided a set of concepts for an analysis.

These can be used to discuss how a challenge compares to other kinds of speech acts and to derive a definition.

What Challenges Are Not: Directives, Assertives, or Commitments

Superficially, a challenge seems like a *demand*. The challenger seems to be demanding a test or proof of some claim. Challenging an election outcome is calling for a recount, and challenging someone to a game of checkers is asking that the individual match his or her skill against yours. Accordingly, a challenge to someone's honor would be a demand to prove that quality. If challenges are really demands, then as speech acts they are in the category of directives (chap. 2), alongside urging, begging, asking, and so on. Partridge (1982) puts them there, and McCawley (1977) makes a point that supports this idea—that they share a grammatical feature with many directives in that they can appear in the imperative case:

> "Send help, I urge you."
> "Ring that doorbell, I dare you."

However, a challenge cannot be a demand in the normal sense. When I demand something, I am implying that I want it, but when a gentleman challenges another to a duel, he might be content to see the other decline. His challenge is not suggesting otherwise. Its point would be accomplished when the other declines—the challenge was not made to bring about a duel, just to test the validity of the other's reputation, perhaps reveal it as counterfeit. A directive that is refused is a failure, but a challenge that is declined achieves its purpose.

If challenges are not demands, are they *assertions?* What are they asserting? They cannot be saying that the other will lose the contest. When someone is challenged to a duel, it is not marksmanship that is at issue, but willingness to participate in the duel. Are challenges the same as assertions that the challenged party's reputation is false? This will not work either, since a valid response to an assertion would be an attempt to disprove it, but the appropriate response to an honor challenge is violence. In 1784, Benjamin Franklin wrote to Dr. Thomas Percival, "Formerly when duels were used to determine Lawsuits from an opinion that Providence would in every instance favour truth and right with Victory they were more excusable. At present they decide nothing. A man says something which another tells him is a Lye they fight, but whichever is killed, the point in question remains unsettled." Franklin was not arguing that the man would be smarter to file a lawsuit; he was assailing the whole institution. He knew that a challenge could not be answered by counterevidence.

Perhaps challenges are *commitments* in which the challenger is promising to participate in the contest. They would then be commissive speech acts, which bind the speaker to a course of action, like offering, accepting offers, promising, surrendering, or saying "I do" at a wedding. McCawley (1977) puts them there, reasoning that they are like bets of the kind, "I bet you won't have the guts to" do such and such. However, the usage of "bet" in this sense is an odd one in which the bettor is not really committing to making a payoff. Daring is like offering a bet only in those cases where "I bet you" is not a commissive.[4]

What Challenges Are, the Class of Provocatives

The essence of a performative is its *illocutionary point,* its characteristic purpose, and performatives with similar illocutionary points should be grouped together. The idea of illocutionary point can be understood by considering a promise, which is meant to obligate the speaker to a certain action to the benefit of the recipient. That is not its purpose on every occasion—someone might make a promise to show off or to relieve a silence in the conversation—but promising has a typical purpose, which is its illocutionary point.

For a challenge, the illocutionary point is to hold a public test of some proposition that the challenged person would like to have generally believed. For some kinds of challenges, like those that involve honor, the test is whether the challengee will engage in a costly or risky contest. Another variety is a *dare,* whose illocutionary point is to test whether the target is bold and fearless. Unlike a challenge, the action is usually performed only by the daree. *Defying* someone challenges that individual to assert authority and thereby tests whether the person has that authority. (Used in the context of a debate, defying has a somewhat different point: to induce the other to try to prove a claim and thereby show that the individual cannot.) Challenging, defying, daring, double daring and the like do not fit any current categorization. They belong in their own group. Naming it would underline this difference, and I will term it the class of *provocatives,* after the Latin *provocare,* to dare.[5] The provocatives have a common illocutionary point: to test some proposition that the recipient wants believed by seeing whether the recipient will or can perform a certain action.

---

4. Fotion (1979) analyzes betting as a speech act.

5. "Challenge," "defy," and "dare" are sometimes not provocatives. To defy, for example, can be simply to declare one's unwillingness to accept the other's authority, not to call for a fight.

A Game of Challenging

This section will examine the provocative of challenging by first showing its function in social interactions and then by embedding it in a simple game. This will lead to a definition of a challenge to honor.

The game of figure 15 *(top)* adds a player to the basic game of honor of the last chapter. This player has only one move, to challenge, and is included only for exposition. Then the challenged player decides whether to bear the cost of a fight. Payoffs for the challenger are omitted, since that player makes no choices, but the player with the moves has payoffs like that of the basic game of honor. It is essentially the basic game, put in a fuller way, and there are two equilibria, as in the basic game. At the pooling equilibrium, the player does not pay the cost, and the audience does not change its view of the player's honor. At the threshold equilibrium, the player does or does not pay the cost depending on his degree of honor, and the audience revises its estimate of honor up or down accordingly. The pooling equilibrium corresponds to a culture where the particular form of challenging used does not work or perhaps where the whole institution of challenges is absent. The threshold equilibrium is one where the mode of challenging is valid and induces expectations all around that a sufficiently honorable person would bear the cost of accepting.

Even after all strategic factors and interests are considered, there are two equilibria, two possible different assemblages of beliefs and actions that are mutually consistent.[6] In each of the equilibria, the player holds beliefs about the audience's beliefs, which influence his utility, and the audience holds beliefs about the player's beliefs and actions, which it uses to assess the player's honor. The existence of multiple equilibria explains the Green Knight's taunt that his mere words have overthrown the Round Table's reputation. Game-theoretical factors cannot determine which of the two equilibria will obtain, so this opens up a role for outside factors, even words. It also explains why challenges can be arbitrary and vary from culture to culture. As a male adult, I cannot effectively dare you to hold your breath for a minute, but in a barroom I can deliver certain formulaic epithets that start a fistfight. Again, the reason a particular form works in a society must lie outside the game, and it often involves symbolic messages or arbitrary conventions.

The Definition of a Challenge to Honor

The definition of a challenge will have three elements. First, it is a communicative act with a certain meaning. Chapter 3 distinguishes different kinds of com-

---

6. This argument corresponds to the second rationale for Nash equilibria in appendix B.

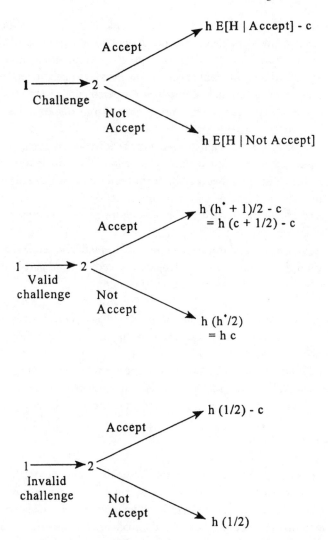

Fig. 15.   The general payoffs for the challenge game *(top)* and for two equilibria, where social customs do and do not support, respectively, the particular form of the challenge.

municative acts by the belief or action they intend the receiver to adopt, and a challenge aims for a change of belief about the challengee's honor. It is unusual among assertive communicative acts in that the direction of belief change depends on whether the challengee accepts. The second element in the definition arises from Schiffer's thesis about performatives (1972, chap. 4) that a core feature that differentiates them is the particular reason they give the receiver to change the belief or perform the action. For example, to "advise" someone to do something is to express one's wish that the individual do it, for the reason that it is in his or her interest. To "order" someone to do something has the same point but it is based on a different reason on the receiver's part: that the orderer has some power or institutional right to have the person do it and has called on the person to do it. The reason for complying when someone "begs" you to do something is your personal sympathy for the speaker. In the case of a challenge, the reason that the audience ought to change its beliefs about the person's honor is that a challenge has been issued, one that is valid in the sense that it will provoke certain beliefs in the audience. With many performatives, the receiver's reason for a new belief or action is brought into being by the performative act itself. This is not the case with advising, but it holds for some others, like ordering, promising, apologizing, and challenging.

Challenging has a third feature, an unusual one that the receiver is typically different from the person being challenged. The receiver, the party meant to adopt new beliefs, is the broader audience, the honor group.

DEFINITION: *X's challenge to Y's honor* to engage in a certain contest is a communicative act whose receiver is the honor group and whose meaning has two components: that X will engage in the contest if Y accepts and that the honor group should raise or lower its estimate of Y's honor according to whether Y accepts or refuses. The reason for the honor group to change its estimate is that the challenge will cause Y to believe that the audience will change its estimate.

Semiforceful Challenges

A challenge takes a form specified by the culture. Examples are reciting a formulaic accusation of lying, or pulling a rival's nose. A restriction is that the words or action be distinctive enough that it will not be missed, and there will be no false alarms.[7] Sometimes, however, the challenge is at the edge of the form supported by the culture. If one twelve year old dares another to eat a worm, it will not work—it is too late. International challenges in particular are often of uncertain validity, since they cannot exploit a common culture. The challengee

---

7. Even within a culture there is ambiguity, and Boehm (1983, 145) describes how it can be exploited to enhance the challenger's honor, "While offering insults was an expected mode of maintaining honor, [a Montenegrin male] also knew that his stronger provocations might get him killed. In the eyes of the tribe, this was exactly what made aggressive behavior commendable in many contexts. . . . if he offered insults that came close to requiring homicidal retaliation, then no one would doubt his courage."

may not be sure whether a response is needed, and the audience may not be sure whether to revise its estimate of honor. For the goal of peace, this is bad news and good news. It means that relatively innocent events might be misperceived as challenges but also that a nation can ignore some intentional challenges. This section discusses why some challenges are only partially forceful.

Again, philosophers of language and linguists have not discussed challenges in this regard, but we can apply what they have written on the general issue of speech acts.[8] Asking what makes a challenge compelling is like asking when a promise really commits its maker or when an order must be obeyed. It turns on three properties of a speech act: its force, strength, and success, which are discussed now.

Success, Force, and Strength: Can I Promise My Cat a Treat?

The *success* of a speech act is the degree to which it achieves its illocutionary point. A challenge succeeds if it gives information about the challengee's honor.[9] Two determinants of success are force and strength. The *force* of a speech act is its innate ability on a given occasion to achieve its illocutionary point. Force is causal potential, and it relates to a speech act's success as mechanical force does to an object's motion. Some bodies have high inertia, and some situations make an illocutionary point much harder to accomplish, even when the speech act is well performed. *Strength* applies purely to the vocabulary used, not the occasion. Other things equal, a stronger performative will accomplish its illocutionary point more fully and more widely. Solemnly promising is stronger than promising in that the receiver is likely to be more convinced that the promise will be carried out. Granted, in some situations asking is more effective than demanding—perhaps the receiver will stiffen up if the sender is too assertive—but the fact that we must come up with an explanation shows our presupposition that demanding is generally more effective.

A traditional example illustrates the difference between force and strength.

---

8. The approach of Searle and Vanderveken (1985) and Vanderveken (1990) will be used. They propose that a speech act possesses features on six dimensions, the six "components of illocutionary force." They are its illocutionary point, the degree of strength of its illocutionary point, its mode of achievement, its propositional content conditions, its preparatory conditions, and its sincerity conditions. They showed that in a well-defined sense their scheme is complete: two performatives possessing identical features on the dimensions would be the same.

9. One could formalize the idea of success by measuring the uncertainty resolved by the challenge. The challenger would choose the cost of the challenge, the optimal cost being the one that maximally reduces uncertainty. In the model of the last chapter, where the prior distribution of honor H was uniform between 0 and 1, the challenger should choose cost $c = \frac{1}{4}$.

Suppose I promise my cat a treat. Is this promise valid? A philosopher assures me that I am not really bound by it, so I try to remedy this by a "solemn" promise to the cat. The philosopher is still leery. I pumped up the strength, but the problem is that the promise was made to a being that could not understand it. Force requires freedom from defects, not stronger words.

To summarize, strength is the general, acontextual ability of the word or phrase to accomplish its purpose; force is innate to the speech act as delivered on a given occasion; success is the achievement of the illocutionary point on the occasion and depends on force and the broader context, including what the speech act is trying to do.

As a Performative, Challenging is Single Strength

For many illocutionary points, the English language offers a sequence of speech acts of increasing strength. Suggesting is weak, asking is moderate, and demanding is strong. Verbal challenges have the unusual feature of having a single value of strength. I can "deeply apologize" or "thank you from the bottom of my heart," but I cannot "strongly challenge you."[10] This could be related to the game of challenging (fig. 15), which has only one equilibrium involving a successful challenge. There is no series of equilibria requiring higher and higher degrees of honor for the individual to accept. Accordingly, the language does not include a sequence of performative words to select each equilibrium.[11]

Another possible explanation for the single strength of verbal challenges is that different strengths are not needed. To separate people of different honors, one can vary the cost, since a more costly contest raises the minimum honor for accepting. Sometimes, however, the challenger has no choice in the cost, which is set by social customs. In some societies a challenge is appropriate only following an insult, and often the severity of the insult determines the cost of the contest. McAleer (1994) describes such a system in nineteenth-century Germany. A consideration against this, however, is that while verbal challenges are single strength, international ones often involve some token harm or symbolic

----

10. Daring seems to have the opposite property—there are daring, double daring, and, especially in the American South, further notions like double dog daring and upward (Cassidy 1991). However double daring is not the same as daring more strongly. One child cannot walk up to another and issue a double dare—it must be a rejoinder after a refusal to accept a dare. Still its existence points up a difference between challenges and dares, and just why children's culture allows many strengths is an interesting issue.

11. It is possible to postulate a prior distribution on an individual's honor H that yields several equilibria setting different thresholds of responding, but for a wide class of distributions, there is only one equilibrium that separates players by honor.

violation of the challengee's rights and their strength depends on the degree of injury. President Wilson stayed at peace after a single American died in a U-boat attack, but when 128 Americans drowned on the *Lusitania,* he declared war.

Challenges as Social Constructions

Since verbal challenges are single strength, strength is not the interesting variable here. It will be the force of challenges that is modeled. A speech act loses force by knowledge of its defects. Someone might impersonate my boss on the telephone, and get me to obey an order. The order is defective but it will succeed unless I know it is defective.

Some speech acts depend crucially on my knowledge of the objective event. If I learn that you are not my boss, your order becomes forceless. Challenges are different. Although a challenge generally has to be performed according to the culture's rules, its success does not turn on this. The objective event of challenging is just a trigger for certain beliefs about beliefs. If these beliefs come into place in some way, they will be self-sustaining and the challenge will be fully forceful. If I knew that the audience would charge me an honor cost for refusing to fight, and if the audience knew that I knew it, then any opinions we might hold about the challenge's objective details would be irrelevant. Conversely a challenge might be done appropriately, but that would not matter if the parties knew that neither would pay any attention to it.

Everyday language portrays a challenge as a physical entity. Making a challenge or accepting one sounds like the parties are dealing with an object, and even the philosophical vocabulary of force suggests that it has physical features. In fact, there is no important sense in which a challenge is real apart from the expectations of the audience and the challengee. A challenge is a *social construction.* The metaphor portrays such a shared social belief as an outside object. It also carries an attitudinal component, suggesting that society constructs a concept such as prostitution, illiteracy, or gender, and adopts an attitude to it. The term is an academic one, common especially in the study of social problems (Berger and Luckmann 1966), but it also arises in regular speech, as one is "loaded down" with responsiblities or "takes" credit or "possesses" honor or "acquires" prestige, and is related to a broader metaphor of an individual's beliefs as objects that he or she possesses (Abelson 1986).

The point of the phrase "social construction" in regard to its belief component is that sometimes a group's beliefs about beliefs form the same pattern that would arise if there really were an outside object. Imagine two people sitting across a table on which a candle is burning. There is the objective fact and also the ladder of beliefs: both people know the candle is there, know they know it, and so on. For social constructions the mutual beliefs are in place but not necessarily because of a candle. The latter can be thought of as filled in by implication, constructed from the social perceptions. Talking this way is an easy code for the structure of mutual beliefs. Searle (1995) uses *social fact* or *self-referential* concept for a similar idea and suggests that most concepts around social institutions are these kinds of social facts. Money, his example, is not money because of its physical properties, but because people think of it as that, which means that they think others will think of it as money, and so on.

The next section presents a model of a social constuction that goes beyond the metaphor in being "partly there" in people's minds. It is stated for challenges but could be adapted for other such concepts.

A Model of Semiforceful Challenges

The social constuction nature of challenges means that there is one approach the model should not take: it should not assign each challenged party and the audience a subjective probability that the challenge is a "valid" one, in some objective sense. The model represents a loss of force as doubt about others' beliefs. This is formalized by the method of interactive belief structures (appendix B.)[12] For simplicity, the model assumes that each player can be of two types. The types of challengees are Ch_I and Ch_{II}, and the types of audience are Aud_I and Aud_{II}. A player's type is not an objective attribute brought to the game. It can be thought of in this way: at the time of the challenge, the players have had different life experiences, which have led them to adopt beliefs about other players' life experiences. The player's type is this life experience. It is nothing more than what that player believes about the other player's type. In conjunction with the strategic aspects of the current game, it determines what the player does in the game.

The joint likelihoods of each type are expressed in matrix 1. The types show probabilistic dependence, but it is not causal dependence. There is no implication that one player's set of beliefs influences the other's. The dependence is evidential—if I have had a certain life experience, I assess different likelihoods for what yours have been.[13]

---

12. The model in this chapter differs slightly from Aumann's approach in that the type does not include the Challengee's knowledge of *h* or the move made. It is a "partial" type. Since it is assumed in this model that beliefs about another's beliefs are independent of *h*, it is easy to move to a player's full type. A more standard form for a challenging model is in appendix B.

13. These probabilities do not refer to proportions of the audience holding each belief—a Challengee believes that the *whole* Audience is of one type or the other.

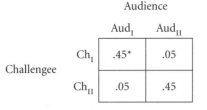

Matrix 1.   **Joint likelihoods of each pair of types, partial common knowledge case**

Assume that the true situation is indicated by the asterisk (*). Types Ch_I and Aud_I are reality, and the other two are hypothetical, included only because each player entertains them as possibilities for the other player. It is assumed that the probability matrix is common knowledge, so each can use it to calculate a distribution over the other's type. The Challengee (who is in reality type Ch_I) believes the Audience is of type Aud_I with probability .9 [= .45/(.45 + .05)] and of type Aud_{II} with probability .1 [= .05/(.45 + .05)]. This situation can be contrasted with a fully forceful challenge, whose matrix implies that each knows with certainty what the other is thinking. In matrix 2, the players assign conditional probabilities to the other's type, given their own, of 0 or 1.[14] A Challengee of type Ch_I holds probability 1 [= .6/(.6 + 0)] that an Audience is type Aud_I. Knowing the other's type constitutes knowing the other's beliefs about one's own type, so here types are more than each player's knowledge: they are their common knowledge.

Returning to the partial common knowledge case of matrix 1, one can calculate Challengee's probabilities for Audience's distribution over Challengee's types and, from this, Challengee's estimate of Audience's probability that Challengee is Ch_I rather than Ch_{II}, and on up. The Challengee holds probabilities .9 and .1 that A holds a .9 and .1 probability of Ch_I, respectively. Therefore Challengee's estimate of Audience's probability of Ch_I is .820 [= .9 (.9) + .1 (.1)]. Further, one can calculate Challengee's estimate of Audience's estimate of that estimate, and so on (appendix B). For matrix 1, the numbers are .820, .705, .631, .574, . . . , converging to .5. The limiting uncertainty .5 is the prior probability of Ch_I, not conditioned on knowledge of the current situation (*).[15] So one's opinion about what the other is thinking dissolves into uncertainty as the level

---

14. The weighting of the nonzero cells with .6 and .4 is arbitrary—when each player reaches the game, the prior likelihood of other types becomes irrelevant.

15. This is always true (Samet 1996).

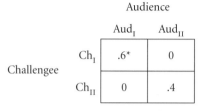

Matrix 2. **Joint probabilities of each pair of types, full common knowledge case**

of metabelief rises. This justifies calling matrix 1 partial common knowledge.[16] (For full common knowledge, matrix 2, the series would be 1, 1, 1, ...)

The full common knowledge game was solved in the preceding chapter—players have a threshold and a pooling equilibrium. What happens with partial common knowledge? The original two equilibria are still there, but a third one appears that depends on players' types. The players believe that the different Challengee types will use different thresholds of personal honor for responding and that different Audience types will come to different conclusions about Challengee's threshold. To add some details, let h, which is Challengee's honor, be uniformly distributed on [½, 1] and let the cost of accepting the challenge be .15. For matrix 1, one equilibrium is for Challengee not to respond and for Audience to exact no cost in honor—the original pooling equilibrium. Ignoring possibilities of arbitrary beliefs the Audience might adopt after an unexpected acceptance, it is as follows.

POOLING EQUILIBRIUM. The Challengee does not accept; the Audience maintains its estimate of h *at .75.*

A second equilibrium is identical to the threshold equilibrium for the full common knowledge case and can be calculated in the same way. The Audience alters its beliefs in response to an acceptance or a refusal, and the Challengee acts differently in response to his personal honor, but neither pays attention to type:

TYPE-INDEPENDENT THRESHOLD EQUILIBRIUM. The Challengee accepts if h > .60; *the Audience estimates* h *at .55 or .80, depending on whether the Challengee does not or does accept.*

The new equilibrium adds a dependence on types.

---

16. Monderer and Samet (1989) give a relevant definition for *degree of common belief.*

Type-dependent threshold equilibrium. *The Challenge accepts if* h >
.705 for type Ch_I, *or if* h > *.992 for type* Ch_{II} ; *a type* Aud_I *audience estimates*
h *at .677 or .867 if the Challengee does not or does respond, respectively; a type*
Aud_{II} *estimates it at .732 or .982.*[17]

It may seem odd that two Challengees with the same honor would behave
differently, but analyzing this equilibrium shows why. A type Aud_I audience sees
the challenge as more forceful and accordingly reacts more strongly. A Ch_I challengee is more ready to accept than a Ch_{II}, because this Challengee holds a
greater belief that the audience is Aud_I.

Doubt about the other's beliefs does more than add diversity to the players. It weakens the challenge. One can calculate that a Ch_I challengee who does
not respond holds an estimate of .6825 for Audience's view of Challengee's
honor, and a Ch_{II}'s estimate is .7265, so neither expects much loss below Audience's prior estimate of .75. In the full common knowledge game, Challengee's
revised estimate of the audience's estimate would show a far greater loss, down
to .55. Assuming that the third equilibrium is in effect, a bit of mutual doubt
about whether the challenge was forceful—a Challengee's probability of .1 instead of 0 that the other is of the tolerant type—has increased both Challengee
types' motivation to decline. This is also reflected in their behavior. With full
common knowledge, 20 percent of Challengees refuse the challenge at the
threshold equilibrium, but with doubt, the numbers rise to 41 percent and 98
percent for Ch_I and Ch_{II}. A grain of doubt makes a challenge less effective as a
test of honor; it saps its force and promotes peace.

The model gives an example of a mathematical representation of a social
construction. The point behind the metaphor is that the entity is not objectively
there but is implied by social behavior. Like all metaphors it has its limits, and
the problem here is its suggestion that there is a one construction out there available for all to see. The difficulty is much like the one that Reddy (1979) saw in
the information-as-a-conduit metaphor. This pattern, discussed in chapter
3, talks as if conveying information is sending a copy of our thoughts to another
person for their perusal. Reddy suggests that it produces a tendency to think that
the receiver can see what we are thinking from the copy we send them. We do
not need to put special effort into communicating, such as putting ourselves in
the other's place to understand how our message is interpreted. The metaphor
allows that our idea might sometimes get mangled in the trip, but in that case

17. The values are calculated as the Audience's estimates of types Ch_I and Ch_{II}'s honors, multiplied by the updated probability that the Challengee is of either type and summed, with the values conditioned on the Challengee's accepting or not accepting. The derivation is in appendix C.

the receiver would see that it has come through damaged, and be aware that he or she is not understanding us. We assume we are understood when we are not. If it becomes clear that we were misinterpreted, we blame the receiver for being stubborn or dense. In fact, he argues, receiving a message is more like detective work, with tests of hypotheses and inferences about what was in the sender's mind. The receiver does not immediately recognize distortion, but does as well as possible to decipher the sender's meaning from the evidence.

Like the conduit metaphor, the construction metaphor of a social belief turns it into an object. The belief is shared by the parties as if it were an external object "constructed" by them, there for all to see. The problem again is that it does not easily handle a partially shared social fact, like a semiforceful challenge. If the edifice is there, there is no reason why it should be perceived differently by the parties, at least within the metaphor. If it is only partly built, all should see that and should not act as if there were a shared understanding. However, groups do not always do this, any more than receivers recognize when a communication is distorted. This shortcoming of the metaphor is ironical because it is this kind of behavior that many writers who use it want to address. The present model gives an example of the situation described nonmetaphorically as an interactive belief system. Incompletely shared social constructions are represented as matrices of partial common knowledge.

For challenges in particular, the model shows the potential benefit of a small amount of cultural ambiguity. But three equilibria exist, and one of them is the same as the full common knowledge case, so this doubt is only potentially helpful. What might induce doubt, and what might point to one or the other will be dealt with next.

How Challenges Lose Force

What could sow a grain of doubt about mutual beliefs and weaken a challenge's force? *Sir Gawain and the Green Knight* has a semiforceful challenge as its opening episode. The poem is carefully crafted—it "moves over an almost flawless structure as smoothly as supple skin moves over the bones of the hand," according to one critic (Loomis 1959, 528)—so one can expect that its representation of partial forcefulness is self-consistent and subtle. It illustrates a series of requirements for fully forceful challenging that will be detailed now. The dismal conclusion will be that modern international challenges do not seem bound by these requirements. Still a central requirement holds internationally and weakens the force of challenges. An earlier story, Sir Gawain's ancestor, is described to illustrate it.

Gawain starts with the Round Table celebrating the 15-day Christmas festival. As King Arthur's courtiers sit down to the feast, an awesome figure rides into the hall, a large man—perhaps a giant, the poet says—handsome, sturdy, finely dressed, and entirely green. He wears no armor but carries a holly bough in one hand and a battle-ax in the other. Even the metal of the ax is bright green. The stranger says he has come to propose a Christmas game. The fame of the Round Table is universal and he hopes that his request will be granted here. Arthur promises that if he wants single combat he will have it, but the Green Knight replies that he did not bring his weapons or armor, and in any case there is no one here who could match him; they are like beardless boys. His mission is different: to challenge anyone to an exchange of blows. Whoever accepts may use his ax to strike the first blow, and the Green Knight will not resist and will demand his turn only after a year and a day. When no one accepts, he taunts the company, declaring that he has exposed its reputation as counterfeit. Pricked by shame and anger, Arthur leaps forward to seize the ax. The Green Knight bares his neck, but before the king can strike, Gawain asks to stand in. The knight says that if he survives the blow, he will tell Gawain where to seek him, but if afterward he can reveal nothing, Gawain is free of obligation. The Green Knight again lifts his long hair to expose his neck. Gawain brings down the ax; it shears through flesh and through bone and the head rolls across the floor and into the crowd, but the body does not stagger or fall. It springs after the head and grabs it, mounts the horse, and holds the head up by the hair. The eyelids open, and the head commands Gawain to appear one year hence at the Green Chapel or be branded a coward. When the hoofbeats have receded into the distance, the company laugh somewhat nervously at the wonder they have seen. After this episode the narrative moves on to Gawain's journey to find the Green Knight, his stay at a castle and his encounter with the lady of his host and her tests of his chivalry, and the knight's final sparing his life.

The Green Knight puts Gawain in a quandary by deliberately making the challenge partially forceful. Why he wanted to do this is never explained, but a likely possibility is that it can be a more stringent test of honor, as the third equilibrium shows. It certainly adds to the drama for the reader. He weakens the force in several ways.

Force Is Weakened if the Challenger's Membership Is Doubtful

In most societies, only a member of the honor group can issue challenges. When a child dares another to swallow a slug, the speech act's success is based on their common membership in children's culture. An adult could not dare another adult to do it, and an adult could not dare a child to do something—daring cannot help parents manage their children's behavior. One man challenges another by virtue of his social role, and challenges coming from below one's social class or from women can be ignored.

To the extent that the Green Knight is seen as a fellow knight, Gawain is bound to accept, but if he is clearly supernatural, the challenge has no force. To make the challenge seem partially forceful, the poet's characterization of the Green Knight hovers between the human and the supernatural. He is large, perhaps a half-giant, says the poet, surely the biggest of men, but in any case handsome. First, his shape and size are described, anchoring us in the impression that he is human, but after a dozen lines of such details, the poet announces that he is bright green. In the passage quoted earlier the Green Knight calls himself a *wyȝe* (315). The term usually denotes a person, but it could mean a living being of any kind (Borroff 1962, 112). In battle, the knight implies, he would defeat his adversary with his weapons, not by magic, and this sounds like a mortal man. When Arthur offers him a fight, he replies that he did not come for that, although at home he has a hauberk, a helmet, a shield, and a sharp shining spear. Cataloging his equipment lets the court know that he possesses the accoutrements of a knight (Burrow 1965) and so is a member of the group. His fine clothing, his articulate speech, his horse described as obedient to the rider's command reinforce this. However, the horse too is bright green. By manipulating the perception of his membership in the group, the knight is manipulating the force of his challenge.

Internationally, this requirement seems to be gone. Challenges are taken as bona fide even when the challenger has no group credentials or could be claimed to have none. In Lyndon Johnson's account, the attack in the Gulf of Tonkin was seen as a challenge even though the United States did not recognize North Vietnam. To support the bombing of Libya, Ronald Reagan spoke of the challenge of terrorists, whom he did not regard as members of the international system.

Force Is Weakened if the Contest Is Unfair

Most speech acts can be seen as accepting a proposition and performing a characteristic operation on it. The proposition that the milk is on the table, for example, could be put into a question, an assertion, a request, or a promise. For a forceful speech act, this proposition must satisfy certain requirements. I cannot promise some event in the past, for example, and I cannot apologize for the weather, since it is not something I did. The damage done to the speech act is a matter of degree—it means something to thank someone "in advance" for something, although it is a good idea to thank the person again afterward.

The speech act "I challenge you to p" requires that p be a proposition describing a competitive activity, with some way of determining a winner.[18] Traditionally a challenge presumes that the game in the proposition is superficially fair. A challenge to a duel where I use a rifle and you use a sword would lack force. The challenge has only to look fair. In nineteenth-century France, a skilled duelist could challenge someone who had no hope of winning (Nye 1993). Even if the Green Knight were human, his contest cannot possibly be fair: someone must go first and someone must go second, so he obscures this with details. He loads the agreement with symmetries: you strike at me, I strike at you; I offer no resistance, neither will you; I sought you out at your abode, you seek me out at mine and come at this same time next year. He would never provoke an unfair contest, he suggests—he would refuse to fight a battle against "berdles boys." All this nods at the fairness requirement and partially saves the challenge's force.

In modern international affairs, the issue of the symmetry of the contest is not raised. A small nonnuclear state can challenge a strong one, and the latter will still lose reputation. It may be that the requirement has survived but has been transformed. If North Vietnamese torpedo boats challenge U.S. ships, the challenge is not to a contest of navies but one of national wills and in this regard the countries are potentially equals. However, if in fact the requirement has been reinterpreted in this way, it puts no effective restrictions on international challenges and does not help the goal of peace.

Force Is Weakened by an Improper Motive for Challenging

Speech acts do many things, but in all of them the speaker asserts some belief. My apology implies that I really am sorry, and my promise implies that I really have a certain intention. A performative's *sincerity conditions* require that the speaker be sincere in these assertions. Intentions are usually unobservable, of course, but sometimes evidence of insincerity is manifest, and then the performative loses force.

Sincerity requirements fall into two types: those involving intention and those involving motive. My daring you, for example, expresses my intention that I will watch whether you perform the action. If I dared you to stand on your head but intended to look away when you do it, my dare would be insincere. My

---

18. Another approach would have the propositional content be that the challengee accepts or declines the challenge. This makes provocatives close to yes/no questions whose propositional content can be taken as that the person answers them yes or no (Vanderveken 1990).

challenging you implies that I am willing to participate in the contest. If I announced that since you have accepted my illocutionary point has been achieved, and there is no reason to proceed—that would be insincere.

Provocatives also put requirements on the sender's *apparent motive.* If social customs supported a challenge by means of burglarizing someone's house and keeping that person's possessions, the purpose of the action would be obscured, and frivolous challenges would proliferate. One child cannot dare another to hand over $5. A challenge with the consequence of simply killing Gawain would be ineffective, so the Green Knight supplies a reason for his proposal—it is a Christmas game or sport. The Round Table has drawn him here by its reputation, and it will lose that reputation, he says, if no one will play. This bolsters the challenge's apparent sincerity.

The distinction between the motives of testing reputation and accumulating gain disappears on the international scene. Judging by some of the examples given earlier, countries can make challenges that are manifestly designed to forward their national interests.

In Some Cultures, a Forceful Challenge
Requires a Prior Insult

Speech acts generally involve certain *preparatory conditions,* presuppositions about the context, without which they would be defective. Double daring requires that the target has already been dared, and defying someone to prove a position requires that the person has already espoused it. In some cultures an insult is a preparatory condition for a challenge. In Renaissance Italy, one had to be insulted before one could "give the lie," and in the U.S. South, a man who simply begins a fight in a bar loses respect—the fight must come from an affront, even if concocted. This institution serves to reduce pointless challenges. International challenges, however, seem to have no such restriction.

How to Stop a Challenge from Starting a Fight—
The Feast of Bricriu

Overall, the international system has made challenging much easier by dropping various requirements for force: membership in the group, the fairness of the contest, the possible motives, and sometimes the need for a prior affront are gone. A reason may be that within a society, an individual is assumed honorable unless proven otherwise, but in the international system, "credibility" or "resolve" is not attributed automatically, and nations may be looking for opportunities to enhance it. One way is to respond as if one was challenged even if one does not believe that was the other's intention. Societies want to restrict challenges, but states can have an interest in inventing them.

Assuming that the a state does not want to respond to a challenge, how can it achieve peace with honor? An effective way might be to use the ambiguity of international culture. What constitutes an international challenge is poorly defined, so the state might pretend that none has occurred. In terms of the model, a semiforceful challenge yielded one equilibrium where no doubt crept in and another where it did. One can send signals that one believes that the latter is in effect.

A bad example, a story of how not to deflect a challenge, comes from an earlier beheading tale, the Old Irish *Feast of Bricriu* (Meyer 1893; Henderson 1899; Thurneysen 1921; Buchanan 1932; O'Neill 1991b). It is an ancestor of *Gawain and the Green Knight,* and was first written down around the eighth century. It was almost as old when the Gawain poet wrote as the latter's work is now. A *bachlach,* a rough-looking giant, walks into the court of the Ulstermen. He says he has traveled the world in search of someone who will give him fair play. He proposes that he will take the first turn and wield his ax on someone's neck. (Note that this is the reverse of the Green Knight's challenge.) Munremar, one of the company, steps up and points out that this is unfair. He wants the order reversed. To Munremar's surprise, the giant accepts immediately. Munremar beheads the giant and the room is awash with blood, but when the giant comes the next night for his turn, Munremar is not to be found. This sequence happens twice more, until the fourth taker, Cuchulainn, keeps the bargain and is recognized as preeminent among the champions.

The story looks like Gawain's, but there is a strategic difference. The giant's motive, it turns out, is to prove Cuchulainn to be the worthy one. He must induce Munremar into accepting the game, even though Munremar lacks honor. He does this by reversing the order of play, inducing Munremar to propose the game that the giant really wants. Munremar does this, and he is trapped. He has endorsed the legitimacy of the challenge on the record, and so bolstered its force. In game terms, endorsing the challenge's legitimacy means increasing the degree of common belief that one is a type Ch_I challengee.

Munremar's mistake has lessons for current leaders. When a state faces a questionable challenge and prefers to avoid war, it should say nothing that bolsters the challenge's force and especially should avoid recognizing it as a challenge. A government that labels an adversary's new missile program or troop deployment as a threat that must be answered is making it one. This is relevant to the potential recipient and also to the potential challenger. If one's action might be taken as a challenge, it should be kept off the record to avoid common belief in a forceful challenge.[19] In October 1950, China was ready to enter Korea, but first it renamed its army. What had been the "Northeastern Border Forces" became the "Chinese People's Volunteer Army" (Yao 1985), and through the war Chinese soldiers fighting in Korea were "volunteers." The suggestion may have been that the war was not a fully official act of the Chinese government. Mao's worry, one that he had discussed with Stalin, was that the United States would attack China with nuclear weapons. The new name may have been meant to diminish the pressure on the United States for a stronger response. In this vein, Israel has possessed nuclear weapons for two decades, and although this fact is widely known, it has never been announced. Keeping its nuclear status off the record may lessen the pressure on surrounding countries to respond in kind. The adversaries are not fooled, of course—they know the objective facts—but whether a certain situation constitutes a forceful challenge is about something other than the objective facts.

19. This consideration is like chapter 5's conclusion of avoiding public events that increase tension. "Off the record" is defined in chapter 9.

CHAPTER 8

Commitments Based on Honor

A constant problem for national leaders is to make their commitments believable. One way is bridgeburning—visibly eliminating the option of backing down (Schelling 1960). In the 1990 Gulf crisis, when George Bush stationed several hundred thousand troops in Saudi Arabia, he made it clearly harder for himself to drop his demands on Saddam Hussein and bring the troops home. Another technique for credibility is to leave the implementation of one's threat to chance or to someone else's control. During the Cold War, U.S. policy was to respond with nuclear weapons to a Soviet nonnuclear attack on Western Europe, but implementing this threat would have risked the destruction of the United States. To make it more credible, German troops were trained in the use of some tactical nuclear weapons. In a crisis the United States could hand over its codes, turning Germany into an instant nuclear power.

These are the dramatic extremes. The usual way that leaders commit themselves is simply by their words. Someone who backs away from a clear statement will lose future credibility and reputation (Pitt-Rivers 1968; James 1986).

(E9) Honor cultures frequently include the institution of oath taking, which allows protection to be extended to interests beyond those already specified as points of honor.

This chapter describes a mechanism of verbal commitment based on honor. (Chap. 10 will discuss how the same function can be achieved by manipulating one's own social face.) The first model involves making promises on one's honor and possibly keeping them. Two plausible equilibria arise, reflecting the fact that the rules of promising vary by culture. Honor-based commitments have other functions than threat credibility: making a credible promise allows one to make an alliance, or an agreement that settles a conflict. A second model deals with the kind of commitment that one makes to an ally, which, in contrast with a promise, imposes an obligation to act only when it is challenged. The model of commitments based on honor is contrasted with recent game models of deterrence and crisis bargaining.

Keeping a commitment is supposed to show that one values honor and to create an expectation that one will keep other commitments in the future. The advantages of commitment making entail a problem. Why should the group draw the conclusion that future commitments will be kept, when any person, honorable or not, would benefit from developing a reputation for honor? This question will be treated here. Other issues are the following: Can a state make a commitment to an entity that is seen as outside the honor group of national states, like the United Nations or the Palestinian people? Which kinds of societies develop honor-based commitments and which do not, and what does this suggest about the kinds of countries that use commitments?

The Difference between Commitments, Promises, and Threats

Schelling (1960) states that a promise is costly when it succeeds and a threat is costly when it fails.[1] The definitions here will be slightly different. My promise means that I will do something you apparently want, and a reason will be that performing the communicative act obliges me to do it. The message incurs the obligation not necessarily because of moral reasons, particularly in the case of a threat. The connection might arise from my sense of honor, the law, people's opinions, or some other element of the context.

DEFINITION: X's *commitment* to Y to action A is a communicative act whose meaning is that X will do A and that X has an obligation to do A by virtue of performing the communicative act. X's *promise* to Y is a commitment where X believes that Y wants A done. X's *threat* to Y is a commitment where X believes that Y does not want A done.

A commitment to defend an ally is both a promise and a threat—it is a promise to that ally and a threat to the potential attacker. It involves two receivers in the role of Y: one wants the commitment fulfilled, and the other does not. The action A in a threat is usually conditional, to be undertaken only if some other event happens, typically a deed by Y; promises can be conditional as

---

1. See also Schelling (1989) and the philosophical literature on promising and threatening (e.g., Downie 1985, Seligman 1995.) Klein and O'Flaherty (1993) use game models to analyze the difference between promises and threats.

well. It might be claimed that a promise also has a moral element, involving the promiser's obligation to keep it. This enters the definition as possible grounds for the receiver to believe the promise will be kept. There may be nonmoral grounds for the same inference—the promiser might feel constrained by public opinion or by the law.

Promising on One's Honor

Figure 16 shows a simple game of promising as a step to the more complicated model of commitment making. If you make a promise, the receiver gives you benefit b, but keeping your promise costs you c. Breaking the promise will not take away the benefit but might diminish your perceived honor. Only one player has a move.

STAGE 1: The player knows his sense of honor *h*.

STAGE 2: The player makes or does not make the promise, the former producing a utility increment *b*.

STAGE 3: A player who has made a promise chooses whether to keep it or not; keeping it produces a utility decrement of *c*. The audience revises its estimate of the player's honor, according to whether the promise was made and kept, made and broken, or not made.

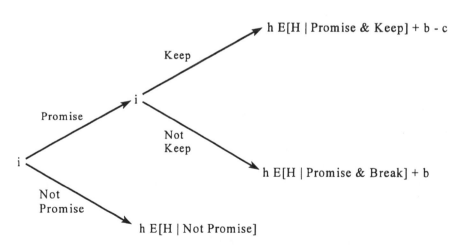

h E[H | Promise & Keep] + b - c

Keep

i

Promise

Not
Keep

i

h E[H | Promise & Break] + b

Not
Promise

h E[H | Not Promise]

Fig. 16.   Individual i making a promise based on honor and keeping it or not

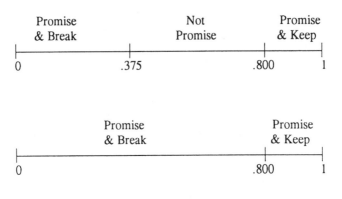

honor, h →

Fig. 17.   Two equilibria in a game of promising

To derive some results, it is assumed that h is selected from a uniform distribution on $[0,1]$, that if the audience sees an action inconsistent with the expected equilibrium, it assigns zero honor (this is usually not essential), and that the utility parameters are $b = .3$ and $c = .4$. The game has several equilibria, but some can be skipped because they render promises unbelievable. At one, for instance, promises are always broken but a player still gets benefit b for making one. Requiring some credibility for a promise leaves two equilibria (fig. 17), derived in appendix C. In one equilibrium, individuals of low honor ($0 \leq h <$ .375) make it and break it; those of middle honor ($.375 \leq h < .800$) do not make it; and those of high honor ($.800 \leq h \leq 1$) make it and keep it. In the other, everyone makes the promise; those of low honor ($h < .800$) break it, and those of high honor ($h > .800$) keep it.[2]

The existence of two equilibria means that the institution of promising is consistent with different social customs. Promises are more credible in the first society, where people sometimes refuse to make them: 35 percent are kept there, compared to 20 percent in the second society. Why do some people refuse to promise? We are familiar with positions based on moral principles, like refusing to take a loyalty oath, but the motive here is different. The player is simply

---

2. The two thresholds are $b/2c$ and $2c$ in the first case and $2c$ in the second. As before, equilibria that differ only in behavior at the endpoints are not distinguished.

weighing the benefit of making the promise against the reputational costs of breaking it and deciding that overall it pays not to promise.

Committing Oneself to Defend an Interest

Commitments have been prominent in U.S. foreign policy (Jentleson 1987), but game models have tended to pass them over.[3] The model deals with using commitments to deter injuries to one's interests. Defender (D) holds a prize desired by a potential Attacker (A) and tries to deter A by announcing an honor-based commitment to defend the prize. The game tree is shown in figure 18.

> STAGE 1: D knows his honor h_D, and A knows his value v_A for the prize; each is uncertain about the other's value. D is commonly known to value the prize at b; A is commonly known to be unconcerned with honor.
> STAGE 2: D makes a commitment to defend the prize or does not make one.
> STAGE 3: If D commits, A can attack or not; if A does not attack, then D keeps the prize.
> STAGE 4: If A attacks, both lose cost c, and D chooses between defending or not; if D defends, both suffer another decrement c and get the prize with equal probability.
> STAGE 5: The audience reevaluates A's honor in the light of A's observed behavior: committing or not and defending or not.

The assumption that player D is uncertain about A's prize value when it decides whether to make a commitment, seems reasonable in that commitments can be made long before the crisis, perhaps before the committer knows who the adversary will be.

For some parameter values, the equilibria in the game lead one to always making a commitment no matter what one's honor or perhaps to never making one. The values here are chosen to yield a more interesting equilibrium. The Defender's honor is uniformly distributed on $(0,1)$, the Attacker's prize is uniformly distributed on $(0, 2)$, and b and c are set at .4. One equilibrium, derived in appendix C, has Defenders of low honor ($0 \le h_D < .078$) not committing,

---

3. Some international relations authors use the distinction between *situational* and *nonsituational* commitments (Weinstein 1969). The former arise because of preexisting objective facts—a country feels compelled to defend its source of oil. For the latter, which are the kind of interest here, the state chooses to make a commitment and binds itself by its declaration.

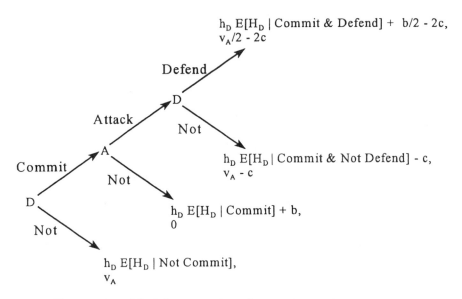

$h_D E[H_D \mid \text{Commit \& Defend}] + b/2 - 2c,$
$v_A/2 - 2c$

Defend

D

Attack

Not

$h_D E[H_D \mid \text{Commit \& Not Defend}] - c,$
$v_A - c$

A

Commit

Not

$h_D E[H_D \mid \text{Commit}] + b,$
0

D

Not

$h_D E[H_D \mid \text{Not Commit}],$
v_A

Fig. 18.   A model of deterrence through commitments based on honor. Uncertainty involves the Defender's honor and the Attacker's value for the prize.

those of middle honor ($.078 \leq h_D < .434$) committing but not defending if attacked, and those in the high range ($.434 \leq h_D < 1$) making a commitment and defending if attacked. The first group lets the prize go from worry about an attack and disinterest in their reputation; the middle group makes a commitment for the sake of reputation and deterrence but backs down when attacked; the high group defends the prize for its value and for their honor. Attackers with prize value less than .932 do not attack in the face of a commitment, and those with value between .932 and 2 attack.

Models of Commitment versus Crisis Signaling Models

The commitment-on-honor approach can be contrasted with crisis signaling models, sometimes called deterrence or crisis bargaining models. They usually involve the following elements (O'Neill 1993): (1) The players are an Attacker A looking for a gain and a Defender D preferring the status quo. (2) A can initiate the crisis, and D then resists or not. (3) A is unsure how motivated D is to fight, but D's initial response resolves some of this uncertainty. (4) This evidence influences A's further decisions of whether to press the attack.

The crisis signaling model begins after a crisis is under way, started by A's initial probe. Each player starts with uncertainty about the other's value for the prize, and this becomes less and less as the player observes the other's moves. In the language of the literature, D's resistance shows that D is "tough" or "hard" or "resolved." However, each side's continuing carries a cost each time. An equilibrium tells the player when to stop depending on his value for the prize.

This kind of generic crisis signaling model can be compared with the honor-based commitment approach. The model focuses on setting up deterrence, not responding to a deterrence failure. In the latter, the commitment decision is made before D knows that there will be a crisis; it is made to prevent one. Both approaches depend on incomplete information about the other side's values but the locus of the uncertainty about the Defender is different. In the crisis signaling model, it is the value for the prize, or sometimes the cost of a conflict. In the commitment model, it is D's honor. Crisis signaling models rely on the argument for costly signaling that willingness to sacrifice cost shows one's motivation. The honor model makes D's initial move the announcement of a commitment, which in itself is cost free unless it is challenged. It reveals D's incentive to defend the interest, but, different from the standard models, it also increases that incentive. This is bridge burning more than costly signaling.

A question for the crisis signaling approach is the following: Why should A take D's earlier resistance as evidence of D's resolve on the main issue? Why does it not reveal D's unexpectedly high utility for winning the earlier conflict, or low cost for engaging in it, or perhaps its optimism about winning on it? The answer is simply that the model is set up that way—A is assumed to be uncertain about only one thing, D's value for the prize, so D's resistance can convey information on only that issue. The conclusion is logical within the model, but in reality there would be many sources of uncertainty, and historical analyses of international signals have found them to be repeatedly misinterpreted (e.g., Thies 1980; Mercer 1996). It would be bad methodology to include all of the uncertainties—the game would be so complicated that one could learn nothing from it—but it is worth considering alternatives like the honor-based commitment model.

Real versus Virtual Honor

If honor pays, then anyone would want an honorable reputation. That puts any claim to honor in doubt, since when a state sacrifices by keeping a commitment, onlookers may suspect that the real motive was the practical benefits of appearing honorable. This section distinguishes two ways in which the quest for honor becomes impure and discusses how one can tell them from the real thing.

To represent an honorable reputation that carries practical benefits, one can start with the basic game of honor. The individual had two choices:

incurring the cost, with utility $h\,E[H\,|\,S] - c$,

not incurring it, with utility $h\,E[H\,|\,N]$.

Here $E[H\,|\,-\,]$ is the audience's estimate of H given what they observe, and S and N stand for making some Sacrifice, like keeping a commitment, or Not Sacrificing, respectively. Finally, c is the cost of the sacrifice.

If an honorable reputation also has a self-interest benefit, these payoffs can be modified to

$$(h_i + k)\,E[H_i\,|\,S] - c$$

and

$$(h_i + k)\,E[H_i\,|\,N].$$

(Here the subscript is added to show that h_i is specific to the individual i and k is not.) Honorable people value external reputation the same as others, it is assumed, so the multiplier is a constant k, the same for all individuals and commonly known, the importance of the self-interest benefit of being seen as honorable. Assuming a uniform distribution on h_i on $(0,1)$, there is a threshold equilibrium: Sacrifice if $h_i > 2c - k$. This holds as long as that quantity is nonnegative; otherwise one finds only a pooling equilibrium. Compared to the proportion $1 - 2c$ in the original game, the proportion of people who sacrifice now is $1 - 2c + k$, which is higher than before. The revised estimate of the honor of a sacrificer is $½ + c - k/2$, which is lower. Introducing a practical benefit of being seen as honorable means that more people will sacrifice, and that sacrificing will do their reputations less good, since their act is attributed partly to expediency.

Some individuals would not have sacrificed except for a nonzero k, and they get a higher reputation than they deserve. The difference in reputation could be termed *virtual* honor. It feeds off true honor in the sense that if the audience were sure that the society were honorless, that $h_i = 0$ for all i, sacrificing would make no difference and no one would pursue virtual honor.[4] Society must believe that true honor is not dead for virtual honor to play a role. In international relations the distinction between true and virtual honor is revealed when there is no tomorrow, as in Herman Kahn's scenario of suicidal nuclear retaliation (chap. 6). No doubt much honor behavior involves caring for the practical benefits of a reputation, but elements of others' behavior and our own introspection suggest that the true version is present. For simplicity, true honor alone is included in the models, with the suggestion that the general conclusions would hold true if the other type were added.

Commitments to Those outside the Honor Group

Gerrard (1994, 6) relates a story from Harriet Jacobs, writing about her life as a young slave in the American South. Her grandmother had loaned money to the mistress.

> [She] had laid up three hundred dollars, which her mistress one day begged as a loan, promising to pay her back. The reader knows that no promise or writing given to a slave is legally binding; for, according to Southern laws, a slave, being property, can hold no property. When my grandmother lent her hard earnings to her mistress, she trusted solely to her honor. The honor of a slave holder to a slave!

The debt was not repaid. Element E2 indicates that honor is like group membership and E8 that challenges from outside can be ignored. A further element can be added.

(E10) Commitments to those outside the group are not binding.

Some states have been disinclined to keep commitments to parties that were not also states in the system. Backing out can be a delicate matter, since one has to explain why the commitment was made in the first place. One way is to put the refusal to keep the commitment in obscure language. An example, related by Robert Keohane, involved an 1814 controversy between the United States and Britain over the terms of the Treaty of Ghent. Hoping to limit U.S. access to Canada, the British diplomats proposed a condition that the boundaries that the United States had accorded to native peoples in a 1795 treaty

---

4. A different model of how "honor pays" posits that people want to be seen as believing that an honorable reputation has practical benefits (as opposed to the model of virtual honor where they really do believe that). The results are much the same as in the original model.

would be made permanent. John Quincy Adams, Henry Clay, and other U.S. cosigners refused, on the grounds that the United States was determined to buy the tribal lands. The explanation they sent to Britain seems self-contradictory, asserting native rights from the earlier treaty but suggesting that the members of the tribes were American subjects, so they would have to give up their lands: "the United States, while intending never to acquire lands from the Indians other than peaceably, and with their free consent, are fully determined, in that manner, to bring into cultivation every portion of the territory contained within their acknowledged boundaries. . . . If this be a spirit of aggrandizement, the undersigned are prepared to admit, in that sense, its existence; but they must deny that it affords the slightest proof of an intention not to respect the boundaries between them and European nations." The United States would not consent to "arresting their [the United States'] natural growth within their own territories, for the sake of preserving a perpetual desert for savages (*American State Papers* 1814, vol. 3, 1719)." Not to say that we do not keep our word, but there are treaties with European equals and treaties with "savages."

Recent events suggest that violating a treaty is easier if the treaty partner does not have membership status in the group of states. One can compare worries about treaty compliance with the Soviet Union and with the United Nations. In the mid-1980s the U.S. administration was eager to conduct research and development activities that would have violated the Anti-Ballistic Missile Treaty with the Soviet Union. The administration pointed to a Soviet treaty violation, the construction of a large radar site at Krasnoyarsk, but was not willing to abrogate the treaty on that account. In the public debate and in Congress, much emphasis was placed on keeping one's treaty obligations, but it was proposed to reinterpret the treaty's language with a unilateral declaration that it actually permitted what had generally been seen as forbidden.

This contrasts with U.S. dealings with the United Nations. In 1994, Congress declared that the United States would pay no more than 25 percent of the cost of UN peacekeeping. This contravened the dues schedule of 31 percent, which followed a formula that the General Assembly had set pursuant to the UN Charter, a U.S. treaty obligation. Concern about keeping this treaty was not reflected in the congressional debate and no excusing rationale was developed. The United Nations, not itself a nation, did not generate a sufficient duty to keep commitments.

Honor-Based Commitments and Offensive Advantage

The discussion so far has suggested that honor serves the purposes of assurance and deterrence. However, it may not the best way to do that, since it leads to continual disputes. Is it a self-perpetuating trap? Do single members feel forced to follow it, as Franklin implied, even though all would benefit by simultaneously abandoning it?

One reason to suspect that there are better alternatives than honor is that often one finds two cultures side by side, with comparable economies and environments, one using honor and the other not. The only explanation would seem to be their histories (Nisbett and Cohen 1996). In the United States, Yankee practicality met the Southern culture of honor. Greenberg (1990, 1996) tells the story of the "Feejee Mermaid," P. T. Barnum's invention of the 1840s, the torso of a monkey sewn onto the body of a fish, which came out looking like a tiny grotesque centaur. When Barnum exhibited the mermaid in Northern states, the public debated whether it was a hoax and took the possibility that Barnum was trying to fool them with humor more than resentment. When he brought his marvel to the South, the controversy took a dangerous turn. In one newspaper debate over its authenticity, each party took offense not at the other's opinion but at the lack of appropriate respect in his expressing it. The controversy became self-referential and almost led to a duel.

What is it about a culture, then, that induces a system of honor? Nisbett and Cohen, extending an idea of Campbell's (1964), suggest that honor develops in societies where the formal institutions of law and punishment are weak and where a person's livelihood can be stolen suddenly and irreversibly. These conditions often hold in societies based on animal herding rather than farming. The theft of livestock can mean sudden and thorough ruin, so one has to deter a transgression rather than try to fix it afterward. A private system of deterrence substitutes for law and requires drawing a wide boundary around one's rights and cultivating an expectation of vengeance for its own sake. The same conditions, especially the absence of law enforcement, hold in U.S. inner cities, they argue.

(E11) Honor systems often arise in societies without an effective law enforcement system, where members face harm to their interests that is sudden, disastrous, and hard to rectify.

An analogy can be made to the international system. There is no supernational body to enforce justice. When the military environment gives an advantage to taking the offensive, nations look to deterrence rather than defense. An emphasis on national honor may then be a response to an offensive advantage, a variable that some international relations theorists have seen as crucial in a nation's security policy (Quester 1977; Jervis 1978; Snyder 1984; van Evera 1984). During the Cold War, for example, the United States' worry with credi-

bility was not that the enemy would attack the U.S. homeland—that seemed un-
likely—but that U.S. distant interests in Europe, Asia and the Middle East, might
be "gobbled up" overnight. The United States took up commitments and other
honor-related behavior because it was in the position of a herdsman instead of
a farmer.

CHAPTER 9

Insults as Assaults on Face

Sir Harold Nicolson (1939) described diplomatic language as "that guarded understatement which enables diplomatists and ministers to say sharp things to each other without becoming provocative or impolite." Insults from diplomats may be rare, but they seem to have been more common as preludes to a war. Many of them were more than a careless phrase provoking an emotional response—they had a strategic point. This chapter explores their strategic basis and their connection to violence.

The chapter starts with examples of insults that provoked wars, at least in the opinion of historians. One account would take them as challenges to honor that force a nation to strike back or lose reputation. Some of them did challenge honor, but others do not fit the pattern. Another link between insults and violence is needed, and this chapter construes them as threats to face that sometimes must be resisted by war.

Face involves the group's common belief about how much deference will be given to someone, especially in interactions that are face-to-face and publicly known. It sets behavior toward the individual by giving each group member expectations about how others will behave and what the individual will accept. If the individual has a higher degree of face, the group is more reticent to impose, it makes requests more carefully, and it offers various public signs of respect. Face-related behavior, or "facework," is prominent in conversational disagreements. The higher person interrupts more, takes less care to qualify opinions or cloak disagreements, and may well have chosen the topic in the first place. Honor puts a person in or out of the group, but face sets a hierarchy within it, and two people's relative positions determine the rules of their interaction.

In this usage, "face" means just about what it does in everyday English, as in "losing face" or "saving face." The goal here will be to define it more clearly and show its strategic aspects. Erving Goffman (1967) treated it as a basis of social interaction, and linguists have applied his ideas to study verbal politeness (e.g., Brown and Levinson 1987). Even though Sir Harold MacMillan expressed his worries about the Russians' face in Cuba, as recounted in the preface, the word is uncommon in international relations discourse, perhaps because "national face" is an odd picture. Facelike practices exist in many societies, however, and it would be surprising if leaders did not use some version of them to regulate their international dealings.[1]

A government loses face when it has to accede to another's will, and accordingly the word comes up around compromising in negotiations. Face can be saved by providing an on-the-record explanation that makes compromising seem voluntary. Good negotiators regard saving each other's face as a mutual cooperative activity, and one way is to arrange for superficially reciprocal moves. That was behind Sir Harold's offer to dismantle his Thor missiles in exchange for the Soviet missiles in Cuba, and it was the point of the famous Walk-in-the-Woods plan to resolve the Intermediate-Range Nuclear Force negotiations (Talbott 1985). Mobile trailers carrying four NATO cruise missiles were to be traded against Soviet SS-20 missiles with three warheads. The clever element was equating the missile-carrying truck with the multiwarhead missile. A problem was that four warheads were on each U.S. truck but three were on each Soviet missile. This was finessed by pointing out that the U.S. weapons were subsonic cruise missiles with longer flight times than the SS-20's. The matching of a truck and a multiwarhead missile was not based on any calculations of military operations analysis; it simply restored a superficial symmetry and made the deal look fair. Although the plan was rejected by both governments, the popular enthusiasm it generated may have increased the demand for an agreement, which was eventually signed.

The chapter starts with examples of international insults that pushed countries toward war. A definition of an insult is then given—it is a communicative act meant to attack face. This requires an explication of the concept of face and, in turn, the subsidiary concept of being "on the record." A model shows how face functions in a social context and how it can be maintained in a group without reference to any objective feature of the group's members. The model gives it a structure different from a simple ranking of people, as it is usually talked about. Members' faces can be regarded as ranges of values rather than exact values. The model is stated in a context of individuals interacting, but applies to relations among nations and delimits the possible hegemonic structures in an international system. Finally, the chapter points out the importance of common

1. McGinn (1971) refined the concept to analyze the U.S. dilemma in Vietnam.

knowledge of the actions that set the hierarchy of face and its relationship to communication in a group.

Insults That Led to War

An affront provoked Sweden's entry into the Thirty Years' War. In February 1629, King Gustav Adolf sent emissaries to Lubeck to observe peace discussions between Denmark and Austria. Germany's Albrecht von Wallenstein suspected an intrigue and induced the emperor to expel the Swedes from the country. King Gustav's resentment erupted in a memorandum to his chancellor listing his reasons for going to war. Number one was "that the commissioners at the Lubeck conference have declared us enemies of the Emperor. The reputation of a king will not allow them to treat us unjustly and disgracefully" (Charveriat 1878, 454; Ringmar 1993). The following June, Swedish troops landed on the northern shores of Germany.

On June 1, 1812, U.S. president James Madison called on Congress to declare war on Britain. He cited five British offenses: the impressment of American sailors, interference with shipping within American coastal territory, seizure of American cargo on the high seas, declaration of blockades against American trade with European nations, and instigation of Indian raids in the Northwest. The issues of seizing cargo and encouraging raids were objective and substantial. However, the other items on Madison's list are in the realm of honor: violations of U.S. coastal sovereignty and the British presumption that the United States had to respect a blockade on the pure basis of a British decree, when the Royal Navy was not able to enforce it and when in fact British merchants themselves were conducting shipping trade. Some historians (e.g., Pratt 1925) have claimed other objective motives for declaring war—the hope of annexing Florida and Canada and expanding into the Northwest—but others have stressed honor as a cause of the war (Risjord 1961). Many Americans viewed the impressment of sailors as the greatest affront of those on Madison's list and the main justification for fighting. In April 1809, the editor of the *Baltimore Whig* wrote, "I trust that no treaty [on trade] will be concluded without their previous release and an agreement that the flag shall henceforth protect the seamen; short of these we ought to be despised for regarding trade as everything—honor and the blood of our citizens as nothing. Next Congress must act like men." In October 1811, as negotiations failed, John Quincy Adams wrote to Secretary of War William Eustis, "The practice of impressment is the only ineradicable wound, which, if persisted in, can terminate not otherwise than by war." When the time came to fight, he said, the country should "declare a war explicitly and distinctly upon that single point, and never afterwards make peace without a specific article renouncing forever the principles of impressing from any American vessel" (quoted in Zimmerman 1925.)

In December 1851, the British representative in Rangoon, a Royal Navy commodore, began a campaign of rudeness toward the local governor. Refusing to visit the governor's residence, he insisted that the governor present himself on the commodore's ship anchored in the harbor. The commodore sent emissaries to the governor, choosing lower officials who demanded an immediate audience without the required protocol. The commodore had been acting largely on his own, but his superiors in London, either fearing a loss of face or sensing an opportunity, demanded that the king of Burma, Pagan Min, express regret for his country's "insult" in not receiving the delegation and pay a large compensation for wrongs that British merchants were claimed to have suffered in Rangoon. The king had given up hope of compromise and refused to answer. In April, British troops landed in Burma (Woodman 1962; Aung 1965; Bruce 1973).

In the 1856 "Incident of the Lurcha Arrow," Chinese police seized a rice-trading vessel near Canton and detained the crew, claiming that they wanted to question a sailor about his father's activities as a pirate. The ship was Chinese owned, but its registry was British, and the boarding party allegedly took down the Union Jack. This act struck the British consul as an "outrage . . . a gross insult to our flag." The emperor's high commissioner was willing to hand the sailors back, but not in the public manner that the consul demanded, and he would not admit to lowering the ensign or apologize for it. British forces seized Chinese forts, ransacked the commissioner's house, and occupied Canton. The conflict escalated into the Second China War of 1856–60 (Bonnersmith and Lumby 1954; Costin 1937).

The spiral of affronts that led to the British invasion of Ethiopia in 1868 was a relatively pure example of insults provoking a war, since, according to documents, the British government had no desire to be there except to "vindicate the honor of the Crown," in Queen Victoria's words. In 1862, King Tewodros had sent letters to the English queen and to Napoleon III expressing his friendship as a fellow Christian monarch and requesting an official acceptance of his gifts (Asfaw, Appleyard, and Ullendorff eds. 1979.) For Britain or France to do this would have been a facsimile of diplomatic recognition. The French reply was noncommittal on the King's request and disrespectful in its form, as it was signed by Napoleon's foreign minister, rather than Napoleon himself. The British Foreign Office behaved worse, failing to answer in spite of Tewodros's repeated inquiries. Tewodros expelled the French consul and locked the British consul in chains. He put off responding to British messages and later detained a delegation seeking the consul's release. The British foreign secretary declared, with inadvertent irony, "we rest our position there on what is vaguely called prestige. . . . we cannot accept an insult from an uncivilized power and merely say we are sorry for it." A British expedition seized Tewodros's fortress, and to avoid the humiliation of capture the king took his own life (Ram 1985; Rubenson 1976).

Some wars were fostered by faked or magnified insults, such as the de Lome Letter of 1897. The Spanish minister in Washington, D.C., wrote to a friend in Havana that President McKinley was "weak and a bidder for the admiration of the crowd." He revealed that Spain's negotiating stance had been insincere. Supporters of Cuban independence stole the letter and passed it to William Randolph Hearst's New York newspaper, the *Journal*, which published an inflammatory translation under the banner "WORST INSULT TO THE UNITED STATES IN ITS HISTORY." U.S. opinion was ready for a war with Spain, and the explosion on the battleship *Maine* a week later set it off (Companys Monchus 1987; Morgan 1963; Offner 1992).

In 1870, the crisis between France and Prussia over Spanish succession had been subsiding when Bismarck received a telegram reporting a chance meeting between the French ambassador and the Prussian king on the boulevard at Ems (fig. 19). He worked over the account to emphasize that the ambassador had placed strong demands on the monarch and the latter had snubbed him, then distributed this to the press (Lord 1966). Bismarck's trick provoked France and Germany into war. Emile Ollivier, France's chief minister just before the Franco-Prussian War, was described by Lord Lyons, the British ambassador in Paris, as "particularly alive to the importance of not exposing France to the appearance of being slighted; in fact he would not conceal from me that in the present circumstances a public rebuff from Prussia would be fatal—'*un echec* (he said) *c'est la guerre*'" (Ollivier 1913). On the Prussian side, the influential theorist and teacher Heinrich von Treitschke later wrote, "If the flag of the state is insulted, it is the duty of the state to demand satisfaction, and if the satisfaction is not forthcoming, to declare war, however trivial the occasion may appear, for the state must strain every nerve to preserve for itself the respect which it enjoys in the international system" (1916). The war was the seventh most lethal in modern times, costing almost 200,000 lives.

In 1889, the French lieutenant governor of Senegal was negotiating over port tariffs in Dahomey. He claimed treaty rights for France on the grounds that the documents had been ratified by the French Republic. In fact, the treaties were forgeries, and Kondo, the heir apparent to the throne of Dahomey, made

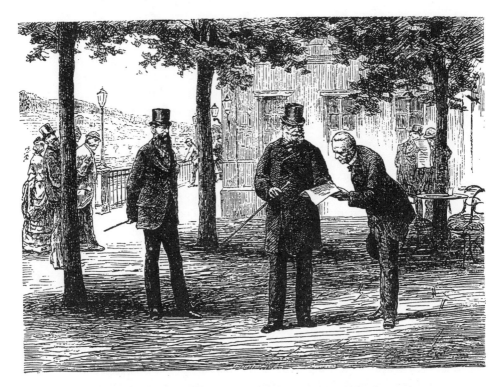

Fig. 19.   Prince Leopold's renunciation of the Spanish throne is announced in the Cologne daily paper. Kaiser Wilhelm and the French ambassador, Count Benedetti, discuss it on the promenade at Ems. The chance meeting led to the Franco-Prussian War. (From Fechner 1890.)

the rejoinder that since France was now evidently under the government of the young and rash, it might be better off returning to a monarchy. He brought up the lieutenant governor's failure to send a message of sympathy on the king's recent death, and forced him to sign as a witness to a document declaring that the treaties were invalid. The French official assembled forces and seized the port, a move that failed militarily but led to a large-scale intervention and the fall of the African kingdom (Hargreaves 1985).

Some prewar moves combined a change in the objective conditions with the element of an insult, one example being the archduke's assassination at Sarajevo in 1914. In their private exchanges, German and Austrian leaders talked of "the outrage," of "settling accounts," and of "teaching Serbia a lesson" (Albertini 1952–57), phrases suggestive more of national honor than realpolitik. The removal of the archduke made a difference politically, but its insult component had a major effect in propelling nations into World War I.

In July 1956, the United States unexpectedly rescinded its offer to Egypt to finance the Aswan Dam. Aiming to undermine President Nasser's leadership of the Arab nations, John Foster Dulles publicly questioned "Egyptian readiness and ability to concentrate its economic resources upon this vast construction program" (Neff 1981, 262). The president of the World Bank compared Nasser's humiliation to that of someone applying for a personal loan and reading in next day's paper that he would be refused for bad credit. The following week Nasser gave a speech lasting nearly three hours, cataloging Western abuses of the Arab world and finally announcing the nationalization of the Suez Canal. His move sparked the 1956 Suez War.

In August 1985, the secretary-general of the West African Economic Community, who was a Malian, gave an interview to a popular African magazine. He contradicted the claims of Burkina Faso's leader, Col. Thomas Sankara, about an embezzlement scandal in the organization. The Burkinabe leader called the Malian's words insulting and disrespectful and expelled him from the country. In the view of several commentators, this tension led the two countries into the "Christmas War" the following December ("Avant le Procès" 1985).

The 1990–91 U.S. confrontation with Iraq before the 1991 Gulf War involved sustained personal invective. George Bush referred to Saddam Hussein as the "mad dictator" and "the rapist of Kuwait" and repeatedly compared him with Hitler. Indeed, he asserted, the Iraqi leader was worse, because Hitler had never seized hostages. Bush referred to his adversary as "<u>Sad</u>-m" instead of "Sa-<u>dam</u>," a mispronunciation that was deliberate, according to a White House source (Canadian Broadcasting Corporation 1991.) Saddam Hussein was more muted, but on occasions referred to Bush as a "liar" and an "enemy of God." The exchange lasted up to the start of the war, and even as bombs were falling on his country, Hussein continued to complain about the language Bush was using against a fellow head of state (*Foreign Broadcast Information Service,* January 17, 1991, pp. 17–19).

Honor versus Face in the Dynamics of Insults

Some of these examples recall the pattern of honor, where the insult is a challenge that calls for a violent response. That explanation seems to cover the War of 1812, the Ems telegram, the assassination at Sarajevo, and the Christmas War between Mali and Burkina Faso. Other prewar insults do not fit the pattern. A challenge to honor is supposed to come from a party of equal rank—someone with honor does not challenge someone without it[2]—but some states issued insults to others they saw as of lesser status. Britain viewed Burma and China as inferior, as the United States did Egypt, and the insults seemed to be their way of saying that the others were not equals. Saddam Hussein repeatedly complained that Bush was not treating him as a bona fide leader (e.g., *Foreign Broadcast Information Service*, November 1, 1990). He saw Bush's insults as sending a message that he would not be treated as an equal and he had better get used to it. Another discrepancy with honor is that some of the insults were directed upward in the hierarchy. A peasant who challenges a noble can be ignored, but some insults are taken all the more deeply when they come from below. The British foreign minister would not tolerate an offense from Ethiopia, an "uncivilized power." It will be seen that both of these practices fit the concept of face.

The Definition of an Insult

A good way to define a typical speech act is to specify what it intends the receiver to believe or, in some cases, to do (chap. 3). The following approach works well for insults: an insult is meant to generate a certain belief in the receiver: the receiver is to believe simply that this very act of insulting is meant to lower the receiver's face. An insult need not say anything in particular about the target. Just as a challenge can take an arbitrary form as long as it is hard to mistake, an insult is whatever the context allows or the culture specifies through convention or symbolism as conveying that intention.

DEFINITION: A (prototypical) *insult* is a communicative act whose meaning is that the sender intends the act to seriously diminish the receiver's face.

Each of the definition's elements are considered now to show that they apply to the ideal concept of an insult. After that, the question will be why a simple message of an intention to diminish someone's face can actually do that. This will come out in the discussion and in the subsequent game model.

---

2. Aristotle (translated by Thomson 1976) divided insults into three types; one of these, often translated as "insolence," was claiming superiority to someone through an insult. In the culture of the antebellum United States the distinction might be expressed by the kind of violence used. A gentleman would duel with a social equal but take a horsewhip to an inferior (Greenberg 1996). Stewart (1994) states that insults between unequals are relevant to "vertical honor," but in this book, this would be called face rather than honor. The difference is more than semantic.

The Definition Is for a Prototypical Insult

The definition is for a "prototypical" insult, meaning that it includes the conditions that are typically expected. Many insults, in extended senses of the word, violate the definition. Sometimes an insult is not communicated to its target, and sometimes it is not intended to lower the other's face or not intended as a message at all. In 1979, Joe Clark, head of Canada's Progressive Conservative Party, made a hasty election promise to consider moving the Canadian embassy in Israel from Tel Aviv to Jerusalem (Leyton-Brown 1981). When he became prime minister, Arab countries and the Palestine Liberation Organization threatened economic reprisals if he followed through. One of his cabinet ministers remarked that "their bark is worse than their bite." This was an unfortunate phrase, as many Arab insults use the dog motif. It was an insult, but not a prototypical one since it was not intentional. Another episode occurred in 1992, when President Bush's nominee for ambassador to Ireland revealed during his confirmation hearings that he misunderstood some basic facts of Irish politics. The *Irish Times* of Dublin labeled the choice an insult to the nation. Even when one does not intend to attack the receiver's face, one can insult in an extended sense by not taking proper care to protect it, in the Canadian case, or by unintentionally revealing one's true opinion, in the case of the ambassador to Ireland.

It is common for words to have a full-fledged usage along with wider meanings—this happens especially with emotionally loaded words like *insult*. Speakers try to exploit their impact in contexts where they do not quite belong. George Lakoff (1987) calls one particular pattern of allied meanings a *radial concept*. It has a hub (or prototypical) meaning along with a group of subsidiary meanings generated by relaxing different conditions in the definition. Lakoff's example is "mother." Prototypically, my mother is the person who gave birth to me, gave me half her genes, cares for me, and is married to my father. However, there are many varieties of mothers that violate one or more of these conditions: stepmothers, biological mothers of adopted children, adoptive mothers, and so on. For every criterion, there is some kind of mother who lacks it, so one cannot produce even a minimal set of conditions that qualify someone as a generic mother. The only way to produce a definition is to specify the hub, then list the subtypes.

A definition counts as the prototypical definition because its conditions are what we expect, so features outside the prototype can be recognized through the "but" test (Lakoff 1987).

The insult is intentional:	I insulted him, but I didn't mean to.
	*I insulted him, but I meant to.

The insult is communicated to the receiver:	I insulted him, but he never found out about it.
	*I insulted him, but he found out about it.

The asterisked sentences seem to call for "and" instead of "but," and this tells us that our expectations are being crossed, that insults that are intentional or communicated to the receiver are the norm. These two conditions are in the prototypical definition. Other conditions found by the "but" test may not be in the definition but are fairly direct consequences of it. Two examples are that insults typically threaten the receiver's self-esteem and that they arouse hostile emotions.

Insults Attack Face

Consider two situations:

1. A husband tells his wife not to try to change a fuse, that he will handle it. She finds his comment demeaning.
2. A professor tells a student that he did poorly on a course paper. The student takes offense.

One can imagine that the husband's remark qualifies as an insult, while the professor's does not. (The husband is not delivering a prototypical insult, since he probably has no intention to diminish face, but it could be an insult in an extended sense.) The crucial element is face. Event (2) is not an insult because the professor's criticism is consistent with a role that the student has accepted, and so it is not attacking the student's claimed face.

An Insult Needs No Semantic Meaning and Can Be
Delivered outside a Language

Some authors have defined an insult as a negative statement about another party (e.g., Stice 1973; Flynn 1977), but it is hard to specify what negative features one is attributing by hanging up the phone on someone, or refusing to shake hands, or not receiving the individual as a foreign visitor at the presidential palace. The premier English sexual insult is indecipherable in its semantic content, since its grammar violates the normal rules.[3] Sometimes it is put into words that explicitly say something negative about the target, but that could not be its essence as an insult, since the same idea could be put in a noninsulting way.

The essence of an insult is not what it literally says, but the intention it communicates. In 1956, President Nasser remarked that he was surprised not by Dulles's refusal to finance the Aswan Dam but "by the insulting attitude with which the refusal was declared" (Neff 1981; Jonsson 1991). An insult is intended to attack face, and the receiver is to believe nothing more than that the sender has that intention in delivering the insult. In theory a prosaic insulter who could think of nothing better might say, "I hereby attempt to diminish your face." Insults are unusual among communicative acts in this aspect: that recognizing their intention is the same as (not just "leads to") recognizing their meaning. With an assertion, in contrast, the definition of a communicative act (chap. 3) requires that it involve first, the utterance: X's making a statement to Y, like "Today is Monday"; second, the recognition of the intention: Y's recognizing that X intends to thereby have Y believe that X believes it is Monday; and third, the consequent belief: Y's believing, based on that recognition, that X believes it is Monday.[4] Insults combine the second and third parts and make X's intention itself what Y is supposed to believe. The intention is the meaning, and when Y recognizes it, there is no need for further inferences. It follows that an insult needs no semantic content.

Communicating an Intent to Attack Face
Is Itself Attacking Face

According to the definition, an insult both expresses an intention to diminish face and tries to carry it out. How could expressing an intention also fulfill it? There are various ways people get face from others: they have their opinions supported, their requests granted, their feelings considered. They also receive face. Possessing face involves, in part, others not trying to threaten one's face. When someone expresses an intention to attack face, this is itself attacking face. It suggests that the insulter will refuse to grant face again in the future, in the same or in other ways, and others who might be watching may follow the precedent that the act is setting. Expressing an intention to attack face is itself attacking face.

---

3. "Damn you" or "curse you" have respectively God and the speaker as the subject, but "fuck you" is a puzzle. Gregersen (1977) believes that the subject was once the devil.

4. Some analyses of assertions would, at this point, have Y simply believe it is Monday.

For the same reason that stating an intention to attack face is an insult, so is a public declaration that face has been attacked. Some accounts of the Ems telegram have it reporting scurrilous remarks from the French side; in fact it was not much more than an account of how the two parties took offense at each other, with little more about what they said to cause that. Ives (Ollivier 1913) paraphrased the attitude of French foreign minister Emile Ollivier: "In Gramont's eyes the insult consisted in the false pretense that there had been an insult." Convincing the world that there had been an insult would have had consequences for face even if no insult had been delivered.

How to Recognize an Insult

By the definition, an insult must be recognizable as such. One way would be to declare that one's remark is an insult when one makes it. As far as the definition is concerned, one could say simply, "I hereby insult you," and nothing more. However, this does not work, at least not in English. How does the definition account for this? One explanation was proposed by Leiber (1979) who points out that there are certain words that name speech acts but cannot themselves be used as performatives. "I hint that . . ." "I insinuate that . . ." or "I provoke you by saying that . . ." or "I insult you by saying that . . ." seems odd. The reason, he argues, is that the meanings of these words require that their illocutionary points be deniable, but including the assertion that one is hinting, provoking, and so on, makes them undeniable. They are "illocutionary suicide," in Leiber's view; one might as well say, "I lie to you that . . .". Insults must be deniable, and this explains why they are often exaggerated or ridiculous—everyone knows that the receiver does not literally "look like a horse's ass."

The present definition gives no role to deniability. On the contrary, as a communicative act, an insult is meant to be understood. One must distinguish denying the content of an insult from denying that an insult is being sent. The content can be ridiculous and deniable, but the fact of an insult is not. The communicative meaning is, according to the definition, not that someone actually looks like a horse's ass but that the sender wants to diminish the receiver's face, and after such a remark there would be no denying that. The present account of insults does not preclude "I insult you" in theory, so it is less powerful than Leiber's argument would be if his went through. It simply says that a language adopts certain conventions of insulting, and in English this phrase is not one of them. The conventions are signals that one is delivering an insult. One is the wild exaggeration of a negative trait. Another is the breaking of a taboo by referring to an improper bodily topic in connection with the receiver. Another is to put a negative message in terms of a personal characteristic: to claim that the other is a liar rather than that he or she lied. Saying only that someone lied allows that there is a solvable problem to work on, but saying the other's words are generally not believable, that his or her personality is defective, is associated with the kind of longer-term disrespect required by the definition of face. Suggesting insanity, as Bush did about Saddam before the Gulf War, does the same. The point is not whether the sender believes these assertions; they are conventionalized signals of the intention.

Face depends on the target's social role, so not granting the target the verbal concomitants of that role is one way to make the insult recognizable. Before the 1991 Gulf War, Bush would not refer to Saddam Hussein as "President Hussein." As in his 1984 television debate with Congresswoman Ferraro, whom he continually called "Mrs. Ferraro," he used the name without the title. The message got through: Saddam constantly emphasized that he was not receiving the respect due a national leader. On his part, Saddam also claimed a discrepancy between the actions of his adversaries and their proper roles. Bush, Baker, and Cheney were going around the world hat in hand for war funds, he stated: "Imagine a state that claims to be the biggest, yet it is begging like street jugglers" (*Federal Broadcast Information Service,* November 30, 1990).

Another way to make an insult recognizable is to abandon the politeness formulas of the language. A criticism or a demand can be a threat to face, and polite communication remedies this by depersonalizing it, by phrasing it in a way that separates it from the individual. In many languages, one politeness strategy is to use the passive voice and thereby omit the agent as an object of criticism (Brown and Levinson 1987). A genteel street sign would read "Spitting is not allowed," instead of "You must not spit." In diplomacy, one depersonalizes a criticism by blaming the national government rather than its leader. Doing the opposite signals an insult, and Bush continually made Saddam Hussein the actor. His opening statement at one news conference (*Washington Post,* December 1, 1990) had 14 points where he could construe his adversary as impersonal (as Iraq or the Iraqi government) or personal ("Saddam" or "the Iraqi dictator.") Ten of the 14 were personalized, and the choice was systematic: negative statements tended to name Saddam ("Saddam's violation of international law"), while hopes for better behavior were put impersonally ("We seek Iraq's immediate and unconditional withdrawal from Kuwait"). Bush's January 16 announcement of the start of the war named Saddam Hussein 20 times (Newhouse 1991). By ignoring the politeness formulas that protect the receiver's face, these statements became recognizable as insults.

Definition of Face

Roughly, face is everyone's expectation about how everyone else will treat the individual. Unfortunately the exact definition must be longer to include the idea that it is a hierarchy. It is defined here as a pattern of behavior that allows a certain measurement scale, as a pattern of deference that can be represented by numbers. Since it is representable by numbers, face is a hierarchy, that is, deference cannot go in circles. Other conditions are that face regulates who accedes to whom, that it is determined by past deference behavior, and that it is kept in place by the common belief that the group is using it to coordinate deference.

DEFINITION: A group *exhibits a hierarchy of face* if its members can be assigned scale values whose relative magnitudes determine the direction of the deference shown in on-the-record interactions in the group. It is also required that present deference to someone in the group is determined by past precedents of deference shown to the person, and that the members expect their current behavior to set such a pattern for the future.

Some associated terms can be added, consistent with Goffman's definitions. The scale values that determine the deference shown to members are their *degrees of face*. If, other things equal, someone would have lost face but some event or action prevents it, the individual *saves face*.[5] If someone saves face in a particular way by skillfully acting as if nothing has happened so as to diminish the common belief that face was lost, he or she has shown *poise*.

To count as face, the deference must be based on past precedent and motivated by the precedent it sets for the future. If I let someone talk more because I want to hear that person's opinion, face is not in operation.[6] Also, the precedent must involve behavior across the group, so that a regularity involving the interactions of only two individuals would not be face.

On versus off the Record

Face deals with the superficial. A folk story from New England tells of a young swell who comes into the blacksmith shop to waste time and chat. Horseshoes,

---

5. McGinn (1971) makes this point. It is similar to Brown and Levinson's concept of "face-threatening acts" (1987).

6. In an extended meaning, face can arise from an individual's actions alone, when the person displays competence or power or proper behavior. The United States lost face when the 1980 Iranian hostage rescue failed, and a country that violates a treaty is also said to lose face. These events determine the group's expectation on how to treat a party in the future, but they are not based on precedents of this treatment. They are analyzed as prestige in chapter 12.

just out of the forge, sit cooling in a row on hooks. He picks one up and quickly drops it. "Hot?" the blacksmith asks. "Nope," the young man answers, "just doesn't take me long to feel a horseshoe."

An element in the definition of face, and therefore of insults, is being "on the record." To say something *on the record* is to perform the communication in a way that generates common belief in the fact that one is saying it. Recall that common belief means that each person believes it, believes that the others believe it, ad infinitum. The definition given here is put in terms of general communicative acts, including symbolic messages, rather than pure speech. A broader common usage is that an on-the-record communication is one where any can render it common belief in the future if desired. This sense of the term takes account of the fact that memories fade or that important parties may not have been present, but a "record" can be produced to inform the group of what happened. Using the phrase "public event" of chapter 5, saying something on the record means deliberately making one's communicative act a public event.

DEFINITION: A communicative act is performed *on the record* when it is meant to generate common belief in the fact that it was performed (or in a broader sense, when it allows members of the group to render it common belief over time, if they wish).

Suppose a sender S leaves a note for a receiver R and that R reads it. Each knows the note might have been lost on the way, and in fact each has common knowledge of this. We then have a communicative act but one that is not on the record. In contrast, if S met R directly and conveyed the message, each could see that the other understood the situation. The event would be communicated on-the-record.

The strategic importance of common belief in a communication arises when there is also common belief that the person is trustworthy and in a position to know, which is assumed in most communication situations. In that case the proposition being asserted (not just the fact that is was asserted) becomes commonly believed. A phrase that fits this context is to "put" something on the record, which carries the suggestion that one's communication is convincing.

Some formalism can clarify the distinction between simply communicating and putting something on the record (under the assumption that one's communications are commonly known to be trustworthy). Let p be the proposition, and B_R p mean that the intended receiver believes p. Also let I_S p mean that sender S intends to bring about p. These terms can be conjoined—for example, $I_S B_R$ p means that S intends that R believe p. The performance of a convincing communicative act produces B_R p (since the communication is convincing), also $I_S B_R p$ and $I_S B_R I_S B_R p$ (since the sender intends the receiver to believe it, and believe it by virtue of recognizing the sender's intention). Putting p on the record means all of these, but it also means $B_S B_R p$, and $B_R B_S B_R p$, and so on.

The strategic point of staying "off the record" is that one's communication cannot be used with confidence in future situations that require higher levels of knowledge of it. If a potentially embarrassing event has happened to someone, that party can display poise, and the onlookers can avoid commenting. Everyone may recognize the event but be unsure that everyone else recognized it. An off-the-record event is usually harder to narrate to third parties. The young man in the blacksmith's shop claimed he was just feeling the horseshoe. The foolishness of his act may have been obvious to anyone present, but when he avoided admitting it, he avoided reinforcing the higher orders of belief. If you tell me that my new suit looks ugly, then we both know what you meant, know that we know what you meant, and so on. But if you say haltingly that my suit "certainly has an unusual color and design," then you are staying somewhat off the record. I know that you dislike it but I am less sure that you know that I got your meaning, and as we ascend to higher levels of beliefs our confidence trails off.

Just why a face-threatening event requires common belief in its occurrence is illustrated by the model of the next section.

A Model of a Hierarchy of Face

This section presents a game model that yields some of the important elements in the definition of face. The group confronts a series of conflicts, which are resolved using a scale that determines deference. Past deference sets the current scale, and current actions influence deference for the future. The game has a large number of players who interact at times $t = 1, 2, 3, \ldots$. At each time, they are paired randomly, the possible matchings being equiprobable and independent from one period to the next. Each pair of players is randomly, independently and equiprobably, assigned roles in the game of figure 20. As the figure shows, player A has the opportunity to Impose on B, which means to take some kind of liberty that violates deferential treatment. The alternative to A Imposing on B is A Deferring to B. Player B can Acquiesce or Resist the Imposition. Acquiescing carries a cost to B alone, while Resisting means a conflict with a greater cost that is mutual. At any point players have common knowledge of who was matched with whom and how they acted. A player aims to maximize the sum of his or her payoffs, with future payoffs discounted by a factor δ in $(0,1)$—a payoff of x units received next period is evaluated now as δx, received two periods from now it is equivalent to $\delta^2 x$, and so on.

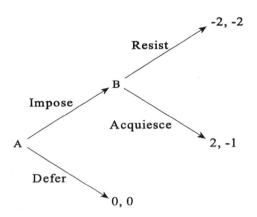

Fig. 20.   Stage game for the basic model of face

If this game were played once, it would have a unique subgame perfect Nash equilibrium, where player A Imposes and B Acquiesces.[7] As a repeated game, for any discount factor one subgame perfect Nash equilibrium is to choose this outcome every time. The equilibrium is an uninteresting one and is "faceless" since past precedents are ignored.

THE FACELESS EQUILIBRIUM: At every matching, the A player Imposes and the B player Acquiesces.

The next equilibrium has players paying attention to the past in a way suggestive of face. It divides them into an arbitrary number of categories ordered highest to lowest—here there will be seven groups. Anticipating the interpretation of the equilibrium, these will be called *face groups*. When two players meet their behavior is determined entirely by their roles as A or B and the two facegroups to which they currently belong. A player X in the role of A will decide whether to Defer or not to a player Y in the role of B, according to a rule $A[f(X),f(Y)]$, where $f(X)$ and $f(Y)$ are X and Y's face groups and the rule A assigns an action, either Defer or Impose. Similarly, the B player's rule at the equilibrium will have the form $B[f(X),f(Y)]$, assigning Resist or Acquiesce. Both rules depend only on the current face groups, so at this equilibrium one's history is summed up in one's face group.

Membership in a face group is not permanent—players can move up and down. Suppose that two players are matched; one Imposes and the other Acquiesces. If the Imposer is lower on the hierarchy than the Acquiescer, possibly

---

7. A subgame perfect Nash equilibrium is one with utility-maximizing behavior even at points in the game that players are sure they will not reach.

the Imposer will gain face and the Acquiescer will lose it.[8] At the equilibrium to be constructed, the new pair of faces will be a function of the old pair of faces plus the actions taken at the matching. The rule for a "shift" is $S[f(X),f(Y)]$, which assigns an ordered pair of faces to the players in the A and B roles, after an Imposition and an Acquiescence. In general, the resulting pair may be different or the same, but it is assumed here that if there is no Imposition and Acquiescence, the faces stay the same.

Behavior in the game is thus influenced by the ordering of the face groups, their initial membership, and the three functions A, B, and S. These factors are not given exogenously; they are part of an equilibrium. The particular equilibrium depends on how one specifies them. One way, which will be termed the *complete-order* equilibrium, says that A players Defer to B players who are higher up but not to B's at or below their own face level. Players in the role of B Resist only those lower down.

$$A[X, Y] = \text{Defer}, \quad \text{if } f(X) < f(Y),$$

$$= \text{Impose, otherwise.}$$

$$B[Y, X] = \text{Resist}, \quad \text{for } f(Y) > f(X),$$

$$= \text{Acquiesce, otherwise.}$$

Here "$<$" and "$>$" mean "lower than" and "higher than" in the order of the face-groups. The two functions A and B are linked in a simple way at equilibrium: no A player would Impose on someone who would Resist. The equilibrium's rule of shifting is that if someone higher Acquiesces to someone lower down, the two switch faces:

$$S[X, Y] = (f(X), f(Y)), \quad \text{if } f(X) < f(Y),$$

$$= (f(Y), f(X)), \quad \text{otherwise.}$$

(A less drastic rule could be used that moves them up or down one level only, or only with some probability, but this one is simpler and should not change the

---

8. This idea is reminiscent of Rashevsky's analysis of status (1947). When two individuals interact the higher-status person passes some status to the lower in the group's eyes. Status was continuous and Rashevsky derived a distribution for the number of people at each value. He drew a parallel with the distribution of energy in a gas with molecular collisions and suggested that if the total status is constant before and after an interaction, then the distribution of status in the population should follow Boltzmann's law.

qualitative conclusions.) It is assumed that at the start of the game there are seven face-groups of equal size (it is assumed that *n* is divisible by 7). At the equilibrium, they will stay equal because players will not move among the face groups. Even if they did, the shifting rule would keep the group sizes constant.

THE COMPLETE-ORDER EQUILIBRIUM: *For the payoffs of figure 20, the following is a subgame perfect equilibrium for any discount factor δ ≥ .824. At the start players are divided into seven ordered face groups of equal size. At a pairing, the A player Imposes on the B player if and only if the B player has an equal or lower face; B Acquiesces if and only if A has an equal or higher face; if (contrary to the equilibrium) a higher player Acquiesces to a lower one, the two switch face levels.* (The proof is in appendix C.)

Subgame perfection requires that if a player of higher face is Imposed upon, that player should have no incentive to Acquiesce, and the form of the shifting rule guarantees this. Acquiescing means losing face and will cost the player in future interactions. To provide the incentive to stay with the equilibrium, Acquiescing must be more costly than a fight. The higher-face B player's decision to Acquiesce (and hence the A player's decision to Impose) is set by the magnitude of the immediate loss of one unit of utility in the stage game (payoff −2 versus −1), compared to the longer-term discounted loss occasioned by moving to a lower face group. Since the latter is a future-oriented consideration, the future must have some minimum importance, so the discount factor is bounded below.

The two equilibria so far can be compared by their benefit to the players. If the discount factor δ = .9, the simple "faceless" equilibrium gives every player a total discounted payoff .5/(1 − .9) = 5. In the complete-order equilibrium, one's payoff depends on where one is in the facial hierarchy. For the seven face-groups, the discounted expected payoffs are, lowest to highest, −3.57, −1.43, .714, 2.86, 5, 7.14, and 9.29. Not surprisingly they are increasing, and each is at least one unit higher than the previous payoff, ensuring that the higher player will fight rather than switch. The average utility is 2.86, which is lower than the faceless equilibrium, and only those with the two highest faces prefer the complete-order arrangement.

In this equilibrium, players' faces were constant, but one can construct another where they change during play.

THE IMPOSE-ON-ONE-LEVEL-UP EQUILIBRIUM: *For discount factors in the range .660 ≤ δ ≤ .789, the following is a subgame perfect equilibrium. At the start, players are in seven ordered face groups of equal size. At any pairing, the A player Imposes on the B player if and only if the latter is no more than one level*

*higher; B Acquiesces if and only if A is no more than one level lower; if a higher-
face player Acquiesces to a lower one, the two switch face levels.*

An A player who has the luck of getting paired with someone exactly one
level higher will Impose, receive Acquiescence, and move to the higher level. For
$\delta = .75$, the expected payoffs from being in each face group are $-.75$, $-.23$, .58,
1.43, 2.27, 3.05, 3.36, for an average of 1.39. At each face level, the next level
down is less than one unit lower, so a player prefers to drop a level rather than
Resist. However, a player would Resist someone two levels down. Subgame perfection requires that future-oriented considerations should exert some influence, but not too much or a one-level-up player will not Acquiesce, so now the
discount factor is bounded above and below. This group has mobility. A player's
face engages in a random walk with a reflection at each endpoint. There is less
deference—the probability of deference between a random pair is $^{15}/_{49}$, compared to $^{21}/_{49}$ in the complete-order case, although the two are not really comparable since the ranges of possible discount factors do not overlap.

Patterns of Deference in a Face-Based Society

So far equilibria with three different deference patterns have been constructed,
and one might wonder what patterns are possible. This can be answered, assuming a shifting rule that says, as before, that when a higher person Acquiesces
to a lower one, they switch faces. For a function that gives an A player's responses, we can define a *deference graph* whose points are the face groups and
whose lines go from one point to another, $f_i \rightarrow f_j$, if and only if the function tells
the former group to defer to the latter. At equilibrium, the response of the B
player follows immediately from this graph. Figure 21 shows the deference
graphs for the two equilibria that involve face. According to the impose-on-one-
level-up graph, A players at level 3 are willing to Impose on B players in face
groups 1, 2, 3, and 4 but not on 5, 6, or 7, and so on.

What graphs are possible as equilibria? A deference graph must be a *semiorder*. This is one that can be generated by assigning to each of its points a closed
interval on a line, such that in the graph $f_i \rightarrow f_j$ if and only if in the line the f_i interval lies entirely below the f_j interval; it is also required that no interval contain another (Fishburn 1985).[9] All the deference graphs must have the form of

---

9. Semiorders arise in the theory of psychological measurement. The partial order might be
one on sensory stimuli, where an arrow indicates that one sound is *noticeably* louder than the other
or one color is noticeably brighter. Our sensory organs are not perfect discriminators, so indifference will not be transitive—if sound A seems the same as B, and B the same as C, possibly A will
seem louder than C.

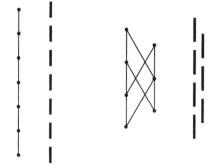

Fig. 21. Deference in the complete-order equilibrium *(left)* and impose-on-one-level-up equilibrium *(right)*. Two representations of each equilibrium are given. A face-group commands deference from another if there is a downward path from the former's node to the latter's in the graph or, equivalently, if its interval lies entirely above the latter's in the interval order.

a semiorder, since at an equilibrium a player will Impose on someone else if and only if the latter is one utility unit or more down. This requirement can be reproduced by assigning to f_i the interval on the line is $[u_i - \frac{1}{2}, u_i + \frac{1}{2}]$, where u_i is the discounted expected utility at the equilibrium for a player who has face level f_i. This gives two ways to think about a hierarchy of face. In one, an individual's face is measured by *an exact number,* the expected utility of being in the face group. One person defers to another as long as the other is *far enough* above. The other way measures someone's face as *a range,* where one defers to another only if the latter's range is *entirely above* on the face scale. The comparison is shown in figure 21.[10]

If the number of face groups is small, all possible semiorders can be generated,[11] using a theorem of Luce (1956) that a partial order is a semiorder if and only if it does not contain certain subgraphs.[12] The partial orders on a given number of points were constructed and examined by a computer routine, and

10. Another way to portray semiorder is in a higher-dimensional space. The elements are assigned coordinates so that one ranks higher in the semiorder if and only if it is higher on all dimensions. Rabinovitch (1978) proves that it is possible to find such a representation in a space of three dimensions or fewer.

11. These intervals are all of equal size. Scott and Suppes (1958) proved that restricting the intervals to a constant size still allows one to represent any finite semiorder.

12. Often it is easier to understand a theory by considering what it rules out. One excluded pattern has group w deferring to x, and y deferring to z, and that is all. The other has a vertical chain of $w \rightarrow x \rightarrow y$ along with a fourth group that gives or receives no deference. It is impossible to set up intervals on a line whose positions reproduce these patterns.

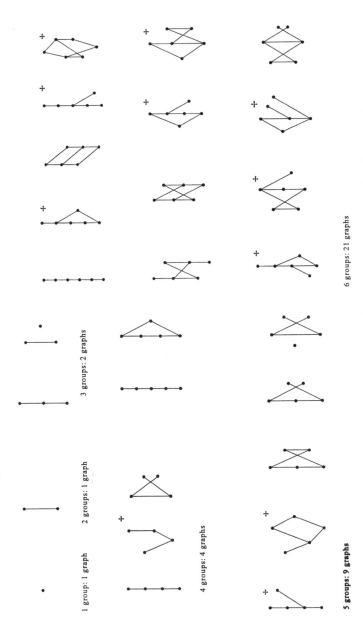

1 group: 1 graph   2 groups: 1 graph   3 groups: 2 graphs   4 groups: 4 graphs

5 groups: 9 graphs

6 groups: 21 graphs

Fig. 22.   The possible deference graphs for one to six groups are these semiorders plus the top-to-bottom reversals of those with vertical asymmetry (marked †). One group commands deference from another if there is a downward path from the former to the latter. The height of the group indicates its face ranking.

those that contain the forbidden graphs were eliminated. Another restriction was added to reduce the number of cases: there should be no two face groups that are symmetrical with each other in the graph. Such groups would be indistinguishable vis-à-vis the deference patterns of the whole society, and in effect they would be the same face group. Thus, for example, the three-group society with one group at the top and two groups that defer to it was excluded since the two groups are one as far as face is concerned. The possible deference graphs with six face groups are shown in figure 22. They are drawn so that the vertical dimension gives their representation as a semiorder.[13] There are 21 of them, compared with 126 six-element partial orders with the same restriction of no equivalent groups, so the model implies a significant limit on the possible deference structures. It limits the possible structures of an international hierarchy within the model.

Insults and Symbolic Deference in the Model of Face

In the model, interactions were important in themselves and set precedents for future deference. It is also possible that interactions with no innate importance could set precedents. They would represent conventional signals of face or else signals of face that were special to the occasion using focal symbolism. Conventions might be removing one's hat, calling someone by the proper title or not doing so, or delivering a deliberate insult. A variation of the game includes this idea. Players confront two kinds of games, randomly and equiprobably chosen, one of which is of real importance as before and the other symbolic (fig. 23).

Symbolically Imposing would mean violating the rule of politeness, so that the other must decide whether to let it pass or engage in a conflict. The symbolic game has no payoff gains from Symbolically Imposing and Acquiescing. The only real payoffs are the costs of Resisting. Resenting an insult, or getting even, is costly, but at an equilibrium players are still ready to do it for fear of the precedent. A higher discount factor is necessary to maintain the hierarchy of face, because benefit comes only from every second game on the average.

COMPLETE-ORDER EQUILIBRIUM WITH SYMBOLISM: *For any discount factor $\delta \geq .903$, the following is a subgame perfect equilibrium. At the start, players are divided into seven ordered face groups of equal size. In the real (symbolic) game, A Imposes (Symbolically Imposes) on B if and only if B is the same face or lower;*

---

13. Inclusion among these graphs is a necessary condition, but nothing here promises that one can construct a deference order of a given graph.

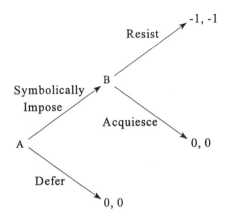

Fig. 23.   Stage game for the model of face with symbolism

B Acquiesces if and only if A is the same face or higher. In either game, when a higher-face player Acquiesces to a lower one, the two switch degrees of face.

Face and Gossip

The model shows why the events that determine face must be not only known but to some extent commonly known, and accordingly it shows why being on the record was part of the definition of a prototypical insult. Suppose that the game has been in progress for awhile, that you and I are now matched, and that you have the opportunity to impose. You need to predict how I would respond to an imposition. This would depend on how I compare our two degrees of face, so your decision requires that you know my belief about your degree of face, which depends on the history up to now. Second-level knowledge, not just simple knowledge, of past moves is required. For models with more complicated stage games, especially those where more than two players interact, higher levels would be needed.

Many studies of animal behavior have based dominance on objective, observable attributes. One contribution of biological game models has been to show that the observable attribute can be otherwise irrelevant to the payoffs (Maynard-Smith 1982; Hammerstein and Selten 1994; Kim 1995), explaining why the controlling element might be whether a gorilla has a silver stripe on its back or whether one speckled wood butterfly is in prior possession of a spot of forest sunlight. The present model goes farther and involves no objective traits at all; it explains the dominance pattern by the players' histories in the game. Still, players must possess higher-level knowledge of the history. This might come from direct observation of the past encounters and observation that others are observing it. It is more accurate, however, to think of it as coming from communication. This requires language, perhaps "gossip"—news about what someone did in his or her confrontations, vis-à-vis the norms and expectations of the group, and also how others reacted to it. Language lets us learn the social order without observation or physical cues. Dunbar (1996) has suggested that a positive loop was a factor in the development of our species: the circulation of "gossip" promoted the development of language, which in turn allowed a more extended social order than occurs in animal species, which in turn generated more communication. The model of the hierarchy of face shows the connection between the group's knowledge of its history and its present social order.

CHAPTER 10

Commitments Based on Face

Face is like honor in that it helps one make a credible commitment. The commitment is reinforced by setting up a situation where backing down would mean losing face before some important audience, such as one's adversary, allies, or domestic groups. This chapter discusses how face can be manipulated to achieve credibility, parallel to the earlier treatment of honor.

The basic idea is that to bolster credibility, one establishes a connection between keeping the current commitment and similar decisions in the future. Often the connection is made by setting up focal symbolism. An example is the Korean tree-cutting incident of August 1976 (Head, Short, and McFarlane 1978; Kirkbride 1989). In the demilitarized zone separating the North and South, a poplar tree was blocking the view from the U.S. observation post, and a party of American soldiers set out to trim it. North Korean soldiers surrounded them and clubbed two Americans to death. Angry diplomatic exchanges followed, and finally, in "Operation Paul Bunyan," the United States dispatched a party of tree trimmers to do the job. Armaments were forbidden in the demilitarized zone, so they were accompanied by 64 Tae Kwon Do experts. As they were cutting the tree down, three B-52s from Guam flew along the border. The North Koreans let the operation proceed.

The idea that B-52s would bomb North Korea over a tree trimming seems far-fetched. Of course, they were not there for their military function. In part, they were a symbolic message, a warning, using a metonymy from the scenario of going to war. More relevant to this chapter, however, the B-52s set up focal symbolism. They were a symbolic precedent that put U.S. credibility in future crises at stake, since backing down now would influence expectations of what the United States would do in more important games of Chicken. The use of bombers strengthened the analogy between the incident and more serious confrontations that might involve strategic war to make the symbolic precedent more important.

Setting up a focal symbol is one way to invest face, and another is to hurl an insult. The insult would not be prototypical by the definition, since it would not be aimed at diminishing the other's face. The face in jeopardy would be the insulter's own. Iklé (1964) states that in early disarmament negotiations, the Soviet delegates often adopted an abusive tone to signal their unwillingness to give in on a particular point. Strong words suggest a strongly held position that the insulter is expected to stick to. Like the symbolism around the tree trimming, insulting is a form of bridge burning. One sets up the situation so that one cannot afford to back down.

The prelude to the 1991 Gulf War put Bush and Saddam in a Chicken contest, each trying to convince the other that he would carry through with the resolute move. Bush put his own face increasingly at stake through the use of stronger and stronger language. When he said early on that Iraq should leave Kuwait, he was investing a small amount of face. When he announced that the annexation of Kuwait "will not stand," the explicitness of his words made it harder to back away from them. When he compared Saddam to Hitler, he committed himself strongly. Insults like these are diplomatic moves, on the continuum with expressions of concern, cancellations of official visits, and solemn declarations. They lie at an extreme position of self-commitment.

The chapter gives a model of how insults could function strategically, in a "war of face." Since backing down from them would be costly, they prove one's willingness to fight for a prize. There are other ways to show one's resolve, such as engaging in a costly arms race or starting a violent conflict, and the chapter asks whether insult trading in the war of face is a relatively cost-efficient way to prove resolve. From an outside viewpoint, the answer seems obvious: real wars cost human lives, arms races cost money, but insults are just about face. From the decision maker's viewpoint, however, all three commodities are valuable. When costs are measured in a common medium, it will turn out that wars of face are no more or less cost efficient than most other ways of conducting the contest, but if the rules could be modified in certain ways, they could be made more cost efficient.

The War of Face

The *war of face* is a game that shows the skeletal structure of self-commitment through face. Two players compete for credibility. Instead of the back-and-forth escalation of the Gulf confrontation, each player chooses one move from the diplomatic continuum of self-commitment. They act simultaneously, then observe each other's move. The one who has chosen the stronger move takes the prize, while the other backs away from the commitment and thereby loses the face it committed. The amount of face committed and the value of the prize are measured in a common medium of money, and losing a certain amount of face is translated into a loss of money.

Players know their own value for the prize but have only a probability distribution over the other's. It will turn out that at equilibrium, there is a one-to-one relationship between the player's value for the prize and the amount bid, so the bid credibly indicates the value. When the bids are revealed, it is assumed that the lower valuer backs down and lets the other take the prize. Starting a conflict for the prize would be a waste at that point, since it is assumed that expectations of who would back down in that conflict have been set by the revelation of who values the prize more. This assumption will be amended later.

To bid, each chooses a nonnegative number, and, as noted, the prize goes to the higher bidder. The game has an unusual feature: only the loser pays. That is, if you made the lower bid, you receive nothing and pay the amount you bid, while the higher bidder pays nothing and gets the prize.[1] This loser-pays rule is the opposite of a normal auction where it is the winner who pays, but it fits the notion of investing face. When the United States prevailed in the tree-trimming incident, it lost no face, but the North Korean government, by backing down, lost face commensurate with the strong language it had used during the crisis. That is the feature of wars of face that the loser-pays rule means to capture.

The game is as follows.

STAGE 1: Each player learns its value for the prize, which is chosen in $[0,1)$, uniformly and independently of the other's value.[2]

STAGE 2: Each simultaneously chooses a nonnegative number as a bid for the prize. Bidding "infinity" is not allowed.

PAYOFFS: The player making the higher bid is the winner, pays nothing, and receives the prize; the player making the lower bid pays the bid and gets nothing. Ties are resolved by choosing the winner equiprobably.

How much should each bid? Each player's strategy will be a function giving the amount to bid depending on the player's value for the prize, and an equi-

---

1. The notion of only the loser paying seems to have been discussed first by Riley and Samuelson (1981), who called it the "sad loser auction." Fearon (1994) gives a version of the game where, like here, the payment is interpreted as the reputational cost of backing down. The present model is dual to Crawford's bargaining model (1982), where the players choose how much to demand and the costs of backing down are then drawn randomly. Here the demands are given as the whole pie, and the players choose their costs of backing down.

2. A prize value of 1 is not allowed, since it would lead to an infinite bid.

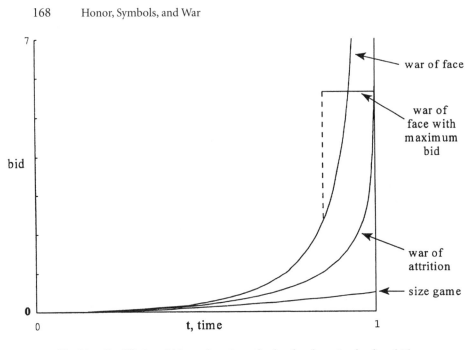

Fig. 24.   Equilibrium bid as a function of value for the prize for four bidding games

librium will be a pair of such strategies. There is a unique symmetrical equilibrium,[3] it turns out, and it tells a player whose value is v to bid $\frac{1}{2} v^2/(1-v)$. This function is shown in figure 24. For $v = \$.10$, which is a low value for the prize, the bid is half a cent, but at $v = \$.90$, one should bid $\$4.05$, several times what the prize is worth. This seems unreasonably high, but someone with a value at the 90th percentile is confident of winning and not having to pay anything. The optimal bid goes to infinity as v approaches its maximum of 1. In fact, it rises so quickly that the mean bid is infinity. This does not mean the auction is infinitely costly to a player, since the higher the bid, the less likely it is to have to be paid. The loser's expected bid, and therefore the expected amount paid, is $\$.33$.

Nicolson's comment (chap. 9) that the art of diplomacy is politeness seems contradicted by the pre–Gulf War exchange. The explanation may be that it was a contest where each was a high value type, so they bid very high to achieve self-commitment. The United States had much at stake compared to past military

3. A symmetrical equilibrium is one where both players use the same strategy. The game also has a family of asymmetrical equilibria where the two players use different functions of their values, and it has extreme equilibria where one player bids a very steep function of its value and the other bids nothing at all (appendix C).

actions, like those in Panama, Grenada, and Libya. It saw a threat to its oil supply and to its credibility at a defining moment in international politics. If B-52s
were appropriate for the tree trimming, it would have wanted a very strong signal to show its motivation in the Gulf. Bush sent troops, recruited allies, and
procured supporting resolutions from the UN Security Council, but still his
concern was "getting the message through." Pronouncements that Saddam was
worse than Hitler may have been issued because of the high demands of bidding in face. Of course, it is not just one's own high motivation that generates a
high bidding—one also must be confident that one is more motivated than the
other. This probably fit the Gulf confrontation, as each side probably saw its reasons as more justified and pressing.

Simple Signaling Contests

The war of face can be understood by comparing it with other games where
players make simultaneous bids to prove their value for a prize. The games in
table 2 share its features, in that they have two bidders whose values for the prize
are uniformly and independently drawn from $[0,1)$. The players bid simultaneously, and the higher bidder wins. However, the rules about who pays differ for
each game. The winner might pay either the winner's bid, the loser's bid, or
nothing, and the loser might pay one of these values. Three choices for each
player give the nine different game rules shown.

The games are listed in order of their "volatility," the average bid made at
the symmetrical equilibrium. The first three games possess no equilibrium but

TABLE 2.   The Nine Simple Signaling Contests, with Statistics for Their Symmetrical
Nash Equilibria, Assuming a Uniform Distribution on $[0,1)$ for Each Player's Privately
Known Value for the Prize (listed in decreasing order of mean bid)

Game	Winner Pays/ Loser Pays	Equilibrium: Bid for Prize Value v	Bid for $v = .9$	Mean Bid	Expected Net Payoff
War of words	Nothing/nothing	... No equilibrium ...			
Reverse sealed-bid auction	Nothing/W's bid	... No equilibrium ...			
Reverse size game	L's bid/W's bid	... No equilibrium ...			
War of face	Nothing/L's bid	$\frac{1}{2}\, v^2/(1 - v)$	4.05	∞	1/6
War of attrition	L's bid/L's bid	$-v - \log_e (1 - v)$	1.40	1/2	1/6
Second-price auction	L's bid/nothing	v	.90	1/2	1/6
Bidding with a public bad	W's bid/W's bid	v	.90	1/2	−1/3
Sealed-bid auction	W's bid/nothing	$\frac{1}{2}\, v$	.45	1/4	1/6
Size game	W's bid/L's bid	$\frac{1}{2}\, v^2$	.41	1/6	1/6

appear at the top since the best response to any bid, no matter how high, is to bid higher. First comes the *war of words:* whoever names the higher number wins, and no one pays anything. In the next two games, each player bids with the other's money and it is not surprising that they have no equilibria. They are the *reverse auction* and the *reverse size game.* Their names come from two more sensible games that appear lower down.

The equilibria of the other games are not always unique, but all have only one symmetrical equilibrium. The *war of face* is next, and with only the lower bidder paying, it puts barely enough accountability on the bids to keep them finite. After that come various well-known games. In Maynard-Smith's *war of attrition* (1974), two animals wait by a watering hole, and one can drink as soon as the other leaves. This is equivalent to an auction where each animal's bid is the maximum time it is willing to wait, and both pay the bid of the loser. Next is the *second-price auction,* where the winner pays the loser's bid. An equilibrium strategy—in fact, a strategy that dominates all others—is to bid exactly the value v that you hold for the prize. This was the reason for Vickrey's interest in the game (1962): that its rules draw out the players' true values. Next is the *game of bidding with a public bad,* where each player pays the winner's bid.[4] It is disastrous; each player has an expectation $-\frac{1}{3}$. Since players bid their true values and pay the winner's bid, the winner gains exactly zero, and the loser has a negative payoff. No one would enter it voluntarily. If they could decide beforehand to throw away the prize instead of holding the auction, they would lose nothing.

The regular *sealed-bid auction* comes next in size of equilibrium bid. The equilibrium is that players bid half their values. It makes sense that they would bid below their values: they can assure themselves at least zero by bidding zero, and they will only bid something in hopes of a profit. Last comes the *size game,* so-named by Maynard-Smith and Brown (1986) for a contest between two animals who want to be physically small for the purpose of surviving on the available food but bigger than their rival. In the war of attrition, one animal stopped waiting as soon as the other left, but an animal cannot observe its rival's size and shrink to an optimum response. The fact that each is stuck with its chosen size is a motive to bid lower than in the war of attrition. The game is often called the "all-pay auction," and Hirshleifer and Riley (1992) discuss it as the "secret arms race," drawing an analogy with the United States and Germany during World War II, where each chose an amount to spend on developing an atomic bomb

---

4. The name would apply as well to any game where the players pay the same amount—one where they pay the sum of their bids, for example.

without knowing the other's amount. It is a continuous and simultaneous version of the dollar auction (O'Neill 1987).

Is the War of Face an Efficient Way to Settle a Conflict?

The conflicts suggested by these games are truly costly, sometimes in dollars and sometimes in human lives. The analysis sidesteps the question of whether it is better to lose face in a war of face or lose lives in a literal war of attrition and asks which rules are least costly. It takes the decision maker's viewpoint in which the various commodities used to bid are valuable, and it compares the cost in the common medium. The last column of the table gives the mean net payoff, that is, what a player would expect to gain averaged over all prize values of the player and the adversary. All but one give the same value, $\frac{1}{6}$. The games in the table have the feature that the players compete for the prize and in doing so reveal their true values for it. The player with the higher value wins, and this promotes efficiency, but the test to determine the higher valuer is a costly one since it involves paying bids. All of them have a lower expectation than random allocation as will be shown. The bidding competition eats up the benefit from correct selection of the winner, and more.

One can compare the table's rules with some other allocation rules that are not auctions. One alternative is to simply give the prize to the player who wants it more. A player's expectation would be $\frac{1}{3}$, as shown in appendix C. It cannot be beaten by any other rule, but it can be implemented only if the judge knows which player has the higher value, and often there is no way to know this. A second possibility would assign the prize randomly to one of the players. Each would have expectation $\frac{1}{4}$ (since a given player gets the prize with probability $\frac{1}{2}$ and has a mean value for it of $\frac{1}{2}$). This is still better than the simple signaling contests in the table.

Almost all the solvable bidding games have the same expectation, $\frac{1}{6}$. This is not a coincidence; it is an instance of a broad fact discovered in the study of auction design, the *revenue-equivalence theorem* (Myerson 1981). It is really a group of related results, using slightly different conditions on the rules of the auction and the information available but coming to a common conclusion that any auction rule in the class extracts the same expected payment from participants. One version (Milgrom and Weber 1982) applies to auctions where the bidders have privately known values for the prize, independently determined according to a single distribution. It states that if two auction mechanisms have equilibria where the prize goes to the player with the highest value, and where a player who values it to the minimum degree of zero gains zero, then the expected payments to the auctioneer are the same at these two equilibria. "Expected payment to the auctioneer" in a literal auction is a simple negative linear function of expected net payoff to a player in our conflict games (since the prize always goes to the higher valuing player). It follows that the expected net payoffs to our players are constant over the allocation mechanisms that satisfy the theorem's conditions.[5]

A good way to understand the revenue-equivalence theorem is to look at an auction rule that violates its conditions. Bidding with a public bad, in the table, evidently does not satisfy the conditions because a player expects $-\frac{1}{3}$, rather than $\frac{1}{6}$. In this game, a player can hold zero value for the prize but still suffer a loss, so it violates a condition of the revenue-equivalence theorem. This fact explains the lower expectation.

Variants of the War of Face

Those who developed the strategic theory of auctions usually took the viewpoint of the auctioneer and were interested in maximizing revenue. They saw the revenue-equivalence theorem as an impediment to taking in more money and often looked for special rules that exempted an auction method from the theorem. In the context of international conflict, the payments go into no one's pocket. They are a waste, so we want to *minimize* "payments to the auctioneer." Some variants of the war of face will be outlined, which are chosen to imitate aspects of real conflicts and possibly reduce the players' costs.[6]

War-of-face variants with expectation different from $\frac{1}{6}$ can be generated by violating different conditions of the revenue-equivalence theorem. In the *war of face with a maximum bid,* the rule is that neither can bid higher than M. This would happen if insults could not go beyond a certain point of nastiness, or if, in some sense, M represented all the face a party has to invest. One can calculate the symmetrical equilibrium, and figure 24 shows it for the case of $M = 6$. A player with v from 0 to $M/(M + 1)$ bids just as it would in the original game, and a player with v from $M/(M + 1)$ to 1 bids the maximum M. Compared to the original game, some players are lowering their bid because they have to, and others are raising their bid to the maximum. The intuition behind the latter be-

5. The equivalence among mechanisms is true not only for the expected gains to players before they know their values for the prize but also afterward.

6. The different signaling contests will have different expectations if the players' distributions are not independent. Milgrom and Weber (1982) provide some results for the first and second prize auction, and Krishna and Morgan (1994) treat the war of attrition and the size game.

havior is that they are taking a greater risk in hopes of tying with the types of players who are clustered at the maximum, who would otherwise beat them. This equilibrium is not constrained by the revenue-equivalence theorem since the prize is assigned randomly when both bid M, and so the higher valuing player may not get it. Would the expected payoff be higher, lower, or equal to $\frac{1}{6}$? It might rise since the higher players are restrained from high bids; on the other hand, it might fall because the middle group is bidding higher than before and because of the inefficiency of the player with a lower value sometimes getting the prize. Overall, it turns out, the first effect outweighs the latter two—a player's expected payoff is higher with a ceiling on the amount of face bid. For a large M, the game is close to the original war of face, and the expectation is only slightly higher than $\frac{1}{6}$, but as M decreases to zero, the expectation rises to $\frac{1}{4}$ as the rule goes effectively to a random allocation.

In the *war of face with unreliable commitments,* each player i tries to commit face but succeeds only with probability $p_i < 1$, as if sometimes an insult does not come off. Failing to commit, which has probability $1 - p_i$, is equivalent to bidding zero. This version violates the theorem's condition that the prize always goes to the higher valuer. At the equilibrium, bids submitted are exactly as in the original game. This makes sense, since the exact value of a nonzero bid makes a difference only when both are successfully committed—in other words, only when chance has them play the original game. The game is more efficient than the original: as both p_i go to 0, the mean payoff goes from $\frac{1}{6}$ up to $\frac{1}{4}$, as the game moves to the random allocation rule.

The original war of face misses one feature of the 1990–91 Gulf crisis. In the game, whoever bids lower backs down, but in the Gulf neither one backed down. The *war of face with the option of not backing down* is close to a game discussed by Fearon (1994). It postulates that after a very strong commitment it is not worthwhile to back down, even if the other has bid higher than you. Suppose the cost of a conflict is C to both, so a side who bids above C and loses will be motivated to let the conflict start, rather than pay the bid. In a conflict, neither player gets the prize. Making a bid in this game is not just sending a credible signal of your value but burning a bridge. Again, the revenue-equivalence theorem does not apply, since the higher valuer sometimes misses the prize. The equilibria are simple and essentially all alike: a player makes a bid according to the original formula, as long as the bid is below C. If the formula calls for a bid higher than C, the player makes some bid or other higher than C. The exact value does not matter since it will not be paid, and in fact the symmetrical equilibrium strategies of the original war of face would do as an equilibrium here too.

The resulting expected net payoff is just below ⅙ for high values of C but goes to zero as C is reduced. Unlike the previous modifications, this is a change that hurts the parties' welfare.

The *war of face with misjudged signals* is also suggested by events around the Gulf War. After an Iraqi threat to retaliate against sanctions, according to the *New York Times* (September 1990), U.S. officials "took pains to note that the threats were conveyed within an established context of intimidating public displays and comments emanating from Baghdad. . . . 'We get a daily diatribe from Saddam and this is another one of them.'" In the model, this could be interpreted as the United States believing that with such talk as standard, Iraq is not really staking much face, and its words should not be seen as high bid. The sender and the recipient might judge the strength of the signal differently. One can imagine a situation in which the strength of i's insult from i's viewpoint is multiplied by some randomly determined constant K_i when j hears it, and j's insult is multiplied by K_j in i's ears. If a side judges its own insult as sent to be stronger than the other's as received, it does not back down. This opens the possibility that neither party backs down or both do. In a stalemate, neither gets the prize and both are charged C, or if they both back down, the winner is chosen at random. Since it is assumed they are unaware of the biases, they see the game as the original one and make bids according to the original equilibrium. A simulation gives some values of a player's expectation as a function of C, assuming that K_i and K_j are independently uniformly distributed on the interval (0,2): for $C = 0$, it is .163; for $C = 1$, it is .075; and for $C = 5$, it is $-.277$. This variant is far worse than the original. Noise in the communication channel is severely harmful.

Dangers in the Diplomacy of Insults

The pre–Gulf War confrontation seems close to a war of face, especially considering the stance of President Bush. In an age of pervasive world news, it is tempting for a president to use this tone—Bush was able to rally domestic support for his policies, appear resolute to allies, and engage in the war of face with Saddam all at once. However, it should be clear that the diplomacy of insults was a failure. Saddam did not withdraw from Kuwait, and Bush, having overcommitted his own face, paid a price at the polls when he did not pursue the war to its end.

Why did the tactic not work? The last variant of the game illustrates a significant problem with insults as commitment devices: that they can get distorted when they cross cultures. Relevant to the Gulf War, much has been written on how the style of insulting in Arabic cultures differs from that of European cultures (e.g., Parkinson 1989; Cohen 1987, 1990; Abu-Zahra 1970), but neither leader seemed to understand the difference well enough to use insults for diplomacy. Some Arabists in the United States were worried about Bush's "worse-than-Hitler" talk, but Bush held little consultation with specialists within his administration. White House aides gave the questionable explanation that the crisis was a global, not a regional, crisis (Goshko 1990).

There is a further danger. In a game of Chicken, each has a motivation to convince the other that it disbelieves its claimed degree of commitment. When a rival dismisses one's insults, the natural response is to raise their intensity. This action-reaction process could run out of control.

Also, each side might misunderstand the other's view of the game. Saddam Hussein's speeches and interviews suggested that Bush's tone was not a tactic to establish self-commitment in the current crisis but a continuation of how Western powers had always treated Arab and Islamic nations and small states.[7] Manuel Noriega had been treated this way, dismissed by Bush as an "amateur" just before the invasion of Panama. Saddam seemed to be interpreting the insults as having the prototypical purpose, that of diminishing his face.

Musing on the ironies of language, Kenneth Boulding liked to tell an up-side-down version of the Tower of Babel. When the builders set to work, everyone spoke different tongues. They would gesture for help and point to what needed to be done, and the building rose toward heaven. To thwart their ambition, God gave them all one language. They fell to bickering, and the work was abandoned. Not all communication is helpful. Insults can have a strategic purpose in theory, but using them that way is unreliable. The models bring out the assumptions that must be satisfied for this tactic to work, and they are far from real politics. Nicolson stated that insults are unusual in diplomacy, and this norm has evolved for a good reason.

---

7. Examples of U.S. insults toward Presidents Nasser of Egypt and Mossadegh of Iran are given by Neff (1981, 258–62), and Parker (1993, 105).

CHAPTER 11

Apologies

An apology is meant to counteract an insult, to help undo the offense and restore harmony. This chapter will discuss how apologies work, how they are connected to honor and face, and how they use symbolism. International apologies often show flaws that would never be tolerated in apologies between friends. The chapter will argue that this difference is due to the decreased importance of communication of attitudes and feelings in the international context and the greater importance of honor and face.

The Relationship of Apologies to Face and Honor

Apologies are linked to honor and face in several ways. When we feel someone owes us an apology, our honor prompts us to demand it. The apology satisfies the needs of honor by helping to right the offense, and failure to deliver it can even be taken as a challenge. When we are in the wrong ourselves, our own honor calls on us to make an apology. In 1995 while the Japanese Diet was debating an apology for the country's actions in World War II, the Chinese newspaper *People's Daily* urged an apology, stating, "there is no greater sin than not to admit a fault, and there is no greater disgrace than not to realize the need for shame" (quoted in *Japan Economic Newswire*, March 23, 1995).

Conversely, if making an apology would serve our practical ends, but we feel we do not owe one, then honor calls on us to refuse to apologize. During the 1980 hostage crisis, Iran demanded that President Carter apologize for the United States' involvement with the shah, but Carter would not, on the grounds of America's "honor and integrity" (*New York Times*, September 19, 1980). Other administration officials talked about avoiding "self-abasement" and "abject apology."

Though apologizing can be the honorable thing to do, it means admitting that we were wrong and on that account losing face. It can generate common expectations that others will take us less seriously. The quests for honor and face are in conflict here, and the fact that we are willing to sacrifice face helps prove that we are sincere, in the fashion of costly signaling. After the Irangate affair, Ronald Reagan made an apology for the actions of his administration but leavened it with expressions of self-tolerance: "By the time you reach my age, you've made plenty of mistakes if you've lived your life properly. So you learn. You put things in perspective" (*New York Times*, March 5, 1987, quoted in Abadi 1990). The face involved in apologizing depends on the culture, but even for a Western leader his stance seemed at odds with the expectation that one takes full responsibility. That means accepting all the consequences, including the appropriate loss of face.

A Budget of International Apologies

To examine how international apologies work, 121 apology incidents between 1980 and 1995 were assembled from the Nexis database of newspaper articles. An apology incident means either a full apology or something weaker, like an expression of regret for a deed, or a demand for an apology, or a refusal to apologize.[1] The database was not restricted to apologies between governments, but the incident had to involve interstate relations. The actors themselves had to make an explicit reference to apologizing or had to use some related term—words or symbolic actions that newswriters interpreted as apologies were not included because their real meaning was uncertain.

Table 3 has some major categories of offenses and some examples. It shows that the offenses generating apologies can be of very different degrees of seriousness. We say that we "owe" an apology, but it is not like a banknote of fixed value. Our cost is in proportion to what we are admitting to. When the sin is small, like misplaying the other's national anthem at a ceremony, leaders apologize readily, as in the perfunctory "I'm sorry" or "Excuse me" when people bump into each other on the street (Abadi 1990). This is simply a reassurance that the event was a mistake and not a manifestation of one's attitude. The apology is announced to the world as well as to the offended party, so that the slight will not cause the offended party to lose face generally.

In other cases, the demand for the apology was strongly felt, as in the de-

---

1. The Nexis database was searched for the words *apology* or *apologize* used at least twice in an entry, in conjunction with some word suggesting an international context, such as *embassy, premier, president, prime minister, secretary of state, minister of foreign affairs,* or *foreign minister.* The great bulk of the returned articles were false alarms.

TABLE 3.   Categories of International Apology Incidents from News Reports, 1980–95 (with counts and examples)

A. Major, protracted acts of violence or abuses of rights (21 apology incidents)
Individual European nations apologize for complicity in the Holocaust.
Japanese officials apologize for offenses during World War II and colonial rule.
Russia apologizes for the detention of Japanese POWs after World War II
   (February 1991).

B. Protracted policies not included in A but harmful to another state (9)
U.S. expresses deep regret to France for shielding war criminal Klaus
   Barbie from French prosecuters (August 1983).
Belgium apologizes for refusing to send arms to its 1991 Gulf War allies
   (June 1993).
Kuwait continues demands that countries supporting Iraq in the Gulf War
   apologize.

C. Specific acts of violence or threats by a state against another state's institutions or
functionaries (24)
Cuba apologizes for its planes sinking a Bahamian patrol boat (May 1980).
Nigeria demands that Cameroon apologize for killing Nigerian soldiers in a
   border incident (May 1981).
Saddam Hussein apologizes to U.S. for missile attack on the USS *Stark*
   (May 1987).

D. Specific nonverbal abuse or violence by another state toward another's citizens
who are not functionaries (10)
Argentina apologizes for detention and abuse of U.S. and British reporters
   (May 1981).
U.S. secretly apologizes to Canada for CIA-run LSD experiments in Canada
   (January 1984).

E. Specific violations of sovereignty (18)
Various countries apologize for unintended overflights, border crossings by
   troops, or ships entering another's waters.
France apologizes to Switzerland for anti-Greenpeace agents forging Swiss
   passports (November 1985).
U.S. apologizes for forcibly entering the Nicaraguan embassy during the invasion
   of Panama (December 1989).
Netherlands demands a South African apology for police entering its embassy to
   seize a fugitive (July 1985).

F. Offensive words and statements (23)
Greece apologizes for its foreign minister calling Germany a "giant with bestial
   force and a childlike brain" (December 1993).

(*continued*)

TABLE 3—*Continued*

U.S. apologizes for accusing Philippian president Aquino of gun smuggling (September 1989).

Malaysian representative "explains" its error to Indonesia in running a TV documentary on East Timor (September 1992).

Japanese police officials apologize to Pakistan's embassy for a police training manual derogatory to Pakistanis (December 1989).

U.S. State Department apologizes to Arab countries for use of the term Abscam ("Arab scam") in a probe of official corruption (February 1980).

G. Specific acts of violence by one's citizens or those in one's domain, not one's functionaries, against another state (4)

Various countries apologize for demonstrators attacking foreign embassies or consulates on their territories.

In an open letter, King Hussein apologizes to Syria for the presence in Jordan of the Moslem Brotherhood, "outlaws committing crimes and sowing seeds of division among people" (November 1985).

H. Lapses of etiquette or protocol (8)

Premier Yeltsin apologizes for canceled visits to Japan (July 1993).

President Bush apologizes for Marine honor guard carrying the Canadian flag upside down at a World Series game (October 1992).

The U.S. ambassador to Britian apologizes for President Reagan announcing his address to Parliament before Prime Minister Thatcher had informed Parliament of the plan (March 1982).

I. Unintentional damage or loss of property (4)

The U.N. apologizes to Japan for losing a pocket watch recording the time of A-bomb explosion from a display (October 1989).

Soviet Union apologizes for fighter crashing in a Belgian town (July 1989).

---

bate about Japanese actions in World War II. This involved admitting a serious fault, renouncing one's past behavior and declaring that one has accepted the other's moral position.

The database suggests that demands for apologies are often expressed in the vocabulary of rights, honor, or face, rather than interests. Instead of saying that an action did it harm, a nation calls it an interference in domestic affairs. There were many apologies for symbolic violations of sovereignty, like overflights or abuse of another country's citizens which are offenses connected with the metaphorical world of honor and face. Apologies were seldom given for cutting foreign aid or raising tariffs. These acts may have caused greater injury but did not fit the script of an attack on a point of honor.

A natural question is whether some nations are more ready to apologize than others. Anthropologists have classified societies as guilt based or shame based, and it would be interesting to see if this distinction has consequences in international affairs. The database shows apologies from every region, with many from Asian countries, but one cannot draw a conclusion. Many variables are uncontrolled, such as how extensively the press reported a country's activities in general or how much that country was involved in conflictual interactions or how many deeds the country had to apologize for.

How International Apologies Differ
from Interpersonal Ones

The apology events in the database differ from interpersonal apologies. This section will state how, then analyze the differing purposes of interpersonal and international apologies to generate an explanation.

The first difference is that many international apologies seem insincere because they are delivered under pressure. An interpersonal apology is a commitment, but it will be seen that like most speech acts, it also contains an assertion of a fact. It asserts that one feels regret. If someone were forced to make it, the sincerity of the assertion would be in doubt. For some reason, this does not matter much on the international level, where apologies are negotiated, even coerced, but are still taken as important, as if uttering the words had significance in itself.

A second oddity about international apologizing is the lack of explicit forgiving. In everyday affairs the two acts are linked—an apology that does not achieve forgiveness is a partial failure.[2] An international recipient, however, will "note the apology" and state that it is "satisfied with the explanation given" or "considers the matter closed," but no statement of forgiveness appears in the database.

The third feature is that international apologies are often from or to third parties. Britain was asked to apologize for expelling the Acadians, which happened centuries ago, and Japan for mistreating Koreans during its colonial rule. Some philosophers and ethicists have debated whether an apology can be delivered to a third party and whether forgiveness can come from one. Simon Wiesenthal (1972) narrates an experience in a Nazi concentration camp. He was working in a military hospital, and a nurse called him to the bed of a young SS

2. Forgiving is in part asserting that there was a wrong, so to avoid putting a potential forgiver in this position, we sometimes apologize in terms of asking for an acceptance—"Would you please accept my apology for" such and such.

officer. The officer confessed that he had taken part in a massacre of Jews, that he knew he was dying, and that he wished to receive the forgiveness of a Jew. Wiesenthal listened to the story but left the room without a word. He was not sure that he had acted correctly, but when he related the event to fellow inmates, they were adamant that he would have had no right to forgive the crime since he was not in a position to speak for its victims.

Most accounts of apologies, including the one to be offered here, agree that one must deliver the apology to the offended party. To a secondary degree, an offense against one member of a group is an offense against all the others, and on this account Wiesenthal did have something to forgive. However, he was not in a position to forgive the primary offense. In the Catholic tradition also, when God forgives our sins against others, this can be interpreted as God forgiving the aspect of the sin in which it was an offense against God, as a violation of our duty of obedience, or it could be God pardoning us, as an authority who can waive punishment. We still owe an apology to the person offended. Whatever holds for person-to-person and even person-to-God relations, international apologizers seem to be free of this constraint.

A Prototypical Scenario of Apologizing

To explain these differences, the first step will be to develop a theory of interpersonal apologies. Then it can be seen which of its elements change in the international setting. Apologies have a prototypical scenario (chap. 3), an expected

TABLE 4.   The Prototypical Scenario for Apologizing

Initial situation
  X and Y are friends;
  X performs an action that is wrong because it offends or injures Y.

Resentment phase
  Y expresses resentment against the offense or injury and demands an apology.

Apology phase
  X feels remorse for the action;
  X apologizes;
  X promises to mitigate the damage.

Forgiveness phase
  Y accepts the apology or forgives X;
  X tries to mitigate the damage;
  X and Y's friendship is restored.

script, as shown in table 4. The three elements in the list are the expression of resentment, the apology, and the expression of forgiveness.[3]

Resenting

Resentment is more than anger. I resent someone's action only if my anger is based on moral grounds. If someone beats me in a competition I might be angry, but if I believed they had cheated I would resent it. A second difference with anger is that I can resent an injustice only if it was done to me. Moral anger over an offense against someone else is *indignation* (Golding 1985). Resentment is thus partly cognitive; it is an emotion including supporting reasons.

Y's *expression of resentment* against X is a communicative act, a directive, whose illocutionary point is to get X to do something. Y wants X to declare on the record that X did A and that A was morally wrong because it harmed or offended Y. An expression of resentment thus presumes certain facts about the situation, its so-called preparatory conditions (Searle and Vanderveken 1985). It presumes that X really did A and that A really was morally wrong because of the harm to Y.

Apologizing

In an apology the offender puts his or her fault and feelings of remorse on the record. Remorse means the feeling that one should not have done it—it is more than regret, which is simply the wish that one had not done it. As defined in chapter 9, putting something on the record means communicating with the goal that the sending of the message becomes common belief. A touch or a wink may be enough in some circumstances, but to apologize with just a phrase like "I'm only human" would undermine the point. People often insist on special marker words like "I apologize." Putting an apology on the record is required because it is more than a transfer of information. It involves matters of face and honor. If one backs away from the apology in the future, it should be at a significant loss of credibility.

DEFINITION: X's *apology* to Y for action A is a communicative act from X to Y

---

3. Philosophy is the discipline that has paid most attention to forgiving, and the account here is most influenced by Haber (1991). His analysis is less religiously oriented than some others, and he looks at forgiving not as a mental state but as a speech act, in line with the general approach of this book. I have modified his treatment in the direction of Downie's definition (1965) and the speech act theory of Searle and Vanderveken (1985).

meaning that X did A, that A caused Y harm or risk and on that account that it was wrong, and that X feels remorse for it.

The definition implies that an apology complies with all the directives in the expression of resentment; it does everything that was called for. Turning this around, an expression of resentment is a demand for an apology. An apology is not defined here as a request for the victim's forgiveness, but it changes the victim's expectations in such a way as to make it more attractive for that person to forgive. If the offender has admitted the fault, there is less chance of recurrence and less need to continue to hold the deed against the offender.

Forgiving

Some writers have defined forgiveness as an expression of one's feelings, a statement that one has overcome the emotion of resentment. In my account it is a commissive, in particular, a promise. When Y *forgives* X for action A, Y is promising to no longer harbor resentment against X because of A. This sounds like a promise to avoid a certain mental feeling, and some philosophers have taken this position, but the interpretation here is different. Y is promising not to use X's misdeed as a *moral reason* for future actions against X, that is, to give up certain considerations as justifications for action against X. In normal circumstances, the victim would owe the offender X fair treatment based on the respect due to other persons, but after the misdeed A, Y's justified resentment allows Y to act otherwise.[4] For Y to forgive X at some later point is to promise to no longer make X a moral exception on the grounds of the offense A.

A case posed by Haber has John offending his friend Mary. He borrows her book and keeps it even though she continually asks him for it. John finally returns it and apologizes to her, and she tells him that she forgives him. Months later, John asks Mary for help, but she refuses, citing the wrong he did to her before. John reminds her that she forgave him. If forgiving were just an expression of her feeling at the time, Mary could reply, "Well, that was how I felt then, but not now." However, John is right. Refusing him as a moral response to his past offense is breaking her promise.

Forgiving is not forgetting, and Mary did not oblige herself to wipe John's action off the record. If he wanted to borrow another book, she could decline on the grounds that he has a bad habit of not returning books. This would not

---

4. The next chapter will discuss a concept of norms in which violating a norm obligates others to adopt a response that is usually counternormative.

be breaking the promise involved in forgiving, since her motive for refusing would not be resentment. To forgive something is to waive the past only as a moral justification.

An expression of resentment, it was argued, is a demand for an apology. Is an apology simply a request for forgiveness? Not in this definition, since it can succeed even if it does not generate forgiveness. However, the relationship between the two acts is very close. An apology prepares the ground for the speech act of forgiveness. Certain assumptions are necessary for forgiveness—harm and responsibility—and the apology puts them on the record. This is an important move, since for Y to express forgiveness to an X who has not apologized is in effect to accuse.

A Partial Order for Partial Apologies

To deliver a full apology, one must satisfy all the elements of the definition. However, many international apologies are partial, and the database shows which elements tend to be absent.

Regretting versus Apologizing

An example of a partial apology is Emperor Hirohito's September 1984 careful statement to South Korean president Chun concerning Japan's colonial rule: "it is indeed regrettable that there was an unfortunate past between us for a period in this century, and I believe it should not be repeated" (*Time*, September 17, 1984). A full apology as defined needs an acknowledgment of the harm done to Y, the moral wrong involved in the action, and X's responsibility for it. The emperor's statement did only one of these—it only acknowledged harm. Prime Minister Nakasone's statement on the same occasion was interpreted as going farther, since it moved from impersonality to naming Japan as the actor. It regretted that "Japan brought to bear great sufferings upon your country and its people" during the colonial period (*Economist*, September 15, 1984). It seems like a short step from this to admitting the deed was morally wrong, but both statements appear phrased to avoid doing this, so both fall short of full apologies.

The gap between what was called for and what Japan delivered was the difference between expressing regret and apologizing. In 1988, after a U.S. cruiser shot down an Iranian Airbus in the Persian Gulf, President Reagan sent a note of "deep regret" but not an apology. In 1985, after an EgyptAir 737 carrying hijackers was forced to land by U.S. fighters, U.S. Envoy John Whitehead said, "we very much regret that developments took the course they did." To regret something is to wish that one had not done it. Mr. Whitehead expressed less than regret, wishing only that it had not been necessary to do it. An apology requires accepting *moral* blame, going beyond lament or regret to remorse.

A Guttman Partial Order

Expressing only regret is one way to semiapologize, and there are others. In fact, partial apologies can be partially ordered, in that performing one element is in effect performing certain others, or implying willingness to do so. A partial order suggested by the data is shown in figure 25. It can be called a *Guttman partial order,* an extension of the standard technique of Guttman scaling, or "scalogram analysis." Regular Guttman scaling applies to a group of actors and a list of behaviors, based on whether each actor engaged in each behavior. A classic study (Stouffer et al. 1950; Coombs 1964) investigated the reactions of soldiers before a World War II battle, as they approached a Pacific island in landing craft. They suffered various symptoms from the ride and their fear of the imminent combat: upset stomachs, dizziness, vomiting, and so on. These symptoms could be ordered top to bottom so that a soldier exhibiting one symptom generally exhibited all the ones below. This pattern was not perfect, in that some soldiers exhibited a more severe symptom but skipped a lesser one. However, an ordering of the symptoms was found that minimized the total discrepancies of this kind. The method simultaneously produced a ranking of soldiers and symptoms. The orders stated which symptoms were most severe and which soldiers were most prone to symptoms, without an a priori judgment by the researcher.[5]

   The soldiers correspond to nations engaged in apology incidents, and their fear behaviors correspond to the different elements that appear in an apology act—whether restitution was offered, whether moral responsibility was expressed, and so forth. A full Guttman scale would not work, the data indicate, but the method can be weakened to require that the behaviors follow a partial order. The one shown in figure 25 fits fairly well and indicates, for example, that nations that regretted an action would be willing to acknowledge that they did it or were ipso facto acknowledging that. The difference between this and a full Guttman scale is the existence here of pairs of actions that have no implication in either direction. A nation may be willing to punish the guilty but not offer restitution or vice versa.

---

5. If one represents the data as a matrix of 0s and 1s, which mean, respectively, engaging or not engaging in the behavior, then a Guttman scale is a reordering of the rows and columns so that all the 1s lie in a triangle in the upper right.

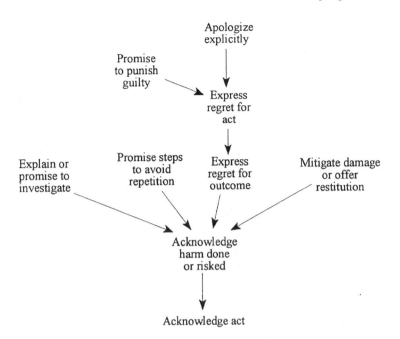

Fig. 25.   A partial order on the elements of an apology

Stouffer's rankings of soldiers and symptoms were objectively based, but figure 25 is my perception of the pattern in the data. A formal scaling method would be better, but the data were not systematic enough. They came from news reports and speeches, and the leaders quoted did not lay out their positions completely, unlike the soldiers filling out their questionnaires. Some of figure 25 is based on an intrinsic analysis of the concept—apologizing fully but adding that one did not do the deed, for example, would make no sense. It is also based on the presence or absence of certain cases from the database. Sometimes a country worked its way up the ordering, such as Japan first recognizing simply that the harm had been done to the Korean women and other women forced to provide sex for Japanese soldiers, then admitting that they were indeed coerced, then apologizing, then offering restitution. This narrowed the possibilities for the partial order.[6]

---

6. A Guttman partial order is a weaker assertion about one's data than a complete Guttman scale since it rules out fewer varieties of apologies. Its strength can be defined as the number of patterns it allows. The weakest claim, saying nothing at all, allows $2^9 = 512$ patterns, since one's apology could include any of the nine behaviors and omit the rest. A complete ordering would allow 10 patterns, from including all nine apology elements to none of them. It can be calculated that figure 25 is somewhere in between, allowing exactly 50 patterns. Another measure of its strength would be

It is hard to find an apology where every element was present and explicit, but one demand for an apology was situated at the top of the partial order. It was in South Korea's speech in the United Nations after the Soviet Union shot down its flight KAL 007 (*UN Chronicle,* November 1983). It called for "a full and detailed account of what exactly had happened. . . . a full apology . . . complete compensation for the loss of the aircraft, as well as to the families of the passengers and crew . . . the Soviet Union must adequately punish all those who were directly responsible . . . guarantee unimpeded access to the crash site to the representatives of impartial international organizations . . . return any remains or debris that might be found . . . give specific, concrete, effective and credible guarantees against recurrence of such violent actions." Almost as complete was Canada's demand for an apology after it discovered that the CIA had arranged for LSD experimentation on Canadian citizens, disguising it as mental health care. It called for every element except punishing the guilty. Apology demands can be strongly felt but still be low on the partial order. The secret Armenian organizations responsible for the continuing assassinations of Turkish officials have generally demanded only an acknowledgment that the massacres happened (Permanent Peoples' Tribunal 1985).

Like a challenge, an apology can be semiforceful in several ways. According to Bean and Johnstone (1994), a frequent use of "I'm sorry" in daily conversation is to initiate an interruption of the speaker. This violates an apology's preparatory condition that the apologizer has already committed the offense. Another common nonapology involves a statement like "I'm sorry that you took offense at what I did." The moral admission must be about something done by the apologizer, not the recipient. International apologies have also misfired and sometimes increased resentment by the wrong choice of the act or the recipient. Japan apologized for its World War II actions, but the apology was directed not to the victims but to the Japanese people.

Symbols and Metaphors in Apologies

An apology can be a symbolic message—a country might apologize to convey friendship. However, this section is concerned with a different connection to symbolism. It discusses symbols that appear in apologies, in their context or their form.

---

the bits of information it conveys, regarding each pattern as equally likely. The maximum uncertainty about what pattern might be used is $\log_2(512) = 9$ bits. Figure 25 would reduce the uncertainty to $\log_2(50) = 5.64$ bits, and a complete ordering would leave $\log_2(10) = 3.32$ bits. Thus figure 25 goes 59 percent of the way to a full Guttman scale. It is a semistrong theory of what counts as apologizing.

A case where the symbolic form was crucial was the Tampico incident of 1914. Mexican soldiers detained several U.S. sailors who had tried to sail their supply boat down a canal. They were soon released, and President Huerta was ready to apologize verbally, but he balked at a further U.S. demand that Mexico deliver a 21-gun salute to the American flag in the presence of U.S. ships in the harbor. The impasse led to a battle costing several hundred lives and to the U.S. occupation of Vera Cruz (Eisenhower 1993.)

Two important symbolic matters are the individual chosen to make the apology and the occasion chosen on which to deliver it. A statement from a monarch or an emperor has the greatest force, one from a prime minister or president is next, then come a foreign minister and a foreign affairs spokesperson. Transgressions that were committed long ago adhere to the nation rather than its current administration, so the emperor or monarch is the appropriate apologizer. Nations calling for a Japanese apology for its World War II actions looked to the emperor. When Queen Elizabeth visited South Africa in March 1995, many Afrikaners wanted an apology for the deaths of thousands of Boer prisoners in British concentration camps, but she rose only to the lowest point on the partial order, referring to the "pain and suffering" felt by the Afrikaner people. In December 1994, she was called on to apologize to Queen Dame Te Atairangikaahu of the Tainui people of New Zealand for the British seizure of their lands in 1865. It was fitting that one queen deliver the apology and another one receive it. Countries that do not have a monarch may be in a worse position for that when they want to rectify an old offense.

Related to the apologies from monarchs is a subtle question about a government's responsibility for the offenses of its predecessor: Who bears the guilt, the people who live on the territory, the government, or some abstract entity? Does present-day France have a duty to apologize for its World War II participation in the murder of tens of thousands of Jewish citizens? In 1993, when President Mitterand established a National Remembrance Day to recognize anti-Semitic persecution in France, he declined to apologize: "If the French nation had been involved in the unfortunate Vichy undertaking, then such an apology would be due" (*Montreal Gazette,* July 15, 1992). Holding to the position of past governments, he pointed to the Resistance and Charles de Gaulle's Free French government-in-exile as the keeper of the two-hundred-year tradition of the Republic. At first glance the existence or nonexistence of a government-in-exile would seem to be irrelevant to a French apology, but the COUNTRY-AS-A-PERSON metaphor clarifies Mitterand's thinking. Continuity is the key—just as people do not disappear and reappear, the "national person" is thought of as continuous. In World War II, France's national person was in England, in Mitterand's view. A similar controversy continues around the massacres of Armenians, the worst of which occurred in 1915, before the Ataturk government. The Permanent Peoples' Tribunal (1985) rejected any Turkish argument like Mitterand's: "the Turkish state must assume responsibility without using the pretext of any discontinuity in the existence of the state to elude that responsibility."

International apologies are more public than interpersonal ones. They acknowledge harm and responsibility to the whole world in order to constrain the apologizer's future assertions and behavior. Only rarely are they secret. An exception was the U.S. apology for the Central Intelligence Agency's LSD experiments on Canadian citizens in the 1950s. Even this event supported the general thesis that international apologies are public, since there is an explanation: the offense being apologized for was itself supposed to remain a secret. The public nature of international apologies influences the symbolism of their context. They are usually given at public gatherings and during speeches. They are not conveyed in letters that are only later released to the press. A strong pattern is for the apologizer to travel to the other's turf. Indonesia's foreign minister apologized for the construction of a road that violated the border of Papua New Guinea on the occasion of a speech at an official banquet in Port Moresby. In March 1995, President Brazauskas of Lithuania used a visit to Israel to apologize for Lithuanian involvement in the Holocaust. Emperor Hirohito was visiting South Korea when he made the statement quoted previously.

If an apology is not carried to the recipient's metaphorical home, it should at least be offered face-to-face. In January 1984, after South African foreign minister Rolef Botha apologized to a Zimbabwean trade official who had had his arm broken at a police roadblock, the Ministry's head of protocol personally visited the official. This behavior taps the COUNTRY-AS-A-PERSON metaphor, in which one person visits the other to deliver an apology, to symbolize respect and show the deliberate and significant nature of the act.

What happens when an apology is demanded but not given? International behavior is again guided by the COUNTRY-AS-A-PERSON metaphor and the scenarios around interpersonal quarrels. The aggrieved state often withdraws its hospitality and refuses to meet or communicate. Until 1988, Indonesia had refused to recognize the People's Republic of China without an apology for its complicity in a 1965 coup attempt. In August 1985, Costa Rican president Luis Alberto refused to meet with his Nicaraguan counterpart without an apology for the killing of two civil guards the previous May. In September 1986, Foreign Minister Antoine Ndinga-Oba of Congo, speaking to the United Nations General Assembly, compared Israel to Nazi Germany. According to the *New York Times* (September 22, 1986), Ndinga was soon told that President Reagan might find it not "convenient" to meet with Congo's president during the latter's forthcoming visit to Washington, D.C., unless the matter were cleared up. The foreign minister apologized.

Models of Apologizing Based on Face and Honor

This section suggests some connection of apologies to face and honor. The processes are separate, and one notable consequence of this is that apologizers can lose face but gain honor.

Apologies' relationship to face is straightforward. To apologize is to grant the other person face, to imply that he or she matters and will get better treatment in the future. To apologize is also to accept blame and possibly lose face oneself. In the model of chapter 9, face rose and fell according to a sequence of encounters where one party imposed and another chose to resist or defer. Apologies can be incorporated into the model by changing the interpretation of some actions in the stage games. Following an imposition, one might add a game between the same players where one can Demand an Apology and the other can Apologize. An equilibrium could be found where apologizing influences the players' public face levels, and refusing to apologize leads to conflictual relations in future games between that pair.

A model of apologizing based on honor might work as follows. Suppose the person has done some act that is morally blameworthy in many people's eyes. Blameworthiness would be represented in the model by the likelihood of someone of each degree of honor being willing to do it under those circumstances. The distributions for the individual and the audience are different—the individual has an opinion about how blameworthy the deed is and so does the audience. Honor calls for an apology when one is due and calls for no apology when one is not due. An honorable person who violates either principle loses payoff in proportion to honor. An apology may change the audience's estimate of the individual's honor—the audience may feel confirmed in its low opinion of the deed, or it may note that an honorable person would offer an apology when one is clearly due.

The next section will clarify how the connection to honor and face allows international apologies to work even when they violate the normal requirements.

Why Do International Apologies Differ from Interpersonal Ones?

Three features mark international apologies: they can be from and to third parties, they can be blatantly insincere, and they seldom lead to explicit forgiveness.

A straightforward explanation for third-party apologies is the COUNTRY-AS-A-PERSON metaphor. Yeltsin's apology that the Soviet Union had been holding Japanese prisoners in Siberia years after the war was not from one leader to another but symbolically from Russia to Japan.

One factor explains all three differences. International and interpersonal apologies emphasize different illocutionary points of apologizing. Interpersonal apologies are largely messages about the apologizer's feelings, meant to inform the other and give confidence in the future of the relationship, but international apologies are aimed at the management of face and honor. They are more communications to the world than to the offended party: their point is to restore the other's face. Also, similar to the self-commitment war-of-face model of the last chapter, uttering penitent words commits one's face before the whole group that the action will not be repeated. Both purposes, transmitting information about one's feelings and managing face and honor, are typical in apologizing, but international dealings emphasize the latter, and this leads to differences in practice.

CHAPTER 12

Prestige, Normative Regimes, and Moral Authority

Someone possesses *prestige* in a group if the members believe that the person is generally admired in the group. The admiration must be seen as having some grounds, such as the individual's deeds or possessions. A third element is that the members expect the person to gain influence in the group from the admiration. A soldier who dies in battle can be said to have gained honor or glory, but not prestige.

Prestige thus is at the second level, of beliefs about beliefs about the facts. As a matter of objective reality, a person is said to have a good quality; at the first level of beliefs the person has a good reputation—the group thinks that the person has a good quality. Prestige means that everyone thinks that everyone thinks the person has the quality. Perhaps no one admires the person, but if each person thinks that the rest do, that constitutes prestige. As in a trick done with mirrors, someone can gain prestige by convincing everyone that he or she has a good reputation—there is no need to possess the quality in question. This possibility recalls the word's Latin root, *praestare,* meaning to create an illusion, as in "prestidigitation."

Since it can confer rights and benefits in the group, prestige functions like face and honor. Roughly, it is in between them—like honor, it involves an innate quality of the person, but like face, it depends on beliefs about what is in others' minds. A person might possess personal honor while others do not know about that quality, but the idea of having unnoticed prestige or face makes no sense.

Prestige involves what each member believes about others' attitudes toward the individual; face is about what each believes about others' disposition to act toward the individual. Prestige and face also differ according to what produces them and who confers them. For face, respectful treatment comes from a record of the same treatment by the group, but prestige usually starts with the individual, with deeds done or objects acquired. For this reason, we speak of prestige being "gained" or "lost." This is in contrast to face, where the individual is in a reactive position. Face is said to have been "saved" or "lost," the latter by failing to respond to a threat to it. As well as these differences in the sources of the two concepts, there are differences in their consequences. Someone with high face gets deference in direct on-the-record interactions; but prestige produces perceived admiration by the whole group and, from this, influence of various kinds.

A distinction can be made between prestige and status. Status suggests a hierarchy with clearly defined positions and an institution that set it up. Instead of looking to others' attitudes as with prestige, with status each party looks to the rules and decisions of the organization. If moral authority derives from normative prestige, the analogue for status is legitimacy. It is the moral right of an actor to be obeyed by virtue of his or her position.

There is no formal structure for the international system, and accordingly *prestige* is usually the better term in that context. "International prestige" is a more common usage than "international status." Midlarsky (1975) and Luard (1992), however, use "status," and just why they do so clarifies the difference. Luard was interested in well-defined rules of diplomatic protocol and Midlarsky in the hierarchy of states based on the ranks of diplomatic officials sent to them by other countries. A state's rank came from a relatively formal system accepted by the whole group, so the choice of these writers is reasonable for their purposes.

This chapter will focus on *normative prestige,* the particular kind that comes from abiding by norms. An important aspect is that good behavior confers influence on related issues.[1] Those who have followed the norms in the past have more influence in pronouncing on what the norms are now in a situation where ambiguity arises. This is called *moral authority* (Lasswell and Kaplan 1950).

The Relationship of Prestige to Symbolism

Prestige can be gained by doing deeds or possessing things. The latter kind of prestige usually involves concrete, publicly visible tokens that suggest power and ability. A nation holds on to its colonies, acquires a naval fleet, buys modern jets for its national airlines, or hosts an important conference (Sagan 1996,

---

1. Weber (1924), Mills (1951, 239), Parsons (1952, 132), Lasswell and Kaplan (1950), and others have analyzed prestige in similar terms, and Nicolson (1937) discusses it in the international context. McGinn (1972) gives the most systematic theory of it so far in the international context, and Milliken (1996) analyzes its use in justifying U.S. persistence in Vietnam.

1997; Eyre and Suchman 1996). In 1987, when India leased a nuclear-powered submarine from the Soviet Union, the national news agency circulated a photograph of Prime Minister Rajiv Gandhi standing on the conning tower. Although the submarine was Soviet built and stayed under Soviet control, it symbolized India's technological progress.

A so-called prestige symbol usually combines three mechanisms. It can be simply a demonstration that the country is able to do something, in which case it is not a symbol at all in the present usage, but an index in Jervis's sense (1971). A prestige symbol can also rely on the mechanism of message symbolism. The message might be from the grantor of the symbol, not its possessor—a large office is the boss's way of saying that the person has a high rank. It is meant to be on the record, in that the boss is letting everyone know that everyone knows that the person has high rank, and so on. The symbol helps establish the person's face in the hierarchy. This is an example of a typical connection among three central concepts of this work, message symbols, prestige and face.

Some prestige symbols rely on the mechanism of focal symbolism. High technology weapons are salient parts of the typical modern and powerful state. The possessor expects to get its way in future games of power politics, and expects others to recognize this and be more ready to defer.

One way to gain prestige is by winning a symbolic contest. This combines the mechanism of a demonstration with that of a focal symbol. The context must have a structure that makes the symbol analogous to a larger contest for which it is meant to set expectations. It functions like the prenegotiation debates about the shape of the conference table (chap. 4), whose outcome could be a self-fulfilling symbolic indicator of the outcome of the real struggle. One example was the space race. The Soviet Union won the first round by launching unmanned and manned earth satellites. The United States landed on the moon and soon retired. America's motive had been the symbolic competition, a demonstration that it was not slipping into technical inferiority after the surprise of Sputnik. It won a round, but after that, other practical benefits did not justify further effort. The Olympic Games are another costly contest over a prestige symbol. Many countries put their funds into them instead of into athletic programs that would benefit significant numbers of their population. Another example of a symbolic contest involved Taiwan and the People's Republic of China competing for diplomatic recognition from other countries. The next chapter will suggest that the nuclear arms race was also largely symbolic.

The focus of the rest of this chapter is on a certain kind of prestige—normative prestige. It is gained from doing appropriate deeds, and very often does not involve symbolism.

Normative Prestige and Moral Authority

Normative prestige yields moral authority. When a country speaks out on a normative issue, its voice has greater legitimacy if it possesses prestige in that context. Costa Rica had a stable democratic system and gained a role in the negotiations for peace in Nicaragua. It acquired moral authority, the self-fulfilling expectation in the group that the group would follow the possessor's normative suggestions. Conversely, when a country commits a normative lapse, it loses moral authority on related issues.[2] In December 1993, Hungary changed its election laws to a system that made it harder for ethnic Germans living there to elect representatives to the National Assembly. According to the BBC, the group Alliance of Germans in Hungary charged that this cast a shadow on Hungary's minority policy and diminished its international prestige. The Hungarian leadership would have no moral grounds, the Alliance said, to raise its voice for the rights of Hungarians beyond its borders.

Normative prestige is illustrated by parallel controversies in Canadian defense policy, 25 years apart. In the early 1960s, Canada was debating whether to acquire nuclear warheads for its fighter-bombers and antiaircraft missiles (Cox 1985). The United States would supply the warheads, and, by U.S. law, would keep ownership and veto power over their use. Proponents argued that unless Canada accepted a nuclear role, it would lose its sway in NATO. Opponents held that acquiring nuclear weapons would weaken Canada's voice against proliferation and the arms race. Both sides were citing moral authority, but they focused on different reference groups, one on the military milieu of NATO, where acquiring the weapons was normative, the other on diplomatic circles striving for arms reductions, where it was not. Lester Pearson's government accepted the weapons, but soon afterward Canada began dropping its nuclear involvement piece by piece, and after a decade, the antinuclear position prevailed. Sagan (1996) describes a similar Ukrainian dilemma about the strategic nuclear weapons left on its territory after the end of the Soviet Union.

In 1985, a dilemma arose for Canada between normative prestige and focal symbolism. A government committee advocated the purchase of 10 nuclear-powered attack submarines. Opposition voices criticized the proposal for undermining Canada's stand against proliferation, and submarine advocates stressed the need to patrol the Arctic. Canada had 20 diesel submarines, but the newer ones could stay submerged long enough to operate under the ice. Even

2. As in message and focal symbols, contrast with the past increases the symbol's power. Haglund (1989) suggests the existence of an "Elmer Gantry phenomenon" around nuclear proliferation that the holier you have been against it, the more harm you do if you start proliferating.

so, the concept of patrolling was a symbolic one, since the submarines' chance of detecting an encroaching submarine was nil. The rationale was that Canadian claims in Arctic territory disputes with the United States would be stronger if Canada had a military presence there (Desjardins and Rauf 1988; Haglund 1989). The normative prestige argument against the submarines competed with an argument based on symbolic dominion. In the end, the plan was rejected as too expensive.

Social Norms and Normative Regimes

In these examples, moral authority came from "good behavior," and the latter concept requires an analysis of social norms and normative regimes. The first thesis concerns a prototypical feature of social norms: a social norm is part of a normative regime. This is a system of norms connected to one another in relationships of mutual support.[3] Compliance with the given norm is bolstered by other norms in the regime, which put individuals under obligation to grant rewards to a norm follower and to punish a norm violator. Others have a positive duty to reward or punish, and sometimes an action that is forbidden in regular circumstances becomes required after a violation. Treating someone inequitably is wrong, unless the person violated a norm, and then he or she deserves it. The 1970s and 1980s saw the growth of an international norm against racism, and states like Britain, that did not act against South Africa, were themselves criticized (Klotz 1995). This support structure is a normative regime, and being part of one is a core feature of a norm.

Apologizing and forgiving are part of a normative regime. When you forgive someone, you are making a promise, and if you do not keep it, it is the forgiven person who has a grievance. Whether a social system of honor constitutes a regime is controversial. Honor is supported by further norms—the members of society are supposed to ostracize a dishonorable person, and if they do not, they too will be punished. Their punishment is not necessarily a loss of honor, but it will take some aversive form, like criticism. Whether honor systems really qualify depends on whether one sees the attitude behind them as a moral concept or as one closer to the kind of self-esteem one has from being athletic or speaking several languages. Gerrard (1994) argues that the attitude supporting honor is close to an aesthetic one.

3. Krasner (1983) defines international regimes in general as "sets of implicit or explicit principles, norms, rules and decision making procedures around which actors' expectations converge in a given area of international relations." Kydd and Snidal (1993) give a summary of game-theory approaches.

The norms invoked when a norm is kept or violated can be called its *supporting norms*.[4] This leads to a puzzle: What keeps the supporting norms in place? If there is a hierarchy of supporting norms, then, there is either an infinite regress or a highest norm with nothing to back it up. In the analysis here, norms do not go off to infinity but rather form loops of support. Diagrams will show how this works.

Normative Regimes for a Repeated Prisoner's Dilemma

The concept of a normative regime will be clarified by comparing it with an equilibrium of a repeated game. The game is a repeated Prisoner's Dilemma, and the equilibria discussed here are Always Defect, the Grim Strategy equilibrium, and Fight-and-Forget.[5] One criterion for a normative regime lies outside game theory and involves feelings of moral approval and disapproval. However other conditions can be stated within the theory and show some of the equilibria to be poor candidates for normative regimes. Always Defect cannot be one, the Grim Strategy is a middling candidate, and Fight-and-Forget is a good one.

A Repeated Prisoner's Dilemma

Suppose the Prisoner's Dilemma game of matrix 1 is played repeatedly, at times $t = 1, 2, 3, \ldots$ to infinity. Each player chooses to Cooperate (C) or Defect (D).

Matrix 1 is the *stage game,* and the whole sequence is the *supergame.* The

---

4. The concept has appeared under different names. Crawford and Ostrom (1995) refer to these as "monitoring" or "sanctioning" norms, on the grounds that people have a duty to watch and punish each other, and Axelrod (1986) terms them *metanorms*.

5. The well-known strategy of Tit-for-Tat (start cooperatively, then duplicate the other's previous move) is not one considered here. Tit-for-Tat generates an equilibrium that is typically not subgame perfect. That is to say, it prescribes non-utility-maximizing behavior in some hypothetical situations. (It still qualifies as an equilibrium since the situations that would yield this behavior never arise if the equilibrium strategies are played, so the player's payoff is not decreased.) If a player chose D at some point, the two would go back and forth: CD, DC, CD, DC, . . . forever. Unless the game has payoffs fixed to give precise equalities at the choice points, either the Row chooser should not cooperate to produce CD, since Row knows that Column will defect, or, if Row is choosing C in hopes of prompting a return to the cooperative path, then Row should not choose D on the next move. One way or the other, Row is not playing optimally. It might be objected that if the players had stuck to Tit-for-Tat as they were supposed to, they would not reach this CD-DC cycle. However, each player's reason for avoiding D is based on the expectation of what would happen after choosing it, and Tit-for-Tat suggests that they expect this illogical play.

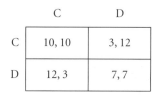

	C	D
C	10, 10	3, 12
D	12, 3	7, 7

Matrix 1. The stage game, a Prisoner's Dilemma.

rules are the standard ones: the players are told each other's move immediately after each stage game and before they choose their next moves. Future payoffs are discounted by a factor δ between 0 and 1, meaning that 10 units received one period from now are valued equal to 10δ units received now, 10 units two periods from now are valued $10\delta^2$, and so on.[6] Each player's goal is to maximize his or her total discounted payoff. Thus, if the players' strategies resulted in cooperation at every stage, each would receive a stream of payoffs 10, 10, 10 $\cdots$ and would assess this at present utility $10 + 10\delta + 10\delta^2 + \cdots = 10/(1 - \delta)$. For $\delta = .9$, a player would value this repeated game at 100. The whole game is thus defined by the stage game, the goal of playing, and the information known at each point.

The Always-Defect Equilibrium

This equilibrium has each player use D on every play, no matter what has happened so far. Both get a stream of payoffs 7, 7, 7, $\cdots$. This pair of strategies is an equilibrium for any discount factor, since no player could do better by switching unilaterally to the other move. The equilibrium is subgame perfect.

The Grim Equilibrium

The Grim Strategy says to Cooperate if no one has chosen Defect so far. If there has been a D chosen, then use D forever. For matrix 1 both players using the Grim Strategy constitutes a subgame perfect equilibrium on the condition that $\delta \geq .4$ and produces an indefinite string of CC pairs, with the payoff stream of 10, 10, 10 $\cdots$. This equilibrium leads to mutual cooperation at as low values of δ as any other equilibrium. Players have the greatest incentive to choose cooperation, since doing otherwise causes the worst consequence.

---

6. The discount factor can also be viewed as the probability that the game will continue after each play, as opposed to simply ending.

Fight-and-Forget

The final equilibrium discussed can be termed *Fight-and-Forget*. It states:

At the beginning of the game or if both Cooperated last time, Cooperate;
if exactly one player Defected last time, Defect;
if both Defected last time, Cooperate.

In other words, the players Cooperate if they played identically last time, either with CC or DD. If they played differently, they get even, then get back to cooperating. A fight would last only a single round, but the negative prospect of this keeps them cooperating each time, as long as the discount factor is high enough. In the previous game, Fight-and-Forget is a subgame perfect equilibrium for $\delta \geq \frac{2}{3}$. The strategy has its advantages and disadvantages. For some Prisoner's Dilemma games it does not give an equilibrium for any discount factor. However, it is an equilibrium in some other types of games, including repeated Chicken. One of its merits is that it responds to a criticism of the Grim Strategy that if a player made a chance error in the Grim Strategy the two players would be stuck indefinitely in defections. With Fight-and-Forget, players who slip from mutual cooperation would return to it in two moves.[7]

The next section will amplify the concept of a normative regime, then these equilibria will be discussed for their properties as normative regimes.

Normative Regimes as Game Equilibria

A normative regime and an equilibrium of a repeated game are similar in certain ways. Both tell people what to do in social situations, and both prescribe behavior that accords with incentives in some sense. A game equilibrium cannot prescribe suboptimal behavior for a player, and somewhat similarly, a culture whose norms urge people to take a certain course and that then punishes them for doing so would be under pressure to change. Also, game equilibria and

---

7. Fight-and-Forget seems to have been published first by Rapoport and Chammah (1965), who called it "Simpleton," on the grounds that getting one of the two better payoffs leads a player to repeat the strategy and getting one of the worse two causes a switch. A stochastic version goes by the name "Pavlov" for the same reason: that it tends to repeat a successful move (although Pavlov's theory of learning actually involved association rather than reinforcement, so a better name would be "Skinner"). Some biologists have found that it does well in computer simulations (Kraines and Kraines 1987; Nowak and Sigmund 1993). Binmore and Samuelson (1993) investigated its evolutionary development under the name Tat-for-Tit, in a version where the initial move was D to discourage the spread of a simpler mutant species that cooperates every time. Fudenberg and Maskin (1990) called it "Win-Stay, Lose-Switch."

normative regimes rules for the current situation are backed up by expectations of hypothetical situations: in a game, players stay on the equilibrium path because of the prospective consequences of going off it, and in a normative regime, people stay on the straight and narrow for fear of being punished. As with the common knowledge assumptions that are often made in solving games, group members recognize that others know the norms.

These are the similarities, but game equilibria and normative regimes are different in several ways.

Norms are linked to feelings of moral approval and disapproval; equilibria do not necessarily involve such feelings. Past definitions of a norm have included four elements, which have been emphasized to different degrees: behavior, beliefs, intentions, and moral attitudes.[8] Axelrod's definition (1986, 1097) stressed behavior, beliefs, and intentions: "a norm exists in a given social setting to the extent that individuals act in a certain way and are often punished when seen not to be acting in this way." Elster's definition involved belief and moral attitude (1989, 105): "A norm . . . is the propensity to feel shame and to anticipate sanctions by others at the thought of behaving in a certain way." The analysis here focuses on beliefs, behavior, and intentions, without negating the importance of attitudes like approval, disapproval, pride, guilt, or shame.

Equilibria apply to actions chosen by people in situations; norms apply to types of actions chosen by types of people in types of situations. In the repeated Prisoner's Dilemma, a norm would not just prescribe cooperation at a certain point in a particular game but rather cooperation in similar points in games of that type. Strictly speaking, norms apply to "game forms" that group situations, people, and moves. They are parallel to scientific laws in this regard. Moral obligation in a normative system corresponds to nomological necessity in an empirical one. According to Hempel (1965), a scientific law cannot refer to a specific place or time. To say that a certain force grows stronger near the North Pole, or as the year 2000 comes, may be a true statement, but it does not have the form of a possible law. Similarly, a norm cannot refer to specific situations or people. A social group might hold different norms for men and women, or for kings and commoners, but the norms cannot refer to a specific king or commoner. Norms must be personally neutral.

Equilibrium behavior is never violated within the model, but normative behavior sometimes is. Within a game model, choosing a nonequilibrium strategy is a contradiction, given the appropriate assumptions on the players' knowledge

---

8. Many definitions have been proposed in political science (Crawford and Ostrom 1995), and others are available elsewhere in the social sciences, in particular sociology.

and utility functions. Situations are grouped for norms, and sometimes two situations that end up together are strategically different. The norm will call for a certain type of action in that type of situation, but players may have different utilities for the outcomes and make a different choice. They would be violating the norm.

A normative regime is socially beneficial; an equilibrium is not necessarily so. In general, a social norm is supposed to benefit the group. In a repeated Prisoner's Dilemma game, the equilibrium of Always Defect cannot be termed a norm since it leads to inefficient payoffs.

A norm is supported by the prospect of intentional reward or punishment by others; players stay with an equilibrium for its costs and benefits, but these do not necessarily arise through others' intentions to reward or punish. Punishment means more than the violator losing benefit. Others must impose the loss deliberately because of their moral disapproval of the violation. Norms require a causal sequence:

> i complies or violates →
> others observe i's action and approve or disapprove →
> others reward or punish i.

This marks the difference between norms and the equilibria generated by many conventions, in Lewis's sense of the word (1969). Suppose Jim and Bob go to an amusement park, arranging that if they are separated they will go to the Ferris wheel. They do get separated, but for some reason Jim goes to the entrance booth, and they have a bad time for the rest of the fair. Jim's violating the convention did not induce Bob to go to the Ferris wheel to punish Jim. Bob had no intention to punish. Their agreement was a convention, not a norm. Simple conventions are *self*-enforcing, which is one reason that we do not hear of "regimes of conventions."[9]

Diagramming a Normative Regime

The Fight-and-Forget equilibrium will be the first example. It can be shown to satisfy all the conditions for a normative regime that can be formulated within game theory. (If it were also true in a certain context that people acted with an

---

9. Behavioral definitions of norms, like Axelrod's and the present one, have others doing the punishing and rewarding. In Elster's definition and similar ones, the norm follower acts from conscience. The approaches are different, but their relation is clear. In some norms, socialization has internalized the punisher.

moral attitude, the situation would be a full normative regime.) First, one must define the action types and the situation types. A game equilibrium analysis would distinguish the moves available at the first stage of play from those at the second and third, but this normative analysis groups moves across stages. The natural choice for the two action types is {Cooperate, Defect}. As to situation types, a reasonable grouping has three: {Start of the game or two C's last time, one C and one D last time, two D's last time}. Fight-and-Forget can then be stated by giving the rule for each situation type:

Start, or two C's last time: *choose C;*
One C and one D last time: *choose D;*
Two D's last time: *choose C.*

For a game, these are rules that define an equilibrium; for a moral situation, they are norms constituting a normative regime.

One can now draw figure 26, the *consequence graph.* Its nodes (circles) are norms. The diagram takes the viewpoint of one player and shows the results of that player's actions. By making a move, the player keeps the situation type as it was or shifts to a new one. The possible shifts are shown by arrows, of which there are two kinds: a solid one showing what happens if the player keeps the norm and a dotted arrow showing the result of violating it. Violating the norm "If two C's last time or the start of the game, *choose C,*" for example, would move play to the situation "One D last time." The arrows are drawn under the assumption that the other player keeps the norm.[10]

Next is constructed figure 27, the *normative regime graph.* The nodes are the same, but the arrows have a new meaning—instead of consequences, they show incentives. If the graph represents a subgame perfect equilibrium, then keeping the norm at each situation is as good as or better than violating it. The incentive to keep or violate the norm is the immediate payoff from doing so, combined with the prospects of the next situation resulting from what one does (possibly the same one as before). A situation resulting from keeping the norm provides *inducement* to keep it, and violating the norm should move the individual to a situation that is less desirable and that, therefore, provides a *deter-*

---

10. Note that the graph is not a depiction of an equilibrium in that it makes the assumption that the other is following a certain strategy. It does not show one necessary element in an equilibrium, what would happen if both players violated the strategy. It resembles the diagrams of Moore machines of automata theory, used by Osborne and Rubinstein (1994) and others to portray evolutionary game strategies, but it is richer than these in that it includes what a player would do after that very player violated the recommended strategy. Moore diagrams do not show this, since automata are not supposed to make mistakes or think hypothetically.

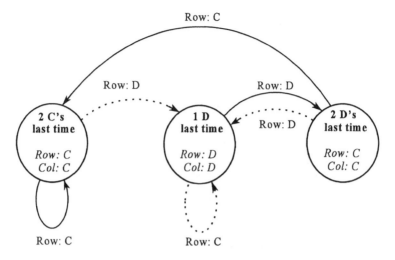

Fig. 26.   Consequence graph for the Fight-and-Forget equilibrium. Norms
are in circles, including the situations and their rules. The graph is from
Row's viewpoint and assumes that Column acts normatively. Solid lines
show the consequences of normative actions by the Row player, and dotted
lines show those of counternormative actions.

rent that motivates the player to keep the current norm. Deterrent and inducement support are the two kinds of normative support, and they are shown by
labeled arrows.

For the case of Fight-and-Forget, the normative regime graph, figure 27, involves taking the consequence graph, figure 26, and reversing all its arrows.
Those arrows that represented normative action in a situation now provide normative support, and the ones that are counternormative move the situation to
an undesirable one, and so provide deterrent support. At the middle situation,
one player or the other has just chosen D. Row is now supposed to choose D,
and expects Column to do the same. (As before the graph is from Row's viewpoint.) This will move Row to the third situation, where Row expects mutual
cooperation. If Row does not act normatively in the middle situation, Row will
stay there. Thus the third situation provides inducement support for Row to
keep the norm in the middle, and the middle situation provides inducement
support for itself.

Figure 27 shows how Fight-and-Forget satisfies the criterion listed for a
normative regime in that each norm gets support from others. Norms are supported directly by a certain set of norms and indirectly by other norms further
removed. A norm can be part of its own supporting set, either directly or indi-

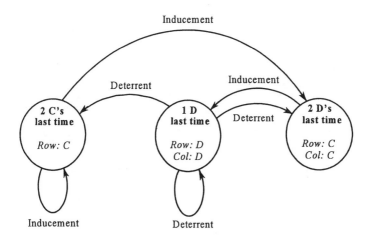

Fig. 27. Normative regime graph for the Fight-and-Forget equilibrium. Norms are in circles, with their situations and rules. Deterrent and inducement support relationships among the norms are shown for the Row player.

rectly, and this answers the earlier puzzle about how norms can support each other without an endless hierarchy. If the structure of normative support in a game is arranged properly to give correct incentives, then at equilibrium the norms can maintain each other in loops.

Why the Always Defect and Grim Equilibria Do Not Yield
Normative Regimes

The Always Defect equilibrium is an equilibrium for the repeated Prisoner's Dilemma, but it is not the basis of a normative regime. Going through the mechanics of constructing its normative regime graph shows why this is so. The graph is figure 28 *(bottom right)* and one finds rules that are self-supporting, not based on the prospect of the rewards and punishments of others. Both players are to play D, but it is not the prospect of future punishment that induces them to do it. As with Jim and Bob at the fairgrounds, it is the current payoff that makes them stay with D. Norms require others to punish a violator in response, and that is not happening here. No matter what a player does in the situation "At least one D," the result is the same situation, so others are not differentially rewarding or punishing based on the player's behavior. If Row were to choose C instead of D, Row would be sorry, but not because Column was punishing Row in reaction to the deviation. Column would have defected anyway.

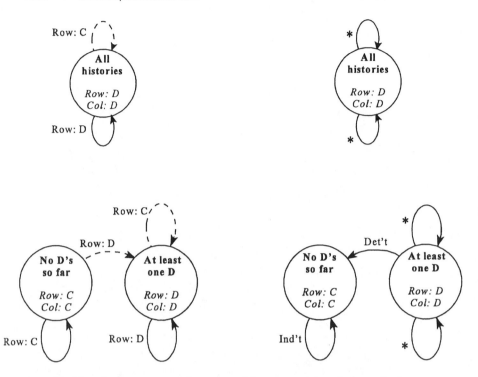

Fig. 28.   Consequence graphs and resulting normative regime graphs for the Always Defect *(top)* and the Grim Strategy equilibria *(bottom)*. In a normative regime, arrows marked (*) would involve deterrent or inducement support, but here the situation always leads to itself and so cannot provide differential reward or punishment.

Regarding the qualifications of the Grim Strategy as a normative regime, first note that it has two situation types. One, "At least one D" is not supported by a norm—it is a subgame that is identical to the Always Defect equilibrium, and the preceding arguments hold for it. One cannot make the argument for the other situation, "No D's so far," so the Grim Strategy could be called a partial normative regime. Players continue to cooperate for fear of switching to the second kind of situation, that is, for fear of a regime breakdown.

A Normative Regime Using Optimal Penal Codes

Another example satisfies the conditions for a full normative regime and shows some more subtle ways that a normative regime can maintain its loops of sup-

	Low	Med	High
Low	10, 10	3, 15	0, 7
Med	15, 3	7, 7	−4, 5
High	7, 0	5, −4	−15, −15

Matrix 2.   The stage game for Abreu's game, a Prisoner's Dilemma supplemented with a dominated row and column

port. It is an especially effective regime, since for the particular game, no equilibrium maintains cooperative behavior at a lower discount factor. Matrix 2, from Abreu (1988), is played repeatedly at $t = 1, 2, 3, \ldots$ with a discount factor δ. Each time, the players choose among three levels of competition, Low, Medium, or High. The matrix is a 2×2 Prisoner's Dilemma game with an added third move. Choosing Low corresponds to cooperation in a normal Prisoner's Dilemma, Medium is defection, and the new High level is an especially uncooperative move. Competing at the High level is so intense that it is dominated by the other two moves. On that account, this move would appear to do no good, but it will turn out to be important as a part of a punishment threat.

An equilibrium is defined by specifying each player's strategies, and here this is done indirectly, by defining *paths of play*. In Abreu's definition, a path of play is a sequence stating the outcome at each stage. Here three paths are necessary to give the equilibrium: the equilibrium path, which the players are supposed to start on, and two punishment paths, one for each player, which they move to following a player's unilateral deviation from the equilibrium path. A player's punishment path is also started if the player deviates unilaterally from a punishment path, either as the punisher or the violator. A punishment path requires certain moves from both the punisher and the violator—the latter must take a role in his or her own punishment. The motivation to cooperate in one's own punishment arises because the path is especially aversive at the beginning, so the violator would rather stay on it than restart it. The simplicity of Abreu's approach is that it does not tailor the punishment to the offense but gives one punishment that serves for all deviations. It is so effective because the punishment is the most severe one that is still credible.[11]

---

11. Fight-and-Forget has this property to some degree, since if either player balks at the mutual Defect outcome, the game lingers in an unresolved state until a mutual defection.

The equilibrium is then as follows.

> Players start on the *equilibrium path*, which is the series of outcomes when both play Low forever, giving the stream of payoff pairs: (10,10), (10,10), (10,10), $\cdots$
>
> If the Row player deviates unilaterally from the current path, players implement *Row's punishment path*, $(-4,5)$, (3,15), (3,15), (3,15) $\cdots$
>
> If the Column player deviates unilaterally from the current path, they implement *Column's punishment path*, $(5,-4)$, (15,3), (15,3), (15,3) $\cdots$
>
> Joint deviations are ignored—the current path is continued.

The two-phase character of the punishment paths, with an initial severe punishment and a second part that continues indefinitely, is somewhat like Prisoner's Dilemma's Fight-and-Forget equilibrium, except that there is no forgetting. To make the punishment more powerful, a deviation has permanent consequences. This equilibrium holds for discount factor $\delta \geq \frac{4}{7}$, and, Abreu shows, no other equilibrium does better. Using the new row and column makes the difference. If one were to ignore them and treat the game as a 2×2 Prisoner's Dilemma, cooperation could be maintained only down to $\delta = \frac{5}{8}$ by use of the Grim Strategy. The particular punishment paths are *optimal penal codes*, in Abreu's vocabulary. The paths are defined so that a player has an incentive to stay on the current path at any point. As figure 29 shows, there are five norms and each one draws support from one or more of the others, so the equilibrium is a full normative regime. In this example, a normative regime is used to produce maximum cooperation.

Moral Authority

An important question for peace and justice involves normative change. Norms against slavery, racism, biological weapons, and other evils were not around from the start but developed. Other norms have disappeared, like those against submarine attacks on merchant ships or the bombing of civilian targets (Legro 1997). Some mechanisms of normative change are precedent (Kier and Mercer 1996), argumentation (Crawford 1993), changing influences originating in culture (Legro 1997), and the self-serving definition of the norms by the hegemonic state. The preceding model suggests another mechanism: an actor gains normative prestige by good behavior and can then specify further norms.

An example of a normative regime in the context of nuclear proliferation shows how this might work. The presentation will be informal, without setting

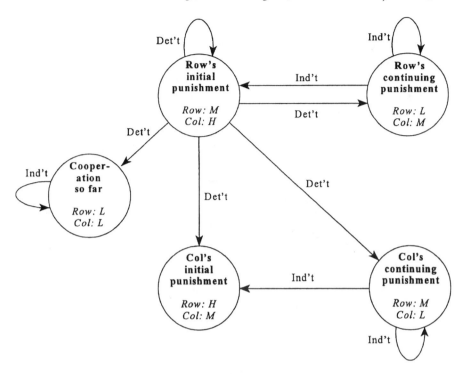

Fig. 29.   Normative regime graph for optimal penal codes in matrix 2. The graph is from Row's viewpoint and assumes Column behaves normatively.

up the full model. States randomly confront situations, and for each situation, the prevailing norm telling the state what to do can be Fuzzy or Clear. States are divided into three groups: those of High, Middle, and Low normative prestige on proliferation. States can move up or down in prestige. They move downward in two ways: for those who are High or Middle, committing a Clear violation puts them into the Low group, and for those in the High group, committing a Fuzzy violation puts them in Middle. States can move upward in prestige in two ways: those in the Low group rise to the Middle by some random process, as long as their recent record has been good on Clear norms. A Middle state moves to High in the same way, as long as its recent record has been good on Clear and Fuzzy norms. The final step is to state the incentives for being in each group. The advantage of being High is that the Highs determine appropriate behavior when any state is confronted with a Fuzzy norm. They get to say what is a violation, and they benefit from having this moral authority. Those in the Low group are pariahs. Some of the situations that states meet are opportunities for pairwise interactions, for example, the sharing of technical information. It is a Clear violation to deal with someone in the Low group.

The key to the analysis of a system like this is the normative regime graph, since it shows an equilibrium's properties as a regime if it is one and shows what is missing if it is not. The examples before this one were unusually tight—in the Prisoner's Dilemma games and in Abreu's game, norms called for a unique action at each situation, and there were no chance events. This example includes these other elements. The normative regime graph must be defined in a different manner, since doing it the previous way would produce something very complicated. First, situations are grouped by ignoring what kind of nation the norm is being applied to. A norm may have different consequences depending on one's prestige group, but the different possibilities are collected in one node. The arrows too are generalized. They now mean that there is some circumstance in which the one norm supports the other (as opposed to the situation in figs. 28 and 29, where it means support at every situation), and they also do not distinguish deterrent from inducement support. The result can be called a *generalized normative regime graph*.

The graph for the proliferation regime is shown in figure 30. It contains five arrows. "Defer to Highs" supports itself because following it sometimes lets a state stay in the High group and keep its moral authority. "Don't Deal with Lows" supports itself since violating it puts a state in the Low group or keeps it there. "Don't Deal with Lows" is supported by "Defer to Highs" since keeping the former norm may allow a state to move into the High group. One cannot say the reverse—that arrow is absent—since not deferring to the authority of the Highs on a Fuzzy norm does not move a state into Low. A state gets motivation to "Follow other Clear norms" (those other than avoiding Lows and deferring to Highs on Fuzzy cases) from the other two norms, and this fact accounts for the final two arrows.[12]

The generalized graph gives a more practical way of looking at support relations and checking for the properties of a normative regime. The activity of constructing it helps one consider the full set of relationships and possibilities.

The benefit of having a High group with this power is that they can sometimes lead the whole group to a better equilibrium. The institution of moral authority can solve the problem of coordination in a group by selecting a leader. At the 1995 conference to renew the Non-Proliferation Treaty, the South African and Canadian representatives became the active leaders (Bunn, personal com-

---

12. One element of moral authority is missing from the model—it does not state that a decision of the Highs on a Fuzzy norm establishes a norm thereafter—but one would expect this to be true by virtue of the precedent set on the occasion.

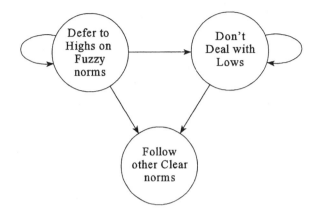

Fig. 30.   Support relationships among norms for a regime based on moral authority and exclusion. The support can be deterrent, inducement, or both, depending on whether the state they apply to is High, Medium, or Low.

munication 1995; Dunn 1995). South Africa had been the first nation ever to give up nuclear weapons and had further prestige for its rejection of apartheid and the biracial character of its delegation. Canada had rejected nuclear weapons in spite of having had the technology to make them. The two countries jointly took on roles of proposing initiatives and lobbying the other delegates. Canada collected signatures on a list of countries willing to extend the treaty, hoping to generate a bandwagon effect, and South Africa led the nonaligned nations to a compromise with the nuclear nations. Their diplomatic skills were important, but their prestige on the relevant issues created an expectation that their leadership would be followed.

Part III
Synthesis

CHAPTER 13

Nuclear Thought-Styles and Nuclear Symbolism

In its issue of November 12, 1945, *Time* made some predictions about the new atomic bomb. One was that countries would not compete in numbers of weapons. "Outproducing the enemy is not much advantage in atomic warfare. Two hundred bombs may be better than 100, but 10,000 is no better than 5,000 because 5,000 would destroy all important targets in a country" (quoted in Bundy 1988, and Jervis 1989). By 1959, however, the United States had several times this number capable of attacking the Soviet Union (Cochran et al. 1989, chap. 2). *Time*'s underestimate was more surprising given the development of hydrogen bombs. These were orders of magnitude more powerful than the original weapons, so that one would assume that fewer would be necessary. The Navy received the smallest share of the buildup, and in 1960 Admiral Arleigh Burke commented on the Air Force's arsenal, "You seldom see a cowboy, even in the movies, wearing three guns. Two is enough" (quoted in Rosenberg 1983, 71).

The importance of understanding the nuclear arms race is more than historical. We must understand why states might want to acquire nuclear weapons in the future. *Time*'s error was the premise that the arms race would be determined by the objective features of the weapons and the logic of strategy and deterrence. This chapter suggests that an important further element was symbolism. Nuclear weapons functioned as symbols in three ways:

as message symbols in response to challenges;
as focal symbols in symbolic competitions over numbers of weapons or the deployment of new technologies;
as focal symbols meant to influence the degree of tension in a crisis.

Symbolic dynamics still cannot explain the nuclear buildup under an objective analysis of nuclear weapons. Symbolism must be combined with an account of nuclear reality as seen by those involved. The chapter starts by discussing organizational "thought-styles," defined as the systematic ways in which a group or an organization "thinks" about its task, as revealed in its statements and actions.[1] The thought-styles define what is admitted as reasonable for discussion in the group versus what is not to be questioned. They are not always false but they are often unsubstantiated, sustained more by organizational forces than by evidence. Members of the organization do not necessarily embrace them privately, but "believe" them in the sense that they follow them in their organizational roles.

This chapter deals with thought-styles and symbolism together because both are based on the same entities—beliefs about others' beliefs. The parties are asking themselves what is in each others' minds, not necessarily what is the objective situation. Since thought-styles and symbols are at the same epistemic level, it seems likely that they would interact, and it will be seen that they do.

The chapter looks at thought-styles and symbolism in the Intermediate-Range Nuclear Forces (INF) episode, the 1980s deployment of intermediate-range missiles in Europe. It was a small copy of the arms race and allows us to examine the dynamics of the whole competition in a more manageable way. The discussion shows that the two phenomena were synergistic—the symbolism made the thought-styles seem more reasonable and the thought-styles prompted the symbolic use of the weapons. Both usually pushed in the same direction: the deployment of more weapons.

Organizational Thought-Styles and Symbolism

Thinking is more liable to stray from reality when there is little historical experience available, as is the case with nuclear operations (Eden 1991). According to March and Simon (1958, 165), organizations "absorb" uncertainty and turn it into fact: "the particular categories and schemes of classification [the organization] employs are reified, and become, for members of the organization, attributes of the world rather than mere conventions."

Organizations also tend to generate unrealistic thought-styles when they are facing impossible or unacceptable objectives. An organization involved with

---

1. Eden uses this term (1990), following Mary Douglas and Ludwig Fleck. Related ideas in the military organization context have received various names. Snyder (1984) speaks of the "cult of the offensive," and Travers (1984, 1992) analyzes the "mental escape hatches" used to preserve the doctrine of offensive superiority before World War I, despite the evidence. Eden also speaks of "organizational frames" (forthcoming) and the "imaginary battlefield" (1991) on which nuclear war is planned. Compared to allied concepts like belief systems, heuristics (Kanwisher 1989), or intuitive deterrence theories (DeNardo 1995), these emphasize the organizational aspect.

nuclear weapons is frustrated by a basic truth: their military use could serve no beneficial purpose. A military organization has traditionally held the duty of defending its country, but in a nuclear conflict it would be called on to take the lives of millions of civilians and to do this to no end, since deterrence would already have failed. Political uses of nuclear weapons, typically involving threats, are more plausible than military ones, but are still problematic. Nuclear weapons can deter an adversary from using its own nuclear weapons against one's own country, but the United States wished to do more, to protect its interests in Europe and elsewhere. Its continuing problem was that the threat to use nuclear weapons for this purpose lacked credibility.[2]

The organizational thought-styles around the arms race fell into four classes:

> treating nuclear weapons as if they were conventional weapons;
>
> using criteria to evaluate nuclear plans that were overly simple and contrary to the evidence;
>
> staying systematically vague about one's nuclear policy, its relationships to one's goals, and the consequent criteria of sufficiency for one's weapons;
>
> cultivating and stressing the role of "irrationality" in nuclear planning, that is, adopting the attitude that either one's country benefits by projecting its belief in a distorted version of nuclear reality, or that the adversary or third parties hold such beliefs, so one must follow their expectations.

Conventionalization

The first group of thought-styles involves *conventionalization,* the tendency to think that nuclear weapons work the same way that regular weapons do. The term was introduced by Morgenthau (1976) and elaborated upon by Jervis (1984, 1989), Kull (1985, 88), and Glaser (1991). One of its subtenets is that *the essence of nuclear war is the destruction of the other's weapons.* One needs fast, accurate missiles to "take out" the enemy's missiles and their supporting systems. The idea is seen in "nuclear exchange" models, which typically calculate the

---

2. The discussion will focus on the American way of thinking, since much more information is available. It would be more accurate to say that there are several American ways of thinking. The image of deterrence and war projected in a presidential speech is different from that in the journal writings of a defense expert, which is different from the criteria by which an air force officer assigns weapons to targets. A typical thought-style spans these groups but takes slightly different forms in each.

number of warheads destroyed but not population deaths. The official and semiofficial literature estimates the consequences of a war in terms of "post-exchange equivalent megatonnage," and so on, and it is hard to find assessments of human losses. What has been published seems understated (Glaser 1991). This thought-style comes into conflict with the idea that the basis of peace is deterrence, since taken together the two propositions would imply that each side is deterred more by losing its missiles than its society.

In line with conventionalization is the *downplaying of fire and radiation*. In official analyses, nuclear weapons are treated as explosives. The Arsenal Exchange Model, the most widely used computer program to simulate nuclear war, drops radiation and fire and concentrates on blast. Eden (forthcoming) argues that this tendency derives from organizational factors rather than any unimportance or unpredictability of fire effects. The experience of the U.S. Air Force during World War II established certain mental categories about how weapons cause damage, and nuclear weapons were fitted into these. Studies of fire destruction were not done because thinking on nuclear war did not need them; conversely, nuclear planning could rationalize ignoring fire on the grounds that so little was known about it.

A third tenet of conventionalization is that *a necessary component of nuclear strategy is defense.* It has promoted the drive to deploy ballistic missile defenses beyond their promise of effectiveness, as well as the emphasis on "damage limitation." The *primacy of control over lack of control* is a fourth aspect of conventionalization. The major nuclear threats would not be believable without a chance factor (Brams and Kilgour 1988), but officially, chance is downplayed. Statements on Intermediate-Range Nuclear Forces (INF), to be quoted later, concealed the importance of chance under deterministic-sounding talk about "links," "coupling," and "flexible response."

Thought-styles are often synergistic, and deemphasizing fire and radiation fits with the tenet that missiles attack missiles, since blast is the main way to destroy a hardened underground silo. Deemphasizing fire and radiation promotes the understatement of civilian deaths, and along with the primacy of control over chance, it fits with the image of nuclear war as a duel of military forces.

Simplifying the Objective

Nuclear thinking typically hedges about the goals of war, so heuristic guides must be constructed to set weapons procurement. These are often simple rules and a common kind is an *index of equivalence.* During the Cold War charts were regularly presented to Congress showing the relative numbers of submarine missiles or nuclear warheads or time trends in these numbers (O'Neill 1988). Officials proclaimed goals of "essential equivalence," assessed the military "balance," and worried about bomber and missile "gaps." The problem is that relative size is not a valid measure of effectiveness (O'Neill 1992). For some missions, a smaller force than the adversary's is adequate, but for others, the force must be much larger. Usually the equivalence was judged by numbers of weapons held, or in more sophisticated analyses like Nitze's (1976, 1976–77) it was defined by weapons left after a nuclear exchange or by relative damage done (Salmon, Sullivan, and van Evera 1989; Kanwisher 1989). This thought-style was embodied in U.S. law, when the 1972 Jackson amendment called for arms negotiations that "would not limit the United States to levels of intercontinental strategic forces inferior to the limits provided for the Soviet Union."

The arms competition was also simplified by *zero-sum thinking,* the notion that in a war adversaries hold no common interests, that what is bad for them is good for us. This is in line with the win/lose vocabulary of the WAR-AS-A-GAME metaphor (chap. 2). It precludes the idea that both sides could mutually benefit by avoiding disastrous losses. At an intellectual level, officials may realize that there can be no victory in a meaningful sense, but the notion of winning is in their vocabulary and creeps back into their thinking. Harold Brown as secretary of defense wrote in the 1982 *Annual Report,* "an improved relative balance would appear to be a minimum condition of 'victory'" (Brown 1982). The "Nitze scenario," discussed subsequently, and many computer models of nuclear war endowed the participants with strictly competitive goals, and weapons were allocated to maximize differences or ratios after the nuclear exchange (O'Neill 1987; a Soviet example is cited by Meyer and Almquist 1985). Some officials switched to a vocabulary that suggested the zero-sum game metaphor without using it explicitly—instead of "winning," they spoke of "prevailing," a usage favored in the early 1980s, or "dominating," or terminating the war "on favorable terms."

A final simplification is to *deploy weapons in numbers set by precedent.* Obsolescent armaments are replaced by newer ones in the same quantity. The rule cannot be applied for a new kind of weapon, so this case makes it especially obvious that the size is not based on analysis and calculation. As ICBMs were introduced, General Thomas Power, commander in chief of the Strategic Air Command, suggested to President Kennedy that 10,000 missiles were required (Enthoven and Smith 1971). Robert McNamara chose 1,000, and this has been roughly the number in place from the 1960s to the end of the Cold War. York (1970) commented that the size of the ICBM force was determined by the digits that evolution put on the human hand. More precise calculations for a new kind of weapon were given by Army Lieutenant General James Gavin in his appearances before the Joint Committee on Atomic Energy in 1956 and 1957. He stated that the army would need 151,000 nuclear weapons (Schwartz 1995). The numbers that were actually deployed have still not been revealed, but from the 1960s until the INF Treaty they seemed to have remained fairly constant at about 7,000 (Daalder 1991). The size level of various elements of the nuclear arsenal stabilized as the years passed, and the arms competition switched to a qualitative one. When part of the U.S. intercontinental ballistic missile force was given multiple warheads, the total warheads roughly doubled, but the number of missiles stayed constant. The level came not from any analysis of real needs but from simple precedent.

Systematic Vagueness about Plans, Goals, and Their Relationship

A further thought habit avoids specifics about plans or goals or the ways in which the plans would promote the goals. When a country is planning its conventional forces, it identifies possible military objectives, such as seizing territory, repelling an attack, or making an attack too costly for the adversary, and it designs its forces accordingly. A statement of the objective in a nuclear war is hard to find. As secretary of defense in the Kennedy administration, Robert McNamara took a step in that direction by specifying what would count as unacceptable damage to the Soviet Union—the loss of 20–25 percent of its population and half its economic potential. His initiative was disdained in military circles, and his successors have avoided precision.[3] Salmon, Sullivan, and van Evera (1989, 200) summarize the goal statements of later secretaries of defense from their annual reports and pronouncements on strategic policy.

> Melvin Laird sought "an adequate strategic nuclear capability," and a "sufficiency" of overall military capability "adequate to prevent us and our allies from being coerced"; James Schlesinger required "the selectivity and flexibility to respond to aggression in an appropriate manner" and "options other than suicide or surrender" that would "shore up deterrence across the entire spectrum of risk"; Donald Rumsfeld required a force that could "survive a first strike, penetrate the enemy's defenses, and destroy a designated set of targets," which he did not otherwise specify; Harold Brown required "the capability to frustrate any ambition that an enemy might at-

---

3. His criterion for a level of destruction lived on among Soviet strategists, who dubbed it a "McNamara unit" or simply "one McNamara" (Horgan 1989).

tempt to realize with his strategic nuclear forces" and "the capability to respond realistically and effectively to an attack on a variety of levels." . . .
Caspar Weinberger posited that American forces must enable American
leaders to "terminate the conflict on terms favorable to the forces of freedom, and re-establish deterrence at the lowest possible level of violence."

All the criteria except Rumsfeld's are thoroughly empty. In the tradition of
vacuity, Secretary William Perry and many other officials have used the formula
in President Clinton's July 1994 *National Security Strategy:* "We will continue to
maintain nuclear forces of sufficient size to hold at risk a broad range of assets
valued by such [hostile] political and military leaders."

Calculated vagueness also permeates discussions of how a nuclear war
would be fought. A fundamental question was whether the United States would
attempt to strike first, or launch its missiles after warning of an immediate attack, or wait until nuclear explosions had given unquestionable confirmation of
a strike. This matters for the types of weapons procured and the plans made, but
it is hard to find consistent analyses of any case. The degree of vagueness about
it should depend on how close the forum of discussion is to those doing the operational details. At the most public level, there is little ambiguity: the policy is
a second strike—U.S. nuclear forces are for deterrence by retaliation. The milieu of defense intellectuals and concerned politicians, however, recognizes that
many weapons have "fast hard-target kill capability"; they are designed to destroy other missiles in silos, not empty silos or cities. In these circles the ambiguity is greater: the question of preemption-versus-retaliation is downplayed.

Higher officials sometimes face a mixed audience of citizens and specialists, and they regularly use an equivocal phrasing: that the United States means
to "hold at risk" the other's weapons. The 1988 *National Security Strategy of the
United States* (White House 1988) stated that INF's purpose was to "serve as a
link to U.S. strategic forces. NATO aircraft will continue to have the capability
to hold at risk a broad range of targets, including those within the Soviet homeland." The phrase appears in recent versions of the document (White House
1996). In the context of global war, the classified but leaked 1989 *National Military Strategy of the Joint Chiefs of Staff* (Tyler 1992) stated that in a nuclear war,
"United States forces will seek out and destroy Soviet naval forces and be prepared to conduct attacks against the Soviet homeland. . . . Our forces will hold
at risk those assets that the Soviet Union would need to prevail in nuclear conflict and dominate in a post war world." In a war of that intensity, one would expect that military actions would be pursued with full vigor, but "holding" Soviet weapons "at risk" combines the tones of doing something and doing
nothing. It would seem to be the worst choice, since it would increase the

Soviet incentive to preempt. The expression is attractive, however, because it allows equivocation over the timing of the launch of the U.S. weapons, part of the planned vagueness in nuclear thinking.

This equivocation would be resolved, one would expect, at the operational level, that is, within the groups that actually target nuclear weapons. They have to know whether their missiles are launched before, during, or after a Soviet attack, so as to know whether certain U.S. weapons would be available for use in the plan and whether Soviet missiles would be in their silos to be struck. To a large extent it has been resolved there, but the resolution seems more a function of organizational procedure than national goals. By the end of the 1970s, the working assumption was effectively a launch on warning of an attack (Blair 1993), to avoid the destruction of command and control. However, planning continues to show the marks of ambiguity over launch timing. There are not three distinct scenarios for a first, simultaneous, or second strike with different schedules and targets for the weapons in each. Basically, there has been only one plan, the SIOP (Single Integrated Operational Plan), and the concepts it uses allow the equivocation on launch timing (Eden 1990). One is *prelaunch survivability* (PLS) which measures the availability of a U.S. missile for use in the SIOP, but in spite of the name, it is not the conditional probability of the missile surviving given an attack. It is the probability that the missile will be available, either because it has survived or because it was not attacked at all. Targeters do not calculate PLS values themselves by weighting the two possibilities; the numbers come to them from outside their organization. *Damage expectancy* (DE) is the criterion of success of the SIOP, a measure of how effective it is as a whole. It gives the SIOP credit for the destruction of a silo, regardless of whether there is a missile in it. The "empty hole problem" is discussed among targeters, but the organizational product, the SIOP, is generated in a way that avoids the question of launch timing. The SIOP is fully specific in terms of what weapons go where, as one would expect, but its relationship to strategic goals is unclear. This disconnection is easier because the makers of policy are separated from its implementers. They communicate through concepts like PLS and DE which do not reflect actual goals.

Cultivating Irrationality in One's Own Group
and Imputing It to the Adversary

The final nuclear thought-style is the toleration of and emphasis on irrationality.[4] It comes in two variants. "Second-level irrationality" acknowledges the er-

---

4. Here "irrationality" means bad judgment, not necessarily a deviation from the rules of decision or game theory. As discussed in appendix A, a person may follow probability theory yet have bizarre beliefs about the world.

ror of some beliefs and thought-styles about nuclear war but suggests that the adversary believes them, so our side must play along. "Third-level irrationality," more sophisticated, suggests both sides are sensible, but that the adversary does not know that for sure. We must feign irrationality to induce a proper degree of caution from the adversary.

In 1983, President Reagan appointed the Scowcroft Commission to survey strategic nuclear matters. As part of an argument for adding one hundred MX missiles, its broad policy section concluded,

> In a world in which the balance of strategic nuclear forces could be isolated and kept distinctly set apart from all other calculations about relations between nations and the credibility of conventional military power, a nuclear imbalance would have little importance unless it were so massive as to tempt an aggressor to launch nuclear war. But the world in which we must live with the Soviets is, sadly, one in which their own assessments of these trends, and hence their calculations of overall advantage, influence heavily the vigor with which they exercise their power. (President's Commission on Strategic Forces 1983, 5)

The commission comes close to explicitly recognizing the military uselessness of nuclear weapons but says that we must worry about the strategic nuclear balance after all because the Soviets believe in it. It does not explain how the Soviet Union could be so irrational, with its scientific cadres and long experience testing nuclear weapons. Perhaps the Soviet Union could be that irrational—I have argued that much of the U.S. perspective is—but it takes mental acrobatics to attribute these errors to the adversary and ignore the degree to which the commission's own government embraces them as reasons to build arms. Another version of the argument has neutrals and one's allies holding that the nuclear balance matters. It is feared that they will shift to the other side unless the United States accommodates their misconceptions (Kull 1985, 1988; Jervis 1989).

Another mode of cultivating nuclear irrationality fits with Herman Kahn's idea that in a Chicken game it helps to "look a little crazy." This is the rationality of perceived irrationality. Kull (1988) interviewed U.S. defense officials and found many taking this line to support the nuclear buildup. The difference between the two modes can be clarified by some formalism. Suppose that "$B_U t$" and "$B_S t$" mean that the United States and the Soviet Union, respectively, believe a certain nuclear truth t. The proposition t might mean that the nuclear balance is unimportant in itself, as the Scowcroft Report implies. Its negation is written "f", for "fallacy." One can then generate statements of beliefs about beliefs: "$B_U B_S t$" means that the United States believes that the Soviet Union believes t.

The simpler version of the rationality of nuclear irrationality is shown in table 5. Under each report are the statements that it expresses directly or implies. The U.S. commission declared something about the external world, that the nuclear balance is really irrelevant ("t"), and the assumption of its sincerity implies also that the commission believes this, $B_U t$. The quoted section of the report implies its belief the Soviet Union believes the fallacy, $B_U B_S f$. The irrationality here is "second level," because f enters only at the second level of beliefs. First-level irrationality would be a report propounding f.

The Scowcroft Commission left open whether the Soviet Union saw the United States as holding to t or f—it did not take a stand on $B_S B_U t$ versus $B_S B_U f$. Doing so would have confronted the question of whether the Soviet Union was simply posturing, perhaps following the advice of a Soviet Scowcroft Commission. If the Scowcroft Commission had chosen between second-level beliefs the symmetry of the situation would have become apparent. It would have been clearer that the proper response was not to add more missiles but to convince the Soviet Union that the United States was realistic about nuclear war.

The next version (table 6) describes Kahn's rationality of irrationality. It starts imputing irrationality at the third level. The United States thinks the Soviet Union thinks that the United States believes in the importance of the balance: $B_U B_S B_U(f)$.

This account of nuclear irrationality has involved interactions between countries but the dynamic can operate within an organization. It would be difficult for the heads of the organization to proclaim t to the members but f to the external world, so actively or silently, they encourage the fallacy. This fact influences the epistemic interactions of the members, who feel they must not contradict the fallacy or their credibility will suffer among the others who believe it. This would be the organizational version of second-level irrationality. Or the third-level model might be operating: I am sure that everyone knows the truth t, but with no one

TABLE 5.   Beliefs and Metabeliefs for Second-Level Irrationality

	Scowcroft Commission	Hypothetical Soviet Commission	
Higher-level beliefs	$\cdots$	$\cdots$	
Second-level beliefs	$B_U B_S f$	$B_S B_U f$	← Attributed Irrationality
First-level beliefs	$B_U t$	$B_S t$	← Attributed Rationality
External world	t	t	

TABLE 6.   Beliefs and Metabeliefs for Third-Level Irrationality

	Hypothetical American Commission	Hypothetical Soviet Commission	
Higher-level beliefs	$\cdots$	$\cdots$	
Third-level beliefs	$B_U B_S B_U f$	$B_S B_U B_S f$	← Attributed Irrationality
Second-level beliefs	$B_U B_S t$	$B_S B_U t$	Attributed Rationality
First-level beliefs	$B_U t$	$B_S t$	
External world	t	t	

saying it out loud, I am not sure that they know that they all know it. I had better avoid openly advocating *t*, since each other member would perceive my credibility to have fallen in the eyes of the rest and would treat me accordingly.[5]

Imputing irrationality is not a nuclear fallacy per se, but it facilitates and amplifies other thought-styles like conventionalization. It protects them from contrary evidence and promotes them as social facts, internationally and within organizations. No one dares to say what everyone knows, and their expectation of the group's reaction induces all to become enforcers of the false belief.

The INF Debate

A particular episode shows the role of symbolism and challenges in interaction with these thought-styles. The intermediate-range nuclear forces debate about the 1980s deployment of U.S. cruise and ballistic missiles in Europe was the nuclear arms competition on a smaller scale.[6] It included the same push to acquire weapons whose use could never promote a practical end, and the same choice

5. The tables indicate the same thing as the interactive belief matrices of chapter 7: that common knowledge is limited. The former exemplify what has become known as the "syntactic" approach, which expresses belief as sentences, as opposed to the latter's "semantic" approach, which uses a set of probabilities. The syntactic approach is somewhat easier to understand here, but the latter allows us to talk about degrees of belief and common belief. A semantic version of the model of nuclear irrationality is example 4 in appendix B.

6. INF's political history is discussed in Thomson (1984), Talbott (1985), Garthoff (1983b, 1994), Risse-Kappen (1988), Nolan (1991), and Eichenberg (1993). Dean (1987) and Talbott (1988) emphasize the negotiations, and Jervis (1984, chap. 4), Freedman (1986), and Peters (1990) the strategic logic.

of fast, accurate, first-strike-capable missiles, in spite of a proclaimed policy of deterrence. The goal was the same as a major one of the overall arms race, to protect Western Europe. Compared to the strategic weapons competition, however, the INF decision was more deliberate and explicit. The larger competition took for granted that the last generation of weapons had to be "modernized," but the INF missiles had no immediate predecessors, and their advocates had to make fuller arguments. Considerable detail is given on these arguments here to show that the decision was based more on symbolism than on objective military factors.

From the start of the Cold War, the Western concern was protecting noncommunist Europe from a Soviet invasion. NATO officials held the view that the Warsaw Pact armies could launch a conventional war and win quickly. Although this now is seen as overly pessimistic, it was NATO's central assumption and generated a continual search for solutions. The 1968 document MC14/3 set the doctrine as "flexible response": if there were a conventional invasion and NATO's conventional forces could not stop it, NATO would initiate nuclear use on some level below strategic weapons (Legge 1983; Daalder 1991). Policy pronouncements did not specify the form of first nuclear use, but it might have been a demonstration shot, or tens of weapons sent against a few battlefield locations, or hundreds across the whole front, or the destruction of Warsaw Pact rear echelons, or strikes inside Soviet territory. European leaders expressed hope that nuclear use might prompt Soviet leaders to reconsider and withdraw their forces, but this was not the official purpose of flexible response. Its agreed aim was to induce a Soviet expectation that a conventional war in Europe would escalate. Foreseeing this, the adversary would have only the alternatives of peace or Armageddon.

Western planners worried whether the flexible response threat was credible enough. It called on the United States to initiate or allow a nuclear strike that might lead to its own destruction. Would the United States continue to follow such a policy when its aim of deterrence had already failed? In the 1970s, the Soviet Union increased NATO's credibility worries by installing new SS-20 missiles aimed at Western Europe. These had three warheads, were more accurate and longer range than their predecessors, were quick to prepare and launch, and were less vulnerable to attack, as they were based on trucks. Germany's prime minister Helmut Schmidt was particularly alarmed, and in 1979, NATO's Nuclear Planning Group proposed a response, that new U.S. missiles would be sent to Europe. West Germany would receive 108 Pershing II ballistic missiles, and 464 ground-launched cruise missiles would be shared by Belgium, England, Germany, Italy, and the Netherlands. This announcement, in turn, alarmed Soviet leaders. NATO already had shorter-range nuclear missiles in place, and NATO aircraft could carry nuclear weapons to Moscow, but if the new deployment plan went through, for the first time since the Cuban crisis, nuclear missiles based in Europe could reach the Soviet capital. The short flight time of the Pershings, in particular, threatened to eliminate the Soviet command and control centers in a preemptive strike, before they could implement retaliation.

The salience of the issue increased with Ronald Reagan's election in 1980. He projected a hawkish, impetuous image to the European public, and the majority came to oppose the INF plan (Den Oudsten 1985; Adler and Wertmen 1980). To undercut the protest, the White House proposed a bilateral ban on the Pershings, cruise missiles and SS-20s (Talbott 1985, 1988). The Soviet Union denounced the U.S. offer in harsh language, arguing that it ignored the British and French missiles and other NATO nuclear systems near its borders. When the first INF missiles arrived in 1983, it moved its own missiles and submarines forward in symbolic counterdeployments and withdrew its representatives from the major arms control negotiations. However, when Mikhail Gorbachev ascended to office he made significant concessions, and in December 1987 he and Ronald Reagan signed the INF Treaty to remove both sides' intermediate-range nuclear missiles and their short-range ones as well. Dismantling the Pershings and cruise missiles started before their deployment was finished. In spite of rumors about SS-20s obtained by Chechen rebels, the best evidence is that the only remaining INF missiles are one U.S. Pershing and one Soviet SS-20 standing side by side at the Smithsonian Institution (fig. 31).

Rationales for the INF Missiles

There were several prominent justifications for the INF missiles. They are grouped according to whether they involved a symbolic element.

> *Nonsymbolic military rationales*
>   promoting flexible response or "escalation dominance";
>   "coupling" a European war to a global one by reducing control over escalation.
> *Nonsymbolic political rationales*
>   providing NATO with a bargaining chip to achieve an arms control agreement;
>   for European nations, maintaining their normative prestige in NATO by fulfilling the duties of membership;
>   reasserting U.S. leadership of the alliance.

Fig. 31.   The sole remaining SS-20 and Pershing II at the National Air and Space Museum, Smithsonian Institution. (Copyright Smithsonian Institution.)

Symbolic rationales
"coupling" a European war to a global one by decreasing crisis stability; demonstrating alliance solidarity in response to the challenge of the SS-20s;
improving the overall nuclear balance.

Military Rationales: Escalation Dominance
and Flexible Response

NATO's concept of flexible response was close to the broader concept of *escalation dominance* (Kahn 1965, 290). In a war, the side that would face a worse military situation at a higher rung of the escalation ladder would be induced to back down now. It was perceived that with its SS-20s, the Soviet Union had seized escalation dominance at the level of a European nuclear exchange, and in the face of a Soviet conventional invasion, NATO would have to yield. More than that, foreseeing its prospects in a war, it would have to yield to Soviet diplomatic threats. "Flexible response," the common expression for this logic in NATO circles, was described in a U.S. State Department INF rationale paper (1979) as

> designed to enable NATO to make an appropriate response to any level of action initiated by an aggressor, from demonstrations of force to full-scale hostilities. . . . If NATO has only the capability to threaten retaliation that is disproportionate to any Soviet initiative, NATO runs the risk that the Soviets may believe that NATO would not carry out its threat. Because of the danger of this Soviet misperception, NATO's strategy of deterrence and defense requires a force structure capable of military responses along a continuum, with credible options at each point and strong links among conventional, theater nuclear and strategic nuclear forces. (U.S. Department of State 1979, 1–2)

The difficulty with this argument is that even if NATO had a relative advantage at the higher level, it would not have a credible threat to escalate to that level. The relevant comparison is not one's own versus the adversary's cost from going to the next level. It is one's cost from yielding at this level versus one's cost from going on to the next level. Escalating to the detonation of nuclear weapons in Europe would not have been a credible threat.[7] If it sounded plausible, this

---

7. Even if the threat to use nuclear weapons was not credible, its probability was not zero—a crisis could have flown out of control. However, that is another argument, to be considered on its own. In the terms of flexible response, escalation would be a deliberate move.

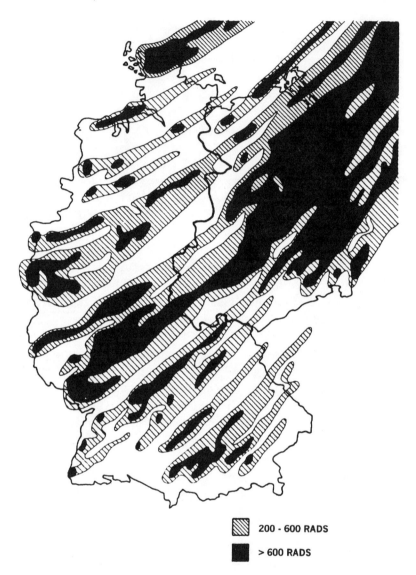

200 - 600 RADS

> 600 RADS

Fig. 32.   An initial nuclear use in Germany. Sample fallout pattern with 200-kiloton groundbursts on 171 targets in East and West Germany. (From Arkin, von Hippel, and Levi 1982.)

was only because of the abstract language of the debate. Examining its actual consequences, Arkin, von Hippel, and Levi (1982) estimated the destruction from an early use of a small fraction of the nuclear weapons held in Europe (fig. 32). The dark areas indicate doses of 600 rads or more, and under wartime conditions, the authors estimated, an exposure of 450 rads would prove lethal to about one-half the population. As horrible as past wars have been, none approached this magnitude of destruction. A U.S. president launching the INF missiles would be risking the same fate for the United States.

The phrase "flexible response" seems to draw on a premise that more options are always better than fewer, but this can be false when the other side is aware of one's new options. In Herman Kahn's vignette of highway Chicken, a driver wins by visibly eliminating an option—by throwing the steering wheel out the window. In fact, what the situation calls for is *inflexibility*, for making the escalation move a forced or an automatic one. Such considerations lead to the idea of coupling, the justification discussed next.

Military Rationales: Coupling by Loss of Control

Flexible response was prominent in official rationales for INF, but it was not a core motive. Raymond Garthoff, former U.S. ambassador to the Soviet Union wrote (1994, 552),

> Despite genuine Soviet concern over the short-time-to-target Pershing II missiles in particular, the INF deployment was not strongly supported in Washington or in NATO for its military value. Rather it was seen initially—in Europe, and in Washington by both the Carter and Reagan administrations—as a step to shore up alliance unity. It was also seen, especially in Europe, as a step to reinforce deterrence by "coupling" American conventional and strategic forces.

The term *coupling*, which was common in NATO circles, is a conditional probability, the likelihood that a Soviet attack on Western Europe with conventional weapons would become a global nuclear war. President Reagan (*New York Times*, October 22, 1981, quoted in Jervis 1984, 91) declared, "The essence of United States nuclear strategy is that no aggressor should believe that the use of nuclear weapons in Europe could reasonably be limited to Europe." According to their proponents, the INF weapons would make escalation more automatic.

The logic of coupling is at odds with flexible response—flexible response requires control of escalation and coupling requires the absence of it. The coupling argument was the more compelling one, since it recognized the importance of chance in a nuclear war and responded to the problem of incredible threats. It tended to intrude even in statements meant to be promoting flexible response. The passage from the State Department rationale paper, quoted previously, ended on an apparent reversal of its logic: "NATO's strategy of deterrence and defense requires a force structure capable of military responses along a continuum, with credible options at each point, *and strong links among conventional, theater nuclear and strategic nuclear forces* [my emphasis]." "Strong links" means that one level of warfare should lead to the next—a conventional war in Europe is just first in a chain. (Other metaphors were a "slippery slope," or a "seamless web of deterrence," and their tension with flexible response is also apparent.) Earlier in the quoted paragraph, the INF missiles were promoted as avoiding this situation—for credibility NATO needed responses that were not "disproportionate" to a Soviet initiative. If intermediate-range nuclear weapons would lead up the ladder anyway, how are they a limited response and so more credible?

Does coupling make sense by itself, apart from its tension with flexible response? Its factual premises seem plausible: surely there is great uncertainty when emotions are triggered by war or when the complex human system for controlling nuclear weapons is activated for the first time. Its difficulty as a reason for INF is that it is double edged. Adding the intermediate stage of INF gives NATO a response to a Soviet invasion that is less harmful to it than global war. However, the response is also less harmful to the Soviet Union, and to this extent it decreases the overall expected cost of an invasion. There is some doublethink in this rationale for INF. NATO would be more likely to launch the missiles because INF use is short of global war, but the Soviet Union would be no less fearful of invading because INF would lead to a global war. In fact, it is not clear whether the new option would have increased or decreased deterrence overall.[8]

Nonsymbolic Political Rationales: Providing Bargaining Chips for Arms Control Negotiations

Especially at the start of the debate, the weapons were promoted as chips to induce an arms control agreement in which the Soviet Union would give up its SS-20s. At the beginning this policy was called the "dual track" decision: simultaneously negotiating and proceeding with deployment. As the episode developed the arms control motive receded. It gained credence again in hindsight, after the INF Treaty was signed, but during the actual debate, before the middle 1980s, no one imagined the foreign policy changes initiated by Gorbachev in particular or his willingness to overlook British and French missiles and accept the extensive verification that led to the treaty. The bargain that was eventually signed was first made as a political move, a proposal to be rejected (Talbott

---

8. By making further assumptions one can derive more specific probabilities. Nalebuff (1986) and Bobbitt (1988) discuss the irrelevance of adding middle options, and in O'Neill (1989) I derive the conclusion that coupling might help or hurt for the case of semicredible threats, in a model based on Selten's analysis of kidnapping (1977).

1985), and various memoirs confirm that its main aim was to assuage the worries of European factions. Former U.S. secretary of state Cyrus Vance (1983) mentions the arms control notion only as "politically essential to contain expected internal opposition" from other NATO countries, and Brzezinski (1983) omits it entirely in his discussion of INF. Its importance is also put in doubt by the report that the number of INF missiles was set in part to have an attractive force left *after* an arms control treaty (Cartwright and Critchley 1985, 15; Thomson 1984, 610). A final difficulty with the bargaining chip rationale became apparent as negotiations dragged on: As well as providing bargaining chips, the INF missiles were meant to show that NATO could stand up to Soviet pressure, which often took the form of arms control concessions that would eliminate INF. It became important to resist these and proceed with the deployment. New weapons could be bargaining chips or shows of resolve but not both.

Nonsymbolic Political Rationales: Maintaining Legitimacy
by Accepting the Duties of NATO Membership

Maintaining one's prestige and voice in NATO was important and each country felt it must play its part. Even in Canada, for example, in spite of domestic protest officials agreed to a U.S. request to test cruise missiles over their soil. Canada was far from the European front and the missiles were an air-launched variety, different from the NATO deployment, but Canadian officials expressed a desire to prove their "reliability" within NATO, when European governments were under fire for accepting INF missiles (Langille 1990).

Nonsymbolic Political Rationales: Bolstering
U.S. Leadership of the Alliance

One rationale was promoting U.S. leadership in the alliance. Carrying the INF decision through would establish a precedent that would promote a focal point for future disagreements among the members. The argument had weight in Washington, but it was not promoted elsewhere, for obvious reasons.

Symbolic Rationales: Coupling Based on Tension
and Crisis Instability

A variant of the coupling mechanism involves crisis instability, which increases the degree of temptation in a crisis to strike first. Each side deploys weapons that are vulnerable to attack and that can destroy the other's weapons, but only if they are launched first. In the event of a crisis each would feel forced to use its weapons for fear the other was about to do so, following the logic of the Stag Hunt game (chap. 5, appendix B). One rationale for INF held that it added a desirable degree of crisis instability (e.g., Kissinger 1982). The Soviet Union would not dare to start a crisis for fear of the mutual incentives that would be generated. Compared to ideas of coupling, in this mechanism escalating is not viewed as a matter of chance and emotion but rather a considered decision prompted by the situation.

The features of the INF missiles were compatible with this argument. The missiles were compelling targets for the Soviet Union, especially the Pershings, which were seen as threats to Soviet command centers. However, the Pershing and cruise missiles were mobile and meant to be hidden in the European woods, and for that reason they might have increased stability. This would be an undesirable consequence within this logic, so their net contribution to instability was uncertain. The argument's other problem is that NATO's missiles might destabilize other crises, including inadvertent ones. Then it might have been U.S. actions that were constrained. The crisis instability argument for INF was rarely offered publicly, probably because it is hard to sell vulnerability as a merit of a weapons system.

Crisis instability depends on the symbolic concept of crisis tension (chap. 5). Certain details make the war equilibrium more salient, and the players' mutual expectations may then generate it. Just as the U-2 flying over Soviet territory increased tension by its analogy with a full-scale war, the more a European war resembles a global one, the more expected the latter becomes, and therefore the more objectively likely it becomes. The Pershing II had properties of both tactical and strategic missiles (those for battlefield use versus strikes on the Soviet homeland). It took the name of the earlier Pershing I, a clearly "European theater" missile, although it was quite different in appearance and operation and under standard practice would have been given a new name. Like tactical nuclear missiles, it was operated by the U.S. Army, rather than the Air Force, but like intercontinental missiles, it was fully controlled by the United States, not under the dual-key system. Also it was multistage, highly accurate, and could reach Moscow. It could be seen as reasonable for use in a limited European war, but once used, its features might invoke symbolic associations of a global war, increase crisis instability, and so bolster coupling.

Rationales Involving Symbolism: A Response
to the Symbolic Challenge of the SS-20s

Ambassador Garthoff stated that "coupling" was a major motive, but he seemed to be using the term differently from the military sense just discussed. His conception was political. Coupling meant proving alliance solidarity in peacetime in order to convince the Soviet Union that the alliance would stand together in war. The importance of this notion in INF is supported by the central role of the SS-20 missiles. It is well documented that they triggered the INF decision, and this is the only kind of coupling that they threatened. They did not decrease military coupling; in fact, they increased it since they looked and functioned like intercontinental missiles and were based inside the Soviet Union. They were in Soviet hands but this made them no less effective in generating crisis instability, since they blurred the European/global war distinction, just as NATO's strategy aimed for.

On military coupling grounds, therefore, NATO should have welcomed them. NATO did not welcome them, and the reason suggested here is that they were seen as a challenge, a test of alliance solidarity and resolve.[9] Their deployment symbolically called on each NATO member to prove that it would stand with the rest. The audience was the potential adversary, as well as the other NATO states. Willingness to defend one's group is an element of honor and must be proved to one's group and to the adversary. Proving it means making a sacrifice, either paying a cost or running a risk. The cost levied by INF took different forms for the different parties. The United States paid for the weapons and accepted a link that would have increased the danger of its destruction in a war. European leaders paid the political costs of accepting them. The growing unpopularity of the deployment threatened an electoral defeat for several governments and convinced many Europeans, especially young people, that the United States bore the responsibility for the arms race (Russett and DeLuca 1983). Interest in alternative modes of European defense grew, which was an unfortunate development from the establishment's perspective. As the controversy swelled, many advocates felt it was all the more important to go through with the deployment (Lunn 1983). This fits the proof-by-sacrifice model of responding to challenges, which suggests that the missiles were deployed not in spite of their political costs but because of them. One reason for including cruise missiles in the deployment was that their longer range allowed them to be based in NATO countries other than Germany—the sacrifice had to be spread across the alliance.

Except for a few grumblings among German and American hawks, the treaty to eliminate the missiles went ahead smoothly (Nolan 1991; Eichenberg 1993). This is inexplicable from a military coupling rationale—on those

9. In the vocabulary of the INF debate, proving one's solidarity to the NATO alliance was "reassurance," while proving it to the Soviet Union was "showing resolve."

grounds discarding both sides' intermediate missiles and the short-range ones as well was the worst possible option. It left the Warsaw Pact with conventional superiority and widened the tear in the "web of deterrence." However, from the viewpoint of a symbolic challenge the end had already been accomplished by NATO's proven willingness to put the missiles in place. The point had been demonstrated and they could be dismantled.

When a challenge is a verbal one, the response can take different forms as specified by the culture. A symbolic challenge is likely to be answered with a symbol. Secretary of Defense Harold Brown treated the Pershing IIs as a symbolic message in an annual report (1982, 64): "TNF [INF] visibly manifest the U.S. nuclear commitment to NATO and our willingness to use nuclear weapons in the defense of Europe if necessary." In their similarity in form to the SS-20s, they tapped the prototype of answering an aggressive act in kind. The planned total number of missiles, 572, seemed chosen to match the Soviet force. A projection of the Soviet intermediate-range missile force in the mid-1980s had been 750–900 SS-20 warheads on launchers plus 50-odd older missile warheads on launchers (U.S. Department of State 1979), from which perhaps a third could be subtracted as they would be deployed in Asia.

Another symbolic feature was the missiles' basing on German soil, the territory they would defend. This draws on an element in the GOING-TO-WAR scenario, in which a state assembles forces at the site to be defended. There were other rationales for placing the INF weapons on land, including accuracy and relative cost (Peters 1990, 182–90), but the symbolic message aspect was important. "Missiles based on European territory would be physically and unambiguously identified with European defence; they 'couple' Europe and the United States in an unmistakable fashion" wrote English parliamentarians Cartwright and Critchley (1985).

If NATO saw the SS-20s as a challenge, a natural question is whether the Soviet Union meant them that way. Garthoff (1983b) notes, "Remarkably, no real analysis of the Soviet purposes in deploying the SS-20s was undertaken by the [NATO High Level Group] or any other body in Brussels or Washington (as many key participants have confirmed in interviews)." This phenomenon has been seen before, where an adversary's move provides an opportunity to prove resolve and is not checked for whether it was really sent as a challenge. Holloway (1983) gave a plausible explanation of the Soviet motive, one consistent with Garthoff's judgment (1983a). Since the 1950s, the Soviet Union had targeted Western Europe with intermediate-range SS-4 and SS-5 missiles, but most Western experts saw these as stopgaps until the Soviet Union acquired a force of intercontinental weapons that could reach the United States. This was achieved in the 1960s, but even into the 1970s, the older missiles stayed in place. Western experts interpreted this as inertia, given the low cost of keeping in place what was already there. It was not expected that the intermediate-range missiles would be "modernized." In fact the Soviet Union had always meant to target Western Europe, but difficulties with a solid-fuel design had delayed the newer missiles. The SS-20s were a belated modernization, but NATO took them as a fresh challenge.

Rationales Involving Symbolism: Symbolic Contests
in Armaments

The relative megatonnage held by the United States compared to the Soviet Union was a major worry through the Cold War. Just as nuclear weapons symbolize power, success in the arms race symbolizes superpower hegemony. Critics argued that nuclear weapons should be judged on an absolute level, based on the requirements of deterring an attack, but Kull (1988) and Jervis (1989) cite many examples of officials worrying about the relative level of armaments and how it would be taken by the adversary and other nations.[10] As a contest, it was an odd type, since the goal was not so much to win as to avoid losing.[11]

Contests like this can be often be interpreted as focal symbolism. One example was the U.S./USSR space race, and another was the long-standing competition between Taiwan and the People's Republic of China for diplomatic recognition by other states. Each spent resources trying to raise its own count of embassies and keep the other's down. Often the numbers were treated as the main concern without much regard to the importance of the country, with Taiwan granting foreign aid to small countries like Belize and treating their diplomatic recognition with great fanfare. Both China and Taiwan preserved the competitive nature of the activity, as each was ready to break relations with any country that recognized the other. Like symbolic prenegotiations, the contest can be viewed as a precursor game that influences the outcome of a conflict with greater consequences. Success in the diplomatic recognition contest sets expectations of who will back down later on in a Chicken-like crisis. Getting the support of other countries in the contest maps into getting the support of allies in the important conflict.

---

10. It was not cheap. Schwartz (1995) estimates that the cost to the United States of its nuclear armaments was at least four trillion dollars measured in 1995 dollars, which was more than three times the procurement costs for World War II.

11. The number of INF nuclear warheads would have been only about 6 percent of the U.S. total, and this amount would have been easier to deploy if the United States had done so on its own soil. This was only a secondary explanation for INF.

The symbolic mechanism was significant even in technical analyses of the arms competition, although it was not always made explicit. One analysis especially worth considering is that of Paul Nitze, since he was a definer of U.S. strategy and his argument for a major U.S. buildup (1976, 1976–77) was effective in the campaign that blocked the SALT II arms treaty. The "Nitze scenario" held that by the early 1980s, the Soviet Union would be able to launch a nuclear war and be sure that it would remain one of weapons against weapons. The Soviet Union would be able to strike U.S. land-based missile silos, bomber airfields, and submarine bases but avoid extensive damage to American cities. These cities would then be hostages against U.S. retaliation against the Soviet population. U.S. counterstrikes would have to be directed against Soviet strategic weapons bases, but in doing so the United States would leave the Soviet Union with a great advantage in nuclear holdings. Nitze measured this advantage by the ratio of throw-weights—the total weight of nuclear weapons available for attack by each side's remaining forces—and provided a model to estimate it. This predicament was coming soon, and to avoid it the United States would have to add accurate war-fighting weapons that would be able to retaliate against the Soviet missiles held in reserve.

Nitze's articles became somewhat unspecific at a crucial point, and some critics misunderstood him as suggesting that, should a U.S. president back down on the demand, a Soviet threat to attack would be a credible one. It would clearly not be. However, in fact, as he saw it, the Soviet Union would not need to carry out a strike—the mere prospect would give it a bargaining advantage (1976, 206). With a prospective advantage in throw-weight after a back-and-forth exchange, the Soviet Union would feel free to extend its power through conventional war or by intimidation.[12]

If the Soviet threat to attack is not credible, what would link the post-exchange throw-weight ratio to a successful Soviet expansion? Although Nitze would probably have avoided the word, the mechanism of symbolism seems necessary to complete his account. Winning a contest over prospective post-attack throw-weight would be symbolically winning the war. Negotiations have many equilibria—they are essentially indeterminate, so a throw-weight advantage could in theory establish a focal point in the Chicken game of negotiation over the Soviet sphere of influence, based on the notion that superior military power generally determines who gives in. This argument by no means proves

---

12. Nitze's associate, T. K. Jones, who did the computer calculations for his article, is more explicit about the prenegotiation relevance of the throw-weight balance (Jones and White 1976). He saw the possibility of the Soviet Union facing starvation because of crop failure and using its nuclear superiority to extract food from the West.

that events would proceed that way, only that the concept of symbolic precedent seemed to be implicitly important in Nitze's thinking.

The Interaction of Nuclear Thought-Styles and Nuclear Symbolism

The story of INF is complicated in its details, but its important aspects show a simple pattern. The SS-20s were seen as a challenge that had to be answered for the traditional purposes of warning the adversary and reassuring the group. This was done by matching them—installing missiles similar in form and number. Matching the SS-20s harmed NATO's strategy of coupling, but it seemed militarily appropriate anyway thanks to the thought-style of conventionalization, in which weapons balance off against each other. INF's apparent military rationale was also facilitated by the other nuclear thought-styles of simplifying the objective, keeping vague about one's goals, and cultivating an atmosphere in which appearing irrational can be helpful. The missiles were accepted by many countries in order to send a costly signal. The special role of West Germany, which alone hosted the Pershings, was a symbolic statement that this soil was the front to be defended.

This chapter began by asking whether nuclear weapons induce overbuilding and the analysis concludes that they do. Because it is so difficult to find a military use for them, they are used in symbolic modes. Their military limitations also prompt the generation of odd thought-styles that promote their symbolic uses. The symbolic aspects of their possession and proliferation have been greatly understudied compared to the technological and economic side. (Exceptions are Jervis 1989; Flank 1994; Eyre 1993; Eyre and Suchman 1996; Sagan 1996, 1997.) Compared to other methods of mass destruction, like chemical and biological weapons, nuclear weapons are more amenable to use as symbols. They are more visible and more costly, which by the present arguments are important factors. They are hurled, they strike and blast, and so fit better with the prototype of war and the tradition of manly violence—in contrast with chemical and biological weapons which suggest poisoning. In this symbolic feature nuclear weapons are synergistic with their stereotypical delivery systems, ballistic missiles, which also have a special attraction for those wanting to project an image of power. How to separate the weapons from their seductive symbolism is an important question; this chapter has attempted at least to identify the problem.

CHAPTER 14

Conclusion

The sociologist Erving Goffman, to whom this book owes a debt, looked at everyday social interactions from a strategic viewpoint. While he did not use mathematics, he had a game-theoretic attitude and talked in terms of goals, strategies, and cooperative endeavors. Some commentators have viewed his explanations as disconnected, noting that he would switch from a strategic viewpoint to a metaphor of theater in which people play out a script, or, having discussed the "strategies" of facework, he would change to the language of ritual, where every person is "a sacred object that must be honored" (Manning 1993). He gave no strategic account of why people followed the ritual. This book analyzes symbolism in a way that unites these modes of thinking by showing how culturally expected scripts, rituals, and symbols can be treated within the strategic approach. This chapter summarizes its conclusions on each of the topics.

Symbols

Symbolic messages are more dramatic than verbal ones, but they are not always clearer. The goal of communication is coordinated thinking, so the receiver must decipher the sender's meaning and the sender must choose a symbol that promotes a correct understanding. For reliability the message should be delivered in an established and expected way. Chapter 2 described some past techniques of generating symbolic messages, summarizing about 680 instances from recent international interactions. The data cannot tell whether individual signals were understood correctly, but they show some patterns that symbolic communicators have taken.

Message symbols are based on metaphors, prototypical scenarios, and metonymies. A metaphor, as the word is used here, is a pattern of thought and speech that maps the domain of interest into a more comprehensible one; a metonymy is the selection of a part to represent the whole; and a prototypical scenario is a generally expected script for a certain kind of event. Most of the international symbolism can be accounted for by a fairly short list of metaphors, metonymies, and prototypes. One common metaphor depicts a country as a particular citizen. This often involves a leader who visits another country to show friendship or acknowledge the other's status or who does a specific task to show that some national policy is important. A related metaphor treats a nation's territory as a house, and accordingly, many symbolic events are conducted at national borders. A common prototypical scenario involved preparing for war and it generated some hostile message symbols in the database, like troop deployments or token acts of violence.

A recurrent problem for national leaders is to get one's action noticed as a symbolic message. National leaders often choose an action that is ineffective for any other function but communication, as when Belize offers military support for U.S. operations in Haiti. The common usage is that something is "purely" or "merely" symbolic, but symbols are not ineffective by nature. Ineffectiveness is a cue that alerts the audience to look for a message.

In chapter 3 a message symbol is defined by two requirements. First, it is a communicative act, meaning that the sender intends the receiver to believe or do something by virtue of recognizing that intention. This kind of "reflexive" intention is an element of all communications, in language or not, symbolic or not, so a second condition is added that qualifies certain messages as symbolic: the act is connected to its meaning by being a part selected either from a prototype alone or from a prototype transformed by a metaphor. Nelson Mandela invited his white jailer to his presidential inauguration as a symbolic call for racial reconciliation. Inviting another to a significant personal event—a marriage or a party—is part of the prototypical scenario for reconciliation. Mandela's action was transformed by the metaphor that regards the group as its leader, so its meaning changed from reconciliation between individuals to reconciliation between races.

No sharp line separates symbolic and nonsymbolic messages. When it is used for the first time, a symbol must be decoded through the steps of metaphors, metonymies, and prototypes, but with repetition it can come to be understood more directly by precedent. It then has changed from a symbolic communication to a conventional one. The history of the Gulf War yellow ribbons shows how the practice of wearing colored ribbons moved back and forth along the symbol/convention continuum over the centuries. With repeated use, the symbolic element weakened but it was reinvigorated when the motif was embedded again in some popular song or story. Using it in a plot, especially in a dramatic and commonly known one, associated the symbol with prototypical actions and emotions and allowed the techniques of prototype and metonymy to be used again. The ribbons moved back toward functioning as symbols but with a slightly different meaning than before. Their history shows some advantages of using message symbols instead of conventional communications: they have greater imprecision of meaning, which can be desirable; they can take a more dramatic form; and most important, they acquire associations and values from the prototypical emotions and scenarios to which they have been linked.

A focal symbol is communication without the requirement of a sender—it needs only receivers. Each one knows what the others are concluding from the symbolic event, knows that the others know that, and so on. The focal symbol establishes a focal point, a common expectation of the outcome of a coming game. It does this symbolically by calling a larger class of events to the observers' minds, typically through the mechanism of analogy. The outcome of the game is one member of this class; what makes the outcome focal is the common belief (in a technical sense of beliefs about others' beliefs) that everyone is thinking along the lines of the analogy.

Often focal symbols spring up around collective action problems—an event occurs that gives watchers confidence to act because others will support them. Another type of focal symbolism is symbolic leadership, exemplified by President Reagan's unfortunate visit to the Bitburg cemetery containing graves of some SS officers. In the world's eyes, the focal symbolism prevailed over his insistence that he was only memorializing the tragedy of war. The event shows that message and focal meanings can be in conflict. Other instances of focal symbolism are the struggles over small points preceding negotiations, which are expected to generate self-fulfilling expectations of who will dominate in the real negotiation. Further instances involve symbolic contests leading to expectations of who will back down in a real confrontation.

Another kind of focal symbol involves crisis tension, a shared worry about an imminent war, which itself contributes to the danger. Tension has been absent as an explicit variable in the recent theorizing about crises, but it has been included by implication, since much theory about nuclear strategy and arms control involves reducing crisis instability. This is interpreted here as the manipulation of focal symbolism. An example of a symbolic event generating tension was the inadvertent U-2 flight over the Soviet Union at the height of the Cuban missile crisis. It was a focal symbol, structurally similar to what would happen in a real war, and so increased the mutual expectation of a war and the temptation to strike. A game model shows how this could work.

The model is compared with the everyday metaphor of tension that treats it as physical stress on a string, where the snapping point corresponds to the out-break of war. The metaphor is mostly valid within the model, but it misses one feature of tension—a string responds to present forces, but leaders look ahead to likely future stress in deciding whether to preempt now. The analysis gives a possible rationale for symbolic arms control and confidence-building measures meant to mitigate future crises, and it suggests the importance of "public" events, defined as those whose occurrence renders them not only known by both sides but known to be known, and so on.

Symbolism of all types—message, value, and focal—proliferates at inter-national ceremonies. Like religious rituals, international ceremonies often reaf-firm the social order, and this fact has generated controversy around the sym-bolism of who should attend a ceremony and in what status. The symbolism sometimes functions to add credibility to promises made at ceremonies, by connecting the current commitment with past and future ones made in like circumstances.

Honor, Commitments, and Challenges

Honor, face, prestige, and moral authority determine whose interests are re-spected or who prevails in a confrontation. They are substitutes for violent con-flict, but they often become the causes of conflict when they are fought over for the benefits they yield. They differ according to their bases: honor refers to a quality within the individual as perceived by the group; face is the group's ex-pectation of how everyone else will treat the individual; prestige is the group's perception of its own attitude toward the individual, based on something the person is or did; and moral authority is the group's self-fulfilling expectation that someone who has abided by the group's norms up to now can set future norms.

Chapter 6 works out a theory of honor that fits the patterns found in soci-eties. The purpose is to allow a judgment of whether honor is reproduced among nations. Possessing personal honor means having a certain bundle of traits whose ingredients vary by culture and by gender. For male honor, which is the relevant kind for international relations, the concept usually includes true-ness to one's word when given in a certain context and willingness to defend one's group and avenge wrongs against it.

One trait in honor's bundle is especially interesting theoretically and dis-tinguishes honor from simple virtue. Honor obliges its possessor to show others that he possesses honor. A man who claims to be honorable but to be unconcerned who knows it is uttering a contradiction. Honor is thus self-referential, and this fact means that the payoffs in games that involve it take an unusual form—they depend on others' beliefs about the person's degree of honor. Honor-conscious societies act as if one trait of honor were an indication that the individual possessed all the rest, so being concerned about being seen as honorable is taken as an indication of really being so. The way to show concern for others' perceptions is to make a sacrifice. When someone's honor is challenged, the individual responds with a costly proof of it, for example, by engaging in a duel or a fight.

A basic game was described in chapter 6 that reproduces most of the features of honor found in societies. It has two equilibria, corresponding to the fact that a certain mode of challenging will work in some cultures but not in others. The game is developed here in several ways to clarify promises, threats, and more general deterrent commitments to defend one's interests. One makes a commitment more credible by putting one's honor at stake. This leads to a different approach to modeling deterrence: by looking at how deterrence is set up before a crisis, rather than during one.

This book argues that states still fight over honor. Further research is planned to investigate this statistically, but here the evidence is qualitative and diverse, involving the parallels between honor-related talk within societies and at the international level. "Honor" is seldom mentioned by name, but leaders talk about "will," "resolve," and "credibility," and these show the same pattern. The speakers typically leave a blank space after them—"will" or "resolve" to do what? The terms are self-referential just as honor is: leaders show resolve to show resolve in the same way that honor means wanting to be seen as possessing honor. Honor's importance is also substantiated by its indirect consequences: related concepts like insults, challenges, commitments, and apologies continue to be central in international matters.

Threats are one kind of international commitment, but promises are also controlled by honor, and an honor-based analysis suggests why certain of them have been treated as binding and others not. Some promises are given on traditional points of honor, such as defense, and are made to members of the group. Promises made to those who are not in the honor group, such as the United Nations or native peoples, are breakable.

The problem with an international system of honor is that it has no single tradition behind it. It is somewhat like a pidgin language, the common denominator of the various forms in the interacting societies. Some components of challenging that are common across cultures are absent or distorted in the international context. Challenges tend to cause fights, and the missing elements at the international level are especially the ones that within a culture dampen the tendency to violence. Unlike most societal challenges, international challenges can come from nonmembers of the group; they can be challenges to blatantly unfair contests; they can arise from clearly self-serving motives; and they do not require a prior affront. Also unlike societal honor codes, national honor does not involve a duty to follow higher authority—on the international scene there is none. This difference is all the worse for peace.

One aspect of international challenges makes them less powerful in provoking violence: with no common culture it can be unclear that a challenge has even occurred. A model suggests that a small amount of doubt about this goes very far in relieving the obligation to respond with a fight. If the challenged party wants peace, it should avoid affirming on the record that a challenge has occurred.

One widespread viewpoint in the social sciences stresses that much of the world that we take as objectively given is socially constructed, in the sense that it is based on common expectations set by culture. Gender or ethnicity or what it means to be sick or drunk or literate are largely socially determined. Searle's example (1995) of a social fact is money, in that something counts as money only because everyone expects everyone to take it as that. Challenges are the example analyzed here. If the audience believes that the challenged individual sees the event as such, and the individual believes the same of the audience, and so on up the ladder of metabeliefs, then it is a challenge. The objective slap on the face may be a trigger to this set of beliefs, but it is no more than that and not an essential part of the challenge. The model of chapter 7 shows what a social construction is without the metaphor of construction. The metaphor suggests that there is an external entity there, perceptible to all, but an analysis using interactive belief systems shows how different individuals may see the social situation in different ways.

Face, Insults, and Apologies

Many writers would dismiss insults as side effects of international conflict. If an insult is followed by a war, the argument goes, the system was already fated for war through objective factors. Historians examining particular cases have disagreed, and the present book cites examples of insults that they saw as leading to wars. Contemporaneous documents show leaders stressing the insult aspect in private and suggest that their complaints about being offended were not just rhetoric to motivate the populace. If the balance of resources and system structure was such that Iraq had to leave Kuwait, one cannot predict from those variables whether this had to happen by diplomatic coercion or by war. Certainly, insults are not long term and abiding as the reasons for wars, but they often seem to have made the difference between peace and war.

Many of the insults that historians have seen as provoking wars fit the pattern of challenges to honor but others do not. Honor challenges can come only from equals, but some of the insults went up or down the hierarchy. In fact, they seemed to be ways to proclaim the target's relative place in the hierarchy. These insults are assaults on face.

In a model of face, a hierarchy of deference emerges as an equilibrium in a repeated game. The game differs from some past approaches, like Shubik's games of status (1971) or Kaneko and Kimura's development of social classes (1992), in that the hierarchy is not based on any objective feature differentiating the players. It emerges from their behavior in the game. The hierarchy is maintained endogenously, based on the history of deference so far. At some equilibria, players rise and fall in their degree of face. An interesting consequence is that representing degree of face as an interval on a line works as well as representing it as an exact point. Someone defers to someone else if the former's interval lies entirely below the latter's. The game shows how insults and symbols can be used to manipulate face.

Like honor, face can be used to establish commitments. If the world sees one put one's own face at stake, it will trust that the commitment will be kept. Delivering a strong insult is a way to do this, and after Bush labeled Saddam a neo-Hitler, it was widely recognized that he would not want to back down in the Gulf. This idea is formalized by a "war of face," a contest used to show one's resolve short of a real war. It is like an auction except that only the loser pays the amount bid. This kind of contest can generate very large bids, like the extravagant insults the world witnessed before the 1991 Gulf War. It is one way to settle a conflict by proving who has the higher motivation to win, and it can be compared with other methods, like wars of attrition or arms races. The comparison is at an abstract level, asking for the perceived cost of each way of settling the same problem without a view to the commodity in which the cost is paid, lives, money, or face. In theory, the war of face seems to be no better or worse than other ways of settling those conflicts, but in practice insulting is inadvisable. It is a relatively dangerous way to engage in facework.

Apologizing is a peacemaking institution, a countervailing force against insulting and challenging. A full apology implies a constellation of statements and requests, and often international apologies worsen the situation when they leave out elements that the recipient is looking for. Simply expressing regrets, for instance, falls short of apologizing and can end up causing more resentment. International apologies are systematically different from interpersonal ones judging by a database of 121 international ones. They are often blatantly insincere; they are often made to and for third parties who did not commit the offense or did not suffer from it; and they do not seem to induce expressions of forgiveness. The explanation offered here is that, compared to interpersonal apologies, their purpose is not to tell the offended party of one's change of heart. They involve more the granting of honor and face in front of the world audience.

Prestige and Moral Authority

Prestige is the degree of belief within the group that the individual is admired by the group for some specific reason. It carries the suggestion that this admiration will lead to influence or power. It sometimes involves symbolism when countries seek prestige by acquiring the kind of weapons that the prototypical powerful state would have. Chapter 12 focuses on normative behavior as a way to achieve prestige and on the consequence of this prestige, moral authority. This lets the prestigious person specify what the norms are in other situations. The dynamic of moral authority is one way that norms emerge and change.

The chapter states a definition of norms, a major element of which is that a norm is supported by other norms that tell people what to do when someone keeps or violates the former. This might suggest an unbounded hierarchy of norms supporting norms, but a game analysis shows how this can be avoided, how norms can be arranged in mutually supporting loops. Susan Strange's comment (1983) that "'Regime' is yet one more woolly concept that is a fertile source of discussion simply because people mean different things when they use it" need not be true. The construction here is one way that the concept can be made more precise. The key is that others grant rewards or inflict punishments *in response to* one's observance or violation of norms, and do this following a further norm, and they do *this* pursuant to a further norm.

Symbolism, Honor, and Arms Building

The final chapter examines symbolism in the nuclear arms race, in particular in one of its subplots, the 1980s deployment of intermediate-range weapons in European NATO nations. It gives a fairly thorough listing of the possible motives for deploying these weapons. The arguments based on military strategy are usually regarded as the hard-nosed ones, but here the symbolic reasons carried more weight in determining the actual decision. The deployment was mainly a symbolic response to the challenge of Soviet missiles. It sprang from the typical motives around honor: willingness to pay costs as a proof that one will be ready to defend the group in the future. The form of the response was also symbolic; it was matching the other's weapons in type and number and placing the missiles on the soil to be defended. Other symbolic motives were using the weapons as moves in a symbolic contest and as influences on crisis tension.

A good account of the INF event has to include nuclear reality as it was defined by those groups making the decision through what are termed nuclear thought-styles. Those in official roles tend to develop special ways of thinking about nuclear weapons, based less on objective considerations, more on what others in the group are thinking. As in any group, members worry about what positions and ideas will be accepted, whatever they may believe in private. Nuclear organizations tend to treat nuclear weapons as if they were conventional weapons; they simplify goals and objectives and stay vague about plans; and they cultivate "rational irrationality" in nuclear thinking. In the INF case, the thought-styles promoted the symbolism, which in turn bolstered the thought-styles.

The U.S./Soviet arms race is over but it is important to determine the causes of overbuilding to know if there is anything about nuclear weapons that prompts arms competitions. The conclusion here is that the nuclear buildup was caused directly by the lack of a practical use for the weapons. It is just because they would do no military good, that governments used them in symbolic modes.

Appendixes

Game Theory and Intangibles in International Relations

Since its emergence in the 1940s, game theory has moved to the center of economics and has entered biology, law, ethics, and other fields. A less conspicuous development has been research on its foundations, suggesting that some of the basic concepts should be reinterpreted with new meanings. The new interpretations have not mattered much for the economic applications, but for other social sciences they have made game theory more flexible and potentially useful. Some of the changes have been

> a recognition of the implications of von Neumann and Morgenstern's redefinition of utility, in which it represents, rather than causes, choices;
> a shift in game theory's concept of probability from objective to subjective; and
> an interest in "interactive knowledge theory," the study of formal systems concerning beliefs about others' beliefs.

This appendix suggests that these developments allow game theory to clarify honor and symbolism. With these changes, game theory cannot be described as the mathematical version of rational choice theory, or the antithesis of constructivism. Finally, the appendix puts this book in one contemporary research stream, the study of how players use extra-game factors to coordinate on a particular equilibrium.

The Redefinition of Utility

Before von Neumann and Morgenstern's book (1953), a numerical utility value was were interpreted primarily as a measure of an internal feeling. It was taken as the intensity of someone's psychological state of satisfaction from acquiring certain holdings. The meaning of a concept is bound up with how it is measured, and the various ways to construct a numerical scale implied that utility was internal satisfaction (Stigler 1950; Ellsberg 1954). A researcher might ask the subject for a numerical estimate: If 10 loaves of bread count as 1, how would you rate 20 loaves? Or the subject might compare differences: Which represents the greater increase, 10 loaves up to 13 loaves or 8 up to 10? The question might be about trade-offs with another commodity, a choice of 8 loaves of bread plus 20 bottles of milk versus 9 loaves and 17 bottles. With the assumption that the total utility is the sum of its components, the subject's series of answers would lead to the construction of a numerical scale.

Von Neumann and Morgenstern, drawing on the approach of F. P. Ramsey two decades earlier, made two changes. First, the old treatment had made no innate connection between utility and uncertainty. In regard to utility per se, its definition and mode of measurement involved no probabilities. To predict someone's choice in the presence of uncertainty or to recommend such a choice, one would have to measure the utilities and then include probabilities, measured separately, as weights according to the usual formula. Von Neumann and Morgenstern included gambles in the definition. The utility scale had to reproduce the individual's choices among outcomes received with certainty as well as gambles involving those outcomes. If one gamble is preferred to another, then the former's expected utility, constructed as the probability-weighted average of the sure-outcome utility values, had to be greater than the latter's. Von Neumann and Morgenstern's contribution was to give conditions on the individual's pattern of preferences guaranteeing that it could be represented by such a numerical utility scale.

The older approach thought of the individual as choosing one action over another because it has a higher utility, but von Neumann and Morgenstern reversed the logical precedence. The individual's utilities represent the preferences rather than cause them. Utility is not inner satisfaction or any other internal state. People choose what they choose, and the question is whether their pattern of choice over the set of prospects can be represented by a numerical scale.

Viewing utility values as representations of decisions rather than their causes has expanded the potential applications of the theory. In the old conception, since utility was a psychological state triggered by objective events, individuals could hold utilities only for events that might influence their lives. In the redefinition, individuals hold utilities for any events that their decisions might influence. It becomes plausible that they seek goals other than pleasure and self-interest. In the applications in this book, people give their lives for honor, and they worry about the future welfare of their country and their own reputation after they die. They hold utilities for outcomes that they will never learn.

An adherent of the old definition might interpret these kinds of preferences as the enjoyment gained from *thinking about* the outcomes. Our posthumous reputation and the welfare of our loved ones are important because we can savor the present thought, the argument would go. This is a distortion of our real goals. We do not take an action with the goal of inducing ourselves to think that a particular outcome will happen—we want it to really happen. If we were offered the choice between the event occurring or swallowing a magical lozenge that induced us to think that it will happen, we would choose the reality.

The redefinition has implications across the social sciences, but they have been slow in being realized. Part of the problem has been old habits of thought and speech, in which utility is still whatever makes us happy. This is congenial to economics applications, which tend to assume that our goal is satisfaction through goods. Likewise, most game applications in international relations are realist oriented and find the older conception adequate. They specify utilities as the population costs of war, or military forces lost, or economic resources expended—the variables that make up the "national interest." The hypothesis that countries hold these goals is plausible, but to view it as the only way to employ utility theory in international relations is to ignore von Neumann and Morgenstern's innovation.

The old attitude has persisted for another reason, a common one in the history of science: the originators themselves did not fully realize what they had done. They embraced the new concept in their mathematics and their general philosophical statements, but in the rest of their discourse they often lapsed into the old mode, talking about utility differences measuring increments in happiness, an interpretation possible only under the old definition. Ellsberg (1954, 551) wrote that von Neumann and Morgenstern were "prone to write in large, clear type about comparing differences and to discard such notions in fine print at the bottom." The true meaning of their utility concept was worked out in the 1950s in writings of Ellsberg, Strotz, Allais, Samuelson, Luce and Raiffa, and others (Fishburn 1989), but von Neumann and Morgenstern's equivocation delayed the understanding of their concept.

Two objections have been raised to the new interpretation. The first accuses it of being tautological, of saying only that people want what they want. The second is that it is false in light of psychological research. Many writers assert both positions, not recognizing that they are inconsistent. Concerning the first objection, one cannot pronounce on the degree of content of a theory by itself. A theory of any depth must be supplemented with postulates that connect its concepts to measurable variables, the so-called auxiliary hypotheses or correspondence rules, which fill in the theory's content. As Duheim and other philosophers of science have noted, Newton's laws of motion and theory of gravity by themselves rule out no possibilities for what might be observed, and any data can be made to fit them by finagling the assumptions about what entities possess mass, how mass changes over time, and so on. In the same way, an application of utility theory requires one to specify the decision makers' goals, beliefs, possible moves, and so forth. When these are added, the whole assemblage, the theory-plus-correspondence-rules, will have content. The question is not whether utility and game theory's content is correct but whether it can form the core of a successful system.

The second objection is that utility theory has been ruled out by psychological research. A large experimental literature has grown up, and it is mostly negative, with studies of the Allais paradox, Tversky and Kahnemann's probability heuristics, and other phenomena (Fishburn 1989). I believe that the implications of this research have been overstated. It has concentrated, quite properly, on designing experiments that the standard theory will fail. This has produced an understanding of utility theory's limits, but it has not given an assessment of how near it is to the truth for typical decision situations. Utility theory may not be exactly true, but it may do well over the situations that are normally encountered.

The negative studies regularly contain a flaw. Instead of observing real behavior, experimenters usually ask subjects what they think they would do in hypothetical circumstances. Subjects state their preferences over various gambles for money, all the while knowing that they will never see any winnings. We often do not know what we will do in a situation until we are in it, and some of the observed discrepancies with utility theory have disappeared when the experimental design became more valid (Luce 1990). Using imaginary money is understandable, but researchers should be demure in announcing conclusions. The manipulations of probability are also often flawed. Many experimenters tell their subjects the probabilities of various states in the experimental decision and assume they will use those probabilities values. In fact, extensive research shows that people distort objective probabilities. Again, the conclusions are based on speculating about decisions, rather than watching real instances.

Any precise simple theory about human beings is wrong, and no experiments are needed to show this. A theory that is wrong for reasons that are not especially interesting may still be worth attending to. Utility theory fails in part because people are poor calculators. If a decision involves several random events in sequence, the decision maker must treat the lottery drawn in stages as identical to one with a single draw according to the appropriately calculated probabilities, but real people cannot do the arithmetic. To be fully accurate, a theory of decision making would need an account of these everyday mistakes, but neither utility theory nor its alternatives, like prospect or regret theory, have done this. It is better that they do not try to include various side issues just for the sake of accuracy. The goal is to understand behavior, not to reproduce it, and adding this complexity would impose too great a cost in understanding. The question is not whether utility theory is exactly right but how accurate it is at its level of simplicity and generality. It is very simple and has a clear basis, and is an approach worth retaining in research programs as long as its limits are recognized.

The Shift from Objective to Subjective Probability

The old view of probability regarded it as just the relative frequency of a repeatable event. A statement that a coin had probability ½ of landing heads was taken as saying something about the objective world: that in a long series of flips, the relative frequency of heads would be ½. The modern view allows a second meaning, subjective probability, in which a probability value reflects an individual's disposition to make choices in the context of uncertainty. For a person to view one event as more probable than another is to prefer to bet on the former rather than the latter. Von Neumann dismissed the subjective concept of probability. His views appear in a correspondence with the philosopher Rudolf Carnap, who was devising a third meaning, probability as degree of belief justified by the evidence (1950, 1952). In his concept of mixed strategies, for example, players use an external randomizing device that they set with certain probabilities. His philosophical position was also evident in his theory of expected utility—the utilities were the subjective viewpoint of the decision maker, but the probabilities were given as objective.

Soon after *The Theory of Games and Economic Behavior,* Savage (1954) and others extended utility theory to include probability as subjective. Game-theory models have moved toward subjective probability, but very slowly, delayed, I believe, by von Neumann's influence. Some of the steps by which game theory came to adopt subjective probability were as follows.

Selten's definition of perfect equilibria (1965, 1975) and subsequent refinements of the Nash equilibrium. Selten noted that certain Nash equilibria depended on one player being willing to carry out a disadvantageous move. The move would be made at a game position that would never be reached if both players used the equilibrium strategies, so it did not lower the player's expected payoff. Nevertheless, such an equilibrium should be eliminated because it implies that players expect that under certain conditions, others would choose suboptimal moves. Only "subgame perfect" equilibria should be retained. Drawing out the consequences of Selten's idea has led to an emphasis on players' subjective expectations of each others' responses. A Nash equilibrium was defined as a set of strategies to be carried out, but a sequential equilibrium (Kreps and Wilson 1982) and other concepts that take account of Selten's arguments include both strategies and beliefs about others' strategies. They require consistency of the entire structure.

Harsanyi's reinterpretation of mixed strategy equilibria as subjective uncertainty about the payoffs (1973). Previously, mixed strategy probabilities were objective settings of the randomizing device. This led to oddities, for example, the fact that when one player uses the equilibrium mixed strategy, the other can deviate with impunity. Given such phenomena, it is hard to make a convincing case that playing an equilibrium is the only optimal thing to do. Harsanyi's approach and later ones turned a player's mixed strategy into the other player's beliefs about the first one's move. (The issues are discussed in appendix B.)

Aumann's treatment of correlated equilibria (1974, 1987). In the original conception of game theory, there was a sharp line between moves of intelligent players and chance events. No prior probabilities were assigned to other players' choices. This fit with the idea of probability as relative frequency, but from the viewpoint of decision theory, it was not clear why some events received no prior assessments. Aumann's approach reconciled game and decision theory, assigning probabilities to all relevant events, including the others' moves.

The objective, relative frequency concept of probability restricted game models by prompting the attitude that players' probabilities have to be reasonable and correct. When probabilities are reinterpreted as each player's perceptions, they become more flexible for applications. One can adopt the subjective viewpoint without discarding the laws of probability. Someone might watch the sun come up in the east each day and hold stronger and stronger expectations that tomorrow it will rise in the west, and such an individual would not be violating the probability axioms, which require only that beliefs be self-consistent in a certain way. They can accommodate this kind of odd reaction to experience. Chapter 13 used probability theory to analyze "cultivated irrationality" involving unevidenced beliefs about nuclear weapons. In the same vein, the shift to subjective probability allows game models to incorporate the findings of psychology concerning probability biases.

Assumptions about Players' Knowledge

A third development in game theory came from the realization that in some games the Nash equilibrium concept was too broad and in other cases it was too narrow. Ellsberg had argued against the minimax solution for zerosum games as too narrow in 1956, but the field generally ignored his views. Since the late 1970s, however, writers have recognized that the right solution depends on the context, and a major determinant is the knowledge that players hold about others' knowledge. The response produced a growth in the number of solution concepts—perfect equilibria, sequential equilibria, correlated equilibria, rationalizable strategies, and others—and an attempt to determine the conditions under which one or the other would be expected to hold. The study of knowledge about knowledge, "interactive epistemology," has become a field in itself, and has led to some techniques used here such as interactive belief systems.

Game Theory, Rational Choice Theory, and Constructivism

These developments refute some old canards about game theory's role in social science. In political science, in particular, game theory is seen as the mathematical version of "rational choice theory." Rational choice theory refers to the general approach that parties pursue their material self-interest, pay attention to objective likelihoods and maximize their expectations in a conscious, calculated way. In fact, game-theoretical models do not necessarily belong to rational choice theory—the models in this book do not. Von Neumann and Morgenstern's original conception was close to rational choice theory, since their probabilities were objective and accurate and their utilities were instinctively close to the older meaning of the concept. However, the only vestige of "rationality" required now is that players judge likelihoods and pursue goals, and this is a weak connection. Players' goals may be far from self-interest, and their probabilities may be quite unreasonable.

The essential elements of utility theory are not that people make sound judgments and pursue their self-interest. They are, first, the use of the concepts of decision analysis: goals, beliefs, actions, and outcomes; and second, the postulate that relationships among these concepts being determined by certain principles of consistency. People's beliefs must be consistent; their actions must be consistent; and the two in combination must be consistent. A general criterion for a principle of consistency is that violating it means that one is ineffective in achieving one's goals in the long run in certain idealized situations, like repeated choices among the same set of gambles. However, no precise criterion of consistency can be given. The principles vary around a certain core, somewhat like the notion of the "radial concepts" defined in chapter 9. Examples of central principles would be transitivity of preferences and the probability axioms, but even these have been dropped—Nash and other writers since have constructed game models with intransitive preferences (Shubik 1982).

A frequently discussed question is whether game theory is justified in assuming "people are rational." In the old interpretation of utility theory, this question went right to the validity of the theory, since it asked directly whether people pursued their self-interest and used objective probabilities to do so. With the new conceptions of utilities and probabilities, it is not clear how this question should be interpreted, and in no case does it seem to be central to the theory. At best it asks which correspondence rules to use, whether to assume that people hold sensible probabilities and self-interested utilities. However, as argued earlier, this is not a necessary assumption of the theory, which is broad enough to allow other goals and beliefs. Another interpretation of "Are people rational?" would see it as asking whether people maximize their utilities whatever those happen to be. However, there is no such thing as having a utility function but not maximizing it. Since utilities represent choices, to have a utility function is to have a certain pattern in one's disposition to make choices, and someone who does not have such a pattern does not have a utility function at all. A third possible interpretation of the question might then be whether people really have utility functions. However equating rationality with possession of a utility function would go far from the normal meaning of the word, since someone can be relatively wise but fail to follow the pattern required by the utility axioms, or alternatively someone who we would call unbalanced might follow the axioms exactly.

The perspective taken in this book is that concern with "rationality" is a red herring. The temptation to use the word almost never arose in the writing and where it does appear, in chapter 13, it refers to possessing wisdom and common sense, not to following the theory.

Game-theory modeling of international conflict has been seen as the mathematical version of "realism" in international relations theory (O'Neill 1994), which holds that the major determinants of actions are material resources and national interests. In fact, there is nothing in game theory implying this stance. It is true that many game models have dealt with deterrence, crisis bargaining, and alliances in terms of interests and power. Also, game models of cooperation and institutions, which are put forward as alternatives to realism, have tended to use the latter's conceptual structure. However, most recent strategic studies in the United States have had this bent anyway, and it is there that game applications are most prevalent so the correlation may not be for theoretical reasons. The philosophy of this book is more allied to the concept of an international society as expressed in the writings of Evan Luard, Hedley Bull, or Fritz Kratochwil. The questions that the book views as important involve language and actors' subjective constructions of international events, more in line with critical theorists like Habermas and like thinkers, who are far from political realism.

Constructivism and allied movements like critical theory, reflectivism, poststructuralism, et al., have concerned themselves with the social world as formed by perceptions and discourse. Recently, some writers have suggested that game theory and constructivism are related or natural allies (Ferejohn 1991; Johnson 1993; Wendt 1999). This book shows that such research can be carried through. The constructivist movement has had a traditional objection to game and decision models: that they are "acontextual," that is, that they exclude psychology, history, and culture. This book's discussion of symbols, honor, face, and challenges explicitly shows where culture, precedent, and psychology enter a game model, determining the player's utility functions or the selection of an outcome from several possibilities.

The book connects with both schools of thought. To political realists, the analysis makes it more plausible that concepts like symbolism, norms, diplomatic language, and various social constructions are important, since they make sense within an accepted paradigm. To constructivists, it shows that the concepts they view as important can be treated precisely in this way.

Coordination through Learning and Communication

The models in this book fit with an ongoing development in game theory, the study of the bases of focal points, that is, how considerations outside the game allow players to choose one equilibrium solution when there are several available. In 1960 Thomas Schelling introduced the idea of focal points and gave examples of how focality might arise, but these were just examples, without a general account. The concept has been invoked often, but a stream of research to explain why one equilibrium should be focal has developed only recently. It is complementary to the literature on refinements, which uses considerations within the game to select one equilibrium out of several, and the study of focal points has developed partly in reaction to the limitations of the refinement approach. (Biglaiser 1994 surveys some approaches.)

There are two strains. In one the game of interest is augmented with a series of preliminary moves, and players' actions in these help them coordinate in the main game. This keeps the analysis entirely within game theory, and coordination becomes a matter of strategy. The previous moves might model preplay communication or might be previous stages of the same game, where players make moves that make an outcome focal, then settle in to play it forever. In the paper of Haller and Crawford (1990) and its developments, if two outcomes are symmetrical within the game, players do not have common knowledge of anything else that distinguishes one from the other. Contrary to the traditional conception, they cannot use the fact that an outcome was written first in the matrix, for example, to coordinate on it, because they do not know the ordering of each other's matrix. The solution is that they make moves in earlier stages to generate a focal point as quickly as possible. Forges (1990) developed another approach, where the players use earlier games to generate a public random variable that influences their choices in the important game. In other approaches, private messages go back and forth to a mediator. The second strain of research asks for the extra-game concepts that allow coordination, using psychological theory or experimentation (e.g., Mehta, Starmer, and Sugden 1994; Bacharach and Bernasconi 1997). The models in this book include elements from both approaches. Some have players make strategic moves in precursor games to coordinate later, as when players engage in contests or use speech acts to establish one equilibrium over the others. Focal symbolism and speech also function as generators of focal points, and these involve issues of psychology and linguistics. The method has been to try to interpret these social institutions within game theory, using what I have called "recent developments in the theory" combined with findings from the empirical social sciences.

Some Basic Game Concepts

This appendix introduces some of the game concepts used in the text. It starts with the basic Chicken and Stag Hunt matrices and discusses their Nash equilibria in pure and mixed strategies. The models for tension, honor, and the war of face involve the further concept of incomplete information about the other player's goals. Here the idea is presented in a simpler form by modifying the elementary Chicken and Stag Hunt games. The appendix goes on to introduce interactive belief systems and gives a series of examples of them, formalizing ideas about symbols, challenges, and cultivated irrationality.

The sections on Nash equilibria focus less on how to calculate them, more on why they are worth calculating—in particular, on assumptions about players' beliefs that imply them. When these assumptions do not hold, there may be no reason to expect the Nash solution, but even then it is worth studying as a way of understanding the game. The goal here is not to confer a full comprehension of these concepts—that would require a more systematic development and practice problems—but to present the basics in a brief and unified way.

Nash Equilibria of a Chicken Game

A class of simple games involves 2×2 matrices, those in which one player chooses a row of the matrix, the other simultaneously chooses a column, and the joint choice determines their payoffs. The simplest examples are the symmetrical games, those that look the same to either player as far as the order of the payoffs is concerned. One is Prisoner's Dilemma (PD) with its familiar story of two prisoners who must decide separately whether to snitch on their partner or keep silent (Tucker 1950). Chicken and Stag Hunt have other stories, leading to different orderings of payoffs and different strategic properties. Example games are shown in matrices 1, 2, and 3, where the convention is that one player

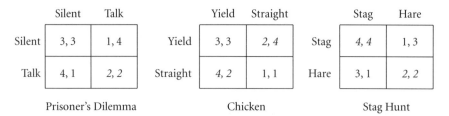

	Silent	Talk
Silent	3, 3	1, 4
Talk	4, 1	2, 2

Prisoner's Dilemma

	Yield	Straight
Yield	3, 3	2, 4
Straight	4, 2	1, 1

Chicken

	Stag	Hare
Stag	4, 4	1, 3
Hare	3, 1	2, 2

Stag Hunt

Matrices 1, 2, and 3.   Three 2 × 2 games. Outcomes from Nash equilibria in pure strategies are italicized.

chooses a row, the other a column, the Row Chooser receives a utility corresponding to the first value in the resulting cell, and the Column Chooser receives one corresponding to the second value.

Prisoner's Dilemma is about avoiding exploitation, but in a Chicken game one person or the other must compromise to avoid a mutual disaster. Each player wants to convince the other that he or she will not back down, and the person who does is "chicken." Calling someone a chicken for cowardice probably goes back at least to the fifteenth century, according to the *Oxford English Dictionary,* but the serious games with that name are from this century and involve automobiles. Ray Bradbury's Chicken game in *Fahrenheit 451* has the driver passing as close as he dares to a lamppost (1953, 27), and Jackson (1961) states that in Denver the driver lets go of the wheel and the first one to grab it, driver or passenger, is the chicken. The 1955 movie *Rebel without a Cause* has two teenagers racing toward the edge of a cliff, with whoever jumps out first being called the chicken. When James Dean asks why do it, his rival, who will soon go over the cliff, tells him, "You gotta do something." Opie and Opie (1969) state that for British children Chicken means a head-on charge on bicycles.

In his 1959 peace manifesto *Common Sense and Nuclear Warfare*, Bertrand Russell made the highway game an analogy for the U.S./Soviet nuclear confrontation. The sport is played by "very rich American teenagers," he related, "young plutocrats," who aim their cars at each other, straddling the white line. Russell added the fine point that if one driver veers off, the other shouts "Chicken!" out the window as he passes. Strategic analysts Herman Kahn (1965) and Schelling, as quoted by Kahn, complained that Russell's analogy was useful, but misleading for nuclear war, since it ignored the back-and-forth possibilities of escalation and negotiation. In turn, Anatol Rapoport (1964, 1965) criticized Kahn and other nuclear strategists for thinking about global war in that manner, and he was the first to attach the name "Chicken" to the familiar 2 × 2 matrix.

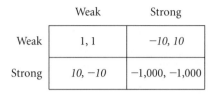

	Weak	Strong
Weak	1, 1	*−10, 10*
Strong	*10, −10*	−1,000, −1,000

Matrix 4.   Rapoport's Chicken matrix

Rapoport's original 1964 Chicken game is matrix 4. Each of the two superpowers can follow a Weak or Strong strategy in the nuclear confrontation. As usual with 2 × 2 games, the convention is adopted of grouping games under one name if they have the same *ordering* of payoffs for each player. Matrix 4 is a Chicken game since it has the same ordering as matrix 2. This grouping leads to a finite number of games (there are 78 different 2 × 2 games if tied payoffs are disallowed) and to a taxonomy—games with the same payoff ordering tend to have the same strategic properties and can be analyzed together (Rapoport, Guyer, and Gordon 1976).

Strategies in general games can be divided into two types: a *pure* strategy is one in which a player chooses one move or the other. In matrix 4 there are two pure strategies for each player. A *mixed* strategy is one in which a player assigns a probability to a certain pure strategy and lets a randomizing device determine which one is actually played. This might involve flipping a coin biased according to the player's selected probabilities. The theoretical motive for introducing mixed strategies is that some games have no equilibria without them. With mixed strategies, any game with a finite number of pure strategies has a Nash equilibrium, as Nash showed.

Recall the definition of a Nash equilibrium: a set of strategies, one assigned to each player, such that no player would gain from switching away from the assigned strategy if the others use their assigned strategies. Thus, any proposed equilibrium must pass a test for each player. Matrix 4, like all Chicken games, has two equilibria in pure strategies. One of these has the Row player using Weak and the Column player using Strong; the other has the reverse. At the outcome (10,−10), for example, Row would not gain from switching from Strong to Weak, since that would decrease Row's payoff from 10 to 1. Column would not gain from switching from Weak to Strong—Column's payoff would drop from −10 to −1,000. Since each player's strategy passes the test, the pair of strategies is a Nash equilibrium.

Chicken games also have one Nash equilibrium where both players use *mixed strategies.* In Rapoport's matrix, both players would use Weak with probability .991 and Strong with probability .009. It can be calculated that each has a payoff of .901 from choosing either strategy. This is a Nash equilibrium since neither can expect to gain from setting the randomizing device at another probability assignment if that player knew the other would play his or her assigned probabilistic strategy.

Nash Equilibria of a Stag Hunt

The Stag Hunt (matrix 3) involves a different ordering of payoffs than Chicken. Like Chicken, it has two equilibria in pure strategies and one in mixed strategies. Its interesting aspect is that one of its pure strategy equilibria is better for both players than the other: the players maximize their payoffs simultaneously by both choosing Stag, but a mutual Hare choice is still an equilibrium. Until recently most formal theorists held the attitude that the game was trivial on this account (O'Neill 1994), but in fact the second equilibrium presents a dilemma that cannot be ignored. If you choose Stag, you are putting yourself at risk. You have no assurance that I will too, and if I do not, you are stuck with your worst payoff. Why would I not choose Stag? Perhaps I am worried about you not choosing it. The joint choice of Hare and the joint choice of Stag are both consistent with the assumption that players are aware what the other will do and are maximizing their utilities, and in some games the joint choice of Hare is the more persuasive equilibrium. If the disaster payoff of 1 in the matrix were decreased, say to −100, choosing Hare would look very risky. If players started with mutual expectations of choosing Stag in that game, those expectations might not be "stable." Each person's fear would be rationalized by the suspicion that the other might be reacting the same way. Moreover, even if the players made promises to each other to choose the Stag move, they would have no reason to believe each other's words when it came time to play. If I intended to choose Hare, I would still say that I am going to choose Stag since I can only gain by tricking you. The lesson is that Nash equilibria may not be self-enforcing.

If Chicken is about threat credibility, Stag Hunt is about promise credibility. Chicken is associated with nuclear crises, and Stag Hunt has arisen in discussions of the social order. Its name was inspired by Rousseau's writing on the evolution of society and its benefits: "Was it a matter of catching a deer, everyone clearly felt that for this purpose he ought faithfully to keep his post; but if a hare happened to pass within reach of one of them, there can be no doubt that he pursued it without scruple, and that having obtained his prey, he cared very little about having caused his companions to miss theirs" (1964, 145). Staying at one's post if the other does that too means half a stag, the highest payoff of all, but waiting there if the other runs after the hare means no food.

Rousseau seems to have been inspired by an Aesopic fable. (Fables, classical and recent, were popular in eighteenth-century France.) A lion comes upon a sleeping hare, but a deer runs by and the lion goes after it instead. He loses the deer, and when he returns the hare is gone. The moral: better to be satisfied with what you have (Vernon Jones 1919). It is a one-person version of the Stag Hunt. In his influential book, *Man, the State and War* (1959, 167–70), Waltz saw this dilemma as the key to Rousseau's ideas on government. Waltz implicitly added to Rousseau's one-sentence tale in the direction of the full Stag Hunt but not enough to fully define the matrix. Lewis (1969) and Ullman-Margalit (1977, 121) also gave verbal arguments suggesting the matrix, but it was Jervis (1978) who put the name Stag Hunt on games with the payoff ordering of matrix 3. He presented it as a model of the security dilemma, where each nation can build a new weapon (Hare) or refrain from doing so (Stag). If each builds armaments attempting to increase its own security, that will decrease the security of both. Since Jervis's article appeared, the game has become widely known in international relations theory. Chapter 5 used a version to model the temptation to preempt in a crisis.

As before, any matrix with the same ordering of payoffs within a player will have the properties of a Stag Hunt—the exact payoff values are not important. Plous (1985) sent questionnaires to politicians asking them to rate the consequences to the United States and the Soviet Union, from the two governments' respective viewpoints, if one or both cut its nuclear weapons. Matrices 5 and 6 came from a Democratic and a Republican in the U.S. Congress. Note that neither Chicken nor Stag Hunt requires that the game look the same to both players, except for the order, and here there is considerable asymmetry from the Soviet and U.S. preferences, as the representatives perceive them.[1]

Chicken with Incomplete Information

Compared to the two pure strategy equilibria, Chicken's mixed equilibrium seems unattractive. First, it needs a randomizing mechanism, which is not only a complication but involves a surrender of control that real decision makers would probably not want to make. Another consideration involves strictness. A *strict*

---

1. The two matrices are illustrations of the Stag Hunt from examples of various games that were returned. Whether an arms race is "essentially" a Stag Hunt or something else depends on the perceiver. In a survey of undergraduates interested in nuclear strategy, DeNardo (1995) found Stag Hunt payoffs in about 6 percent of the responses that fully ordered the cells. About 12 percent took the order of PD payoffs. (The order depended on the type of weapon to be hypothetically cut or kept.) The respondents gave payoffs only for the U.S. side, so the full game might have been neither one. This, he argued, was an indication that there is no typical pattern.

	SU cuts	SU keeps			SU cuts	SU keeps
U.S. cuts	10, 6	−10, 3		U.S. cuts	10, 10	−10, 5
U.S. keeps	5, −10	−8, −6		U.S. keeps	5, −5	−2, 2

Matrices 5 and 6.   The payoffs for unilateral and bilateral arms cuts, as perceived by a Democrat and a Republican in the U.S. Congress, surveyed by Scott Plous (personal communication 1986). Payoffs are to the United States and the Soviet Union. Both games are Stag Hunts.

Nash equilibrium is one where a player's payoff level goes down when that player deviates. Strictness is a desirable property since it makes the equilibrium more self-enforcing. However, for these mixed strategy equilibria, players stay at the same level by deviating from their assigned probabilities. The Row player in matrix 7 might just as well switch to either pure strategy if Column is sure to use the mixed strategy prescription. No matter what Row does, the expected payoff is 5.2. This is unsatisfactory, since it suggests that the only reason the players are using the mixed equilibrium is some extraneous desire to end up at an equilibrium, when they really have only the goals specified by the payoff matrix.

The third problem with the mixed equilibrium is that it behaves oddly in response to the changes in the matrix. Suppose Column's payoff of 2, marked with an asterisk (*) in matrix 7, were reduced to 0. Row's payoff there stays at 2. Since the disaster outcome is now worse for Column, one would think Column would play more carefully and Row more aggressively. In fact, Column's mixed strategy does not change, and it is Row who becomes more cautious, assigning a probability of .57 to Yield, increased from .40. The mixed strategy equilibrium in Stag Hunt shows the same anomaly, with one side turning more cautious when its payoff from choosing Stag alone rises. There is nothing wrong with a theory coming up with surprises, but we should be able to work back and see why the surprise is actually reasonable, and here no explanation comes to light. This puts the mixed strategy equilibrium under some suspicion.

The motive for introducing mixed strategies was to ensure that all finite games possess equilibria, that there should always be something sensible to do. One resolution would be to use a mixed strategy equilibrium only in games with no equilibria in pure strategies. The trouble is that for Chicken, in the end such a theory would be saying only that one player or the other will prevail, and who knows which. The mixed strategy relates the likelihood of fights to payoffs, and for that it is more interesting.

	Yield	Straight
Yield	7, 7	4, 10
Straight	10, 4	2, 2*

Matrix 7.   A Chicken game

A slightly better resolution is to convert the game to one of *incomplete information*. Here one or both players privately know some features of the game before they move. In the typical model, each player has knowledge of his or her own payoffs, but these values are uncertain to the other. Suppose matrix 7 were altered to give the disaster outcome (*) a payoff higher or lower than 2 for each player. Row knows what Row would receive, but Column knows only that Row's payoff is in the interval (0,4) and holds a distribution spread evenly over these values. The same holds for Column's possible disaster payoff and Row's beliefs about it. This new game has three equilibria, the two pure strategy equilibria of the original game with one player or the other prevailing, and a third, which goes as follows: if one's value for the disaster outcome is between 0 and 1.73, choose Yield; if it is between 1.73 and 4, choose Straight.[2] This has the form of many equilibria in games of incomplete information, with instructions that are conditional on the player's private knowledge, often with a threshold value for switching from one strategy to another.

The incomplete information approach avoids the first objection to mixed equilibria—it does not call on players to surrender control to a random device. First, the player's move is no longer random but rather a function of the player's private goal. For strategic purposes, the move is still unpredictable to the other, just as if it had come from a random device. If the interval of uncertainty in the preceding example were narrowed from (0,4) to $(2 - \varepsilon, 2 + \varepsilon)$ for some small ε, the equilibrium probabilities would approach the mixed strategy equilibrium (Harsanyi 1973), and this fact suggests the commonality of the mixed strategy and incomplete information approaches. The second difficulty is also resolved since the equilibrium in the incomplete information game is strict, except for the rare case when a player's disaster utility is exactly at the threshold of 1.73. The player will generally lose by switching away from the prescribed strategy.

The incomplete information approach does not solve the final difficulty of mixed equilibria: that they respond oddly to changes in the payoff matrix. It solves the problem only insofar as the changes are private knowledge, in the

---

2. Strategies differing only at events with probability zero, like behavior just at the threshold, are regarded as the same here.

sense that a player who draws a lower disaster payoff as private knowledge behaves more cautiously than a player with a high one. However, changes that are known to both players still have the paradoxical consequences. Eliminating this difficulty requires a reinterpretation of the meaning of the mixed strategy equilibrium, not as one player's action but as the other player's belief about that action. This conception is explained in the next section.

Rationales for the Nash Equilibrium

The Nash equilibrium has been the most commonly applied solution theory,[3] but writers seldom gave truly careful arguments about why it should be followed. The idea has grown up outside and inside game modeling that the Nash equilibrium is no less than game theory's hypothesis about behavior. This book takes the approach that game theory does not have a central hypothesis about the world. Compared to the theory of relativity or the theory of cognitive dissonance, it is not fully a theory in the empirical sense, but is a body of proofs that allows one to go from axioms to theorems. A better term within the social science lexicon would be *approach,* since it can be applied in many different ways to the same question. There is no such thing as *the* game-theory answer.

In line with this thinking, recently theorists have put greater emphasis on asking when the Nash equilibrium is justified and what contexts call for other solutions. By definition, at a Nash equilibrium no one player would want to change his or her strategy if that player knew what the others were doing. Why should "if that player knew what the others were doing" be the criterion? Players do not have such knowledge since the moves are made simultaneously.

In his founding articles (1950, 1951), Nash spent little effort justifying his concept, calling it only a "theory" of how people play these games. He showed that it had some desirable mathematical properties—every game has such an equilibrium as long as one allows mixed strategies, plus any game where some players have identical roles has an equilibrium that treats those players alike. He wrote as if his concept were convincing only for certain games, which he termed *solvable.*[4] Over the years his restriction has been dropped.

Those who apply the Nash equilibrium in the social sciences face a skepti-

---

3. The concept goes back to the market competition theories of the French mathematician Antoine Cournot, published in 1833 (Leonard 1994), and generalizes von Neumann and Morgenstern's solution (1944) for two-person zero-sum games to the n-person non-zero-sum case.

4. A game was "solvable" only if its strategies were interchangeable, in the sense that two equilibria with strategy pairs (s_1, s_2) and (s_1', s_2') implied the existence of two more equilibria (s_1, s_2') and (s_1', s_2), in the two-person case.

cal audience and must justify it. The common way has been one akin to von Neumann and Morgenstern's argument for their two-person zero-sum solution: if there is a good thing for a player to do, the other player is smart enough to see the situation from that player's viewpoint and figure out what it will be. Each strategy should be an "optimal reply" to the other's, even though they are chosen simultaneously. Strategic thinking by knowledgeable, intelligent entities means that the game will be played *as if* each observed the other's choice before moving. Normal logic would be to describe a rule of choice and then show why it is a good one, but von Neumann and Morgenstern assumed there is a good choice and then derived what it is. For this reason, they called it the "indirect proof." A problem is that many games, including Chicken and Stag Hunt, have several Nash equilibria. How can a player know which the other intends to play? Their argument falters here, since its validity turns on one small word in the premise: the existence of *a* good thing to do is taken as meaning a *unique* good thing.

Some recent justifications for the Nash equilibrium have avoided this problem, but they have other difficulties. Nash equilibria are described as "self-enforcing," in the sense that mutual expectations of a Nash equilibrium do not immediately undermine it by giving the players an incentive to do something else. However, Stag Hunt shows that an equilibrium might not be self-enforcing (O'Neill 1987; Aumann 1990). Another approach has been to talk as if the players have two problems, one of figuring out the equilibria of the game and a second one of "coordinating" on one of them. This seems to give them a motivation beyond what is assigned to them in their payoffs. Also, the mutual choice of Hare in the Stag Hunt is an equilibrium, but it would not be realized if players coordinated.

Rationales for the Nash equilibrium turn on a certain premise that is often unspecified. Will the players be coming to their decisions only from the properties of the abstract game, or will they use other contextual knowledge available to them? The first approach has been called the *tabula rasa* assumption, and the latter could be called the *relevance of context*. An example of the former is Harsanyi and Selten's attempt to find a unique solution for the widest possible class of games based only on the abstract properties (1988). Recent advances (e.g., Aumann 1987) came from the explicit use of the latter premise, but one must be careful in specifying just what players know outside the game, or the result will not be a Nash equilibrium. The issue is treated by Hillas and Kohlberg (forthcoming).

This book embraces the relevance-of-context approach, and following Aumann and Brandenburger (1995), this section presents two rationales for the

Nash equilibrium based on contextual knowledge. The first essentially repeats the definition of an equilibrium, but it is worth stating because it is appropriate in some contexts, and makes a step to the second rationale.

RATIONALE FOR A NASH EQUILIBRIUM BASED ON EACH PLAYER'S KNOWLEDGE OF THE OTHER'S STRATEGY: In a two-person game, if each player knows what pure strategy the other player will use, the outcome of the game will be a Nash equilibrium in pure strategies.

If, through extra-game factors, players know what they will do, then what will happen must be an equilibrium. To see why, assume that the situation were otherwise: that each player in matrix 7 knew that the other would choose Yield, which would not be an equilibrium. Row would then have an incentive to switch to Straight, contrary to the assumption that Column knows Row will choose Yield.

When is it reasonable to expect that each has definite knowledge about what the other will do? This would happen if the game were an instance of a regular situation, repeated so often that definite expectations developed. Driving on the left side of the road is an equilibrium in England. Drivers do not go through any logic of think and doublethink—there is a convention, and they simply know what the others will do. Among the models here, this rationale might apply to societal challenges to honor, but it would be a poorer justification for the crisis tension model in chapter 5. It would be unreasonable to think that a convention will control the other's strategy there. Calculating the Nash equilibrium might still be useful in the tension model by showing that its surprising result, that players attend to payoff-irrelevant symbols, could arise even for players with this extra information. If hyperintelligent players do this, mortals might do it too. Tracing the explanation for the phenomenon in the model can show what to look for in the real situation.

The first rationale for the Nash equilibrium was simple but somewhat uninteresting. It recognized the relevance of extra-game factors but relied on it to an excessive degree and moved the issue entirely outside of game theory. The players knew each others' moves by experience and observation and did not put themselves in each other's minds. The second rationale, however, involves higher levels of knowledge.

RATIONALE FOR A NASH EQUILIBRIUM AS ONE'S KNOWLEDGE OF THE OTHER'S BELIEF ABOUT ONE'S OWN STRATEGY: In a two-person game, if X knows what Y believes about the strategy X will use and vice versa, then these beliefs describe a Nash equilibrium, in pure or mixed strategies.

To say that X knows Y's beliefs means that X knows the exact probability Y holds for X's coming choice. For example, in matrix 7, suppose that Row knows that Column expects Row to choose Straight (with probability 1), and that Column knows that Row expects Column to choose Yield (with probability 1). This pair of beliefs about beliefs describes a Nash equilibrium. What was a player's move in the straightforward interpretation of an equilibrium here becomes the other's subjective belief about that move.

To see why the second rationale leads to equilibria, again assume the players have such a belief but one that does not correspond to an equilibrium. In the case of a pure strategy equilibrium, assume that Row knows that Column knows that Row will play Yield and vice versa. This is an impossibility. From what Row knows, Row would conclude that Column would play Straight, and this contradicts the starting assumptions. Therefore Row did not really "know" that Column would play Yield after all. (The same argument can be made for a mixed strategy equilibrium.)

This rationale for Nash equilibria has two advantages over the first. First, it makes sense of mixed strategies without introducing a random device. In matrix 7, suppose Row knows that Column holds a (.4, .6) probability distribution (the mixed strategy) over Row's moves and vice versa. This is no contradiction, because this set of beliefs corresponds to the mixed strategy equilibrium. There is a subtle but important shift in the meaning of the probabilities. In the standard conception, X sets a randomized device to objective probabilities of .4 and .6. Here however, X chooses one move or the other without randomizing (X knows which), and the probabilities .4 and .6 are subjective ones, Y's beliefs about X's moves. Randomness in one player's objective action has been transformed into uncertainty in the other's subjective belief about that action. The oddity of mixed strategies pointed out in the last section, that worsening a disaster payoff makes that player more aggressive, is sidestepped, since the mixed strategy probabilities no longer describe the player's actions.

Compared to the first rationale, this one involves strategic thinking among the players. Its logic fits with that of the models in the book, which heavily emphasized beliefs relative to actions. The crisis tension model described each player as watching external cues and inferring by focal symbolism what the other is thinking and what action the other will therefore take. The same holds for the arguments behind the honor, face, and commitment models. In some of the honor-related models, in fact, one party has no moves—all the audience does is change its beliefs—so the first rationale would be vacuous. A player is not simply observing past external behavior and generalizing but rather viewing the situation from the other's standpoint, that is, treating the other as an intelligent entity.[5] To the extent that a player can use symbolism, culture, and other knowledge to infer what others expect that player to do, a Nash equilibrium will be justified.

Interactive Belief Systems

The theory of games has given a progressively larger role to players' subjective beliefs (appendix A). The notion that takes this the farthest is an interactive belief system. It establishes a simple conceptual structure for hierarchies of knowledge, which would otherwise be confusing. It allows the modeler more flexibility in postulating players' beliefs and theorizing about them. It was used at several points in the book and will be described here following to a large extent Aumann and Brandenburger's presentation. The examples give a more precise form to some models in the text: those concerning weak symbolism, semiforceful challenges, and attributed irrationality.

Interactive belief systems can be contrasted with traditional games and with games of incomplete information. The traditional conception of a game in matrix form comprises these entities:

> *a set of* n players,
> *for each player,*
>> *a set of strategies,*
>> *a payoff function assigning an expected utility to each* n*-tuple of strategies (one strategy from each player's set).*

In the Chicken game, for example, two players have two strategies each and have the payoffs specified in the matrix. Each player is assumed to know these elements. A solution to the game involves stipulating a strategy to be used by each player in the older approach or the stipulation of probabilities specifying beliefs and actions in the newer ones.

A *game of incomplete information,* introduced by Harsanyi (1967–68), adds a set of "types" for each player. Players know their own types but not necessarily others' types. A type includes a payoff function and a probability distribution over the other players' types.[6] A solution now involves assigning a strategy

---

5. A frequent justification for Nash equilibria has been to stipulate common knowledge, often without specifying just what is commonly known. Note that neither of these rationales requires common knowledge. However, they apply only to two-player games, and for greater numbers of players one must add conditions that involve higher levels of knowledge (Aumann and Brandenburger 1995).

6. It may also involve uncertainty over states of nature, but for simplicity, here this feature is absorbed into the expected utilities in the payoff function.

to each type. In the incomplete information Chicken example discussed previously, a player's type was his or her utility at the disaster outcome. Each type of player had the same beliefs over the other's types in that example: a uniform distribution on (0,4). The Nash equilibrium told a player what to do for each value held for the disaster outcome. In other words, it told each type of a player what to do.

An *interactive belief system* extends a player's type to include the strategy that the player chooses. It is then

> *a set of* n *players*
> *for each player,*
>   *a set of strategies,*
>   *a set of types, each type comprising*
>   *a strategy from the player's set,*
>   *a theory, defined as a probability distribution over the joint types of the other players,*
>   *a payoff function assigning to each* n-*tuple of strategies (one from each player's set) an expected utility.*

Each player knows his or her type, that is, his or her own strategy, theory, and payoff function. Since a type includes a probability distribution over the others' types, each type will have a probability distribution over the others' strategies. It will also imply a distribution over every other player's beliefs about one's own type. A central concept is a *state of the world,* or simply a "state," which is an assignment of types to all the players.[7] At a particular state, a given player's probability distribution over the others' types generates a distribution for that player over the sets of joint moves that the others will make. In contrast to a theory, which was the distribution over players' types, the distribution over moves is called the player's *conjecture.*[8]

A Belief System for a Stag Hunt

The Stag Hunt of matrix 8 has three Nash equilibria. Two of them, italicized in the matrix, involve pure strategies (Left, Up) and (Down, Right), and the third involves mixed strategies, where each player chooses the first or second strate-

---

7. If we extended the structure to include chance events, these too would be specified in the definition of a state, as they are in example 3 subsequently.

8. In some models in the book, one player had no strategic choices. This is represented in an interactive belief system as a strategy set with only one member, which we could call "do nothing."

	Left	Right
Up	8, 8	0, 5
Down	5, 0	1, 1

Matrix 8.   Payoffs for a Stag Hunt game

gies with probabilities ($\frac{1}{4}$, $\frac{3}{4}$). Matrix 9 posits three types for each player. A type specifies the player's beliefs and strategy. The first two types of the Row player are Row$_1$ & U and Row$_2$ & U. They have beliefs labeled Row$_1$ and Row$_2$, respectively, which are the conditional probabilities in those rows. These types choose the move Up in matrix 8. The third type, Row$_3$ & D, has a different belief, and also a different move, Down. The corresponding situation holds for the Column chooser's three types. (The convention here is to put a player's utility type and belief type as subscripts on the role and append the action type.) Here the matrix is symmetrical, but this is not required in general. Matrices 8 and 9 together form the interactive belief system.

According to the entries in matrix 9, the first type of Row assigns likelihoods $\frac{1}{2}$, $\frac{1}{2}$, and 0 to Column's three respective types. This is the "theory" held by the first Row type. A Column type's conditional probabilities are the second entries in each cell and are read vertically. Column's third type, for example, assigns 0, $\frac{1}{5}$, $\frac{4}{5}$ to Row's three respective types. The states of the world are the cells of the matrix. Each cell is a description that is complete relative to the system, since it gives the actions and beliefs of both players in a particular world.

Matrix 9 portrays the player's types as correlated. In the current world (*) Column's third type has probability 0, but if we assumed that the third type of Row held, then Column's third type would be very likely. It is important to rec-

	Col$_1$ & L	Col$_2$ & L	Col$_3$ & R
Row$_1$ & U	$\frac{1}{2}$, $\frac{1}{2}$*	$\frac{1}{2}$, $\frac{1}{2}$	
Row$_2$ & U	$\frac{1}{2}$, $\frac{1}{2}$		$\frac{1}{2}$, $\frac{1}{5}$
Row$_3$ & D		$\frac{1}{5}$, $\frac{1}{2}$	$\frac{4}{5}$, $\frac{4}{5}$**

Matrix 9.   Players' types and theories for an interactive belief system incorporating Matrix 8. The cell entries are conditional probabilities. Empty cells are understood as 0,0.

ognize that this dependence is probabilistic, not causal. It is purely a matter of what constitutes evidence for what. When Row's first type, Row_1 & U, is considering whether to play Up or Down, it does not say "if I were to play Down, then Column's third type would be more likely" that Row type uses the same probabilities in the calculation of either of its moves—(½, ½, 0) as specified in its theory about Column. Matrix 9 means simply that there are three varieties of Row players contemplated by the players in the model. The three have differing opinions about who else is in the world with them.[9]

Matrix 9 can be used to calculate players' conjectures and then to determine what conditions of higher-level knowledge hold in the system. At the state marked (*), the Row player believes that the Column player will choose L for sure. This is Row's conjecture at that state. Row knows how Column will move, and likewise Column knows how Row will move. However, neither knows that the other knows this, since Row allows some positive probability (½) that Column is of a type that is uncertain about Row's move. The same holds, mutatis mutandis, for Column. Thus, at (*) they have mutual knowledge of each other's moves but not knowledge at the next level. They are far short of common knowledge. At the state of the world, marked (**), for example, they lack even mutual knowledge of each other's moves.

In principle, a player type can hold any conditional probabilities over the other's types—matrix 9 can be filled in arbitrarily. However, stipulations involving a player's knowledge, either knowledge of the other's utilities or of the other's knowledge, restrict the probability matrix. If players have common knowledge of each other's utility functions, for example, neither can assign a nonzero probability to a type that is making a suboptimal choice. That would contradict the meaning of a utility function.[10] Further, no Row type can assign a nonzero probability to any Column type that assigns a nonzero probability to a Row type that makes a suboptimal choice, and so on, up the ladder of beliefs about beliefs. What counts as a "suboptimal" choice? As usual, a choice is suboptimal for a given type only if it yields less than the maximum expected utility, based on the conditional probabilities in matrix 9 and the utilities in matrix 8.

---

9. Some authors introduce causation indirectly with a third factor to justify the correlation. One player thinks the other will act the same because they both went through the same school. This leads to problems, and is in fact unnecessary. Even without a third cause, the ability to make inferences from evidence requires that similar events be correlated.

10. I prefer this formulation, "common knowledge of utilities," to the expression used by most authors, which is that players have common knowledge of "the game" and also "rationality." This is redundant. If payoffs are utilities, as is usually the case, utilities are by definition what the players maximize. It would be self-contradictory to say that a player knows that another holds certain expected utilities but is not choosing the highest one.

Suppose, for example, that the players are at state (*). Then it can be shown that their beliefs and actions are consistent with common knowledge of the utilities of all types. The first Row type ascribes positive probability to the first and second Column types, and the second Column type ascribes positive probability to the first and third Row types. All three types are either seen as possible, or seen to be possible by players who are seen as possible, and so on. If players have common knowledge of the utilities then all three types must be utility-maximizers. When this is checked it is found to be true. The first type of Row, for example, is sure that Column will choose Left and is making a best reply to that in choosing Up, based on the probabilities (½, ½, 0). The second type of Row chooser is not sure of Column's move but calculates an expected utility of ½ 8 + ½ 0 = 4 for staying with the move Up and ½ 5 + ½ 1 = 3 by switching to Down. Thus, it makes sense to choose Up. The third type of Row can make a similar calculation and justify staying at Down.[11] A conditional probability matrix like matrix 9 satisfying this condition throughout is a *subjective correlated equilibrium* (Aumann 1987).

The Common Prior Assumption

Matrix 9 shows each type's probabilities over the other's types. How might these have been formed? Perhaps the two players started out with a similar view of the world in terms of the likelihoods of its states, then they went their ways, had different experiences, updated their likelihoods, and brought these revised probabilities to the game. A matrix consistent with this story satisfies the *common prior assumption* (CPA). Note that it holds or not depending on whether the probabilities are consistent with such a story; it does not assert this happened as their actual history.

Only some conditional probability matrices satisfy the CPA, but those that do can be specified by giving only the prior probabilities, which is a simpler way to formulate an interactive belief system. Matrix 10 gives a possible common prior. It is a distribution over the set of joint types of the players, so it has only one number in each cell. Matrix 10 is the particular one that generates the conditional probabilities of matrix 9. Assume that originally, before Row gains the evidence of experience, Row's distribution over Column's types is (⅖, ⅖, ⅕). (These numbers are the "marginals," generated by adding down the columns of

---

11. In general, to test whether a matrix satisfies common knowledge of utilities at a state (*), we look at what states are *reachable* from (*), in the sense of making steps along rows and vertically on columns to cells involving positive conditional probabilities. A situation where every reachable type of player is a maximizer is consistent with common knowledge of utilities.

	Col_1 & L	Col_2 & L	Col_3 & R
Row_1 & U	1/9	1/9	
Row_2 & U	1/9		1/9
Row_3 & D		1/9	4/9

Matrix 10. A common prior distribution that generates the conditional probabilities of matrix 9

Matrix 10.) If life experiences yield the third Row type, for example, that type will update its prior on Column's types to $(0, \frac{1}{5}, \frac{4}{5})$. Thus the fact that one can construct matrix 10, with single values in its cells, shows that matrix 9 is consistent with the CPA. Aumann (1987) and Geanakoplos (1994) discuss the CPA's justification. One reason for interest in it is that it leads to a Nash equilibrium in many contexts, and almost all incomplete information game models in economics and elsewhere, use it implicitly. The interest in it here is also for its simplicity. As a mathematical entity, a matrix satisfies common knowledge of utilities and the CPA yields a correlated equilibrium.

An IBS Model of a Semipowerful Focal Symbol

Interactive belief systems allow us to quantify some notions that were treated in the text qualitatively. The definition of focal symbolism (chap. 4) required an increase in players' common expectation of the outcome being symbolized. A typical game involved a Stag Hunt, as in matrix 11, where a symbol promoted

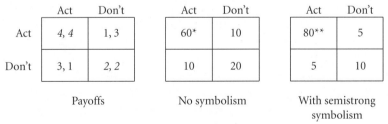

	Act	Don't
Act	4, 4	1, 3
Don't	3, 1	2, 2

Payoffs

	Act	Don't
Act	60*	10
Don't	10	20

No symbolism

	Act	Don't
Act	80**	5
Don't	5	10

With semistrong symbolism

Unconditional probability weights

Matrices 11, 12, and 13. Utilities and probability matrices for a collective action problem without symbolism and with semistrong symbolism. Probability weights are given. To derive normalized probabilities, they are divided by 100.

the jointly cooperative equilibrium. In chapter 4 the two Latvians held opinions about what the other would do in response to the symbol, and, following the second rationale, this led to a Nash equilibrium. These opinions were held with certainty, but symbols can be "semistrong," meaning that the observers might hold only likelihoods about how each other will interpret them. Interactive belief systems allow us to model this. At state (*) in matrix 12, each player holds probability $6/7$ for mutual cooperation. (In this example the CPA is used for simplicity, and only the unconditional probabilities are given in the matrix. Also for convenience, here and from now on, *nonnormalized* probabilities are shown: the entry "60" means "$60/100$.") Players then witness a symbolic event that changes their distribution to matrix 13, and they now assign probability $16/17$ to mutual cooperation.[12] This is an example of a symbol of partial strength, strength being measured by the difference in conditional probabilities. It can be calculated that matrices 12 and 13 are consistent with common knowledge of utilities. Partial focal symbolism can be explicated within a strategic paradigm.

An IBS for a Semiforceful Challenge

Belief systems can also be used in the semiforceful challenge model. To a degree, they were already used in that way in chapter 7, by virtue of the matrix in that model implying partial common knowledge but the presentation there did not quite conform to the way they are described here, since a player's type only included some of the player's private knowledge. Here, a model is presented that is not as rich but does not "cut any conceptual corners." Chapter 7 assumed a continuum of honor, but here the individual may have two possible states: Honorable (H) or Dishonorable (D), the value of honor h equaling 1 or 0, respectively. Each is assumed to be equally likely. The individual can Accept (A) the challenge at a cost .2 or Refuse (R) it. A player's utility for Accepting is then $h\,E[H \mid A] - .2$. The game starts after the challenge has been issued. The Audience and the challenged player may view the challenge as Forceful (F) or Weak (W). The Challengee's types are shown as the rows of matrix 14. The type $Ch_{H\&F}$ & A for instance, represents a Challengee who has high honor, sees the challenge as Forceful, and Accepts the challenge. There are two possible types of Audience. One (Aud_F) sees the challenge as Forceful, the other (Aud_W) sees it as Weak. These two kinds of Audience revise their beliefs about honor in different ways depending on whether the Challengee Accepts, as shown in the ma-

---

12. In this example, any two types of player act differently. In this case the belief system is equivalent to a correlated equilibrium.

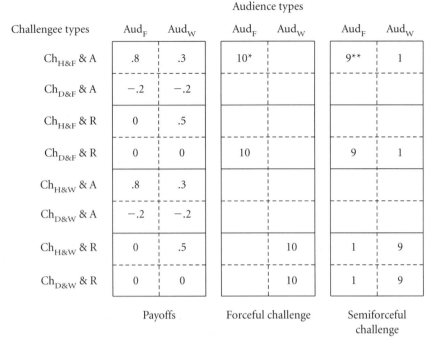

Audience types

Challengee types	Aud$_F$	Aud$_W$	Aud$_F$	Aud$_W$	Aud$_F$	Aud$_W$
Ch$_{H\&F}$ & A	.8	.3	10*		9**	1
Ch$_{D\&F}$ & A	−.2	−.2				
Ch$_{H\&F}$ & R	0	.5				
Ch$_{D\&F}$ & R	0	0	10		9	1
Ch$_{H\&W}$ & A	.8	.3				
Ch$_{D\&W}$ & A	−.2	−.2				
Ch$_{H\&W}$ & R	0	.5		10	1	9
Ch$_{D\&W}$ & R	0	0		10	1	9

| Payoffs | Forceful challenge | Semiforceful challenge |

Unconditional probabilities

Matrices 14, 15, and 16.   Two situations involving fully forceful and semi-forceful challenges. Empty cells represent probabilities of zero; to normalize the probabilities they must be divided by 40.

-trix. The first Audience type takes acceptance as a criterion of honor; the second does not. Thus, a "weak" challenge according to the matrix means one that is entirely forceless. The utilities to the Challengee, which are functions of the cost incurred, and the Audience's assessment of *h* are shown in matrix 14. Matrix 15, at state (*), shows the case of a challenge that is fully forceful, in that it establishes common knowledge of the connection between the Challengee Accepting and the change in the Challengee's assessed honor. (Matrices 15 and 16 contain a number of states that the players commonly know to be impossible. They are included for simplicity and comparability and do not affect the analysis.) Matrix 16, on the other hand, at (**), allows that each might be unsure of how the other perceives the challenge. Here there is no common knowledge of the other's beliefs. The utilities remain as in matrix 14. Again, all types of common knowledge of utilities hold, as can be calculated.

The language of forceful challenges seems to describe some external and objective reality. In fact, it describes a relationship among the beliefs of the parties and is the relationship represented in matrix 15.

An IBS Model of Nuclear Irrationality

Nuclear "irrationality" is an individual or organization's cultivation of unsupported thought patterns about the feasibility of nuclear war. Chapter 13 treated it as propositions that organizations fully believe or disbelieve and included no intermediate degrees of belief. Here, an interactive belief system lets us state the beliefs quantitatively and shows how they interact with utilities.

The model assumes that there is a point of no return in a crisis, when each side must compromise (labeled "Comp") or hold to a position that risks war ("War"). It is to each side's advantage to risk War if it is sure the other side will choose Compromise. However, if they both risk War that will bring mutual disaster, with expected payoffs -10 to each. One or both sides may believe incorrectly that war would be less severe than that, that it would lead to payoffs of $-4, -4$. Belief in the former proposition corresponds to t in chapter 13, and the latter corresponds to f. Belief in t or f by a certain player type is shown by a subscript. (Truth or falsity is specified here to connect with the discussion of nuclear thought-styles in chap. 13—in fact, the validity of the proposition plays no formal role.) The interactive belief system has the expected utilities of matrix 17. Each player, X and Y, has four types depending on the belief held and on the move chosen in the crisis. Unlike in previous examples, their perceived utilities here depend on their types.

The next step is to define the probability component of a belief system so

	Y_T & Comp	Y_F & Comp	Y_T & War	Y_F & War
X_T & Comp	0, 0	0, 0	$-5, 5$	$-5, 5$
X_F & Comp	0, 0	0, 0	$-5, 5$	$-5, 5$
X_T & War	5, -5	5, -5	$-10, -10$	$-10, -4$
X_F & War	5, -5	5, -5	$-4, -10$	$-4, -4$

Matrix 17.   Expected utilities for the four types of each player

	Y_T & Comp	Y_F & Comp	Y_T & War	Y_F & War
X_T & Comp	10*		10	30
X_F & Comp				
X_T & War	10			
X_F & War	30			10

	Y_T & Comp	Y_F & Comp	Y_T & War	Y_F & War
X_T & Comp	8*		4	7
X_F & Comp				
X_T & War	4			3
X_F & War	7		3	64

Matrices 18 and 19.   Unconditional probabilities that generate the second- and third-level versions of nuclear irrationality. To normalize the probabilities, they are divided by 100.

that it reflects "irrationality." Two alternative matrices, 18 and 19, are given to model the two types of irrationality introduced in chapter 13. The matrices assume the CPA and show joint probabilities of the states. Cells associated with types X_F & Comp and Y_F & Comp have probability zero, since the Comp move has a lower expected utility than risking War, given belief in f, and the assumption is made here that the utilities of the types are common knowledge (in other words, "the game" is known). At the state (*), each has particular beliefs about the other's beliefs. Table 7 shows X's probability of t, as well as X's estimates of Y's probability, and so on.[13]

---

13. The value for an nth level of belief in table 7 is $A^n(1,1) + A^n(1,3)$ where A is the conditional probability matrix based on matrix 18 or 19. The limiting value of the sequence $P_X(t)$, $E_Y P_X(t)$, $E_X E_Y P_X(t) \ldots$ is .6, equal to the prior probability of $P_X(t)$ before X or Y know their type. This is characteristic of systems with a common prior and can be understood as doubt about the other's type taking over as the levels go up (Samet 1996).

TABLE 7.   Probabilities and Estimated Probabilities for T According to Matrices 18 and 19 (probabilities and expectations are the same for $P_Y(T)$, mutatis mutandis)

Belief Level	Belief	Matrix 18	Matrix 19
1	$P_X(t)$	1	1
2	$E_X P_Y(t)$	.400	.635
3	$E_X E_Y P_X(t)$	.730	.436
4	$E_X E_Y E_X P_Y(t)$	.519	.345
5	$E_X E_Y E_X E_Y P_X(t)$	.651	.301
	$\cdots$		
∞	Limit	.600	.260

These values show the second- and third-level forms of irrationality. In matrix 18, X believes t (X's probability for t is 1), but X believes that Y believes f (X's estimate of Y's probability of t is .4, less than ½). Irrationality begins at the second level. In matrix 19, X believes t (probability is 1), X believes Y believes t (X's estimate is .635), but X believes that Y believes that X believes f (X's estimate of Y's probability of t is .436). Here irrationality begins at the third level.

The analysis clarifies the temptation to build arms. Arms building can be seen as an attempt to increase certain probabilities in matrix 18. For crisis purposes, X wants those in the bottom row, which involve a possible X type's belief in f, to be as high as possible. In fact, at the actual state (*) X does not hold these probabilities, but X believes that Y might see X as possibly holding them. Setting up an arsenal as if one believed that a nuclear war could be fought, it could be argued, increases those probabilities and induces Y to back down. Whether the adversary really responds in that way is another matter, but the belief system approach lays out the logic of this way of thinking, which has often been used to justify weapons building, and lets us compare it with reality.

Certain human traits, like our ability to recognize faces, are hard to put into words. Thinking about others' thinking is the same. Social interaction requires us to do this, and the ability shows up in the higher apes. In children, it seems to emerge around age four, as illustrated by a classical experiment using two dolls, Sally and Anne (Astington 1994). The dolls are introduced to the child. Sally has some candy that, with the child's help, she puts under a sofa cushion. Anne "leaves the room," and while she is away, the candy is moved from the sofa to Sally's pocket. Anne is brought in again. Where does Anne think the candy is? the child is asked. The answer depends on age: up to four years old, it is that Anne thinks the candy is in Sally's pocket, but after that, abruptly and decisively, it is that Anne thinks it is under the sofa cushion. The child's thinking comes to the idea that others see the world differently than he or she sees it. Dunbar (1996) calls it possessing a "theory of mind."

Beliefs about other's beliefs and beliefs at higher levels are crucial to our socialization. These ideas have been neglected in most of the social sciences, probably because they lead to a verbal tangle. Interactive belief systems allow us to model and manipulate them.

Methods of Calculation and Proofs

International Tension (chap. 5)

EXAMPLE 1: CONTINUOUS-TIME BRINKMANSHIP WITH COMPLETE INFORMATION, DERIVATION OF THE EQUILIBRIUM

Consider a player whose randomizing device calls for dropping out at t and assume the other uses a uniform distribution for dropout times. When t arrives, the player notes that waiting until $t + dt$ occasions an expected gain of $(+1)dt/(1 - t)$, the prize times the probability that the other will give in during the small interval, and waiting brings an expected loss of $(-1)dt/(1 - t)$, the loss of war times probability that it will break out in the interval. The net gain from waiting is thus zero. Thus the player will be indifferent between dropping out at any two times and willing to use a uniform distribution over all times. A pair of uniform distributions is an equilibrium. In general, the players' use of the same distribution that governs the outbreak of war guarantees that they will be neutral over dropout times.

EXAMPLE 2: CONTINUOUS-TIME BRINKMANSHIP WITH INCOMPLETE INFORMATION

Assume that the time of a war is chosen at the start of the game, so that it is defined even if war is averted. Let W be this random variable and let player 1's value be v, 1's dropout time be t, and player 2's strategy be $f(v_2)$. We will look for a function f that is differentiable and strictly increasing. It can be shown following the method of Fudenberg and Tirole (1986) that f must have this form. Then player 1 gets -1 if $W < f(v_2) < t$ or $W < t < f(v_2)$ and gets v if $f(v_2) < W < t$ or $f(v_2) < t < W$, zero otherwise. Player 1's expected payoff is then

$$\prod_1(t \mid v, f) = -\int_0^{f^{-1}(t)} f(v_2)dv_2 - t[1 - f^{-1}(t)]$$

$$+ v \int_0^{f^{-1}(t)} [t - f(v_2)]dv_2 + vf^{-1}(t)(1 - t).$$

The derivative with respect to t is

$$-t(f^{-1})'(t) - 1 + t(f^{-1})'(t) + f^{-1}(t) + vt(f^{-1})'(t) + vf^{-1}(t)$$
$$- vt(f^{-1})'(t) + v(1 - t)(f^{-1})'(t) - vf^{-1}(t)$$

$$= (f^{-1})'(t)(v - vt) + f^{-1}(t) - 1.$$

For the first-order condition on f, set this to 0 at $t = f(v)$. (We also use $(f^{-1})'(t) = 1/f'(v)$, which $t = f(v)$ implies.)

$$f'(v) = [1 - f(v)]/(1 - v).$$

Solving this differential equation by a series expansion around 0 with the boundary condition $f(0) = 0$ gives $f(v) = (v - 1) e^v + 1$. Substitution in the payoff function verifies that 1 maximizes the payoff by using it, given 2 uses it.

The instantaneous tension, the rate at which a war starts given the crisis still continues, is $1/(1 - t)$, inversely proportional to the time left. The prospective tension could not be calculated in closed form, but it can be graphed. Let $v_m = \text{Min}(v_1, v_2)$. If the crisis is still on at time t, let v be defined such that $t = f(v)$. It is the value of the prize to the player who, using strategy f, drops out at t. The value v will be well defined since $f(0) = 0$ and f is continuous and increasing. Then $v < v_m$. The prospective tension will be the probability that war breaks out before someone drops out, that is, the probability of war between times $f(v)$ and $f(v_m)$. The density function for v_m is $2(1 - v_m)/(1 - v)^2$, as it is the minimum of two random variables uniformly distributed on $(v,1]$. Given $W > f(v)$, the probability that also $W < f(v_m)$ is $[f(v_m) - f(v)]/[1 - f(v)]$. At time $f(v)$, the probability of an eventual war is then

$$\int_v^1 P[W \in (f(u), v_m)] \, P[v_m \in (u, u + du)] \, du$$

$$= \int_v^1 \frac{f(u_m)-f(v)}{1-f(v)} \frac{2(1-u_m)}{(1-v)^2} du_m = \frac{11 - 11v + 5v^2 - v^3 - 4e^{1-v}}{(1-v)^3}.$$

Figure 8*b* in chapter 5 was generated with the Mathematica command ParametricPlot, using $f(v)$ on the time axis and the previous expression vertically, and varying v as a parameter.

EXAMPLE 3: SYMMETRICAL EQUILIBRIA OF THE CONTINUOUS-TIME STAG HUNT WITHOUT SYMBOLISM

Under the assumption that a symmetrical equilibrium exists, we will construct one from necessary conditions, and afterward it can be verified to be an equilibrium. Let $f(a)$ be the time at which a player drops out as a function of the value a for striking first. Based on experience with these games, we will look for an equilibrium of a certain form, one that is positive and strictly decreasing in t for $a \in (0, D)$, then drops to $t = 0$ for some D and $a \in [D, 1)$. The following method determines the shape of the function and the value of D. Suppose player 1 expects player 2 to play f and suppose peace is set to arrive at time P. The four possibilities that give player 1 a nonzero payoff are $P < t < f(a_2)$ and $P < f(a_2) < t$, which yield 1, and $t < P < f(a_2)$ and $t < f(a_2) < P$, which yield a_1. For a_1 and a_2 in $(0, D]$, the expected payoff to 1 for dropping out at t, assuming that 2 uses f, is

$$\prod{}_1(t\,|a_1,f) = (1-e^{-t})f^{-1}(t) + \int_{f^{-1}(t)}^D [1 - e^{-f(a_2)}]da_2$$

$$+ a_1 \int_0^{f^{-1}(t)} [e^{-t} - e^{-f(a_2)}]da_2 + a_1 \int_0^{f^{-1}(t)} e^{-f(a_2)}da_2.$$

Simplifying this and setting its derivative with respect to t equal to zero for a first-order condition, gives $(1 - a_1) e^{-t}f^{-1}(t) + a_1e^{-t}df^{-1}(t)/dt = 0$. Setting $t = f(a_1)$ gives $df(a_1)/da_1 = -1/(1 - a_1)$, which has the solution $f(a_1) = \log(1 - a_1) + c$. Substituting this in the expression for $\prod_1$ gives $D - a_1 e^{-c} + e^{-c}\log[(1 - D)/(1 - a_1)]$. This is continuous in a_1, so to find D we can equate it, evaluated at $a_1 = D$, to 1's expectation from choosing $t = 0$, also evaluated at $a_1 = D$, which is $D(1 + D)/2$. The result is $D = 1 - 2 e^{-c}$. The lower limit on c of $\log(2)$ comes from the requirement that D be nonnegative.

Instantaneous tension is calculated more easily by assuming that peace will not break out at all. The impossibility of peace will not alter the probability of an immediate attack while the crisis is still on, when players are assumed to still use their equilibrium strategies. At $t = 0$, each has probability D of not striking, so immediate war has probability $1 - D^2 = 4e^{-c}(1 - e^{-c})$. If the crisis continues, no one attacks until $t = \log(2)$, so the tension during that period is 0. For $t \in [\log(2),c]$, the probability $G(t)$ that an attack will come before t is the likelihood that one player or the other has a higher a value than someone who would attack at t:

$$G(t) = P[\text{Max}(a_1, a_2) > f^{-1}(t) \mid a_1, a_2 < D].$$

If two prize values are uniform on $[0, D)$, the probability that their maximum is greater than a is $1 - (a/D)^2$. Substituting $f^{-1}(t) = 1 - e^{t-c}$ as the inverse of the equilibrium strategy, then $G(t) = 1 - [(1 - e^{t-c})/D]^2$, and the instantaneous tension is the hazard rate $G'(t)/[1 - G(t)] = 2e^t/(e^c - e^t)$, shown in figure 11 of chapter 5.

Finding the prospective tension at each t involves analyzing the different phases of the crisis at this equilibrium—the decision whether to attack immediately, the hiatus, then the renewed possibility of attack. It is best to start with the last phase and work backward. For $t \in [\log(2),c]$ the possible endings are peace or one or the other attacking. Given that the crisis has lasted until time t, the time of peace has density $e^{-(s-t)}$ for s in (t, ∞), and the times of the latter two events have density $e^{s-c}/(1 - e^{t-c})$ for $s \in [\log(2), c]$, since each player uses the strategy $f(a)$, where a is uniform on $(0, f^{-1}(t))$. One can use the latter density to show that the probability that a player attacks between time t' and c is $(e^{t'} - e^c)/(e^t - e^c)$. Thus the probability that an attack comes before peace, given that the crisis has reached $t \in [\log(2), c]$, is

$$1 - \int_t^c e^{-(s-t)} \frac{e^s - e^c}{e^t - e^c} \, ds = \frac{2e^t[(c - t - 1)e^c + e^t]}{(e^c - e^t)^2}. \tag{1}$$

Graphing this as a function of t gives the prospective tension during the final phase.

During the second phase, that is, for $t \in (0, \log(2))$, the probability of ultimate war is the product $[1 - P(\text{Peace during } (t,\log(2)))] [P(\text{ultimate war, given that the crisis lasts until } \log(2)]$. The first factor is $e^t/2$, and the second is expression (1) evaluated at $t = \log(2)$. This yields $2e^t[(c - \log(2) - 1)e^c + 2]/(e^c - 2)^2$. Finally, the probability of war at time $t = 0$ is the probability of immediate war, $1 - D^2$, plus the probability of no immediate war, D^2, times the previous formula evaluated at $t = 0$. The result is $2[1 + c - \log(2)]/e^c$.

EXAMPLE 4: THE SYMMETRICAL EQUILIBRIA OF THE CONTINUOUS STAG HUNT WITH SYMBOLISM

Suppose that the payoffs of striking first are a_1 and a_2 and let $X(t)$ be the value of the cue event. The model assumes $X(0) = 1$ and that the crisis ends at a time T, defined as the time when $X(T)$ arrives at 0. Let the random variable M be the maximum of $X(t)$ in $[0, T]$. This value will be sufficient information about $X(t)$ to determine its influence on whether there is war or peace. A standard calculation for Brownian motion shows that the distribution and density of M are $H(m) = 1 - 1/m$, and $h(m) = 1/m^2$ for m in $[1,\infty)$. We will look for a symmetrical equilibrium function $f(a)$ that specifies a cue threshold for a player attacking and that is strictly decreasing for $a \in (0, D]$, then drops to 0 for $a \in (D, 1)$. (This form is suggested by experience with these kinds of games.) Let x be the threshold value for $X(t)$ chosen by player 1 as a trigger to attack. Four alternative events give 1 positive payoffs: $M < f(a_2) < x$ and $M < x < f(a_2)$ yielding peace payoff 1 and $x < M < f(a_2)$ and $x < f(a_2) < M$ yielding the first-strike payoff a_1. For a_1 in $(0, D]$, multiplying the payoffs by their probabilities and summing,

$$\prod_i(x, a_i, f) = \int_{f^{-1}(x)}^{D} H(f(a_2))da_2 + H(x)f^{-1}(x)$$
$$+ a_1 \int_0^{f^{-1}(x)} [H(f(a_2))-H(x)]da_2 + a_1 \int_0^{f^{-1}(x)} [1-H(f(a_2))]da_2.$$

Differentiating this with respect to x and setting the result to 0:

$$h(x)f^{-1}(x) - a_1 h(x)f^{-1}(x) - a_1 H(x) df^{-1}(x)/dx + a_1 df^{-1}(x)/dx = 0.$$

Substituting $x = f(a_1)$ gives

$$h[f(a_1)]a_1 - a_1^2 h[f(a_1)] - a_1 H[f(a_1)] da_1/df(a_1) + a_1 da_1/df(a_1) = 0,$$

and thus

$$h[f(a_1)] - a_1 h[f(a_1)] - H[f(a_1)] da_1/df(a_1) + da_1/df(a_1) = 0.$$

Substituting the formulas derived from H and h:

$$da_1/(1 - a_1) = -df(a_1)/f(a_1)$$

yielding $f(a_1) = c(1 - a_1)$.

To calculate D, note that the payoff Π_1 from using threshold $f(a_1)$ at $a_1 = D$ is $D(1 - 1/c)$ and from using threshold 0, it is $(1 - D)D/2 + D^2$. Equating the two gives $D = 1 - 2/c$. In all, this implies that each player sets the threshold at $c(1 - a_i)$ as long as this value is greater than 2 but that if the value is less, each player sets the threshold at 0.

Instantaneous tension cannot be defined in this model. If one used a finite approximation to Brownian motion, immediate war would have a positive likelihood just at those times when the cue was higher than ever before. In the infinite limit, the set of such times is like a random Cantor set. One can define a distribution function (the likelihood of war before a certain time given that one knows the cue's path but not players' payoffs) but not a corresponding density function of time of war, which would be needed to calculate the instantaneous tension. Concerning the prospective tension, first consider the case in which the players get past the opening of the crisis with no war. In this case, both first-strike payoffs are in the interval $[0, D]$. The probability of peace is a function of the current state of the cue variable as well as its history, but only one aspect of its history is relevant—the highest value $X_m(t)$ it has reached so far. The likelihood of eventual war is the likelihood that $X(t)$ will reach zero before it reaches $\text{Min}[f(a_1), f(a_2)]$. By a standard calculation this is $X(t)/\text{Min}[f(a_1), f(a_2)]$. This is the probability assuming that we know a_1 and a_2, but we have only distributions on these. We have to calculate the probability unconditional on a_1 and a_2. For $X_m(t) < 2$ the denominator is the minimum of two random variables each with support $[2, c]$, and each of which is uniform on that interval because of the linear solution function f. For $X_m(t) > 2$, the denominator is the minimum of two random variables with supports $[X_m(t), c]$. The probability of an eventual war is calculated to be, for $X_m(t) > 2$:

$$\frac{2X(t)}{[c - X_m(t)]^2} \int_{X_m(t)}^{c} \int_{X_m(t)}^{a_1} X_m(t) / a_2 \, da_2 \, da_1$$

$$= \frac{2X(t)[X_m(t) + c \log(c) - c \log(X_m(t)) - c]}{[c - X_m(t)]^2}. \tag{2}$$

For $X_m(t) < 2$, it is (2) with $X_m(t)$ set to 2. The probability of eventual war right at the start of the crisis is the probability of immediate war, plus the probability of eventual war given there is no immediate war: $1 - D^2 + D^2 K$, where K is (2) with $X(t) = 1$ and $X_m(t) = 2$.

Challenges to Honor (chap. 7)

Equilibrium for the Semiforceful Challenge Model

The type-independent equilibrium is found as in the basic model of chapter 6. To calculate the type-dependent equilibrium, let h_I and h_{II} be the thresholds for responding to a challenge with a fight for Challengees of types I and II respectively. Let $E_{AI}[H \mid F]$ be a type I Audience's estimate of a Challengee's honor, given that the Challengee accepts and Fights, with corresponding designations for the other estimates. The expectation $E_{AI}[H \mid F]$ will be calculated as the estimated honors of type I and II Challengees who Fight, weighted by the type I Audience's probabilities that the Challengee is of each type. The latter probabilities are updated given the observation that the Challengee Fights. The corresponding values for each type of Audience and Challengee behavior are

$$E_{AI}[H \mid F] = [.9(1 - h_I)/(1/2)\,(1 + h_I)/2 + .1(1 - h_{II})/(1/2)$$

$$(1 + h_{II})/2]/[.9(1 - h_I)/2 + .1(1 - h_{II})/2],$$

$$E_{AI}[H \mid N] = [.9(h_I - 1/2)/(1/2)\,(1 + h_I)/2 + .1(h_{II} - 1/2)/(1/2)$$

$$(1 + h_{II})/2]/[.9(h_I - 1/2)/2 + .1(h_{II} - 1/2)/2],$$

$$E_{AII}[H \mid F] = [.1(1 - h_I)/(1/2)\,(1 + h_I)/2 + .9(1 - h_{II})/(1/2)$$

$$(1 + h_{II})/2]/[.1(1 - h_I)/2 + .9(1 - h_{II})/2],$$

$$E_{AII}[H \mid N] = [.1(h_I - 1/2)/(1/2)\,(1 + h_I)/2 + .9(h_{II} - 1/2)/(1/2)$$

$$(1 + h_{II})/2]/[.1(h_I - 1/2)/2 + .9(h_{II} - 1/2)/2].$$

A type I Challengee's estimate of the Audience's estimate of the Challengee's honor given that the Challengee Fights, is designated $E_{CI}[S \mid F]$ ("S" for Socially perceived honor.) Then,

$$E_{CI}[S \mid F] = .9\, E_{AI}[H \mid F] + .1\, E_{AII}[H \mid F],$$

$$E_{CI}[S \mid N] = .9\, E_{AI}[H \mid N] + .1\, E_{AII}[H \mid N],$$

$$E_{CII}[S \mid F] = .1\, E_{AI}[H \mid F] + .9\, E_{AII}[H \mid F],$$

$$E_{CII}[S \mid N] = .1\, E_{AI}[H \mid N] + .9\, E_{AII}[H \mid N].$$

The threshold conditions equate the payoffs from Fighting and not Fighting at the thresholds for each Challengee type. They are $h_I\, E_{CI}[S \mid F] - c = h_I\, E_{CI}[S \mid N]$ and $h_{II}\, E_{CII}[S \mid F] - c = E_{CII}[S \mid N]$. With $c = .15$, as assumed, these are nonlinear equations in h_I and h_{II}. Solving them numerically in the interval $[.5, 1]$ gives one solution that is type independent, $h_I = h_{II} = .6$, another that is type dependent, $h_I = .705$ and $h_{II} = .992$, and a third is the reverse, of course. The various expectations in chapter 7 can be calculated from these values.

Commitments Based on Honor (chap. 8)

Equilibria in the Promise Model

The three strategies in the game are making a Promise and Keeping it (PK), Not promising (N), and making a Promise and Breaking it (PB). An equilibrium must include a nonzero probability of PB behavior, since those with honor close to 0 will seek the benefit b of promising. Since it was stipulated that promises are made and must have some credibility, some portion of players must also use PK. This leaves two possible sets of behavior patterns present in an equilibrium, $\{PB, N, PK\}$ and $\{PB, PK\}$.

Consider the first case of all three behaviors. The audience's estimate of the honor of a player who uses PB is lower than that of one who uses N, which is in turn lower than that of one who uses PK, since the decreasing payoffs of these three strategies must be compensated by higher honor estimates or not all of them would be used. Similarly, the true honor of any player using PB is lower than any choosing N, which is in turn lower than that of any player choosing PK. The continuum of honor is thus divided into three intervals $[0, h_1), (h_1, h_2),$ and $(h_2, 1]$ containing those who, respectively, choose PB, N, and PK. (As usual we ignore considerations of the intervals' endpoints.) Since a player's payoff from a given move is a continuous function of honor, the positions of the endpoints can be found by equating the payoffs for someone whose honor takes those values. The equations are

$$h_2\,(1 + h_2)/2 - .25 = h_2\,(h_1 + h_2)/2$$

and

$$h_1^2/2 + .15 = h_1 (h_1 + h_2)/2,$$

which lead to the values in figure 17 in chapter 8. The equilibrium for strategies {*PB, PK*} can be calculated similarly.

An Equilibrium in the Commitment Model

We will look for an equilibrium in which defenders of highest honor commit and defend, the next highest group commit and do not defend, and those of the lowest honor do not commit and in which attackers of highest value attack. In this case we can draw a rectangle whose axes are the values privately known by each player, and the threshold values for each strategy are assigned unknowns, as shown in figure 33.

By the usual method, citing the fact that the payoffs of the players are continuous functions of their private information variables, the expectations for

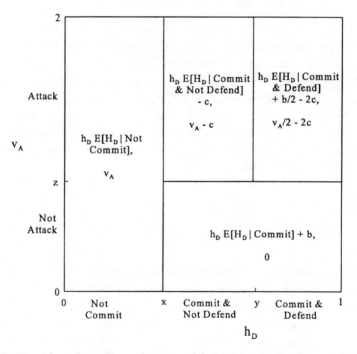

Fig. 33. Players' payoffs as a function of their joint types for the commitment model

each strategy can be equated for a player at the threshold, yielding three equations for x, y, and z:

D's indifference at $h_D = y$: $y(1 + y)/2 + b/2 - 2c = y(x + y)/2 - c$.

A's indifference at $v_A = z$: $(y - x)(z - c) + (1 - y)(z/2 - 2c) = 0$.

D's indifference at $h_D = x$: $(2 - z)/2\ [x(x + y)/2 - c]$

$$+ z/2\ [x(1 + x)/2 + b] = x^2/2.$$

The first can be solved for x; this expression is then substituted in the second, which is then solved for z and the result substituted in the third, whose solution for y can be found numerically.

Insults as Assaults on Face (chap. 9)

Equilibria in the Model of a Hierarchy of Face

To calculate the expected payoffs and admissible discount factors in the complete-order equilibrium, let the discounted payoff for being in group i be u_i, for $i = 1$ to 7. A player has four possible encounters at the current stage, determined by the role assigned and whether there is imposition or deference. The roles are equiprobable, and the probability of imposition or deference is determined by the player's face level. The payoff from each of the four kinds of encounters is set by the payoff it confers immediately plus the discounted value of continuing in that face-group. Multiplying by the probability of each encounter gives seven equations, each with the form:

$$u_i = (2 + \delta u_i)\ \tfrac{1}{2}\ (i/7) + (0 + \delta u_i)\ \tfrac{1}{2}\ (7 - i)/7 + (0 + \delta u_i)\ \tfrac{1}{2}\ (i - 1)/7$$

$$+ (-1 + \delta u_i)\ \tfrac{1}{2}\ (8 - i)/7.$$

Each can be solved for u_i as a function of δ. Bounds on δ are, as mentioned in the chapter, determined by the requirement that membership in each face-group have expected utility at least one unit higher than the next.

For the impose-on-one-level-up equilibrium, there is movement among face-groups, and this method generates seven linked linear equations, which again can be solved for the variables u_i.

Commitments Based on Face (chap. 10)

Equilibria of the Simple Signaling Contests

For any of the games, one can show that a symmetrical equilibrium strategy is differentiable and increasing, following, for example, the argument of Tirole and Fudenberg (1986). If $f(v)$ is a symmetrical equilibrium strategy giving the bid for prize value v, then f^{-1} is well defined. Player 1's expected payoff from bidding x when 1 has value v for the prize and 2 uses strategy f, is

$$\Pi_1(x|f, v) = \int_0^{f^{-1}(x)} (v - \text{winner's payment})\, dy$$
$$+ \int_{f^{-1}(x)}^1 (- \text{loser's payment})\, dy.$$

The winner's and loser's payments take the values x, y, or 0, depending on the game considered. Sources cited in the text treat the equilibria of all but two of the games in table 2 in chapter 10 that have equilibria. The exceptions are the war of face and the game of bidding with a public bad.

For the war of face, $\Pi_1(x|f, v) = vf^{-1}(x) - x(1 - f^{-1}(x))$. Differentiating this with respect to x gives $v(f^{-1})'(x) - 1 + f^{-1}(x) + x(f^{-1})'(x) = 0$. With $x = f(v)$ and the identity $(f^{-1})'(f(v)) = 1/f'(v)$, this becomes $v/f'(v) - 1 + v + f(v)/f'(v) = 0$, yielding $f'(v) = [v + f(v)]/(1 - v)$. This differential equation in f has a unique solution on $(0,1)$, given the initial condition that $\lim f(v) = 0$ as $v \to 0$. A Taylor-series expansion gives the formula in the table, $f(v) = \frac{1}{2} v^2/(1 - v)$. This calculation leads to a symmetrical equilibrium if one exists, but it does not represent a sufficient condition for an equilibrium. To prove it is in fact an equilibrium, one can substitute it for f in the preceding expression for Π_1 and show that it maximizes Π_1 at $x = f(v)$.

Asymmetrical Solutions for the War of Face

A family of asymmetrical solutions of the war of face is found in a way similar to the method of Ammann and Leininger (1996). Assuming the players' strategies are f and g, and that these are strictly increasing on $(0,1)$, the payoff functions become

$$\Pi_1(x|g, v_1) = v_1 g^{-1}(x) - x(1 - g^{-1}(x))$$

and

$$\Pi_2(y \mid f, v_2) = v_2 f^{-1}(y) - y(1 - f^{-1}(y)).$$

Calculating the first-order conditions by differentiating with respect to x and y and setting $v_1 = f^{-1}(x)$ and $v_2 = g^{-1}(y)$ gives

$$f^{-1}(x)(g^{-1})'(x) - 1 + x(g^{-1})'(x) + f^{-1}(x) = 0,$$

$$g^{-1}(y)(f^{-1})'(y) - 1 + y(f^{-1})'(y) + g^{-1}(y) = 0.$$

These are conditions on any equilibrium functions f and g and hold for all x and y. Substituting $x = y = f(v)$ gives

$$v(g^{-1})'(f(v)) - 1 + f(v)(g^{-1})'(f(v)) + g^{-1}(f(v)) = 0$$

and

$$g^{-1}(f(v)) (f^{-1})'(f'(v)) - 1 + f(v) (f^{-1})'(f(v)) + v = 0.$$

Three substitutions are made. First, let $k(v) = g^{-1}(f(v))$. In words, if player 1 has value v, $k(v)$ gives the prize value for a player 2 at the equilibrium who uses the same strategy. Also, note that $k'(v) = (g^{-1})(f(v)) f'(v)$ and $(f^{-1})'(f(v)) = 1/f'(v)$. This yields

$$v k'(v)/f'(v) - 1 + f(v) k(v)/f'(v) + k(v) = 0 \qquad (3)$$

$$k(v)/f'(v) - 1 + f(v)/f'(v) + v = 0. \qquad (4)$$

Equation (4) gives

$$k(v) = (1 - v)f'(v) - f(v). \qquad (5)$$

Substituting this as well as the resulting expression for $k'(v)$ in (3) gives

$$[v + f(v)] f''(v) + [f'(v)]^2 + [(-1 - 2v - 3f(v))/(1 - v)] f'(v) = 0. \qquad (6)$$

With the restriction that $f(0) = 0$, (6) is a second-order differential equation with a one-parameter family of solutions. To construct a pair of functions constituting an equilibrium, one determines an $f(v)$ by finding a solution for (6), then calculates $k(v)$ by equation (5), to allow the numerical construction of $g(v)$. One analytical solution is the symmetrical equilibrium function already found, where $k(v) = v$. All solutions have the general shape of the symmetrical one—concave, starting at 0, and going to infinity at $v = 1$. A solution to equation (6) alone is $f(v) = v/(1 - v)$, and it is the limiting case—for all solutions to both equations, one player's strategy lies at or between the symmetrical solution and this function. The other player's strategy lies at or between the symmetrical one and $f(v) = 0$. This strategy does not itself give a solution to both equations, since its corresponding function k and thus 2's strategy g are not increasing. Still it yields an equilibrium if player 1 uses it and player 2 makes no bid at all. No matter how high the latter's value for the prize, it is not worthwhile for 2 to bid anything. Any player 1 strategy that is greater than $v/(1 - v)$ on the $(0,1)$ interval, and player 2 bidding zero, is also an equilibrium.

Equilibrium in the Public Bad Game

For the public bad game, 1's expected payoff is

$$\prod_1(x|f, v) = (v - x)f^{-1}(x) + \int_{f^{-1}(x)}^1 - y \, dy.$$

Differentiating with respect to x and setting the result equal to zero gives $f^{-1}(x)(v - x) = 0$, which is satisfied only by $x = f(v) = v$, since f^{-1} cannot be identically zero. This can be shown to maximize $\prod_1$ as a response to the strategy used by player 2.

Mean Bids and Payoffs

Finding the mean bids of the games is straightforward. Concerning expected payoffs, first consider the nonauction allocation rule that simply gives the prize to the player with the higher value. To find the expected prize value of that player, note that the higher player's value is uniform between the lower player's and 1, so its mean is halfway between the lower player's value and 1; likewise, the lower player's mean value is halfway between 0 and the winner's value. This is satisfied only by a higher player's expected value of ⅔ and a lower player's of ⅓. A player's expectation in the allocation rule that gives the prize to the higher player is then ½(⅔) + ½(0) = ⅓.

One can find the players' expected payoffs by integration in the auction games, but an easier way uses the revenue-equivalence theorem. (I am indebted to Jeremy Bulow for this simple derivation.) In the second-price auction both bid their values, and these bids being linear functions of the values, the expected net payoff of the winner is the winner's expected prize value, found in the preceding paragraph, minus the loser's expected bid. The latter is the loser's expected prize value, already found. So the winner's expected net payoff is $\frac{2}{3} - \frac{1}{3} = \frac{1}{3}$ and that of the loser is, of course, 0. The overall expectation is the average, $\frac{1}{6}$. In the other five auctions covered by the revenue-equivalence theorem, a player's expectation is therefore $\frac{1}{6}$. For the public bad game, the winner's expected value and therefore expected bid, given the linear equilibrium strategy, is $\frac{2}{3}$. The loser can expect to gain $-\frac{2}{3}$. Therefore, a player's expectation over all values is $\frac{1}{2}(\frac{2}{3} - \frac{2}{3}) + \frac{1}{2}(-\frac{2}{3}) = -\frac{1}{3}$.

A Symmetrical Equilibrium for the War of Face with a Maximum Bid

The bid will be monotonically increasing in the player's value. Define L such that those players with $v \in [L, 1]$ bid the maximum M. For a player with value less than L, the value of the maximum, or even the existence of a maximum, will be irrelevant, since that player's probability of winning and the amount paid will be the same as in the original unconstrained game. Thus players either use the original function or bid M. The exact value of L at which players bid M can be calculated by equating the payoff of a player just at that value from bidding by the original function with that of a player of that value bidding M. The first gets payoff $L(L) - (1 - L) \frac{1}{2}L^2/(1 - L)$. Bidding M yields $[L + \frac{1}{2}(1 - L)]L + \frac{1}{2}(1 - L)(-M)$, and equating them yields $L = M/(M + 1)$.

Prestige, Moral Authority, and Normative Regimes (chap. 12)

Limits of Discounting for the Grim Strategy and Fight-and-Forget

Staying with the Grim strategy gives $10 + 10\delta + 10\delta^2 + \cdots + = 10/(1 - \delta)$. Violating it once gives $12 + 7\delta + 7\delta^2 + \cdots = 12 + 7\delta(1 - \delta)$. The first exceeds the second as long as $\delta \geq .4$.

For Fight-and-Forget to be a subgame perfect equilibrium, players must have an incentive to follow it at each of the three kinds of subgames—where there has been cooperation, where there has been a unilateral defection, and where there has been a mutual defection. In the first case staying with the strategy yields $10 + 10\delta + 10\delta^2 \cdots$. Violating it once yields $12 + 7\delta + 10\delta^2 + 10\delta^3 + \cdots$. The first exceeds the second if $10 + 10\delta > 12 + 7\delta$, or $\delta \geq 2/3$. For the second situation, staying with the equilibrium by choosing D yields $7 + 10\delta + 10\delta^2 + 10\delta^3 + \cdots$. Violating it by using C yields $3 + 7\delta + 10\delta^2 + 10\delta^3 + \cdots$. At this subgame, the first is clearly better, so a sufficient condition for the equilibrium is that $\delta \geq 2/3$.

References

Abadi, Adina. 1990. "The Speech Act of Apology in Political Life." *Journal of Pragmatics* 14:467–71.

Abelson, Robert. 1986. "Beliefs are Like Possessions." *Journal for the Theory of Social Behavior* 16:223–50.

Abelson, Robert, and Milton Rosenberg. 1958. "Symbolic Psycho-Logic: A Model of Attitudinal Cognition." *Behavioral Science* 3:1–13.

Abreu, Dilip. 1988. "On the Theory of Infinitely Repeated Games with Discounting." *Econometrica* 56:383–96.

Abu-Zahra, N. M. 1970. "On the Modesty of Arab Muslim Villages, a Reply." *American Anthropologist* 72:1079–88.

Adams, Cecil. 1994. *Return of the Straight Dope*. New York: Ballantine.

Adler, K., and D. Wertmen. 1980. "Is NATO in Trouble? A Survey of European Attitudes." *Public Opinion* 50:8–12.

Albertini, Luigi. 1952–57. "Austro-German Intentions after the Sarajevo Drama." In *The Origins of the War of 1914*. London: Oxford University Press.

Ambrose, Stephen. 1989. *Nixon*. Vol. 2. New York: Simon and Schuster.

Ammann, Erwin, and Wolfgang Leininger. 1996. "Asymmetric All-Pay Auctions with Incomplete Information: The Two-Player Case." *Games and Economic Behavior* 14:1–18.

Anderson, Elijah. 1994. "The Code of the Streets." *Atlantic Monthly* 273 (May): 81–94.

Anonymous. 1945. "Twelve Points." *Time Magazine* 46:28, November 12.

Aristotle. 1976. *Nichomachean Ethics*. Trans. J. A. K. Thomson. New York: Penguin.

Arkin, William, Frank von Hippel, and Barbara Levi. 1982. "The Consequences of Nuclear War in Europe." *Ambio* 11:163–73.

Asfaw, Girm-Selassie, David Appleyard, and Edward Ullendorff, eds. 1979. *The Amharic Letters of Emperor Theodore of Ethiopia to Queen Victoria and Her Special Envoy*. London: Oxford University Press.

Astington, J. W. 1994. *The Child's Discovery of the Mind*. London: Fontana.

Aumann, Robert. 1974. "Subjectivity and Correlation in Randomized Strategies." *Journal of Mathematical Economics* 1:67–96.

Aumann, Robert. 1987. "Correlated Equilibrium as an Expression of Bayesian Rationality." *Econometrica* 55:1–19.

Aumann, Robert. 1990. "Nash Equilibria Are Not Self-Enforcing." In *Economic Decision-Making: Games, Econometrics and Optimization,* ed. J. J. Gabszewicz, J. F. Richard, and L. Wolsey, 201–6. Amsterdam: Elsevier.

Aumann, Robert, and Adam Brandenburger. 1995. "Epistemic Conditions for Nash Equilibrium." *Econometrica* 63:1161–80.

Aung, U Htin. 1965. *The Stricken Peacock.* The Hague: Nijhoff.

Austin, John. 1962. *How to Do Things with Words.* Cambridge, Mass.: Harvard University Press.

"Avant le Procès, le Secrétaire Général de le CEAO Parle." 1985. *Jeune Afrique* 1283 (August 7): 34–36.

Avramides, Anita. 1989. *Meaning and Mind: An Examination of the Gricean Account of Meaning.* Cambridge, Mass.: MIT Press.

Axelrod, Robert. 1986. "An Evolutionary Approach to Norms." *American Political Science Review* 80:1096–1111.

Bacharach, Michael, and Michele Bernasconi. 1997. "The Variable Frame Theory of Focal Points: An Experimental Study." *Games and Economic Behavior* 19:1–45.

Bean, Judith, and Barbara Johnstone. 1994. "Workplace Reasons for Saying You're Sorry: Discourse Task Management and Apology in Telephone Interviews." *Discourse Processes* 17:59–81.

Berger, Peter, and Thomas Luckmann. 1966. *The Social Construction of Reality.* New York: Doubleday.

Bergeron, Gerard. 1971. *La Guerre Froide Inachevée.* Montreal: Les Presses de l'Université de Montréal.

Bernheim, B. Douglas. 1994. "A Theory of Conformity." *Journal of Political Economy* 102:841–77.

Biglaiser, Gary. 1994. "Coordination in Games: A Survey." In *Problems of Coordination in Economic Activity,* ed. James W. Friedman, 49–65. Boston: Kluwer.

Binmore, Ken. 1992. *Fun and Games: A Treatise on Game Theory.* Lexington, Mass.: Heath.

Binmore, Ken, and Larry Samuelson. 1992. "Evolutionary Stability in Repeated Games Played by Finite Automata." *Journal of Economic Theory* 57:278–305.

Blair, Bruce. 1993. "Launch on Warning." In *The Logic of Accidental Nuclear War.* Washington, D.C.: Brookings Institution.

Bobbitt, Philip. 1988. *Democracy and Deterrence.* New York: St. Martin's Press.

Boehm, Christopher. 1983. *Montenegrin Social Organization and Values.* New York: AMS Press.

Bonnersmith, D., and E. W. R. Lumby, eds. 1954. *The Second China War, 1856–1860.* London: Navy Records Society.

Boose, Linda. 1993. "Technomuscularity and the Boy Eternal, From the Quagmire to the Gulf." In *Gendering War Talk,* ed. Miriam Cooke and Angela Woollacott, 67–108. Princeton: Princeton University Press.

Borroff, Marie. 1962. *Sir Gawain and the Green Knight: A Stylistic and Metrical Study.* New Haven: Yale University Press.

Bradbury, Ray. 1953. *Fahrenheit 451.* New York: Ballantine.

Braithwaite, Richard. 1955. *The Theory of Games as a Tool for the Moral Philosopher.* Cambridge: Cambridge University Press.

Brams, Steven, and Marc Kilgour. 1988. *Game Theory and National Security.* New York: Basil Blackwell.

Brecher, Michael. 1980. *Decision in Crisis: Israel, 1967 and 1973.* Berkeley: University of California Press.

Brecher, Michael. 1993. *Crises in World Politics: Theory and Reality.* New York: Pergamon.

Brecher, Michael, and Jonathan Wilkenfeld. 1997. *A Study of Crisis.* Ann Arbor: University of Michigan Press.

Brecher, Michael, Jonathan Wilkenfeld, and Sheila Moser. 1988. *Crises in the Twentieth Century.* Vol. 2. New York: Pergamon.

Brown, Harold. 1982. *Department of Defense Annual Report.* Washington, D.C.: Government Printing Office. Quoted by Charles Glaser, "Why Experts Disagree about Nuclear Policy," in Lynn Eden and Steven Miller, eds., *Nuclear Arguments: Understanding the Nuclear Arms and Arms Control Debate* (Ithaca: Cornell University Press, 1989), 38.

Brown, Penelope, and Stephen Levinson. 1987. *Politeness.* New York: Cambridge University Press.

Brown, Roger. 1965. *Social Psychology.* New York: Free Press.

Bruce, George. 1973. *The Burma Wars.* London: Hart-Davis.

Bryson, Frederick. 1935. *The Point of Honor in Sixteenth-Century Italy: An Aspect of the Life of the Gentleman.* New York: Columbia University Press.

Brzezinski, Zbigniew. 1983. *Power and Principle, Memoirs of the National Security Adviser, 1977–1981.* London: Weidenfeld and Nicolson.

Buchanan, Alice. 1932. "The Irish Framework of Gawain and the Green Knight." *PMLA* 48:315–39.

Bulow, Bernhard von. 1914. *Imperial Germany.* London: Cassell.

Bundy, McGeorge. 1988. *Danger and Survival.* New York: Random House.

Burckhardt, Jacob. 1929. *The Civilization of the Renaissance in Italy.* London: Harrad.

Burrow, John Anthony. 1965. *A Reading of Sir Gawain and the Green Knight.* London: Routledge and Kegan Paul.

Campbell, John K. 1964. *Honour, Family and Patronage: A Study of Institutions and Moral Values in a Greek Mountain Community.* Oxford: Clarendon.

Canadian Broadcasting Corporation. 1991. *Mediafile.* July.

Carnap, Rudolf. 1950. *The Logical Foundations of Probability.* Chicago: University of Chicago Press.

Carnap, Rudolf. 1952. *The Continuum of Inductive Methods.* Chicago: University of Chicago Press.

Carr, William. 1991. *The Origins of the Wars of German Unification.* New York: Longman.

Cartwright, John, and Julian Critchley. 1985. *Cruise, Pershing and SS-20: The Search for Consensus: Nuclear Weapons in Europe.* London: Brassey. Quoted in Susanne Peters, *The Germans and the INF Missiles* (Baden-Baden: Nomos, 1990).

Cassidy, Frederic G., ed. 1991. *Dictionary of American Regional English.* Vol. 2. Cambridge, Mass.: Belknap Press.

Charveriat, E. 1878. *Histoire de la Guerre de Trente Ans.* Paris: E. Plon.

Chilton, Paul. 1989. "The Container Concept of Security, a Cognitive Linguistic Approach." Center for International Security and Arms Control, Stanford University.

Chilton, Paul. 1996. *Security Metaphors: Cold War Discourse from Containment to Common House.* New York: Peter Lang.

Chong, Dennis. 1993. *Collective Action and the Civil Rights Movement.* Chicago: University of Chicago Press.

Clark, Herbert. 1985. "Language Use and Language Users." In *Handbook of Social Psychology,* ed. Gardner Lindzey. New York: Random House.

Cleveland, Grover. 1913. *The Venezuelan Boundary Dispute.* Princeton: Princeton University Press.

Cochran, Thomas, William Arkin, Robert Norris, and Jeffrey Sands. 1989. *Nuclear Weapons Databook.* Vol. 4, *Soviet Nuclear Weapons.* New York: Harper and Row.

Cohen, Norm. 1981. *The Long Steel Rail: The Railroad in American Folksong.* Urbana: University of Illinois Press.

Cohen, Raymond. 1987. *The Theater of Power: The Art of Diplomatic Signaling.* New York: Longman.

Cohen, Raymond. 1990. *Culture and Conflict in Egyptian-Israeli Relations.* Bloomington: Indiana University Press.

Cohn, Carol. 1987. "Sex and Death in the Rational World of Defense Intellectuals." *Signs* 12:687–729.

Cohn, Carol. 1993. "Wars, Wimps and Women." In *Gendering War Talk,* ed. Miriam Cooke and Angela Woollacott, 228–46. Princeton: Princeton University Press.

Cohn, Carol. 1994. "Sex and Death in the Gulf." Mimeo, Bowdoin College.

Companys Monchus, Julian. 1987. "La Carta de Dupuy de Lome." *Boletín de la Real Academia de la História* 184:464–81.

Congressional Record. 1917. 65th Cong., Vol. 55, pt. 1.

Connaughton, Richard. 1988. *The War of the Rising Sun and the Tumbling Bear: A Military History of the Russo-Japanese War.* London: Routledge.

Coombs, Clyde. 1964. *A Theory of Data.* New York: Wiley.

Costin, William. 1937. *Great Britain and China, 1833–1860.* Oxford: Clarendon.

Cox, David. 1985. *Canada and NORAD, 1958–1978, A Cautionary Retrospective.* Ottawa: Canadian Centre for Arms Control and Disarmament.

Crawford, Neta. 1993. "Decolonization as an International Norm: The Evolution of Practices, Arguments and Beliefs." In *Emerging Norms of Justified Intervention,* ed. Laura Reed and Carl Kaysen, 37–62. Cambridge, Mass.: American Academy of Arts and Sciences.

Crawford, Sue, and Elinor Ostrom. 1995. "A Grammar of Institutions." *American Political Science Review* 89:582–99.

Crawford, Vincent. 1982. "A Theory of Disagreement in Bargaining." *Econometrica* 50: 607–37.

Daalder, Ivo. 1991. *The Nature and Practice of Flexible Response: NATO Strategy and Theater Nuclear Forces since 1967.* New York: Columbia University Press.

Dean, Jonathan. 1987. *Watershed in Europe: Dismantling the East-West Military Confrontation.* Lexington: Lexington Books.

Demosthenes. 1993. *On the Crown, De Corona.* Trans. S. Usher. Warminster: Aris and Phillips.

DeNardo, James. 1995. *The Amateur Strategist: Intuitive Deterrence Theories and the Politics of the Nuclear Arms Race.* New York: Cambridge University Press.

Den Oudsten, E. 1985. "Public Opinion." In *SIPRI Yearbook on World Armaments and Disarmament,* 31–38. London: Taylor.

Derogy, Jacques. 1990. *Resistance and Revenge.* New Brunswick, N.J.: Transaction.

de Saussure, Ferdinand. 1922. *Course de Linguistique Générale.* Paris: Payot.

Desjardins, Marie-France, and Tariq Rauf. 1988. *Opening Pandora's Box: Nuclear-powered Submarines and the Spread of Nuclear Weapons.* Aurora Papers no. 8. Canadian Centre for Arms Control and Disarmament, Ottawa.

Dickens, Samuel. 1980. Testimony before the House Committee on Foreign Affairs, Subcommittee on Inter-American Affairs. US Policy toward El Salvador. 97th Cong., 1st sess. Quoted in Lars Schoultz, *National Security and U.S. Policy toward Latin America* (Princeton: Princeton University Press, 1987).

Donaldson, I. 1982. *The Rapes of Lucretia.* Oxford: Clarendon.

Downie, R. S. 1965. "Forgiveness." *Philosophical Quarterly* 15:128–34.

Downie, R. S. 1985. "Three Accounts of Promising." *Philosophical Quarterly* 35:259–71.

Dunbar, Robin. 1996. *Grooming, Gossip and the Evolution of Language.* London: Faber and Faber.

Dunn, Lewis. 1995. "High Noon for the NPT" *Arms Control Today* 25, no. 6: 3–9.

Dunn, Dana. 1991. "Tie a Yellow Ribbon: A Case of Social Proof during the Persian Gulf War." *Contemporary Social Psychology* 1:189–90.

Eco, Umberto. 1984. "Symbol." In *Semiotics and the Philosophy of Language.* Bloomington: Indiana University Press.

Eden, Lynn. 1990. "The Hypothetical Organization: Organizational Learning and Interpretation in US Strategic Nuclear Targeting." Paper presented at American Political Science Association Convention.

Eden, Lynn. 1991. "Sterilizing Destruction: The Imaginary Battlefield in Contemporary US Nuclear Targeting." Paper presented at the American Historical Association annual meeting, Chicago. (Center for International Security and Arms Control, Stanford University.)

Eden, Lynn. Forthcoming. *Constructing Destruction: Organizations, Knowledge and the Effects of Nuclear Weapons.* Ithaca: Cornell University Press.

Eichenberg, Richard. 1993. "Dual track and double trouble, the two-level politics of INF." 42–76 in Peter Evans, Harold Jacobson and Robert Putnam, eds. *Double-Edge Diplomacy: International Bargaining and Domestic Politics.* Berkeley: University of California Press.

Eisenhower, John. 1993. *Intervention: The U.S. in the Mexican Revolution, 1913–17.* New York: Norton.

Ellsberg, Daniel. 1954. "Classic and Current Notions of 'Measurable Utility.'" *Economic Journal* 64:528–56. Quoted in Peter Fishburn, *Interval Orders and Interval Graphs: A Study of Partially Ordered Sets* (New York: Wiley, 1954).

Elster, Jon. 1989. *The Cement of Society.* Cambridge: Cambridge University Press.

Enthoven, Alain, and K. Wayne Smith. 1971. *How Much is Enough?* New York: Harper and Row.

Eyre, Dana. 1993. Review of *Trappings of Power: Ballistic Missiles in the Third World,* by Janne Nolan. *Armed Forces and Society* 20:152–56.

Eyre, Dana, and Mark Suchman. 1996. "Status, Norms and the Proliferation of Conventional Weapons, an Institutional Theory Approach." In *The Culture of National Security: Norms and Identity in World Politics,* ed. Peter Katzenstein, 79–113. New York: Columbia University Press.

Fearon, James. 1994. "Domestic Political Audiences and the Escalation of International Disputes." *American Political Science Review* 88:577–93.

Fechner, Hermann. 1890. *Der Deutsch-Franzosische Krieg.* Berlin: G. Grote'sche.

Ferejohn, John. 1991. "Rationality and Interpretation: Parliamentary Elections in Early Stuart England." In *The Economic Approach to Politics: A Critical Reassessment of the Theory of Rational Action,* ed. Kristen Monroe, 279–305. New York: Harper-Collins.

Firth, Raymond. 1973. *Symbols, Public and Private.* London: Allen and Unwin.

Fishburn, Peter. 1985. *Interval Orders and Interval Graphs: A Study of Partially Ordered Sets.* New York: Wiley.

Fishburn, Peter. 1989. "Retrospective on the Utility Theory of von Neumann and Morgenstern." *Journal of Risk and Uncertainty* 2:127–58.

Flank, Steve. 1994. "Status, Prestige, Legitimacy and Indian Nuclear Weapons Development: International Sources of Domestic Politics." Paper presented at the thirtieth annual convention of the International Studies Association.

Fleury, Rick. 1992. "The Most Powerful Icon of the 90s?" *Brandweek* 33 (November 20):14–15.

Flynn, Charles. 1977. *Insults and Society: Patterns of Competitive Interaction.* Port Washington: Kennakut Press.

Foreign Broadcast Information Service. *Daily Report, Middle East.* Washington: FBIS. 1990–1991.

Foreign Relations of the United States. 1964–68. Washington, D.C.: U.S. Government Printing Office.

Forges, Francoise. 1990. "Equilibrium with communication in a job market example." *Quarterly Journal of Economics* 105:375–98.

Fotion, Nicholas. 1979. "I'll Bet You $10 That Betting is Not a Speech Act." In *Possibilities and Limitations of Pragmatics,* ed. Hermann Parret, Marina Sbis'a, and Jef Verschueren, 211–12. Amsterdam: Benjamin.

Freedman, Lawrence. 1986. "Flexible Response and the Concept of Escalation." In *The Price of Peace: Living with the Nuclear Dilemma,* 130–60. New York: Holt.

Freedman, Lawrence, and Virginia Gamba-Stonehouse. 1991. *Signals of War.* Princeton: Princeton University Press.

Friedell, Morris. 1967. "On the Structure of Shared Awareness." Working paper no. 27, Center for Research on Social Organization, University of Michigan.

Friedell, Morris. 1969. "On the Structure of Shared Awareness." *Behavioral Science* 14:28–39.

Fudenberg, Drew, and Eric Maskin. 1990. "Nash and Perfect Equilibria of Discounted Repeated Games." *Journal of Economic Theory* 51:194–206.

Fudenberg, Drew, and Jean Tirole. 1986. "A Theory of Exit in Duopoly." *Econometrica* 54:943–60.

Gamlen, Elizabeth, and Paul Rogers. 1993. "U.S. Reflagging of Kuwaiti Tankers." In *The Iran-Iraq War,* ed. Farhang Rajaee, 123–49. Gainesville: University of Florida Press.

Garthoff, Raymond. 1983a. "The Soviet SS-20 Decision." *Survival* 25:110–19.

Garthoff, Raymond. 1983b. "The Decision on NATO Theater Nuclear Forces." *Political Science Quarterly* 95:197–214.

Garthoff, Raymond. 1994. *The Great Transition: American-Soviet Relations and the End of the Cold War.* Washington, D.C.: Brookings Institution.

Geanakoplos, John. 1994. "Common Knowledge." In *Handbook of Game Theory,* ed. Robert Aumann and Sergiu Hart, vol. 2, 1438–96. New York: Elsevier Science.

Geanakoplos, John, David Pearce, and Ennio Stacchetti. 1989. "Psychological Games and Sequential Rationality." *Games and Economic Behavior* 1:60–79.

Gentner, Dedre. 1989. "The Mechanisms of Analogical Learning." In *Similarity and Analogical Reasoning,* ed. S. Vosniadou and A. Ortony. New York: Cambridge University Press.

Gerrard, Steven. 1994. "Morality and Codes of Honour." *Philosophy* 69:69–84.

Gilboa, Itzhak, and David Schmeidler. 1988. "Information-Dependent Games: Can Common Sense Be Common Knowledge?" *Economics Letters* 27:215–21.

Glaser, Charles. 1989. "Why Experts Disagree about Nuclear Policy." In *Nuclear Arguments: Understanding the Nuclear Arms and Arms Control Debate,* ed. Lynn Eden and Steven Miller. Ithaca: Cornell University Press.

Glaser, Charles. 1991. *Analyzing Strategic Nuclear Policy.* Princeton: Princeton University Press.

Goertz, Gary. 1994. *Contexts of International Politics.* Cambridge: Cambridge University Press.

Goffman, Erving. 1967. *Interaction Ritual: Essays on Face-to-Face Behavior.* Garden City, N.J.: Doubleday.

Golding, Martin. 1985. "Forgiveness and Regret." *Philosophical Forum* 16:121–34.

Goldmann, Kjell. 1974. *Tension and Detente in Bipolar Europe.* Stockholm: Esselte Studium.

Goldstone, R. L., D. L. Medin, and Dedre Gentner. 1991. "Relational Similarity and the Non-independence of Features in Similarity Judgements." *Cognitive Psychology* 23:22–62.

Goshko, John. 1990. "Bush Seen as Seeking Little Advice from US Experts on the Arab World." *Washington Post,* November 24, p. A26.

Greenberg, Kenneth. 1990. "The Nose, the Lie and the Duel in the Antebellum South." *American Historical Review* 95:57–75.

Greenberg, Kenneth. 1996. *Honor and Slavery.* Princeton: Princeton University Press.

Gregersen, Edgar. 1977. "A Note on English Sexual Cursing." *Maledicta, The Journal of Verbal Aggression* 1:2.

Grice, H. Paul. 1957. "Meaning." *Philosophical Review* 66:377–88.

Haber, Joram. 1991. *Forgiveness.* Savage, Md.: Rowman and Littlefield.

Haglund, David. 1989. The SSNs and the Question of Non-Proliferation. In *The US-Canada Security Relationship,* ed. David Haglund and Joel Sokolsky, 239–66. Boulder: Westview Press.

Haller, Hans, and Vincent Crawford. 1990. "Learning How to Cooperate: Optimal Play in Repeated Coordination Games." *Econometrica* 58:571–96.

Hallin, Daniel, and Todd Gitlin. 1993. "Agon and Ritual: the Gulf War as Popular Culture." *Political Communication* 10:411–14.

Hammerstein, Peter, and Reinhard Selten. 1994. "Game Theory and Evolutionary Biology." In *Handbook of Game Theory,* ed. Robert Aumann and Sergiu Hart, vol. 2, 929–93. New York: Elsevier-Science.

Hardin, Russell. 1995. *One for All: The Logic of Group Conflict.* Princeton: Princeton University Press.

Hargreaves, John D. 1985. *West Africa Partitioned*. Vol. 2. Madison: University of Wisconsin Press.

Harman, Gilbert. 1974. Review of *Meaning*, by Steven Schiffer. *Journal of Philosophy* 71:224–27.

Harsanyi, John. 1967–68. "Games with Incomplete Information Played by 'Bayesian' Players." *Management Science* 14:159–82, 320–34, 486–502.

Harsanyi, John. 1973. "Games with Randomly Disturbed Payoffs: A New Rationale for Mixed Strategy Equilibrium Points." *International Journal of Game Theory* 2:1–23.

Harsanyi, John, and Reinhard Selten. 1988. *A General Theory of Equilibrium Selection in Games*. Cambridge, Mass.: MIT Press.

Hasluck, Margaret. 1981. *The Unwritten Law in Albania*. Westport, Conn.: Hyperion Press.

Hayes, Margaret Daly. 1980. "Security to the South: U.S. Interests in Latin America." *International Security* 5:130–51. Quoted in Lars Schoultz, *National Security and U.S. Policy toward Latin America* (Princeton: Princeton University Press, 1987).

Head, Richard, Frisco Short, and Robert McFarlane. 1978. *Crisis Resolution: Presidential Decision-Making in the Mayaguez and Korean Tree Incidents*. Boulder: Westview Press.

Heilbronn, Lisa. 1994. "Yellow Ribbons and Remembrance: Mythic Symbols of the Gulf War." *Sociological Inquiry* 64:151–79.

Hempel, Carl. 1965. *Aspects of Scientific Explanation*. New York: Free Press.

Henderson, George, ed. and trans. 1899. *Fled Bricrend, The Feast of Bricriu*. London: Early Irish Texts Society.

Hilberg, Raul. 1986. "Bitburg as Symbol." In *Bitburg in Moral and Political Perspective*, ed. Geoffrey Hartman, 15–26. Bloomington: Indiana University Press.

Hillas, John, and Elon Kohlberg. Forthcoming. "Foundations of Strategic Equilibrium." In *Handbook of Game Theory*, ed. Robert Aumann and Sergiu Hart, vol. 3. Amsterdam: Elsevier-Science.

Hirshleifer, Jack, and John Riley. 1992. *The Analytics of Uncertainty and Information*. Cambridge: Cambridge University Press.

Holloway, David. 1983. *The Soviet Union and the Arms Race*. New Haven: Yale University Press.

Holls, Frederick. 1900. *The Peace Conference at the Hague*. New York: MacMillan.

Holsti, Ole. 1962. "The Value of International Tension Measurement." *Journal of Conflict Resolution* 7:609–17.

Holsti, Ole. 1969. "Time, Alternatives and Communications: The 1914 and Cuban Missile Crises." In *Quantitative International Politics*, ed. J. David Singer. New York: Free Press.

Holsti, Ole. 1972. *Crisis, Escalation, War*. Montreal: McGill University Press.

Holsti, Ole, and Alexander George. 1975. "Effects of Stress on Foreign Policy Decision Makers." *Political Science Annual* 6:255–319.

Holyoak, Keith, and Barbara Spelman. 1992. "If Saddam Is Hitler, Then Who Is George Bush? Analogical Mapping between Systems of Social Roles." *Journal of Personality and Social Psychology* 62:913–33.

Holyoak, Keith, and Paul Thagard. 1995. *Mental Leaps: Analogy in Creative Thought*. Cambridge, Mass.: MIT Press.

Horgan, John. 1989. "Land-locked." *Scientific American* 261:17.

Iklé, Frederick C. 1964. *How Nations Negotiate*. New York: Harper and Row.

Jackson, James L. 1961. "Have Present Teenagers 'Gone Ape' or 'Chicken'?" *American Speech* 36:149–51.

James, Mervyn. 1986. "English Politics and the Concept of Honour, 1485–1642." In *Society, Politics and Culture, Studies in Early Modern England,* ed. Mervyn James, 308–415. New York: Cambridge University Press.

Janis, Irving L. 1989. *Crucial Decisions: Leadership in Policymaking and Crisis Management.* New York: Free Press.

Jentleson, Bruce W. 1987. "American Commitments in the Third World: Theory vs. Practice." *International Organization* 41:667–702.

Jervis, Robert. 1971. *The Logic of Images in International Relations.* Princeton: Princeton University Press.

Jervis, Robert. 1978. "Cooperation under the Security Dilemma." *World Politics* 30:167–214.

Jervis, Robert. 1984. *The Illogic of American Nuclear Strategy.* Ithaca: Cornell University Press.

Jervis, Robert. 1989. *The Meaning of the Nuclear Revolution.* Ithaca: Cornell University Press.

Johnson, James. 1993. "Is Talk Really Cheap? Prompting Conversation between Critical Theory and Rational Choice." *American Political Science Review* 87:74–88.

Johnson, Lyndon. 1965. *Public Papers of the President of the United States: Lyndon Johnson, 1963–1964.* Vol. 2. Washington, D.C.: GPO.

Jones, T. K., and L. R. White. 1976. "The Strategic Nuclear Balance Measured in Terms of Relative Post-War Strength." In *Measuring the Strategic Balance,* ed. Anthony Cordesman, 128–53. London: International Institute of Strategic Studies.

Jonsson, Christer. 1991. "The Suez War of 1956: Communication in Crisis Management." In *Avoiding War: Problems in Crisis Management,* ed. Alexander George, 160–90. Boulder: Westview Press.

Kagan, Donald. 1995. *The Origins of War.* New York: Doubleday.

Kahn, Herman. 1965. *On Escalation: Metaphors and Scenarios.* New York: Praeger.

Kahn, Herman. 1984. *Thinking about the Unthinkable in the 1980's.* New York: Simon and Schuster.

Kaneko, Mamoru, and Toshiyuki Kimura. 1992. "Conventions, Social Prejudices and Discrimination: A Festival Game with Merrymakers." *Games and Economic Behavior* 4:511–27.

Kanwisher, Nancy. 1989. "Cognitive Heuristics and American Security Policy." *Journal of Conflict Resolution* 33:652–76.

Karklins, Rasma, and Roger Petersen. 1993. "The Decision Calculus of Protesters and Regimes: Eastern Europe, 1989." *Journal of Politics* 55:588–614.

Kier, Elizabeth, and Jonathan Mercer. 1996. "Setting Precedents in Anarchy: Military Intervention and Weapons of Mass Destruction." *International Security* 20:77–107.

Kim, Yong-Gwan. 1995. "Status Signaling Games in Animal Contests." *Journal of Theoretical Biology* 176:221–31.

Kirkbride, Wayne. 1989. *DMZ, The Story of the Panmunjom Axe Murder.* Elizabeth, N.J.: Hollym International.

Kissinger, Henry. 1979. *The White House Years.* New York: Little, Brown.

Kissinger, Henry. 1982. "Nuclear Weapons and the Peace Movement." *Washington Quarterly* 5:31–39.

Kissinger, Henry. 1984. *Report of the National Bipartisan Commission on Central America*. Washington, D.C.: U.S. Government Printing Office.

Klein, Daniel, and Brendan O'Flaherty. 1993. "A Game-Theoretic Rendering of Promises and Threats." *Journal of Economic Behavior and Organization* 21:295–314.

Klingberg, Frank L. 1965. "Studies in Measurements of the Relations among Sovereign States." In *International Politics and Foreign Policy: A Reader in Research and Theory*, ed. James Rosenau. New York: Free Press of Glencoe. First published in *Psychometrika* 6 (1941): 335–52.

Klotz, Audie. 1995. *Norms in International Relations: The Struggle against Apartheid*. Ithaca: Cornell University Press.

Kovecses, Zoltan. 1986. *Metaphors of Anger, Pride and Love: A Lexical Approach to the Structure of Concepts*. Philadelphia: J. Benjamins.

Kovecses, Zoltan. 1990. *Emotion Concepts*. New York: Springer-Verlag.

Kraines, David, and Vivian Kraines. 1987. "Pavlov and the Prisoner's Dilemma." *Theory and Decision* 26:47–70.

Krasner, Stephen. 1983. "Structural causes and regime consequences: regimes as intervening variables." *International Organization* 36:1–21.

Krasno, Jean. 1994. "The Role of Belief Systems in Shaping Nuclear Weapons: Policy Preference and Thinking in Brazil." Ph.D. diss., City University of New York.

Krepon, Michael. 1995. *A Handbook of Confidence-Building Measures for Regional Security*. Washington, D.C.: Stimson Center.

Kreps, David, and Robert Wilson. 1982. "Sequential Equilibria." *Econometrica* 50:863–94.

Krishna, Vijay, and John Morgan. 1994. "An Analysis of the War of Attrition and the All-Pay Auction." Department of Economics, Pennsylvania State University.

Kull, Steven. 1985. "Nuclear Nonsense." *Foreign Policy* 58:28–52.

Kull, Steven. 1988. *Minds at War: Nuclear Reality and the Inner Conflicts of Defense Policymakers*. New York: Basic Books.

Kydd, Andrew, and Duncan Snidal. 1993. "Progress in Game-Theoretical Analysis of International Regimes." In *Regime Theory and International Relations*, ed. Volker Rittberger, 94–111. Oxford: Clarendon.

Lakoff, George. 1987. *Women, Fire and Other Dangerous Things: What Categories Reveal about the Mind*. Chicago: University of Chicago Press.

Lakoff, George. 1991. "Metaphor and War: the Metaphor System Used to Justify War in the Gulf." *Journal of Urban and Cultural Studies* 2 (1991). Reprinted in *Quarterly Review of Doublespeak* (July 1993): 9–12. First published in Brien Hallet, ed., *Engulfed in War: Just Peace and the Persian Gulf* (Honolulu: Matsunaga Institute for Peace, 1991).

Lakoff, George, and Mark Johnson. 1980. *Metaphors We Live By*. Chicago: University of Chicago Press.

Lalande, A., ed. 1926. *Vocabulaire Technique et Critique de la Philosophie*. Paris: Presses Universitaires de France.

Langille, Howard Peter. 1990. *Changing the Guard: Canada's Defence in a World in Transition*. Toronto: University of Toronto Press.

Larsen, Lotte. 1994. "The Yellow Ribboning of America, a Gulf War Phenomenon." *Journal of American Culture* 17:11–22.

Lasswell, Harold, and Abraham Kaplan. 1950. *Power and Society*. New Haven: Yale University Press.

Lebow, Richard Ned. 1981. *Between Peace and War*. Baltimore: Johns Hopkins University Press.

Legge, J. Michael. 1983. "Theater Nuclear Weapons and the NATO Strategy of Flexible Response." Report R-2964, RAND Corporation, Santa Monica.

Legro, Jeffrey. 1997. "Which Norms Matter? Revisiting the 'Failure' of Internationalism." *International Organization* 51:31–64.

Leiber, J. 1979. "Insulting." *Philosophia, Philosophical Quarterly of Israel* 8:549–71.

Leng, Russell. 1993. *Interstate Crisis Behavior, 1816–1980: Realism versus Reciprocity*. Cambridge: Cambridge University Press.

Leonard, Robert. 1994. "Reading Cournot, Reading Nash: The Creation and Stabilisation of the Nash Equilibrium." *Economic Journal* 104:492–511.

Levkov, Ilya, ed. 1987. *Bitburg and Beyond*. New York: Shapolsky.

Lewis, David. 1969. *Conventions*. Cambridge, Mass.: Harvard University Press.

Lewis, Helen. 1971. *Shame and Guilt in Neurosis*. New York: International Universities Press.

Leyton-Brown, David. 1981. "External Affairs and Diplomacy." In *Canadian Annual Review of Politics and Public Affairs, 1979,* ed. Rod Byers, 183–266. Toronto: University of Toronto Press.

Lohmann, Susanne. 1992. *Rationality, Revolution and Revolt: The Dynamics of Information Cascades*. Graduate School of Business Research paper no. 1213a, Stanford University.

Lohmann, Susanne. Forthcoming. *Stand Up and Be Counted: Mass Complicity and Mass Action in East Germany, 1949–1998*.

Loomis, Laura Hibbard. 1959. "Gawain and the Green Knight." In *Arthurian Literature in the Middle Ages,* ed. R. S. Loomis, 528–40. New York: Oxford University Press.

Lord, Robert. 1966. *Origins of the War of 1870*. New York: Russell and Russell.

Luard, Evan. 1986. *War in International Society*. New Haven: Yale University Press.

Luard, Evan. 1992. *Balance of Power: The System of International Relations, 1648–1915*. New York: St. Martin's Press.

Luce, Duncan. 1956. "Semiorders and a Theory of Utility Discrimination." *Econometrica* 24:178–91.

Luce, Duncan. 1990. "Rational versus Plausible Accounting Equivalences in Preference Judgments." *Psychological Science* 1:225–34.

Lunn, Simon. 1983. "INF and Political Cohesion in NATO." In *The European Missiles Crisis,* ed. Hans-Henrik Holm and Nikolaj Petersen, 208–31. New York: St. Martin's Press.

Manning, Philip. 1993. *Erving Goffman and Modern Sociology*. Cambridge: Polity Press.

March, James, and Herbert Simon. 1958. *Organizations*. New York: Wiley.

Maynard-Smith, John. 1974. "The Theory of Games and the Evolution of Animal Conflicts." *Journal of Theoretical Biology* 47:209–21.

Maynard-Smith, John. 1982. *Evolution and the Theory of Games*. New York: Cambridge University Press.

Maynard Smith, John, and R. L. W. Brown. 1986. "Competition and Body Size." *Theoretical Population Biology* 30:166–79.

McAleer, Kevin. 1994. *Dueling: The Cult of Honor in Fin-de-Siècle Germany*. Princeton: Princeton University Press.

McCaffree, Mary Jane, and Pauline Innis. 1985. *Protocol: The Complete Handbook of Diplomatic, Official and Social Usage.* Washington, D.C.: Devon.

McCawley, James. 1977. "Remarks on the Lexicography of Performative Verbs." In *Proceedings of the Texas Conference on Performatives,* ed. Andy Rogers, Bob Wall, and John Moore, 13–25. Arlington: Center for Applied Linguistics.

McEvoy, Catharine, and Douglas Nelson. 1984. "Name and Instance Norms." *American Journal of Psychology* 95:581–634.

McGinn, Robert. 1971. "About Face." *Social Theory and Practice* 1:87–96.

McGinn, Robert. 1972. "Prestige and the Logic of Political Argument." *Monist* 56:100–115.

Medin, Douglas, and Brian Ross. 1992. *Cognitive Psychology.* Fort Worth: Harcourt Brace Jovanovich.

Mehta, Judith, Chris Starmer, and Robert Sugden. 1994. "The Nature of Salience: An Experimental Investigation of Pure Coordination Games." *American Economic Review* 84:658–73.

Mercer, Jonathan. 1996. *Reputation and Deterrence Theory.* Ithaca: Cornell University Press.

Meyer, Kuno. 1893. "The Edinburgh Version of the *Cennach ind Ruanado* (Bargain of the Strong Men)." *Revue Celtique* 10:455–59.

Meyer, Stephen, and Peter Almquist. 1985. *Insights from Soviet Strategic Force Modeling.* Defense Advanced Research Projects Agency.

Midlarsky, Manus. 1975. *On War: Political Violence in the International System.* New York: Free Press.

Milgrom, Paul, and Robert Weber. 1982. "A Theory of Auctions and Competitive Bidding." *Econometrica* 50:1089–1121.

Miller, William. 1993. *Humiliation and Other Essays on Honor, Social Discomfort and Violence.* Ithaca: Cornell University Press.

Millett, Richard. 1982. "The Best of Times, the Worst of Times: Central American Scenarios—1984." In *The Central American Crisis: Policy Perspectives,* ed. Abraham Lowenthal and Samuel Wells, Jr. Working paper no. 119, the Wilson Center, Washington D.C. Quoted in Lars Schoultz, *National Security and U.S. Policy toward Latin America* (Princeton: Princeton University Press, 1987).

Milliken, Jennifer. 1996. "Metaphors of Prestige and Reputation in American Foreign Policy and American Realism." In *Post-Realism: The Rhetorical Turn in International Relations,* ed. Francis Beer and Robert Hariman. East Lansing: Michigan State University Press.

Milliken, Jennifer, and David Sylvan. 1991. "Soft Bodies, Hard Targets, and Chic Theories: US Bombing Policy in Indo-China." Draft paper for the XVth World Congress of the International Political Science Association, Buenos Aires.

Mills, C. Wright. 1951. *White Collar.* New York: Oxford University Press.

Monderer, Dov, and Dov Samet. 1989. "Approximating Common Knowledge with Common Beliefs." *Games and Economic Behavior* 1:170–90.

Moore, Sally, and Barbara Myerhoff. 1977. "Introduction: Secular Rituals, Form and Meaning." In *Secular Ritual,* 1–24. Assen, Netherlands: Van Gorcum.

Morgan, H. Wayne. 1963. "The De Lome Letter: A New Appraisal." *Historian* 26:36–49.

Morgenthau, Hans. 1976. "The Fallacy of Thinking Conventionally about Nuclear

Weapons." In *Arms Control and Technological Innovation,* ed. David Carlton and Carlo Schaerf, 255–64. New York: Wiley.

Myerson, Roger. 1981. "Optimal Auction Design." *Mathematics of Operations Research* 6:58–73.

Nalebuff, Barry. 1986. "Brinkmanship and Nuclear Deterrence: The Neutrality of Escalation." *Conflict Management and Peace Science* 9:19–30.

Nalebuff, Barry. 1991. "Rational Deterrence in an Imperfect World." *World Politics* 43: 313–35.

Nalebuff, Barry, and John Riley. 1985. "Asymmetric Equilibria in the War of Attrition." *Journal of Theoretical Biology* 113:517–27.

Nash, John. 1950. "Equilibrium Points in N-Person Games." *Proceedings of the National Academy of Sciences* 36:48–49.

Nash, John. 1951. "Non-Cooperative Games." *Annals of Mathematics* 54:286–95.

Neff, Donald. 1981. *Warriors at Suez.* New York: Linden.

Newcombe, Alan, and James Wert. 1972. "An Internation Tensionmeter for the Prediction of War." Oakville, Ont.: Canadian Peace Research Institute.

Newhouse, John. 1991. "Misreadings (Iraq)." *New Yorker* 66 (February 18): 72–79.

Nicolson, Harold. 1937. *The Meaning of Prestige.* Cambridge: Cambridge University Press.

Nicolson, Harold. 1939. *Diplomacy.* Oxford: Oxford University Press.

Nisbett, Richard, and Dov Cohen. 1996. *Culture of Honor: The Psychology of Violence in the South.* Boulder: Westview.

Nitze, Paul. 1976. "Assuring Strategic Stability in an Era of Detente." *Foreign Affairs* 54:207–32.

Nitze, Paul. 1976–77. "Deterring Our Deterrent." *Foreign Policy* 25:195–210.

Nobili, Flaminio. 1550. *Discorsi sopra le piu importanti questioni nella materia dell'honore.* Bologna. Quoted in Frederick Bryson, *The Point of Honor in Sixteenth-Century Italy: An Aspect of the Life of the Gentleman* (New York: Columbia University Press, 1935).

Nolan, Janne. 1991. "The INF Treaty." In *The Politics of Arms Control Treaty Ratification,* ed. Michael Krepon and Dan Caldwell, 355–98. New York: St. Martin's Press.

Nowak, Martin, and Karl Sigmund. 1993. "A Strategy of Win-Stay Lose-Shift That Outperforms Tit-for-Tat in the Prisoner's Dilemma Game." *Nature* 364:56–58.

Nye, Robert. 1993. *Masculinity and Male Codes of Honor in Modern France.* New York: Oxford University Press.

Offner, John. 1992. *An Unwanted War: The Diplomacy of the United States and Spain over Cuba, 1895–1898.* Chapel Hill: University of North Carolina Press.

Ollivier, Emile. 1913. *The Franco-Prussian War, Its Hidden Causes.* Translation and notes by George Burnham Ives. Boston: Littlewood. Quoted in William Carr, *The Origins of the Wars of German Unification* (New York: Longman, 1991).

O'Neill, Barry. 1986. "International Escalation and the Dollar Auction." *Journal of Conflict Resolution* 30:33–50.

O'Neill, Barry. 1987. "A Measure of Crisis Instability, with an Application to Space-Based Anti-missile Systems." *Journal of Conflict Resolution* 31:631–72.

O'Neill, Barry. 1988. "Pentagon Graphsmanship: Who's Ahead in Nukes? It Depends on Where You Draw the Line." *Washington Post,* December 27, p. L5.

O'Neill, Barry. 1989. "The Intermediate Nuclear Force Missiles: An Analysis of Coupling and Reassurance." *International Interactions* 15:345–63.

O'Neill, Barry. 1991a. "Rush-Bagot and the Upkeep of Arms Treaties." *Arms Control Today* 21:20–23.

O'Neill, Barry. 1991b. "The Strategy of Challenges: Two Beheading Games in Mediaeval Literature." In *Game Equilibrium Models,* ed. R. Selten, vol. 4, *Social and Political Interaction,*124–49. New York: Springer-Verlag.

O'Neill, Barry. 1992. "Measures of the Worth of Weapons." Mimeo. York University, Toronto.

O'Neill, Barry. 1993. "Are Game Models of Deterrence Biassed towards Arms-Building?" *Journal of Political Theory* 4:459–77.

O'Neill, Barry. 1994. "Game Models of Peace and War." In *Handbook of Game Theory,* vol. 2, ed. Robert Aumann and Sergiu Hart, 995–1090. New York: Elsevier-Science.

Opie, Iona, and Peter Opie. 1969. *Children's Games in Street and Playground.* Oxford: Clarendon.

Osborne, Martin, and Ariel Rubinstein. 1994. *A Course in Game Theory.* Cambridge, Mass.: MIT Press.

Osgood, Charles. 1962. *An Alternative to War or Surrender.* Urbana: University of Illinois Press.

Parker, Richard. 1993. *The Politics of Miscalculation in the Middle East.* Bloomington: Indiana University Press.

Parkinson, Dilworth. 1989. "Egyptian Arabic Abuse." *Maledicta, the Journal of Verbal Aggression* 10:143–61.

Parsons, Gerald. 1981. "Yellow Ribbons: Ties with Tradition." *Folklife Center News,* nos. 4 and 8–12.

Parsons, Gerald. 1991. "How the Yellow Ribbon Became a National Folk Symbol." *Folklife Center News,* nos. 9–11 and 13.

Parsons, Talcott. 1952. *The Social System.* Glencoe, Ill.: Free Press.

Partridge, John Geoffrey. 1982. *Semantic, Pragmatic and Syntactic Correlates: An Analysis of Performative Verbs Based on English Data.* Tubingen: Gunter Narr Verlag.

Patrizi, Francesco. 1553. *Dialogo dell'honore.* Venice. Quoted in Frederick Bryson, *The Point of Honor in Sixteenth-Century Italy: An Aspect of the Life of the Gentleman* (New York: Columbia University Press, 1935), 47.

Peirce, Charles S. 1931. *Collected Papers.* Vol. 2. Cambridge, Mass.: Harvard University Press.

Perez de Cuellar, Javier. 1997. *Pilgrimage for Peace.* New York: St. Martin's Press.

Peristiany, J. G., ed. 1996. *Honour and Shame: The Values of Mediterranean Society.* Chicago: U⁻˙ ⋅rsity of Chicago Press.

Peristiany, J. G., ａⅰ.d Julian Pitt-Rivers. 1992. "Introduction." In *Honor and Grace in Anthropology,* 1–18. New York: Cambridge University Press.

Perla, Leo. 1918. *What is "National Honor"?* New York: Macmillan.

Permanent Peoples' Tribunal. 1985. *A Crime of Silence: The Armenian Genocide.* London: Zed Books. Quoted in Jacques Derogy, *Resistance and Revenge* (New Brunswick, N.J.: Transaction, 1990).

Peters, Susanne. 1990. *The Germans and the INF Missiles.* Baden-Baden: Nomos.

Peterson, V. Spike, ed. 1992. *Gendered States.* Boulder: Lynne Reinner.

Pitt-Rivers, Julian. 1968. "Honor." In *International Encyclopedia of the Social Sciences,* ed. David Sills, vol. 6, 503–11. New York: Macmillan.

Plous, Scott. 1985. "Perceptual Illusions and Military Realities: A Social Psychological Analysis of the Nuclear Arms Race." *Journal of Conflict Resolution* 29:363–69.

Powell, Robert. 1988. "Nuclear Brinkmanship with Two-Sided Incomplete Information." *American Political Science Review* 82:155–78.

Powell, Robert. 1990. *Nuclear Deterrence: The Search for Credibility.* New York: Oxford University Press.

Pratt, Julius. 1925. *The Expansionists of 1812.* New York: Macmillan.

President's Commission on Strategic Forces. 1983. *Report of the President's Commission on Strategic Forces (Scowcroft Report).* Washington, D.C.: Goverment Printing Office.

Quester, George. 1977. *Offense and Defense in the International System.* New York: Wiley.

Rabinovitch, I. 1978. "The Dimension of Semiorders." *Journal of Combinatorial Theory Part A* 25:50–61.

Ram, K. V. 1985. *The Barren Relationship, Britain and Ethiopia, 1805 to 1868.* New Delhi: Concept Publishing.

Rapoport, Anatol. 1964. *Strategy and Conscience.* New York: Harper and Row.

Rapoport, Anatol. 1965. "Chicken à la Kahn." *Virginia Quarterly Review* 41:370–89.

Rapoport, Anatol, and Albert Chammah. 1965. *The Prisoner's Dilemma.* Ann Arbor: University of Michigan Press.

Rapoport, Anatol, Mel Guyer, and David Gordon. 1976. *The 2 × 2 Game.* Ann Arbor: University of Michigan Press.

Rashevsky, Nicholas. 1947. *Mathematical Theory of Human Relations.* Bloomington: Principia Press.

Reagan, Ronald. 1983. Address to a Joint Session of Congress. *Weekly Compilation of Presidential Documents,* May 2.

Recanati, Francois. 1993. *Direct Reference: From Language to Thought.* Cambridge, Mass.: Blackwell.

Reddy, Michael. 1979. "The Conduit Metaphor." In *Metaphor and Thought,* ed. Andrew Ortony, 284–324. Cambridge: Cambridge University Press.

Riley John, and William Samuelson. 1981. "Optimal Auctions." *American Economic Review* 71:381–92.

Ringmar, Erik. 1993. "Words that Govern Men: A Cultural Explanation of the Swedish Intervention into the Thirty Years War." Ph.D. diss., Yale University.

Risjord, Norman. 1961. "The War of 1812: Conservatives, War Hawks and the Nation's Honor." *William and Mary Quarterly* 18:196–210.

Risse-Kappen, Thomas. 1988. *The Zero Option: INF, West Germany and Arms Control.* Boulder: Westview Press.

Rohrer, Tim. 1995. "The Metaphorical Logic of (Political) Rape: the New Wor(l)d Order." *Metaphor and Symbolic Activity* 10:115–37.

Rosch, Eleanor. 1978. "Principles of Categorization." In *Cognition and Categorization,* ed. E. Rosch and B. B. Lloyd, 27–48. Hillsdale, N.J.: Erlbaum.

Rosch, Eleanor, C. Mervis, W. Gray, D. Johnson, and P. Boyes-Braem. 1976. "Basic Objects in Natural Categories." *Cognitive Psychology* 2:382–439.

Rosenberg, David Alan. 1983. "The Origins of Overkill: Nuclear Weapons and American Strategy, 1945–1960." *International Security* 7:3–71.

Rousseau, Jean-Jacques. 1964. *The First and Second Discourses.* Ed. and trans. Roger and Judith Masters. New York: St. Martin's Press.

Royce, Josiah. 1914. *War and Insurance*. New York: Macmillan.

Rubenson, Sven. 1976. *The Survival of Ethiopian Independence*. London: Heinemann.

Rumelhart, David, and James Levin. 1975. "A Language Comprehension System." In *Explorations in Cognition*, ed. Donald Norman and David Rumelhart, 179–205. San Francisco: Freeman.

Russell, Bertrand. 1959. *Common Sense and Nuclear Warfare*. London: Allen and Unwin.

Russett, Bruce, and Donald DeLuca. 1983. "Theater Nuclear Forces: Public Opinion in Western Europe." *Political Science Quarterly* 98:179–96.

Sagan, Scott. 1993. *The Limits of Safety*. Princeton: Princeton University Press.

Sagan, Scott. 1996. "Why Do States Build Nuclear Weapons? Three Models in Search of a Bomb." *International Security* 21:54–86.

Sagan, Scott. 1997. "The Causes of Nuclear Proliferation." *Current History* 96:151–58.

Salmon, Michael, Kevin Sullivan and Stephen van Evera. 1989. "Analysis or Propaganda? Measuring the American Strategic Nuclear Capability." In *Nuclear Arguments*, ed. Lynn Eden, and Steve Miller, 179–205. Ithaca: Cornell University Press.

Samet, Dov. 1996. "Common Priors and Markov Chains." Mimeo. Tel Aviv University.

Santino, Jack. 1992. "Yellow Ribbons and Seasonal Flags, the Folk Assemblage of War." *Journal of American Folklore* 105:19–33.

Sapir, Edward. 1937. "Symbolism." In *Encyclopaedia of the Social Sciences*, 492–95. New York: Macmillan.

Savage, Leonard. 1954. *The Foundations of Statistics*. New York: Wiley.

Schelling, Thomas. 1960. *The Strategy of Conflict*. Cambridge, Mass.: Harvard University Press.

Schelling, Thomas. 1989. "Promises." *Negotiation Journal* 4:113–18.

Schiffer, Stephen. 1972. *Meaning*. Oxford: Clarendon.

Schmitt, Raymond. 1989. "Sharing the Holocaust: Bitburg as Emotional Reminder." In *Studies in Symbolic Interaction*, ed. Norman Denzin, vol. 10, 239–98. Greenwich, Conn.: JAI Press. Quoted in Robert Jervis, *The Meaning of the Nuclear Revolution* (Ithaca: Cornell University Press, 1989).

Schoultz, Lars. 1987. *National Security and U.S. Policy toward Latin America*. Princeton: Princeton University Press.

Schuessler, Alexander. 1994. The Logic of Expressive Action. Manuscript.

Schwartz, Stephen. 1995. "Four Trillion Dollars and Counting." *Bulletin of the Atomic Scientists* 51 (November): 32.

Scott, Dana, and Patrick Suppes. 1958. "Foundational Aspects of Theories of Measurement." *Journal of Symbolic Logic* 23:113–28.

Searle, John. 1995. *The Construction of Social Reality*. New York: Free Press.

Searle, John, and Daniel Vanderveken. 1985. *Foundations of Illocutionary Logic*. London: Cambridge University Press.

Sebeok, Thomas, ed. 1986. *Encylopedic Dictionary of Semiotics*. New York: Mouton de Gruyter.

Seligman, David. 1995. "A Threat or a Promise." *Southern Journal of Philosophy* 33:83–96.

Selten, Reinhard. 1965. "Spieltheoretische Behandlung eines Oligopolmodells mit Nachfragetragheit." *Zeitschrift fur die gesamte Staatswissenschaft* 121:301–24, 667–89.

Selten, Reinhard. 1975. "Re-examination of the Perfectness Concept of Equilibrium Points in Extensive Form Games." *International Journal of Game Theory* 4:25–55.

Selten, Reinhard. 1977. A Simple Model of Kidnapping. In *Mathematical Economics and Game Theory: Essays in Honor of Oskar Morgenstern,* ed. R. Henn and O. Moeschler, 139–55. Berlin: Springer-Verlag.

Shubik, Martin. 1971. "Games of Status." Behavioral Science 16:117–29.

Shubik, Martin. 1982. *Game Theory in the Social Sciences.* Cambridge, Mass.: MIT Press.

Singer, J. David. 1958. "Threat Perception and the Armament-Tension Dilemma." *Journal of Conflict Resolution* 2:90–105.

Skorupski, John. 1976. *Symbol and Theory: A Philosophical Study of Theories of Religion in Social Anthropology.* New York: Cambridge University Press.

Smyth, Albert H., ed. 1905–7. *The Writings of Benjamin Franklin.* Vol. 9. New York: Macmillan.

Snyder, Glenn, and Paul Diesing. 1977. *Conflict among Nations.* Princeton: Princeton University Press.

Snyder, Jack. 1984. *The Ideology of the Offensive: Military Decision Making and the Disaster of 1914.* New York: Cambridge University Press.

Soens, A. L. 1992. "The Yellow Ribbons: The Bawdy Balladry Behind the Manufactured Popular Piety." Paper presented to Popular Culture Association Meeting, Louisville.

Stein, Janice Gross. 1985. "Calculation, Miscalculation and Conventional Deterrence I: The View from Cairo." In *Psychology and Deterrence,* ed. Robert Jervis, Richard Ned Lebow, and Janice Gross Stein. Baltimore: Johns Hopkins University Press.

Stein, Janice Gross. 1989. "Getting to the Table: the Triggers, Stages, Functions, and Consequences of Prenegotiation." In *Getting to the Table: the Processes of International Prenegotiation,* 239–68. Baltimore: Johns Hopkins University Press.

Steinberg, Blema. 1991. "Shame and Humiliation in the Cuban Missile Crisis: A Psychoanalytic Perspective." *Political Psychology* 12:653–90.

Stewart, Frank Henderson. 1994. *Honor.* Chicago: University of Chicago Press.

Stice, Jeris W. 1973. "Verbal Aggression in State of the Union Messages during Wartime and Non-Wartime." Ph.D. diss., Florida State University.

Stigler, George. 1950. "The Development of Utility Theory." *Journal of Political Economy* 58:307–27, 373–96.

Stouffer, Samuel, Louis Guttman, Edward Suchman, Paul Lazarsfeld, Shirley Star, and John Clausen. 1950. *Measurement and Prediction, Studies in Social Psychology.* Princeton: Princeton University Press.

Strange, Susan. 1983. "Cave! Hic Dragones: A Critique of Regime Analysis." In *International Regimes,* ed. S. Krasner. Ithaca: Cornell University Press.

Strawson, P. F. 1964. "Intention and Convention in Speech Acts." *Philosophical Review* 73:439–60.

Stuart, Kathleen. 1993. "Boundaries of Honor." Ph.D. diss., Department of History, Yale University.

Sutterlin, James, and David Klein. 1989. *Berlin: From a Symbol of Conflict to a Keystone of Stability.* New York: Praeger.

Talbott, Strobe. 1985. *Deadly Gambits.* New York: Vintage.

Talbott, Strobe. 1988. *The Master of the Game: Paul Nitze and the Nuclear Peace.* New York: Knopf.

Taylor, Shelly, and Susan Fiske. 1978. "Salience, Attention and Attribution: Top of the

Head Phenomena." In *Advances in Experimental Social Psychology,* ed. Leonard Berkowitz, vol. 11, 250–89. New York: Academic Press.

Terraillon, Eugene. 1912. *L'Honneur; Sentiment et Principe Moral.* Paris: F. Alcan.

Thayer, William. 1918. *Out of Their Mouths.* New York: Appleton.

Thies, Wallace. 1980. *When Governments Collide.* Boulder: University of Colorado Press.

Thomson, James. 1984. "The LRTNF Decision: Evolution of US Theatre Nuclear Policy." *International Affairs* 20:601–14.

Thurneysen, Rudolf. 1921. *Die Irische Helden- und Konigsage bis zum Siebzehnten Jahrhundert.* Halle: Niemeyer.

Tilly, Charles. 1978. *From Mobilization to Revolution.* Englewood Cliffs: Prentice-Hall.

Tolkien, J. R. R., and E. D. Gordon, eds. 1925. *Sir Gawain and the Green Knight.* Oxford: Clarendon.

Travers, Timothy. 1984. *The Killing Ground: The British Army, the Western Front and the Emergence of Modern Warfare, 1900–1918.* Boston: Allen and Unwin.

Travers, Timothy. 1992. *How the War Was Won: Command and Technology in the British Army on the Western Front, 1917–1918.* New York: Routledge.

Tsumagari, Maki. 1994. "The Power of Symbols, Government Officials' Visits to Yasukuni Shrine, Tokyo, Japan." Course paper, School of Organization and Management, Yale University.

Tucker, A. W. 1950. "A Two-Person Dilemma." Mimeo. Stanford University.

Tucker, Robert. 1981. *The Purposes of American Power: An Essay on National Security.* New York: Praeger. Quoted in Lars Schoultz, *National Security and U.S. Policy toward Latin America* (Princeton: Princeton University Press, 1987).

Tuleja, Tad. 1994. "Closing the Circle: Yellow Ribbons and the Redemption of the Past." *Journal of American Culture* 17:23–31.

Turner, Victor. 1967. *The Forest of Symbols: Aspects of Ndembu Ritual.* Ithaca: Cornell University Press.

Tyler, Patrick. 1992. "While Fear of Big War Fades, Military Plans for Little Ones." *New York Times,* February 3.

Ullman-Margalit, Edna. 1977. *The Emergence of Norms.* Oxford: Clarendon.

Ulriksen, Ann Schult. 1994. "The Peace Brokers: The Role of Norway in Middle Eastern Conflict Resolution." Course paper, Yale School of Management.

U.S. Department of State. 1961. *Bulletin.* November 12. Washington, D.C.: Government Printing Office.

U.S. Department of State. 1964. *Bulletin.* August 24. Washington, D.C.: Government Printing Office.

U.S. Department of State. 1979. "Modernization and Arms Control for Long-Range Theater Nuclear Forces." Mimeo. October 16. Washington, D.C.

U.S. Department of State. 1979. *Report on INF.* Washington, D.C.: Government Printing Office.

Vagts, Alfred. 1956. "Armed Demonstrations." In *Defense and Diplomacy,* 231–63. New York: King's Crown.

Vale, Malcolm. 1981. "Chivalric Display." In *War and Chivalry.* London: Duckworth.

Valmarana, Paolo Antonio. 1598. *Trattato dell'offese et del modo di far le pace.* Vicenza. Quoted in Frederick Bryson, *The Point of Honor in Sixteenth-Century*

Italy: An Aspect of the Life of the Gentleman (New York: Columbia University Press, 1935).

van Evera, Steven. 1984. "The Causes of War." Ph.D. diss., Political Science Department, University of California, Berkeley.

Vance, Cyrus. 1983. *Hard Choices: Critical Years in America's Foreign Policy.* New York: Simon and Schuster.

Vanderveken, Daniel. 1990. *Meaning and Speech Acts.* Vols. 1 and 2. New York: Cambridge University Press.

Veblen, Thorstein. 1917. *An Inquiry into the Nature of Peace and its Terms of Perpetuation.* New York: Macmillan.

Verkuyten, Maykel. 1995. "Symbols and Social Representations." *Journal for the Theory of Social Behaviour* 25:265–84.

Vernon Jones, V. S. tr. 1919. *Aesop's Fables.* New York: Doubleday, Page & Co.

Vickrey, William. 1962. "Auctions and Bidding Games." In *Recent Advances in Game Theory,* ed. Oskar Morgenstern and Alfred Tucker. Princeton: Princeton University Press.

von Neumann, John, and Oskar Morgenstern. 1953. *The Theory of Games and Economic Behavior.* Princeton: Princeton University Press.

von Treitschke, Heinrich. 1916. *Politics.* Trans. Blanche Dugdale and Torben de Bille. London: Constable.

Waltz, Kenneth. 1959. *Man, the State and War.* Cambridge, Mass.: Harvard University Press.

Warman, Cy. 1911. *Songs of Cy Warman.* Boston: Rand Avery.

Weber, Cynthia. 1994. "Something's Missing: Male Hysteria and the US Invasion of Panama." *Genders,* no. 19:171–97.

Weber, Cynthia. 1995. "Masquerading America and the U.S.-Led Intervasion into Haiti." Mimeo. Purdue University.

Weber, Max. 1924. *Gesammelte Aufsatze zur Sozial- und Wirtschaftsgeschichte.* Tübingen: Mohr.

Weinstein, Franklin. 1969. "The Concept of a Commitment in International Relations." *Journal of Conflict Resolution* 13:39–56.

Wendt, Alex. 1999. *The Social Theory of International Relations.* New York: Cambridge University Press.

Whitehead, Alfred North. 1927. *Symbolism, Its Meaning and Effect.* New York: Macmillan.

White House. 1988. "National Security Strategy of the United States." Bulletin 88:1–31. Washington, D.C.: Government Printing Office.

White House. 1996. "A National Security Strategy of Engagement and Enlargement." Bulletin. Washington, D.C.: Government Printing Office.

Wiegele, T. C. 1973. "Decision Making in an International Crisis, Biological Factors." *International Studies Quarterly* 17:295–335.

Wiegele, T. C. 1985. *Leaders under Stress: A Psychophysiological Analysis of International Crises.* Durham: Duke University Press.

Wiesenthal, Simon. 1972. *The Sunflower.* London: W. H. Allen.

Woodman, Dorothy. 1962. *The Making of Burma.* London: Creset.

Wright, Quincy. 1957. "Proposal for a World Intelligence Center." *Journal of Conflict Res-olution* 1:93–97.

Yao Xu. 1985. *From Yalu to Panmunjom.* Beijing: People's Press.

York, Herbert. 1970. *Race to Oblivion.* New York: Simon and Schuster.

Zimmerman, William. 1925. *The Impressment of American Seamen.* New York: Colum-bia University Press.

Zinnes, Dina. 1972. "The Expression and Perception of Hostility in Prewar Crisis: 1914." In *International Crises: Insights from Behavioral Research,* ed. Charles Hermann, 85–117. New York: Free Press.

Index

INF missiles. *See* Intermediate-Range
Nuclear Force (INF) missiles
Innis, P., 22, 60
Instantaneous tension. *See* Tension, international, instantaneous
Insults, 139–63, 174–75
  Arabic culture, 175
  Aristotle's categories, 146n. 2
  definition, 146–50
  causes of war, examples, 141–45
  challenges, as precursors to, 114–15,
  124
  curses, 149n. 2
  definition of, 146–50
  deniability not a requirement for,
  150–51
  Duck Soup, 85
  expressing intent to attack face, 150–51
  face and, 145–46, 148–49, 161
  honor versus face in, 145–46
  "I insult you," impossiblity of, 149–51
  investments of face, as, 166
  lack of semantic content, 148–49
  nonverbal, 148
  personalizing blame, by, 151
  prototypical versus extended conception of, 147–48
  recognizing, 150–51
  referring to bodily parts, 151
  summary of findings, 246–47
  unintended, 147
  See also Apologies; Face; War of face
Intangibles in international relations
  theory, 253–62
Intentions
  components of, 27
  in insults, 149–50, 152–54
  reflexive, 26n. 1, 27–28
Interactive belief systems (IBS), 116–20,
  223–25, 274–85
  basic example, Stag Hunt game,
  275–78
  challenging model, 116–20, 280–82
  cultivated nuclear irrationality model,
  223–25, 282–84
  focal symbolism model, 279–80

syntactic versus semantic approach,
  225n. 5
Interactive epistemology. *See* Common
  knowledge
Intermediate-Range Nuclear Force (INF)
  missiles, 225–39
  bargaining chips, 232–33
  costly signals, 234–37
  coupling, 218, 227, 231–32, 234–35
  European public opinion, 227, 235
  military rationales, 227, 229–32
  number of missiles, 233, 236
  political rationales, 227, 232–39
  rationale for Soviet SS-20 missiles,
  236–37
  symbolic rationales, 233–39
  symbolism in treaty ceremony, 59
Intuitive deterrence theories, 216n. 1. *See
  also* Organizational thought-styles
Iran, 175n. 7, 185
  hostage crisis, 46, 90, 101, 152n. 6, 177
  See also Yellow ribbons
Irangate Affair, 178
Iraq, 12, 16–17, 21–22, 46
Isomorphism in analogies, 52–55
Israel, 14, 15, 17, 126, 190–91
Italy, Renaissance, honor in, 88, 97, 101,
  124
Ives, G., 150

Jackson, Henry, 86, 219
Jackson, J., 264
Jacobs, Harriet, 135
James, M., 89, 107, 127
Janis, I., 66
Japan, 14, 20, 64–65
  apologies for actions in World War II,
  179, 180, 187, 188, 190
Jervis, R., 6, 46, 54, 61, 78, 92, 137, 195,
  215, 217, 223, 225n. 6, 231, 237, 239,
  267
Johnson, J., 261
Johnson, Lyndon, 102–3, 122
Johnson, M., 32, 52
Johnstone, B., 188
Joll, J., 143

Leyton-Brown, D., 147
Libya, 16
"Life is like a Mountain Railroad" (song), 41
Lion and Hare (Aesopic fable), 267
Lithuania, 60, 190
Livy (Titus Livius), 88
Locutionary speech acts, 26n. 1
Lohmann, S., 49
Loomis, L., 120
Lord, R., 143
Love expressed symbolically, 51
Luard, E., 101, 194, 260
Luce, R., 159, 255–56
Lucretia, rape of, 88, 97
Lumby, E., 142
Lunn, S., 235
Lurcha Arrow Incident, 142
Lusitania, sinking of, 102, 115
Lyons, Lord, 143

MacMillan, Sir Harold, xi, 140
Madison, James, 141
Magruder, Gail, 38, 40–43
Magruder, Jeb, 38, 40
Maine (U.S. battleship), 143
Major, John, visit with Clinton, 28–30
Malaysia, 179
Mali, 145
Mandela, Nelson, 13, 51
  invites jailer to inauguration, 6, 25, 29, 33–36
Manning, P., 241
Mao Tse Tung, 126
March, J., 216
Marx, Groucho, 85, 91
Maskin, E., 200n. 7
Masters, R. and J., 266
Maturity applied to states, 12
Maynard-Smith, J., 162, 170
McAleer, K., 114
McCaffree, M., 22, 60
McCawley, J., 108, 109
McEvoy, C., 49n. 5
McGinn, R., 85, 140n. 1, 152n. 6, 194n. 1
McKinley, William, 143

McNamara units, 222n. 3
McNamara, Robert, 219, 220
Meaning
  communicative (utterance), 26–28
  convention, by, 36
  natural, 26–27
  of performatives, as reason to believe or act, 111–12, 146
  semantic, 26
Medin, D., 30, 52
Mehta, J., 47, 262
Mercer, J., 133, 208
Message symbols, 9–44
  conventions and, 36–44
  definition, 29
  focal symbols and, 46–47
  summary of findings, 241–43
  See also Symbolism
Meta-beliefs. *See* Common knowledge
Metanorms, 198n. 4
Metaphors, conceptual. *See* Conceptual metaphors
Metonymies
  definition, 11, 32
  focal symbolism and, 49–50
  message symbolism and, 16, 28–30, 37–44
Mexico, 189
Meyer, K., 125
Meyer, S., 219
Middle East War (1967), 86
Midlarsky, M., 194
Milgrom, P., 171, 172n. 6
Miller, Mitch, 39
Miller, W., 90, 97
Milliken, J., 12, 33, 34, 105, 194n. 1
Mills, C. W., 194n. 1
Mitterand, François, 13
  declares National Remembrance Day, 189–90
  visits Sarajevo, 25, 29, 34
Mixed strategies, interpretation of, 258, 265–66, 267–70, 272–73. *See also* Equilibria
Monderer, D., 118n. 16
Montenegro, honor in, 87, 112n. 7